Crosscurrents in American Culture

Crosscurrents in American Culture

A READER IN UNITED STATES HISTORY

VOLUME 2: SINCE 1865

Bruce Dorsey
Swarthmore College

Woody Register
Sewanee: The University of the South

HOUGHTON MIFFLIN HARCOURT PUBLISHING COMPANY

Boston   New York

For Sophie and Tim

Publisher: Suzanne Jeans
Senior Sponsoring Editor: Ann West
Senior Marketing Manager: Katherine Bates
Senior Discipline Product Manager: Lynn Baldridge
Senior Development Editor: Lisa Kalner Williams
Senior Project Editor: Bob Greiner
Senior Media Producer: Lisa Ciccolo
Senior Content Manager: Janet Edmonds
Art and Design Manager: Jill Haber
Cover Design Director: Anthony L. Saizon
Senior Photo Editor: Jennifer Meyer Dare
Senior Composition Buyer: Chuck Dutton
Project Manager: Susan Peltier
Marketing Associate: Lauren Bussard
Editorial Production Assistant: Laura Collins

Cover Art: *Traveling Carnival, Santa Fe, NM*, 1924 by John Sloan. Smithsonian Museum of American Art, Washington, D.C./Art Resource, N.Y.

Text Credits: Credits appear on pages 341–45, which constitute an extension of the copyright page.

Printed in the U.S.A.

Library of Congress Catalog Number: 2007941710

Instructor's exam copy:
ISBN-10: 0-618-73230-6
ISBN-13: 978-0-618-73230-2

For orders, use student text ISBNs:
ISBN-10: 0-618-07739-1
ISBN-13: 978-0-618-07739-7

1 2 3 4 5 6 7 8 9 –EB– 12 11 10 09 08

Contents

CHAPTER 2

New and Old Frontiers: 1877–1900 44

CHAPTER 3
Order and Disorder: 1890–1920 80

Mothering Modernity: Women and Progressive Reform 82

An Enchantment and a Snare: The Modern Department Store 96

Progressive Playgrounds: Amusement Parks and Dance Halls 103

CHAPTER 4

The Profits and Perils of Prosperity: 1915–1934   115

The Great War and Beyond   117

Rural Values: Debating the Destiny of Modern American Culture   128

CHAPTER 5

Bad Times and Good Times:
The Era of the Depression: 1929–1942   154

CHAPTER 6

"Why We Fight": World War II and American Culture: 1941–1945   188

Keep America Beautiful:
Fashioning the New Environmental Consciousness   *297*

The Virus in Our System: AIDS and the Culture Wars   *306*

CHAPTER 10

American Culture
at the Turn of the Twenty-First Century *317*

Family Values: Marriage, Parenthood, and Children
in Recent American History   *318*

Electronic Frontiers: Radical Individualism, Virtual
Community, and the Internet   *331*

Preface

Crosscurrents in American Culture offers an innovative approach to the study of U.S. history that conforms to the new directions of historians' research and students' interests. The idea for this project arose from our own classroom experiences as college teachers. With all the readers available, we have been unable to find a comprehensive collection of historical documents that supported the cultural approach and sensibility that we used in our classes. We have designed this collection to solve this problem. This U.S. history reader is the first devoted to primary-source cultural history texts, images, and documents. Many of the materials in these volumes are those that we ourselves have collected and used in our American history classes. From experience, we know them to be effective not only in teaching the subject of U.S. history, but also in exciting students' interest in the study of history.

Crosscurrents explores a broad range of themes and topics, some familiar and some unfamiliar to surveys of U.S. history. Our aim is not to be novel, but to incorporate sources that represent various and alternative voices and perspectives: women, people of color, residents of cities and the countryside, artists and novelists, people in business, entertainment, advertising, and sports. At the same time, the significant events in the history of the United States, from the American Revolution to Reconstruction to the late twentieth-century culture wars, are all addressed with the fresh and new perspectives made possible through a critical reading of cultural documents. These materials raise the kinds of questions that many historians today are directing at the American past. Social conflicts can be examined in accounts of the popular violence provoked over the question of how to perform Shakespearean drama in antebellum America; shifts in the political understandings of citizenship rights can be plotted in the letters ordinary women wrote to the First Lady pleading, during the era of the Great Depression, for help in adopting a child so that they, too, could be mothers. Questions about economics and the family are posed by the comical stories of wily pre–Civil War Yankee peddlers suckering rural families into purchasing their overpriced wares; for a later era, the same questions can be explored in Ruth Handler's autobiographical account of the keen stratagems she used to override the objections of men to give birth to her creation, the *Barbie* doll.

As these examples suggest, we define "culture" broadly to encompass many of the various segments of expression between which scholars usually have drawn boundaries: the material artifacts and fashions of everyday life that are categorized as "consumer" or "mass culture"; the arts and other modes of expression that are popular among ordinary working people and their families, and are categorized as "folk" or "popular culture"; celebrated examples of "high culture," like the Hudson River

School paintings of the mid-nineteenth century, as well as the often ignored categories of low culture, from the pulp novels of antebellum America to late-twentieth-century rock 'n' roll music and video games. Moreover, we present the literary, visual, and aural materials in an integrated fashion. We hope this approach will discourage students from regarding images or music as mere "illustrations" of themes that are more legitimately investigated in written primary texts. On the contrary, we encourage students to treat all of these cultural forms as historical evidence for significant questions about the past.

This reader is also the first in step with today's generation of college students, who are already accustomed to think with and about culture. *Crosscurrents* taps into students' orientation toward images, sounds, and visual texts, but does so in a manner that deepens their sense and appreciation of the degree to which their world has been made by the past. It challenges students and teachers alike to think critically about the importance and power of culture in shaping lives in the pasts as well as in our own times.

Crosscurrents follows the contours of general surveys of American history. The chapters are organized in chronological order, and each chapter is divided into thematic sections. In addition to the editors' introductions to each section, the documents are preceded by "Problems to Consider," questions designed to stimulate thoughtful reflection on and possible discussion of the historical significance of that text. With the "problems" in the study of American history included in *Crosscurrents*, we try to open up discussion and inquiry, not to close them off by directing students toward a particular answer or solution. The "problems" approach of these volumes reflects our position that studying the past is less about coming to final answers to questions than about wrestling with the problems posed by the evidence.

ᦰ ACKNOWLEDGMENTS

We would like to thank our own students who have helped us to refine our own critical assessment of American culture. We are especially grateful for the assistance of student research assistants Sarah Yahm, Timothy Stewart-Winter, Peter Wirzbicki, Margaret Hughes, and Katherine Rogers. We are also grateful for the assistance of the many librarians who guided us, including the staff of the Library Company of Philadelphia, the Friends Historical Library, Swarthmore College Library, and Sewanee's du Pont Library. Kevin Reynolds and the interlibrary loan staff at Sewanee deserve special mention and thanks. This project relied on the guidance, perseverance, and patience of Terri Wise, Margaret Manos, and Lisa Kalner Williams at Houghton Mifflin. As our respective spouses, Martha Hodes and Julie Berebitsky, well know, we are most deeply indebted to them. Both are talented historians and generous partners who have shaped how we think about history and how we imagined and constructed this reader. The collection itself we dedicate to Tim Dorsey and Sophie Register. Anyone who knows them will understand how they have inspired and taught us to be better teachers and human beings.

Instructors from around the country provided us with valuable feedback on the various drafts of *Crosscurrents*. We heartily thank the following reviewers for their comments: Scott E. Casper, University of Nevada at Reno; Lyde Cullen Sizer, Sarah Lawrence College; Nancy Davis, DePaul University; Kathleen DuVal, University of North Carolina at Chapel Hill; Christopher Johnson, Palomar College; Carol A. Keller, San Antonio College; Carolyn J. Lawes, Old Dominion University; Scott Miltenberger, University of California, Davis; Krystyn R. Moon, Georgia State University; Janet Moore Lindman, Rowan University; Richard Moss, Purdue University; Jonathan Nashel, Indiana University South Bend; Scott A. Sandage, Carnegie Mellon University; Lisa C. Tolbert, University of North Carolina at Greensboro; and Daniel Wickberg, University of Texas at Dallas.

Bruce Dorsey
Woody Register

Crosscurrents in American Culture

Introduction: Reading Culture

In NOVEMBER 2004, in the midst of the U.S. war in Iraq, the *Los Angeles Times* published a photograph of a young, unnamed Marine resting "after more than twelve hours of nearly nonstop deadly combat." Within days, the unknown soldier's face—smeared with dirt and camouflage paint, a bloody scrape on his nose, and, dangling from his lips, a legibly labeled Marlboro cigarette—had appeared on network television and in more than a hundred newspapers. The tabloid *New York Post* made the image its front-page cover, under the banner headline "SMOKIN'." CBS News anchorman Dan Rather showcased the image on the evening news. "This," he told viewers, "is a warrior with his eyes on the far horizon, scanning for danger. See it, study it, absorb it. Think about it. Then take a deep breath of pride." By that point, the soldier had been identified as Lance Corporal James Blake Miller, and the attention he was receiving because of the photo had become a story in itself. In his rural Kentucky hometown, Miller was a local hero, and his mother was thrilled by her son's fame. Elsewhere, women wrote to the *Los Angeles Times* asking for the mailing address of the soldier whose "gaze [was] warm but deadly." The newspaper boasted that the image of "the Marlboro Man" (as he was called) had "moved into the realm of the iconic."

That assessment seems fairly straightforward, but is it? What gave an image of a battle-weary man smoking a cigarette such significance? What made it work? An "iconic" photograph, as the newspaper used that word, is more than a popularly recognized image that generates a lot of positive emotional response. An iconic image expresses recognizable and agreed-upon truths and values that seem to be eternal, essential, and natural dimensions of the human experience. It stands for something universal. To accomplish this task, the image has to fit into or remind us of a story that we all know and that tells us something about ourselves as a people.

A major source of this image's explanatory power appears in the name assigned to the soldier before his actual identity was established. He was not just any American man, but the world's best-known cowboy: "the Marlboro Man," the globally advertised emblem of the Philip Morris cigarette. If we are to understand what makes this photograph work—why it makes some people swell with pride—we have to follow some of Dan Rather's advice. We have to look at "the Marlboro Man" image, study it, and think about it. We have to break it down, examine its parts, and ask questions: Would it have worked in the same way or as well if the soldier had been a woman or an African American man? What if he were smoking Camels or Virginia Slims? What if he were not smoking at all? In other words, how do our expectations about gender, race, and class shape what we see in this photograph? These are the kinds of questions that cultural historians bring to historical materials from America's past. They also are the types of questions that we hope you will ask of the documents and images in this book as you seek to wrestle with the problems of understanding American history.

Marine Lance Corporal James Blake Miller on the front page of the *New York Post*, November 10, 2004.

Studying history is often thought of as a matter of mastering information about what happened and when. That kind of factual record is important, but we believe it is insufficient by itself. *Crosscurrents in American Culture* encourages students of American history to engage in a lively, critical, and analytical examination of the cultural record of the American past. "Culture," in this sense, refers to the many forms of expression that surround people in their everyday lives: stories, plays, movies, songs, art, political rituals, cartoons, propaganda, dance steps, amusement park rides, billboards, TV marketing pitches. The list could go on indefinitely. Professionally trained scholars often have written off these dimensions of life as unworthy of their or anyone else's serious attention. We, however, regard such materials as the very "stuff" of history. When we use the word "culture," then, we mean not just things but also the ideas, values, behaviors, and meanings that any given people share. How is it that they come to share these cultural constructs? This is accomplished through the forms of expression that we have begun to list here. These cultural materials communicate meaning and represent reality for that group.

Historians are always interested in discovering the meaning and significance of any evidence from the past. To understand *meaning*, we try to reconstruct what a document might have meant in its own time, to its creator or author, and to its viewers or readers. To ascertain its *significance*, we use our critical judgments and our store of knowledge about the past to determine why this document was important and how it related to other texts or events and concerns in that era. To borrow the words of the historian James Axtell, we seek "to imagine the imaginations" of people who lived in the past. Because something is imagined does not mean we should dismiss it. On the contrary, many historians today treat people's imaginations as the "solid facts" of history. People in the past—no less than ourselves today—were predisposed to see the world in particular, although often conflicting, ways. Reflecting on the European "discovery" of America beginning in the fifteenth century, the historian Richard White reminds us that, in a cultural sense, there is no such thing as *terra incognita*, or "unknown land," even for those shiploads of Europeans who saw the fauna and flora of the New World for the first time. The new, White observes, "always arrives to the eye fully stocked with expectations, fears, rumors, desires, and meanings." Those expectations influence how people see the landscape, explain the world and its human relations, and defend or resist the social changes and conflicts that are enacted in their everyday lives. That is why we treat all cultural materials, whether those documents are words in print or visual images on canvas, film, or video, as "texts"—that is, as virtual transcripts from the past that we can read. Such documents are the evidence of how people thought and acted in the past.

The emphasis on *action* is worth repeating. Cultural history should do more than explain what people in the past thought, believed, and feared, or the meaning of the things with which they surrounded themselves. It also should help us examine how cultural texts shape actions, and how actions take the form of cultural texts. Cultural history should enable us to see how people put ideas to work to justify, to preserve, or, as often was the case, to resist particular social orders or arrangements. For instance, when English Puritans cleared the woodlands of New England to build villages in the 1630s and 1640s, their actions were guided by culturally specific ideas about the landscape and its appropriate uses. These ideas determined the shape of their fields and the architecture of their houses. These beliefs also bolstered the colonists' claims to their rightful ownership of the land, since in their minds, native inhabitants were not using the land in a legitimate way. The Puritans did more than settle a new land; they sought to impose their "story," with all its meanings, on the land itself, despite the resistance of native peoples who had their own, very different stories about the land and its use. Cultural history helps us see how military, political, diplomatic, and economic conflicts took the form of conflicting stories and that they were, in fact, cultural conflicts.

Culture, as we use the word, also defines what is normal, moral, appropriate, and natural, as well as what is abnormal, strange, barbarous, and unnatural. Culture gives meaning to concepts such as "the nation" and "the enemy," civilization and wilderness, "a man's work" or "a woman's place." In doing so, it sets the stage for conflict as well as harmony because such sharply drawn opposites always are subject to being challenged or defended. We want you to reflect on the ways people put ideas—stories—into action in their daily lives and in many of the most important moments of conflict and of unity that have shaped the history of the United States.

Crosscurrents in American Culture presents a cultural history of the United States through the lens of a diverse collection of documents from the past. You will find familiar topics in American history—slavery, industrialization, the Civil War and Reconstruction, the Great Depression, the environmental movement—but you will learn about these topics through less conventional sources. Novelty, however, is not our sole aim. We wish to incorporate materials and perspectives that raise the kinds of questions that many historians today are directing at the American past. We use popular entertainment, advertising, Shakespearean plays and pulp fiction, the words of founding fathers such as Thomas Jefferson and of innovative mothers such as Ruth Handler (inventor of the Barbie doll). To investigate antebellum slavery, we look at folktales told by slaves and proslavery fiction written by their masters. To explore how Americans made sense of the

Great Depression, we examine the era's best-selling self-help book, stories from America's leading pulp magazines, and episodes from the decade's most popular radio program.

To make this approach clearer, let's briefly put it to use in investigating more closely the artifact and question we started with: what makes "the Marlboro Man" work? The answer is not as obvious as it seems. Most Americans living a century ago, when a self-respecting man smoked nothing but a "lusty pipe or cigar," would have read Miller's cigarette as a sign of weakness, even effeminacy and degeneracy. Such danger signs were on the mind of Ernest Thompson Seton, the founder of the American Boy Scouts, when he worried that modern life was turning the nation's "robust manly, self-reliant boyhood into a lot of flat-chested cigarette smokers with shaky nerves and doubtful vitality." America's entry into World War I (1917–1918) did more to change that message (and tobacco history) than anything else. At that point, tobacco companies had the technology to mass-produce cigarettes, but there was very little demand for them. When war came, these companies gave away tons of ready-made cigarettes, cigarette tobacco, and wrapping papers to U.S. forces. Besides becoming addicted, American doughboys found that cigarettes, which are easily lit and quickly enjoyed, were more convenient to smoke than cigars or pipes. Industrial technology and smart marketing tactics, in combination with the circumstances of modern warfare, invigorated the cigarette-smoking American man. By the late 1920s, he seemed manfully modern compared with men who indulged in the "lazy" cigar. The point here is that cigarettes (or any other cultural artifact) are not in themselves masculine or feminine. They acquire these meanings, which are unstable and impermanent, in culture. Thus, cigarettes did not lose their gender signification. They still said something about the men who smoked them. However, gender distinctions were redrawn, and in ways that made "the Marlboro Man" conceivable.

But other changes had to occur first. For one, the Marlboro cigarette is much older than the Marlboro Man. Philip Morris introduced it in the 1920s for the stylish woman. By the early 1950s, when it sported a red filter tip to hide lipstick stains, hardly anyone was buying it, least of all men. In 1954, Philip Morris hired Chicago adman Leo Burnett to reinvent the brand. Burnett called it a "sissy smoke" and determined to change its image. "What is the most masculine figure in America?" he asked his ad writers. When someone suggested "cowboy," the Marlboro Man was born.

To symbolize the brand, Burnett wanted an authentic man, like the "cowboy" whose rugged close-up he remembered from the cover of *Life* magazine back in 1949. The photo was of C. H. Long, the foreman of a big Texas ranch

"Cowboy" C. H. Long from the cover of *Life* Magazine (1949).
(Leonard McCombe/Time Life Pictures/Getty Images.)

whom *Life* described as one of a dying breed of uniquely American types: "undiluted individuals clinging with some ferocity" to the rough life of the frontier West. *Life* observed that, in modern America, these men were being replaced by a "feebler" breed who worked in offices and tended suburban home fires at night. Burnett's ad campaign identified Marlboro's "man-size flavor of honest tobacco" as the choice of men who did not mind getting their hands dirty. But Marlboro was aimed at city-dwelling men who envied the cowboy's "freedom," not at rural or working-class men. Overnight, Marlboro became a man's smoke and was well on its way to becoming the most popular brand on earth. The Marlboro Man was crafted to represent qualities that seem uniquely American: manly independence; honest, productive work performed close to the soil; and, to quote a Marlboro poster, the "strength of self-confidence."

But does he epitomize those qualities? A cigarette or a cowboy does not mean anything until we imagine those meanings. History and cultural influences prepare us to imagine what we see in certain ways, although what people imagine often proves hard to control. That observation brings us back to Corporal Miller. Everyone, it seemed, recognized in his photograph the text of "the Marlboro Man." More important, they also knew that this text told a story about the United States that explained what Americans were trying to achieve in Iraq. For the *New York Post*, the story explained military success in terms of American machismo: "Marlboro men kick butt in Fallujah." The picture "motivated the heck out of me all day," said a Marine recruiter in Long Island, New York. But the image did not make everyone swell with pride. Some objected that the image was misused to rally support for an unpopular and wrongheaded war. Even worse, in some people's minds, "the Marlboro Man" made smoking cigarettes look really cool. "Lots of children, particularly boys, play 'army' and like to imitate this young man," a writer complained to the *Houston Chronicle*. "The clear message of the photo is that the way to relax after a battle is with a cigarette." Even Miller's mother, who relished her son's celebrity, imagined something else when she saw the photo. She wished he would stop smoking. The story of both Miller and the photograph, however, did not end there. He returned from Iraq and was medically discharged from the Marines exactly one year after his face first appeared in newspapers and on television screens around the world. Now suffering from post-traumatic stress disorder, Miller has struggled to rebuild his life after combat and to reconcile his own pain and personal loss with the famous image of him. The photograph of the "Marlboro Marine" has still retained its power to move Americans. Viewed through the context of Miller's circumstances and faltering public support for the Iraq War, it now poignantly suggests to many observers not what has been won in Iraq, but what has been lost. Cultural symbols, then, are open to numerous interpretations, and these interpretations may change dramatically over time. They also inspire conflicting responses and actions, including those their creators did not intend or imagine. One of the strengths of cultural history is its sensitivity to this ambiguity. In studying the various ways in which the meanings of things have been imagined, we can achieve a richer and more complicated understanding of the past.

CHAPTER I

A Second American Revolution: 1865–1877

THE CIVIL WAR was a seismic event in the social and political landscape of the United States. It produced catastrophic destruction as well as triumphant emancipation. With slavery's demise, the familiar world for the South's white and black population was gone forever. Four million black men, women, and children were now free, ushering in a time of exhilarating promise of education, landownership, political participation, and self-determination. The war also permanently reconfigured the economic and political map of both the North and the South. White southern planters found their political dominance challenged by the increased political consciousness of black freedmen and poorer whites. An unrivaled era of large-scale consolidated industrial capitalism ("big business") was born out of wartime profits in the North. And the unprecedented empowerment of the national state meant that ultimate authority rested with the federal government. *The Nation*, a magazine founded by antislavery activists in 1865, proclaimed that the war confirmed "by the blood of thousands of her sons" the triumph of "the consolidation of nationality under democratic forms."

Not since 1776 had the political universe in America been turned on its head. As the New York *Herald* stated, the nation had to recognize that "we have passed through the fiery ordeal of a mighty revolution, and that the pre-existing order of things is gone and we can return no more." Beginning with the Freedmen's Bureau and Civil Rights Acts of 1866, followed by the Fourteenth Amendment and the Reconstruction Acts of 1867, Congress divided the former Confederacy into five military districts; established that readmission to the Union depended on the recognition of black citizenship rights, or else former Confederates would be barred from political officeholding; and gave the federal Freedmen's Bureau the authority to void labor contracts that forced former slaves into work situations that resembled slavery. Senator Lott Morrill of

Maine called these acts of legislation "absolutely revolutionary." But then, Morrill noted, "are we not in the midst of a revolution?" It is these seismic shifts in the political landscape that have led historians to consider the Reconstruction era as the "second American Revolution." Ironically, the last veteran of the first American Revolution died during the same months that Congress was deliberating the Reconstruction Acts of 1867.

This revolution focused on the identity of the nation's citizenry. For the first time since the nation's founding, the United States grappled with the question, as abolitionist Wendell Phillips phrased it, of "what makes or constitutes a citizen." The battle would continue for years after the war's end. Neither the Emancipation Proclamation, the North's victory, nor the Thirteenth Amendment, which abolished slavery, guaranteed the rights of citizenship for former slaves. Yet the emancipation of slaves prompted protests by other Americans—white women in the North, white southerners, and native-born laborers in the West—who felt that the new revolution had omitted them from the promise of liberation and citizenship.

☙ *Free at Last! The Black Man's Vote and Woman's Suffrage* ☙

Like the first American Revolution, Reconstruction proved more revolutionary for men than for women. Its overriding concerns focused on landownership and voting, both of which were privileges extended principally to men and denied entirely to married women under existing laws. Freed slaves immediately demanded the right to vote as one of their essential rights as new citizens. A delegate to North Carolina's Freedmen's Convention in 1865 outlined the rights new black citizens expected: "First, *the right to testify in courts of justice*, in order that we may defend our property and our rights. Secondly, *representation in the jury box*. . . . Thirdly and finally, *the black man should have the right to carry his ballot to the ballot box*." Not without difficulty, the Republican Party gradually tied its future to the citizenship and voting rights of black men in the South. Republicans were caught in a dilemma on this issue. First, only a few Radical Republicans wanted to extend voting rights to the North's free black residents. Second, even the Radicals in the party were divided between those who wanted to use black suffrage to change "the whole fabric of southern society" and those who thought black suffrage would be the quickest and least painful method for northerners to avoid any long-term national responsibility for governing race relations in the South. As *Harper's Weekly* explained, once blacks had the vote, "the 'Negro Question' will take care of itself." When Radical Republicans took control of reconstructing the South, black voting became their political goal and their tool for social reform.

The enfranchising of black men created a dilemma of its own for women's rights activists such as Elizabeth Cady Stanton and Susan B. Anthony. After all, these women began their careers in the abolitionist movement and for years had understood that the enslavement of African Americans was equivalent to their own subjugation under male-dominated laws and social conventions. With emancipation, women's rights activists pursued a strategy of demanding universal suffrage, an inseparable and simultaneous appeal for voting rights for both blacks and women. However, northern antislavery politicians, who were now wedded to the fortunes of the Republican Party, dismissed women's demands as a distraction from their first concern—votes for black men. In August 1865, Stanton wrote to Anthony describing her continual arguments with abolitionist-Republicans: "I fear one and all will favor enfranchising the negro without us. Woman's cause is in deep water." In response to abolitionist Wendell Phillips's declaration before the American Anti-Slavery Society that "this hour belongs to the negro," women suffrage activists girded for a fight.

Letter to the Editor (1865)
FRANCES D. GAGE

This Is the Negro's Hour (1865)
ELIZABETH CADY STANTON

Frances Gage was the first to respond to this impending abandonment of white women's suffrage in favor of black men's voting rights in a letter she wrote to a national abolitionist newspaper. Gage was strongly committed to racial equality. She had volunteered for the first efforts to assist slaves' transition into freedom on South Carolina's Sea Islands during the Civil War, and after the war she became a chief agent of the Freedmen's Bureau. (Gage is perhaps most famous for penning the words "Ar'n't I a Woman," attributed to former slave Sojourner Truth.) A month after Gage's letter, Elizabeth Cady Stanton wrote her own response to Wendell Phillips's declaration that it was "the negro's hour." At this moment, Gage and Stanton were still firmly behind the strategy of universal suffrage, and both insisted that African American women would be denied full emancipation under the Republicans' strategy of black male suffrage. Stanton summarized her position in an acerbic letter to Phillips, asking that he answer one question: "Do you believe the African race is composed entirely of males?"

PROBLEMS TO CONSIDER

1. On what grounds did women suffrage activists assert a woman's right to vote? Can you also discern the arguments against women's suffrage that activists such as Gage and Stanton needed to confront?
2. What was the case these women made for universal, as opposed to just male, citizenship rights?

LETTER TO THE EDITOR

Sir, . . . Can any one tell us why the great advocates of Human Equality, such men as Wendell Phillips and Wm. L. Garrison, who a few years ago were bold champions for equality before the law for women, and gave eloquent lectures in behalf of the sex — more than one-half of the people of the United States, oppressed by unjust laws and partial legislation — now wholly ignore that part of the subject, and forget that once when they were a weak party and needed all the womanly strength of the nation to help them on, they always united the words, "without regard to sex, race, or color"? Who ever hears of sex now from any of these champions of freedom?

Are the four or five millions of hard working women at the North, whose half-priced labor reduces them almost to the dead line of starvation, of no account? Will the two millions of emancipated women of the South be fully protected against the cruel practices of their old tyrants by giving a vote only to male citizens?

Every day we hear arguments in favor of negro suffrage, urged on the ground that he has held the bayonet during this last war. Have the women of the North done nothing to help the nation forward to its present position? Have they who gave husbands and sons[,] time, money, strength, health — all that makes life desirable for their country, no claim to broader privilege? Is it so unjust for a colored man to work for poor wages, such as voting landowners or capitalists may compel, and yet no injustice to women? Is taxation without representation tyranny to them and not to us? . . . And please tell us, while you are about it, why justice to *all* is not better for a nation and a people than injustice to the majority. . . .

N.B. — My sense is *too short* to see the justice of some of the arguments I read in these days of majestic enthusiasm for liberty with woman left out.

FRANCES D. GAGE

National Anti-Slavery Standard, November 29, 1865.

THIS IS THE NEGRO'S HOUR

Sir: — By an amendment of the Constitution, ratified by three-fourths of the loyal States, the black man is declared free. The largest and most influential political party is demanding suffrage for him throughout the Union, which right in many of the States is already conceded. Although this may remain a question for politicians to wrangle over for five or ten years, the black man is still, in a political point of view, far above the educated women of the country. The representative women of the nation have done their uttermost for the last thirty years to secure freedom for the negro, and so long as he was lowest in the scale of being we were willing to press *his* claims; but now, as the celestial gate to civil rights is slowly moving on its hinges, it becomes a serious question whether we had better stand aside and see "Sambo" walk into the kingdom first. As self-preservation is the first law of nature, would it not be wiser to keep our lamps trimmed and burning, and when the constitutional door is open, avail ourselves of the strong arm and blue uniform of the black soldier to walk in by his side, and thus make the gap so wide that no privileged class could ever again close it against the humblest citizen in the republic?

"This is the negro's hour." Are we sure that he, once entrenched in all his inalienable rights, may not be an added power to hold us at bay? Have not "black male citizens" been heard to say they doubted the wisdom of extending the right of suffrage to women? Why should the African prove more just and generous than his Saxon compeers? If the two millions of Southern black women are not to be secured in their rights of person, property, wages, and children, their emancipation is but another form of slavery. In fact, it is better to be the slave of an educated white man, than of a degraded, ignorant black one. We who know what absolute power the statute laws of most of the States give man, in all his civil, political, and social relations, demand that in changing the status of the four millions of Africans, the women as well as the men shall be secured in all the rights, privileges, and immunities of citizens.

It is all very well for the privileged order to look down complacently and tell us, "This is the negro's hour; do not clog his way; do not embarrass the Republican party with any new issue; be generous and magnanimous; the negro once safe, the woman comes next." Now, if our prayer involved a new set of measures, or a new train of thought, it would be cruel to tax "white male citizens" with even two simple questions at a time; but the disfranchised all make the same demand, and the same logic and justice that secures suffrage to one class gives it to all. . . . This is our opportunity to retrieve the errors of the past and mould anew the elements of Democracy. The nation is ready for a long step in the right direction; party lines are obliterated, and all men are thinking for themselves. If our rulers have the justice to give the black man suffrage, woman should avail herself of that new-born virtue to secure her rights; if not, she should begin with renewed earnestness to educate the people into the idea of universal suffrage.

ELIZABETH CADY STANTON

_____

Elizabeth Cady Stanton, "This Is the Negro's Hour," *National Anti-Slavery Standard*, December 26, 1865, in *History of Woman Suffrage*, 6 vols., edited by Elizabeth Cady Stanton et al. (Rochester, N.Y.: Susan B. Anthony, 1881–1922), 2:94–95.

ᔜ

Speech Before the National Woman Suffrage Convention (1869)
ELIZABETH CADY STANTON

The Republicans succeeded in passing the Fourteenth Amendment to the Constitution in 1866, as women's rights activists anticipated. It not only defined freedmen as citizens and guaranteed them equal protection under the law but also reduced a state's representation in Congress if it denied any of its "male inhabitants" the right to vote. For the first time, the Constitution defined a voting citizen as "male" and inscribed sexual discrimination into the fundamental law of the land. Abolitionist and feminist women felt betrayed. Supporters of women's suffrage became increasingly critical of the Republican Party, which shunned their demands in favor of black suffrage. By 1869, Radical Republicans in Congress succeeded in passing the Fifteenth Amendment, which committed the federal government to prohibiting any state from disfranchising its citizens on the basis of race. Democrats called the Fifteenth Amendment "the most revolutionary measure" ever conceived by Congress.

The Fifteenth Amendment created a permanent rift in the white female constituency of the suffragist movement. Elizabeth Cady Stanton and Susan B. Anthony severed the historic ties of women's suffrage to abolitionism and the Republican Party and formed an independent political movement, the National Woman Suffrage Association (NWSA). They called their newspaper the Revolution. *Another faction, led by Lucy Stone, Julia Ward Howe, and abolitionist-Republican men, remained loyal to the Republican Party and formed the American Woman Suffrage Association. (This division among suffragists would not be healed until 1890.) During the debates over the passage of the Fifteenth Amendment, the NWSA began to petition for the adoption of a sixteenth amendment, penned by Anthony, calling for the right of suffrage to all citizens regardless of their sex. This turn of events led Stanton and Anthony further from the position of universal suffrage and racial equity, as evidenced in Stanton's address before the National Woman Suffrage Convention in 1869.*

PROBLEMS TO CONSIDER

1. Compare Stanton's 1869 speech to her 1865 essay: Did her position on the interdependence of black and woman suffrage change during these four years?
2. How and why did Stanton build her argument for women's equality on the basis of the supposed sexual differences between women and men?

Those who represent what is called "the Woman's Rights Movement," have argued their right to political equality from every standpoint of justice, religion, and logic, for the last twenty years. . . . There are no new arguments to be made on human rights, our work to-day is to apply to ourselves those so familiar to all; to teach man that woman is not an anomalous being, outside all laws and constitutions, but one whose rights are to be established by the same process of reason as that by which he demands his own.

. . . The same arguments . . . used by the great Republican party to enfranchise a million black men in the South, all these arguments we have to-day to offer for woman, and one, in addition, stronger than all besides, the difference in man and woman. Because man and woman are the complement of one another, we need woman's thought in national affairs to make a safe and stable government.

The Republican party to-day congratulates itself on having carried the Fifteenth Amendment of the Constitution, thus securing "manhood suffrage" and establishing an aristocracy of sex on this continent. . . .

This fundamental principle of our government—the equality of all the citizens of the republic—should be incorporated in the Federal Constitution, there to remain forever. To leave this question to the States and partial acts of Congress, is to defer indefinitely its settlement. . . . Hence, we appeal to the party now in power, everywhere to end this protracted debate on suffrage, and declare it the inalienable right of every citizen who is amenable to the laws of the land, who pays taxes and the penalty of crime. We have a splendid theory of a genuine republic, why not realize it and make our government homogeneous, from Maine to California. The Republican party has the power to do this, and now is its only opportunity. . . .

I urge a speedy adoption of a Sixteenth Amendment for the following reasons:

1. A government, based on the principle of caste and class, can not stand. The aristocratic idea, in any form, is opposed to the genius of our free institutions. . . . While all men, everywhere, are rejoicing in new-found liberties, shall woman alone be denied the rights, privileges, and immunities of citizenship? . . . While here, in our own land, slaves, but just rejoicing in the proclamation of emancipation, ignorant alike of its power and significance, have the ballot unasked, unsought, already laid at their feet—think you the daughters of Adams, Jefferson, and Patrick Henry, in whose veins flows the blood of two Revolutions, will forever linger round the camp-fires of an old barbarism, with no longings to join this grand army of freedom in its onward march to roll back the golden gates of a higher and better civilization? Of all kinds of aristocracy, that of sex is the most odious and unnatural; invading, as it does, our homes, desecrating our family altars, dividing those whom God has joined together, exalting the son above the mother who bore him, and subjugating, everywhere, moral power to brute force. Such a government would not be worth the blood and treasure so freely poured out in its long struggles for freedom. . . .

2. I urge a Sixteenth Amendment, because "manhood suffrage" or a man's government, is civil, religious, and social disorganization. The male element is a destructive force, stern, selfish, aggrandizing, loving war, violence, conquest, acquisition, breeding in the material and

moral world alike discord, disorder, disease, and death. . . . The male element has held high carnival thus far, it has fairly run riot from the beginning, overpowering the feminine element everywhere, crushing out all the diviner qualities in human nature, until we know but little of true manhood and womanhood. . . .

People object to the demands of those whom they choose to call the strong-minded, because they say, "the right of suffrage will make the women masculine." That is just the difficulty in which we are involved to-day. Though disfranchised we have few women in the best sense, we have simply so many reflections, varieties, and dilutions of the masculine gender. The strong, natural characteristics of womanhood are repressed and ignored in dependence, for so long as man feeds woman she will try to please the giver and adapt herself to his condition. To keep a foothold in society woman must be as near like man as possible, reflect his ideas, opinions, virtues, motives, prejudices, and vices. . . .

We ask woman's enfranchisement, as the first step toward the recognition of that essential element in government that can only secure the health, strength, and prosperity of the nation. Whatever is done to lift woman to her true position will help to usher in a new day of peace and perfection for the race. . . . But government gains no new element of strength in admitting all men to the ballot-box, for we have too much of the man-power there already. We see this in every department of legislation, and it is a common remark, that unless some new virtue is infused into our public life the nation is doomed to destruction. Will the foreign element, the dregs of China, Germany, England, Ireland, and Africa supply this needed force, or the nobler types of American womanhood who have taught our presidents, senators, and congressmen the rudiments of all they know?

3. I urge a Sixteenth Amendment because, when "manhood suffrage" is established from Maine to California, woman has reached the lowest depths of political degradation. So long as there is a disfranchised class in this country, and that class its women, a man's government is worse than a white man's government with suffrage limited by property and educational qualifications. . . . If American women find it hard to bear the oppressions of their own Saxon fathers, the best orders of manhood, what may they not be called to endure when all the lower orders of foreigners now crowding our shores legislate for them and their daughters. Think of Patrick and Sambo and Hans and Yung Tung, who do not know the difference between a monarchy and a republic, who can not read the Declaration of Independence or Webster's spelling-book, making laws for Lucretia Mott, Ernestine L. Rose, and Anna E. Dickinson. . . . This manhood suffrage is an appalling question, and it would be well for thinking women, who seem to consider it so magnanimous to hold their own claims in abeyance until all men are crowned with citizenship, to remember that the most ignorant men are ever the most hostile to the equality of women, as they have known them only in slavery and degradation. . . .

It is a startling assertion, but nevertheless true, that in none of the nations of modern Europe are the higher classes of women politically so degraded as are the women of this Republic to-day. . . . In our Southern States even, before the war, women were not degraded below the working population. They were not humiliated in seeing their coachmen, gardeners, and waiters go to the polls to legislate for them; but here, in this boasted Northern civilization, women of wealth and education, who pay taxes and obey the laws, who in morals and intellect are the peers of their proudest rulers, are thrust outside the pale of political consideration with minors, paupers, lunatics, traitors, idiots, with those guilty of bribery, larceny, and infamous crimes.

History of Woman Suffrage, 6 vols., edited by Elizabeth Cady Stanton et al. (Rochester, N.Y.: Susan B. Anthony, 1881–1922), 2:349–55.

ꝫ

The First Vote (1867)

Frederick Douglass Addresses the American Equal Rights Association (1868 and 1869)

"Slavery is not abolished," Frederick Douglass told a group of abolitionists in 1865, "until the black man has the ballot." Black demands for suffrage affirmed traditional American principles that equated manhood and military service with citizenship and voting rights. Since the nation's founding, one's claim to have fought for the nation gave one the right to deliberate in the nation's political decision making. Douglass phrased it in this way: "To say that I am a citizen to pay taxes . . . obey laws . . . and fight the battles of the country, but in all that respects voting and representation, I am but as so much inert matter, is to insult my manhood." Many black Civil War veterans shared those sentiments. An illustration, entitled "The First Vote," for a cover of Harper's Weekly *in 1867, captured that perspective. However, Douglass did not rest his arguments for black suffrage on sexual difference alone, nor did he oppose the right of women to vote. For almost two decades prior to Reconstruction, Douglass could be heard speaking out at women's rights conventions when few other men (white or black) were anywhere to be found. So there was nothing unusual about Douglass addressing the annual meeting of the American Equal Rights Association in 1868 and 1869; but at that moment, he articulated his reasons for insisting that the right to vote for black men was a more urgent demand than suffrage for white women.*

PROBLEMS TO CONSIDER

1. What do the various men in "The First Vote" illustration symbolize? And what does the image reveal about the thinking of some white northerners about black men's suffrage?
2. Explain why Frederick Douglass thought that black suffrage was more urgently needed than women's voting rights. Is his an argument about race, human rights, or class?

ADDRESS (1868)

The call upon me for a speech on this occasion has been unexpected, and unsought, and I have no lengthy or elaborate remarks to offer. But I must say that I know of no argument that can be adduced in favor of the right of man to suffrage which is not equally forcible, and equally applicable to woman. If it be essential to the dignity of man; if it be necessary to protect the rights of man, it must be equally essential and necessary to woman. If it have the effect to elevate a man,

to inspire within him higher ideas of duty, and of honor, it will necessarily have the same influence upon woman.

I am sorry to say that the race to which I belong have not generally taken the right ground on this question. The idea of obtaining their own rights has so occupied their minds as to exclude the thought of what justice demanded for others. Or if they thought of it, they were not ready to acknowledge the right in the case of women. But, after all, there is a great deal of human nature exhibited in this feeling. It is

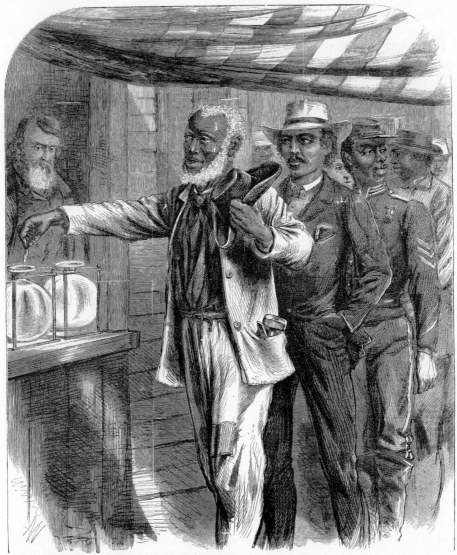

"THE FIRST VOTE."—Drawn by A. R. Waud.—[See next page.]

"The First Vote," *Harper's Weekly*, November 16, 1867.

(The Granger Collection, New York.)

eminently natural and habitual in men and women too to be clamorous for their own rights while they ignore or deny the existence of the same rights in others.

What our Government now needs is more honesty, more goodness, more virtue in its coun-

cils, and for this reason I advocate the admission of the votes of the women of the land. . . . I presume that woman is about like man in these respects—that is, the instincts of the human heart in woman are substantially the same as those in man. And I see no better way than to take in the women, in order to make our government pure. . . .

Since the termination of the war the popular sentiment is crying, "Down with the Rebellion!" and advocating the freedom of the slave, but they do not want them *quite* so free as themselves, they are willing to leave upon their limbs a few links of their chains to remind them of the rock out of which they have been hewn. There is no such thing as instantaneous emancipation; true, the links of the chain may be broken in an instant, but it will take not less than a century to obliterate all traces of the institution. Our Government must be the best and strongest in the world if it be only made consistent with genuine Republicanism, the principle of deriving its power from the consent of a people governed, taxation and representation going side by side. No man should be excluded from the Government on account of his color, no woman on account of her sex; there should be no shoulder that does not bear its burden of the Government, and no individual conscience debarred of chance to exercise its influence for good on the National councils. Then will our Government be the strongest ever seen, and be lasting until the end of the world. I do not expect that the extension of the franchise to my race and to woman is going to suddenly accomplish all this good, but it will accomplish in the end some great results. To the race to which I belong the ballot means something more than a mere abstract idea. It means the right to live and to protect itself by honest industry. You women have representatives. Your brothers, and your husbands, and your fathers vote for you, but the black wife has no husband who can vote for her. . . . The impeachment of the President *[Andrew Johnson]* will be a hopeful indication of the triumph of our right to vote. It will mean the negro's right to vote, and mean that the fair South shall no longer be governed by the Regulators and the Ku-Klux Klan, but by fair and impartial law.

New York Daily Tribune, May 15, 1868.

ADDRESS (1869)

Mr. Douglass:—I came here more as a listener than to speak, and I have listened with a great deal of pleasure. . . . There is no name greater than that of Elizabeth Cady Stanton in the matter of woman's rights and equal rights, but my sentiments are tinged a little against *The Revolution.* There was in the address to which I allude the employment of certain names, such as "Sambo," and the gardener, and the bootblack, and the daughters of Jefferson and Washington, and all the rest that I can not coincide with. I have asked what difference there is between the daughters of Jefferson and Washington and other daughters. (Laughter.) I must say that I do not see how any one can pretend that there is the same urgency in giving the ballot to woman as to the negro. With us, the matter is a question of life and death, at least, in fifteen States of the Union. When women, because they are women, are hunted down through the cities of New York and New Orleans; when they are dragged from their houses and hung upon lamp-posts; when their children are torn from their arms, and their brains dashed out upon the pavement; when they are objects of insult and outrage at every turn; when they are in danger of having their homes burnt down over their heads; when their children are not allowed to enter schools; then they will have an urgency to obtain the ballot equal to our own. (Great applause.)

A voice:—Is that not all true about black women?

Mr. Douglass:—Yes, yes, yes; it is true of the black woman, but not because she is a woman, but because she is black. (Applause.) Julia Ward Howe at the conclusion of her great speech delivered at the convention in Boston last year, said: "I am willing that the negro shall get the ballot before me." (Applause.) . . . I am in favor of woman's suffrage in order that we shall have all the virtue and vice confronted. . . .

Miss Anthony:—The old anti-slavery school say women must stand back and wait until the negroes shall be recognized. But we say, if you will not give the whole loaf of suffrage to the entire people, give it to the most intelligent first. (Applause.) If intelligence, justice, and morality are to have precedence in the Government, let the question of woman be brought up first and that of the negro last. (Applause.) . . . When Mr. Douglass mentioned the black man first and the woman last, if he had noticed he would have seen that it was the men that clapped and not the women. There is not the woman born who desires to eat the bread of dependence, no matter whether it be from the hand of father, husband, or brother. . . . (Applause.) Mr. Douglass talks about the wrongs of the negro; but with all the outrages that he to-day suffers, he would not exchange his sex and take the place of Elizabeth Cady Stanton. (Laughter and applause.)

Mr. Douglass: — I want to know if granting you the right of suffrage will change the nature of our sexes? (Great laughter.)

History of Woman Suffrage, 6 vols., edited by Elizabeth Cady Stanton et al. (Rochester, N.Y.: Susan B. Anthony, 1881– 1922), 2:382–83.

๛

๛ White Terror and Racial Violence ๛

Black voting in the South was truly revolutionary. After the Reconstruction Acts of 1867, more than 700,000 black voters were registered in ten southern states; four-fifths of them voted in the elections of 1867 and 1868. African Americans were elected to every state legislature and even constituted a majority in the South Carolina legislature. Between 1868 and 1876, southern states elected fourteen black U.S. congressmen, two U.S. senators, and six lieutenant governors. Even if these numbers did not constitute parity (keep in mind that in five states blacks actually constituted a majority of the electorate), these were extraordinary gains, especially compared with the complete denial of political rights to African Americans under slavery.

A counterrevolutionary movement emerged in the South during Reconstruction. It manifested itself as a loosely organized, but ruthlessly violent, domestic terrorist campaign. White southerners who refused to acquiesce to the new social and political order of Radical Reconstruction turned to the Ku Klux Klan and similar organizations, such as the Knights of the White Camellia or the White Brotherhood, to try to reverse the revolutionary changes in their midst.

The Ku Klux Klan was a vigilante, paramilitary force dedicated to using violence and intimidation (under the cover of night and disguise) to overturn Republican Party rule and restore white supremacy. Violence now became the new reality of politics, and the Klan emerged as the violent arm of the Democratic Party. Klansmen targeted not only blacks who voted Republican or won elections to political office but also so-called "uppity" blacks, who taught in schools, refused to accept unfair labor contracts, acquired land or livestock, or rejected the deferential behavior demanded under slavery. In Camilla, Georgia, four hundred armed whites opened fire on a black election parade, killing and wounding more than twenty. In two separate massacres, in Saint Landry Parish (1868) and Colfax (1873) in Louisiana, Klan mobs killed more than 200 and 280 blacks respectively.

The Ku Klux Klan was founded in Pulaski, Tennessee, in 1866, but as the Reconstruction Acts of 1867 took effect in the spring of 1868 and a presidential election neared, Klan organizations and violence sprang up in nearly every southern state. Some areas of the former Confederacy remained largely untouched by the Klan. Its activity tended to flourish in the piedmont regions where small farms and nearly equal racial populations and political party strength made white violence an effective weapon for intimidating freedmen and Republicans. Night riding and violence effectively broke up the Republican Party in Georgia and Louisiana, but the party's presidential candidate, Ulysses S. Grant, still carried all of the other southern states in the 1868 election.

Klansmen and their sympathizers created a culture of terror in the Reconstruction South. Night-riding terrorist episodes spilled over into popular racial ideologies, which found their way into print as folktales, off-color jokes, and political oratory. Newspapers and books have too rarely been examined for their role in developing a popular consumer culture of white terror. By examining this culture, we can discover the powerful legacy of minstrelsy humor as an instrument of terror. Moreover, we also expose the new ways that white supremacists sexualized political discourse and created a counterrevolutionary ideology that justified violence against blacks as a safeguard against an alleged sexual threat of black men's political freedom in the South.

✌ THE KLAN AS MINSTRELSY: HUMOR AND TERROR

The Klan's own origin legend states that it began as a social club for young Confederate veterans returning home only to find no prospects for business and a complete absence of "amusements and social diversions." Klansmen maintained that their original purpose was to "have fun, make mischief, and play pranks on the public." Of course, by "the public" they meant their white Republican enemies and a newly freed black population. In light of the violence that followed, we should not lose sight of the cultural significance of how the Klan entwined humor with terror to accomplish its goals. Agents of white terror exploited forms of comic discourse for the consumption of a white public, offering them a palatable ideology for reasserting racial dominance once legalized slavery—the foundation of their earlier domination—had been abolished. We need not psychoanalyze this phenomenon to affirm Freud's observation that jokes can often express "brutal hostility, forbidden by law."

Southern newspapers and humorists combined to create a receptive climate for acts of Klan violence. The staple of their humor involved comic tales of black fright and flight. White folktales of pranks and scares were placed side by side with depictions of disfigured black bodies and performances of Klan night riders who donned outrageous costumes and posed as the wartime dead. Americans already had an indigenous form of humorous entertainment designed to reinforce a racial hierarchy—the popular shows of blackface minstrel performers (see chapter 8)—and minstrelsy played an important role in the reception of the Klan. In the years before the Civil War, minstrel companies regularly visited southern towns, and their popularity continued after the war. Black fright and cowardice, as we have seen, were typical comic ploys of minstrel shows, as were slapstick routines that made scares and violence part of the jokes that audiences and performers shared. During Reconstruction, a sympathetic print culture turned racial cruelty into popular comedy whose significance was apparent to all southern people, whether white or black.

A Terrified Negro (1868)

Ku-Klux in a Safe (1868)

K.K.K.K. (1868)

As they had been throughout the nineteenth century, newspapers during Reconstruction were published to advance the interests of a political party. Thus, it was Republican papers that recorded most of the atrocities committed by the Klan, while Democratic papers encouraged more lighthearted attitudes toward Klan activity. For instance, the Pulaski Citizen, *published in the Klan's birthplace, circulated legends of Klansmen consuming human flesh, advertised for a local "Ku Klux Soda Fount," and even jokingly threatened to send the Klan after readers who failed to pay their subscriptions. Even more common, Democratic newspapers such as the* Nashville Union and Dispatch *published tales depicting Klansmen frightening blacks with practical jokes that combined humor with terror, drawing on stereotypes of African American superstitions about ghosts, as well as comic slapstick routines from minstrel shows.*

PROBLEMS TO CONSIDER

1. How might this humor have shaped the way white southerners discussed black politics? Why was it important that readers laugh at these episodes of terror?
2. What does the emerging market for Klan commodities suggest about the relationship between politics and the consumer economy in the South?

A TERRIFIED NEGRO

A negro was met by one of the Ku-Klux near Franklin a few days ago, and the cowled knight of the black cross and scarlet robe cordially offered to shake hands. The negro grasped the extended palm, but no sooner had he touched it than it dropped off, leaving nothing but the bleeding stump of a gory wrist. Sambo, with a mingled shriek and yell of horror and fright, took to his heels and never once stopped until he had reached home, a distance of some five miles, where he curled up on his cabin floor, remaining in that position several hours before he could recover sufficiently to relate what had occurred.

"A Terrified Negro," *Nashville Union and American*, March 1, 1868.

KU-KLUX IN A SAFE

Night before last, the clerks at the Chattanooga Depot perpetrated a fearful joke upon a darkie employed there, who goes by the name of General Butler. One of them, wrapping himself in a newly washed sheet, and donning a tall hat constructed of blotting paper, placed himself inside of a big safe, and at a late hour the negro was sent to the safe with two books, which he had orders to deposit. As he slowly swung the door on its hinges, a deep groan that seemed to come from the door itself in complaint at being disturbed, nearly lifted poor Butler from his boots. Almost simultaneously, a shriek, as from some yawning grave, fell upon his ear, and a ghostly figure rushed toward him. With a loud yell of horror and dismay, the darkie sank upon the floor, where he doubled himself as if of India rubber, and lay till the graceless scamps who had imposed upon him could bring to bear the proper restoratives, and lay the mischievous ghost who had come so near being the death of him.

"Ku-Klux in a Safe," *Nashville Union and Dispatch*, April 3, 1868.

K.K.K.K.

The genius and enterprise of some people is truly astonishing. Since the "Ku Klux fever" was at its highest pitch in our midst, we have had "Ku Klux Music" from the Music houses, "Ku Klux hats" from Furnishing emporiums, "Ku Klux Cocktails" from the different saloons, together with the many little "Ku Klux etceteras" not in mind. And to cap the climax we now have the genuine "Ku Klux Klan Knife," with cabalistic letters and the terrible symbols of the order on its blade. That sterling firm, Craighead, Breast & Gibson, Exclusive Wholesale Hardware Merchants, 45 Public Square, conceived the happy idea some weeks since and yesterday a large invoice of *their express designings* from their trans-Atlantic manufacturers, Frederick Ware & Co., Sheffield, England, was received at their warerooms in this city.

"K.K.K.K.," *Nashville Union and Dispatch*, June 26, 1868.

ᷓ

Testimony Taken by the Sub-Committee of Elections in Louisiana (1870)

Members of the Ku Klux Klan were sworn to secrecy and waged most of their acts of terror after nightfall in rural areas, where the only witnesses were the victims of violence, who lacked printing presses to tell their stories. Fortunately, the Klan's terrorist campaign forced northern Republicans to intervene. A series of Enforcement Acts, followed by the Ku Klux Klan Act of 1871, brought the federal courts into action and led to lengthy investigations of Klan activity by congressional committees. These congressional testimonies gave voice to black perspectives on the Klan, even as they confirmed the Klan's intertwining of practical jokes and terror. Some former slaves likened the Klan to antebellum slave patrols, but many others knew that Klan violence far exceeded the ferocity of slave patrols and that it stemmed from the new social and political circumstances that followed emancipation.

PROBLEMS TO CONSIDER

1. How does this testimony help us understand the reasons that Klansmen terrorized black southerners?
2. How did black men and women in the South understand the actions and performances of the Klan?

George Washington (colored) sworn and examined.
. . .

Question. Where were you during the late election?—*Answer.* I was home, but I did not go to the polls.

Q. Why didn't you go?—*A.* Because it was too dangerous.

Q. Why was it considered too dangerous?—*A.* Because there were so many threats out against the republican party.

Q. Who made those threats?—*A.* The white people. Just before the election, Mr. Don Williams told me he heard fifty men in Mansfield swear they would kill me if I made my appearance. . . .

Q. Did you run on the republican ticket for any office?—*A.* I was on the republican ticket in the election previous to the last election, but was not a candidate at the last election.

Q. Why did these men say they would kill you?—*A.* Because I was in a party opposite against them.

Q. Because you were a republican?—*A.* Yes, sir.

Q. Had you done anything to make them angry with you personally?—*A.* Not at all. . . .

Q. How is it with the parties up there on the question of suffrage? Are the democrats up there satisfied to let the colored people vote?—*A.* I believe they are perfectly willing for them to vote, provided they vote as they want them to vote. . . .

Q. Were there any threats of violence?—*A.* There was plenty of that from time to time. One thing that was frequently said was, that you could not vote against a man and eat out of his smoke-house: another, that you could not vote against a man and expect to receive justice from him at all. This has been pretty much the talk; and against me as the leader, they made mighty heavy threats.

Q. Was there anything said up there amongst the colored people about the Ku-Klux?—*A.* Oh, yes, sir; there was Ku-Klux up there.

Q. What was said about them?—*A.* The Ku Klux went to some of their houses once or twice. They had not got to killing at that time, but they were so disguised you could not state whether they were men or not. They passed as spirits, and pretended to raise the dead rebel soldiers. They went to the graveyard and frightened one woman very bad. They charged right through the graveyard on horseback.

Q. How did the Ku-Klux appear when they came?—*A.* I never got my "eye-sight" on them, but I saw people that did. They passed for ghosts—for men raised from the dead. They would come round and tell a man "Hold my head till I fix my backbone right"; and the colored people didn't know whether they were ghosts or not, because one of them went to a man's house and called for a drink of water. He drew three buckets of water and carried to him, and he drank every drop of it. He had to go to the pump and start it fresh three times, and when he came back the bucket each time was empty. I never saw them, but there were some of the worst disguised people you ever saw. Some of them had sheets round them. . . .

Q. What did they do when they first came out?—*A.* One man saw one of the Ku-Klux and though he was a spirit, and raised his gun and was going to shoot at him when the man said "Look out; don't shoot me, sir;" and then he knew he was a man, and rode off. They had not commenced killing people when they first came out. I took it for a sort of fun, and didn't believe they would hurt anybody.

Q. Afterwards what did they do?—*A.* Afterwards they came to a man's house and killed him. They didn't play with him then. . . .

Q. Were they afraid of them?—*A.* Yes, sir; and I don't blame them for being afraid.

Q. Did they understand that this had anything to do with politics?—*A.* They very well knew that it all arose from politics, because we never heard of such a thing before.

Isham Buckhalter (black man) sworn and examined on behalf of Mr. Sypher.

I live in Franklintown, Washington Parish, I am working a farm on shares. I have lived there for twenty-three or twenty-four years. . . . I voted the democratic ticket at the November election. I am not a democrat. That is not my principles. I was bound to vote the democratic ticket or to do worse.

Question. How did you expect to do worse?—*Answer.* I expected to be flung out of employment into the woods.

Q. Why did you think so?—*A.* I had reason to think so. I tried all I could to vote my way, and could not do it. I had to vote the other way. I had republican tickets but I was afraid to distribute them. I was afraid of the whole democratic party of the parish.

Q. Did they ever threaten you?—*A.* Yes; they Ku-Kluxed my house and knocked down one leaf of the door. I got away out of the house. They came in and inquired for the radical tickets that I had. They happened to be in my purse, and I had it in the pocket of my pants. There were some old tickets there, which they took and burned up. I cannot tell you who these men were. They were disguised. They were dressed in sheets, and wore false faces. They fired off a gun and pistol while they were in my house.

Q. Are you a leading man up there among the colored people?—*A.* They call me a leading man among them. . . .

Question. How many Ku-Klux came to your house?—*Answer.* About fifteen or twenty, not less than fifteen. My father-in-law was there, but he was disabled; he could not get up without crutches. My family were all in the house; my little boy got frightened, and every now and then since he has spasms, and will cry out, "Look, papa, Ku-Klux!" When I hear that, I tell you it hurts me through. The Ku-Klux looked like people. Some had hats, and some caps. They had false faces and white sheets all over their horses.

. . . I heard the Sunday evening before that they had killed John Kemp and another colored man. I thought to myself that they would kill me, too, as they called me a leading colored man. I believe to-day that they would have killed me if they had caught me. . . .

Q. Were the colored people much afraid of them?—*A.* They were bound to be afraid of them. What could they do but be afraid? Certainly they were afraid. If it had not been for them, they would have voted as they wanted to vote. They did not think they were ghosts. Any sensible human would know that they were not ghosts. I never heard of ghosts jumping off their horses and knocking down doors, and taking such shapes as that. We knew they were men. . . .

Q. What did you colored men understand by their doings?—*A.* That they were going around scaring us to make us vote their way.

41st Congress, 2d Session, House of Representatives, *Testimony Taken by the Sub-Committee of Elections in Louisiana* (Washington, D.C.: Government Printing Office, 1870), Part 1, 150, 153–54, 400–401.

ᔓ

Sut Lovingood's Allegory (1868)
GEORGE WASHINGTON HARRIS

One of the South's most popular humor writers, George Washington Harris, a Tennessee native, rose to prominence and produced most of his best-known work at the same time as the Klan's insurgency. Harris's collection of comic sketches entitled Yarns Spun by a Nat'ral Durn'd Fool *featured the country bumpkin Sut Lovingood. The tales were published just as Congress was passing the Reconstruction Acts and the Klan's popularity was spreading throughout those areas most receptive to Harris's sketches. Sut Lovingood stories appeared in Klan-sympathizing newspapers, including those that capitalized on the Klan sensation, such as the* Ku Klux Kaleidoscope *(Goldsboro, N.C.). Literary critics and other scholars, however, have usually dismissed Harris's humor as a regional folk genre, a form of rowdy frontier humor. Too little attention has been focused on the interrelationship between Harris's comic sketches of racial violence and the Reconstruction counterrevolution during which the Klan flourished. White southern readers were apt to consume Harris's Sut Lovingood tales as part of a print culture that included comic newspaper stories, such as the ones reproduced earlier in the chapter. An example of a Sut Lovingood yarn is this brief allegory in which Harris uses a black goat (goats were a common folk symbol for sexual disorder and adultery) to represent the black Republican social order brought on by Reconstruction. Most of Harris's tales involve Sut's violent pranks against actual freed slaves, rather than an animal allegory, and contain graphically offensive racist language.*

PROBLEMS TO CONSIDER

1. How might Harris's tales be seen as part of a culture war during Reconstruction?
2. How do Harris's tales relate to "The First Vote" illustration at the beginning of this chapter, or to other aspects of the South's social and political revolution?

I was just thinking boys, while Sut was speaking, whether we are the gainer by the discoveries — inventions — innovations, and prayers, of the last forty years. Whether the railway — telegraph — chloroform — moral reform, and other advancements, as they are termed, have really advanced us any, in the right direction or —

"Stop right thar, George, an' take my idear ove the thing, fresh from water. I know powerful well that I is a durn'd fool, an' all that — but I can *see*, by golly! Don't the Bible tell about them seekin' out many strange inventions?" . . .

"No, boys, we aint as *good* as we wer forty years ago. We am too dam artifichul, interprizin an' *sharp* — we know too much. We ought to be sarved like Old Brakebill sarved his black billy goat. We desarve hit, mos' all ove us." . . .

Well! Sut if you will not let me talk, suppose you tell us how Brakebill served his black billy goat. And let us draw no comparisons between the lost past and the present, which we must endure.

"Oh! I dont know much about hit. Only hearsay, from the old folks, you know. Hit seems that he had, what would be call'd now a days, a progressive billy goat — a regular, walkin insult to man, an' beast; he strutted, with his hine laigs, and munched, like a fool gall with hir fore ones. An' then his tail — hit said, 'you-be-dam,' all day long, an' him as black as a coal cellar, at midnight at that. He would a suited our day to a dot tho', an' our day would a suited him. He could a hilt his own, ever agin the 'business men.' . . .

"But, he wer altogether too dam smart for Brakebill, or Brakebill's day, an' generashun beyant all sort of doubt. That ar meterfistickal, free will, billy goat wer forty years ahead ove *his* day. As they say in praise ove some cussed raskil, when he gets a million in a week, when at the gineril rate ove fortin makin, hit had orter took him sixty days. He had been showin many marks ove progress, an' higher law, for a good while, without attractin much notice anyway. Sich as buttin old misses Brakebill, bucket an' all, belly down, clean thru onder the cow, as she stoop'd to milk her. An' then buttin the cow herself out ove her slop tub, so that he could wet his own beard in her supper. That wer 'higher law,' warnt hit? Or he'd watch for the old man to go from the crib to the hog pen, with thirty big ears of corn, piled on his arm. When he'd make a demonstrashun in the rear, that would send the old feller, spread eagle fashion, plowin gravel with his snout, while he impudently munch'd the hog's corn. That were financeerin, I s'pose. . . .

"But at last Mister Benny overdid the thing; he got to be a little too durn'd progressive for old Brakebill and his times. His sin foun' him out, an' he wer made to simmer down to a level surface with the loss ove all, that makes life wholesome to a goat. The fac' is, like mos' ove these yere human progress humbugs, he jis' played h—l with hissef.

"Old Brakebill got to noticin that thar was something wrong with his sheep. The ewes butted at the ram, spiteful like, butted one another an' behaved powerful bad ginerally. Arter a while, on 'zaminin he foun' that some ove the lambs had patches ove coarse har in their wool, an' wer sproutin' beards. Nex' he found' his young pigs behavin' curious to be dutch hog's children. Rarin' up strait on thar hine laigs, clost fornint one another. Walkin' on top ove the fences—climbin' onto the shed roof ove the milk house, an' then buttin' another off agin. An' every now an' then, one would hist his tail as strait up as a stack pole, an' put on a stiff strut. . . . Misses Brakebill left the plantation, an' the very devil was to pay generally. If you had a wanted to a bought the farm, you would a axed that dam goat the price ove hit, from his airs an' impudent ways, while the owner looked like a scared dorg, or a stepchild on the out aidge ove sufferance. Now, all this troubled the poor old Dutchman a power. He know'd that at the rate things were gwine on, his stock, very soon, wouldent be worth a tinker's durn. . . . You must bar in mind that the poor feller dident know the fust durn'd thing about 'progress.' At last, by the livin' jingo! the *true* idear struck him, as hit mus *us* some time. So one mornin' arter drams, he come acrost a bran new, curious, little cuss, lookin' like a cross atwixt the devil an' a cookin' stove, standin' on hit's hine laigs, a suckin' the muley cow. Arter brainin' hit with a wagon standard, he jist sot down, an' whetted his knife, ontil it would shave the har off his arm. Now, boys, that's about all that anybody now livin' knows ove the matter. Only this much was noticed thararter: That Mister Benny, billy goat, instid ove chawin his cud, with a short, quick, sassey nip, nip, nip, arter that mornin', an' plum on, ontil he dried up, an' died in a sink-hole, he chaw'd hit arter the fashion ove an old, lazy cow, when she is standin' onder the shade ove the willers, bellyfull, an' bellydeep in the creek. His tail never agin flauntd the sky, surjestin 'youbedam.' He wer the very last one that you'd a thought ove axin about the price ove the farm. An *he dident raise any more family.*"

George Washington Harris, *Sut Lovingood's Yarns*, edited by M. Thomas Inge (New Haven: College and University Press, 1966), 315–20.

⟿

⌁ THE SEXUALIZATION OF POLITICS AND THE WORK OF WHITE SUPREMACY

As "Sut Lovingood's Allegory" reveals, white southerners expressed their fears of the new freedoms and independence of African Americans in the language of heightened anxiety about the sexual agency of black men. Southerners, white and black, admitted that black men associated voting with an assertion of their manhood. Joseph H. Rainey, a black congressman from South Carolina, declared on the floor of the U.S. House of Representatives that southern white men wished to deny suffrage to black men because they knew it "had a tendency to make him feel his manhood." "Just as soon as we begin to assert our manhood and demand our rights," Rainey concluded, "we become objectionable, we become obnoxious, and we hear this howl about social equality." In the face of the rapid dismantling of centuries of restraint over every aspect of former slaves' lives, many white southerners latched onto the phrase "social equality" to express their hostility to black and white people intermingling in public and private spaces. For many, that phrase was meant to hoist up a warning flag against sexual encounters between black men and white women.

If we conjure images of white southerners' responses to sex between white women and black men, a picture of unflinching hostility and immediate violence, typified by lynchings or Klan raids, commonly appears. But this was not a timeless phenomenon; rather, it sprang from the unique social and political developments that shaped the history of the South after the Civil War. Before the war, southern communities tolerated a variety of liaisons between black men and white women, and only rarely did such relationships result in violent or extralegal retribution. The legal institution of slavery prevented that. The bodies of slave men belonged to their master, and their property status guaranteed a certain degree of toleration. But once the bulwarks of white supremacy were swept away by slavery's demise, those who wished to maintain a system of racial dominance needed to build a new foundation for it in the South.

In the nineteenth-century South, power, politics, freedom, and citizenship rights were tied intimately to the racial constructions of gender and sexuality. White patriarchs of the slave South could measure their dominance by the freedom with which they could sexually abuse black women with impunity. Not surprisingly, they exploited fears that manhood rights for black men might now include access to white women, and they tied those fears to the violent counterrevolution against Reconstruction politics.

U.S. Senate Investigation of the Ku Klux Klan, Testimony of Thomas Tate and J. R. Smith (1872)

The U.S. Senate's investigation of Klan activities in the early 1870s brought together the voices of white and black southerners, Republicans and Democrats, Klan supporters and its opponents. Frequently, witnesses testified to the connections between politics and gender and sexuality. Reproduced here are excerpts of the testimonies of Thomas Tate, a former member of the Klan in North Carolina, and J. R. Smith, a white Republican postmaster in Meridian, Mississippi.

PROBLEMS TO CONSIDER

1. Explain all of the references to both politics and gender in the Klan's oath read at the beginning of Tate's testimony. What does it reveal about the social order that opponents of Reconstruction desired?
2. What do these testimonies reveal about the role of race or class in constructing the meaning of the term "social equality"?

TESTIMONY OF THOMAS TATE
Raleigh, North Carolina, January 1872

COUNSEL. Mr. Tate, listen to this:

"I, before the great immaculate God of heaven and earth, do take and subscribe to the following sacred binding oath and obligation: I promise and swear that I will uphold and defend the Constitution of the United States as it was handed down by our forefathers, in its original purity. I promise and swear that I will reject and oppose the principles of the radical party in all its forms, and forever maintain and contend that intelligent white men shall govern this country. I promise and pledge myself to assist, according to my pecuniary circumstances, all brothers in distress. Females, widows, and their households shall ever be specially in my care and protection. I promise and swear that I will obey all instructions given me by my chief; and should I ever divulge, or cause to be divulged, any secret, signs, or passwords of the Invisible Empire, I must meet with the fearful and the just penalty of the traitor, which is death, death, death, at the hands of the brethren."

Did you ever hear that before?

Answer. Yes, sir.

Question. Where did you hear this?

Answer. At our meetings.

Question. The Invisible Empire?

Answer. Yes, sir; at Horse Creek Den. . . .

Question. How did you come to have disguises, any way?

Answer. It was ordered by the chief to have them. . . .

Question. Did you ever go on any raid?

Answer. Yes, sir; three of them.

Question. Where?

Answer. The first on some colored man, Robert McKinney, and Widow Bridges.

Question. What did you understand it was for?

Answer. That was the orders. I was not at the meeting and didn't know why. I didn't help to whip them. . . .

Question. What was the purpose of the society?

Answer. It was to keep down the colored un's from mixing with the whites.

Question. How?

Answer. To keep them from marrying, &c., and to keep them from voting.

TESTIMONY OF J. R. SMITH
Washington, D.C., June 27, 1871

J. R. SMITH sworn and examined. . . .

Question. Is there not considerable apprehension on the part of the poor white people of that region in regard to negro equality and social equality? . . .

Answer. No, sir; there are remarkably few negroes that show a disposition to—

Question. Is not that the point upon which the democratic leaders always try to stir up the white people?

Answer. That is the means adopted by the leaders of the democratic party.

Question. That is what I mean.

Answer. Oh, yes; they talk much of that idea, and endeavor to instill it into the minds of the white people generally, and are successful to a very great extent.

Question. I want to get at the method by which they arouse the feelings of the poorer white men.

Answer. That is the burden of their argument; this question of equality that they say is endeavored to be forced upon them by the republican party, putting the negro everywhere, and putting him into position.

Question. How do they talk about this subject?

Answer. They put it in very plain terms. They say that the object of the republican party and of the Government is to put the negro in control, to make a sort of negro supremacy, to give him the control of the affairs of the Government, to put him in office, and gradually to force him into social relations with the white people. That is the argument they make use of, to the exclusion of almost every other argument, when they come before the poorer classes of the white people. That has been the case for the last three years, and it does affect the opinions of a large number of the poor white men who are really and honestly republicans, and friends of the Government. But that thing is pressed upon them so strenuously by these leaders that it has had its effect.

Question. Not only political but social equality?

Answer. Yes, sir.

Question. Marrying the whites to blacks?

Answer. Yes, sir; they take the position that putting colored men into office, in positions of prominence, will gradually lead them to demand social equality, and to intermingle by marriage with the whites.

Question. Do the negroes themselves attempt anything of this kind?

Answer. They do not; not in my section of the State. There has been very little, if any, effort on the part of any negro to force himself forward, socially, upon the whites.

U.S. Congress, Joint Select Committee on the Condition of Affairs in the Late Insurrectionary States, *Testimony Taken by the Joint Select Committee to Inquire into the Condition of Affairs in the Late Insurrectionary States*, 13 vols. (Washington, D.C.: Government Printing Office, 1872), 2:434; 11:63, 76.

ᴈ

U.S. Senate Investigation of the Ku Klux Klan, Testimony Regarding Jourdan Ware (1871)

The following Senate testimony revolves around a successful former slave, Jourdan Ware, who lived near Rome, Georgia. Ware was severely beaten by "disguised men" and forced to move off his farm. And although these witnesses were not aware at the time, Ware would be beaten to death in a later encounter with the Klan.

PROBLEMS TO CONSIDER

1. What is the connection between politics, Ware's economic success, and accusations of inappropriate sexual remarks by Ware in these testimonies?
2. How did class influence the way politics became sexualized?

TESTIMONY OF P. M. SHEIBLEY
Washington, D.C., July 10, 1871

[*Sheibley was the white Republican postmaster at Rome, Georgia.*]

P. M. SHEIBLEY sworn and examined. . . .

Answer. . . . At present, disturbances are still greater and violence occurs. This violence is done by disguised men, and generally toward the colored people, threatening them that they shall not vote; shall not interfere in the elections; that they must not vote the radical ticket. In several instances where I have known outrages to be committed, the parties have come to me; I did not myself see the outrages committed, because I was not with the band. But two different negroes have come to me and asked what they should do—what could be done for them. One of these negroes was named Jourdan Ware, and lived about two and a half miles from Rome. He was taken out of his house, and beaten and abused; he came to my office with his head mangled. . . .

Question. How long had you known him?

Answer. Ever since he registered. The registration took place in 1867, I believe. . . .

Question. What is his reputation and character?

Answer. So far as I know, his reputation was good.

Question. Did you ever hear him charged with any offense or violation of law?

Answer. No, sir; I never did. . . .

Question. Was he to any extent a leading man, a prominent man among the colored people?

Answer. Rather so. The Ware family is one of some prominence; old Mr. Ware, the old man of all, had owned a great many slaves. . . .

Question. What did he tell you in reference to the particulars of that transaction?

Answer. I have stated that it was on account of his politics.

Question. Was this assault committed upon him by a band of disguised men?

Answer. Yes, sir; by disguised men.

Question. Did he say that they told him it was on account of his politics?

Answer. Yes, sir; and then an additional reason, which he mentioned, was to get possession of his place; that is, "to break him up," as the common phrase is. He was fixed very comfortably there. He had rented a place from a lady living in town, and was cultivating about thirty acres of land, and was taking care of the place for her at a specified rate.

Question. Was it because somebody else wanted to get possession of that property, or did they merely want to break him up and drive him off?

Answer. This band wanted to break him up. In connection with telling him that he was a radical, and should not vote the radical ticket any more, they told him that he must go away from there.

Question. What became of this man Ware?

Answer. I have not seen him more than once or twice since, and I do not know what has become of him. He has left the place, however, and is not in possession of it. . . .

Question. Did you ever hear from anybody that there was any allegation against this man Ware, that he had committed any offense against anybody?

Answer. No, sir.

TESTIMONY OF B. F. SAWYER
Atlanta, Georgia, November 1, 1871

[Sawyer was a Democratic newspaper editor in Rome.]

B. F. SAWYER sworn and examined. . . .

Question. What was the case of the negro Jordan [Ware] to which you allude here?

Answer. The case as reported to me by an ex-Federal soldier, a gentleman by the name of Helmcamp, was this: I asked him why they whipped Jordan. It was done on the premises where he was. He said Jordan had insulted a white lady a few days before, and they had whipped him for that. That is all I know about it. . . . I asked him what he would have done. He said, "I should not have waited until night to have whipped him, but I would have blowed his brains out that day."

Question. What was the insult given?

Answer. He had made lecherous advances to the lady.

Question. In what way?

Answer. By speaking to her, and also by his acts.

Question. What had he said to her?

Answer. He called her "wife," and thrust out his tongue at her. The lady ran away very much frightened.

Question. That was the information you had?

Answer. That was the information Mr. Helmcamp gave me.

Question. You spoke of him as an ex-Federal soldier. Why did you mention that fact in connection with what you say was his statement to you?

Answer. I thought that you would regard him as good authority, at any rate as one who would not be apt to be biased.

Question. What are his politics?

Answer. He was a republican, I think, until the last election; at the last election he voted the democratic ticket.

TESTIMONY OF Z. B. HARGROVE
Washington, D.C., July 12, 1871

[Hargrove was a white attorney in Rome.] . . .

Z. B. HARGROVE sworn and examined. . . .

Question. What were you during the war?

Answer. I was an officer in the confederate army for nearly two and a half years. I was a rebel, and a true one, I reckon, if there ever was one. . . .

Question. What have been your political opinions since the war?

Answer. My antecedents are all democratic. . . . I was a reconstruction man, though that was rather in antagonism to my party. . . . I will say that the reason they gave for beating Jourdan Ware was that he had made some insulting remark to a white lady—a lady with whom I am well acquainted. Previous to that time he had borne the reputation of being an humble and obedient negro. He had a little farm, and was doing well, and was comfortable, though in a neighborhood surrounded by the poorer class of white people, who did not like his residence there. He may or may not have made some insulting remark to a white lady; I do not say whether he did or did not, though, from my knowledge of him, my opinion is that he did not.

Question. Let me understand the character of the allegation against him. You say that he made some insulting proposal to a white lady?

Answer. O, no; that he had just made some insulting remark. He remarked, "How d'ye, sis," or something of that kind, as the young lady passed down the road. She was a sister of the lady of whom he had rented the place on which he was living. He was driven away from his home, and came very near being killed. . . .

U.S. Congress, Joint Select Committee on the Condition of Affairs in the Late Insurrectionary States, *Testimony Taken by the Joint Select Committee to Inquire into the Condition of Affairs in the Late Insurrectionary States*, 13 vols. (Washington, D.C.: Government Printing Office, 1872), 6:43–45, 73–75; 7:878, 885.

⌁

⌁ Tracks of Conflict: Railroads and Chinese Immigration ⌁

The contested question that Wendell Phillips raised—"what makes or constitutes a citizen"—was not limited to conflicts between the North and South or between whites and blacks after the Civil War. The identity and privileges of citizenship also reared its head in heated battles between industrial capitalists and American laborers, and between white native-born workers and Chinese immigrant laborers, as the North's economic culture was crowned the victor after the war.

Perhaps the most significant development after the Civil War was the rapid expansion of railroads in the United States. In the eight years after the war ended (1865–1873), railroad companies in America laid 31,000 miles of track and capped that achievement with the completion of a transcontinental railroad in 1869. Its western road (the Central Pacific) was built almost entirely by the labor of 12,000 Chinese immigrant workers. Chinese immigrants were welcomed when their labor was needed, but even their employers balked at the idea of admitting them into the body politic. Central Pacific executive Charles Crocker, who probably hired more Chinese immigrants than anyone else, told a legislative committee in 1877, "I do not believe they are going to remain here long enough to become good citizens, and I would not admit them to citizenship." Even if they so desired, Chinese immigrants could not become citizens because the federal Naturalization Act of 1790 restricted naturalized citizenship to "white persons." That racial restriction certainly posed no problems to Americans before the Civil War, given that Indians had been forcibly removed and the vast majority of blacks were enslaved. But with Reconstruction, the possibility of nonwhite citizenship became a more pressing concern for white Americans.

The documents in this section reveal the transformative power of the railroads in American culture and expose the hostilities directed against Chinese immigrants in the years leading up to the Chinese Exclusion Act of 1882, as well as the growing cleavage between labor and big business during the great railroad strike of 1877.

Humors of Railroad Travel (1873)

THOMAS WORTH

Railroads transformed American life in the nineteenth century. Everything suddenly moved faster. The sounds, smells, and smoke of railroad engines became an indelible feature of the American landscape. Railroads represented the enormous energy of progress, and as John Gast's painting reveals (see chapter 8), they also became symbols of racial "manifest destiny." When a delegation of Americans led by Commodore Matthew C. Perry visited Japan in 1854 to open its ports for trade, they transported and built a quarter-scale model railroad on a circular track to demonstrate the irresistible strength of American technology. Railroads were also the source of repeated conflicts in the United States. As early as the 1840s, Ralph Waldo Emerson called the railroad "that work of art which agitates and drives mad the whole people." In his 1873 cartoon entitled "Humors of Railroad Travel," the illustrator Thomas Worth captured the bumps, bustles, and confusions that went along with railroad travel. By the 1870s, populists and labor activists also came to see railroads as the country's greatest source of corruption, exploitation, and monopoly privilege.

PROBLEMS TO CONSIDER

1. Is this cartoon an endorsement or a criticism of railroad travel?
2. What are the principal themes of the humor in this cartoon?

Thomas Worth, "Humors of Railroad Travel," *Harper's Weekly*, September 20, 1873.
(The Granger Collection, New York.)

The Chinese in California (1869)

HENRY GEORGE

Many years after the transcontinental railroad had been built, Henry George liked to recall that during the 1850s he went to a theater in San Francisco, and at a climax in the performance a curtain was dropped with a bold painting depicting the overland railroad wending its way to the Pacific. The audience sprang to their feet with thunderous applause. But George recalled that he stopped and wondered whether the railroad would actually improve the lives of laborers. "As the country grows, people come in, wages will go down," were his thoughts. George was a young newspaper editor when the railroad neared completion. In 1868, he published an essay entitled "What the Railroad Will Bring Us." A year later, he focused his concerns on the "Chinese problem" caused by industrialists' desire for cheap Chinese immigrant labor and wondered what would be the consequences when thousands of Chinese workers had completed their work on the railroads. A decade later, George published Progress and Poverty *(1879), the most widely read radical book of the nineteenth century. In it he devised a scheme—the "single tax"—to strip the wealthy of their monopoly on land, make laborers into farmers, drive up wages, and end unemployment and periodic industrial depressions.*

PROBLEMS TO CONSIDER

1. Unlike other racist anti-immigrant sentiments, George offers a fairly positive appraisal of Chinese immigrants. In his opinion, why does this make them even more dangerous?
2. Whom does George blame for the "Chinese problem"?

CHARACTER OF THE ASIATIC IMMIGRATION—THE PROBLEM OF THE PACIFIC COAST

Look at the swarming that is possible from this vast human hive! Consider that if all humanity were marshaled, every third man in the line would wear the queue and the blouse of a Chinaman: that this half billion people could throw off annually six, ten, twenty millions of emigrants, and this not merely without feeling the loss, but without there being any loss. . . .

According to the count of the six great Chinese Companies—to one or the other of which all, or nearly all of the Chinese upon the Pacific Coast belong—there are some 65,000 Chinamen in California and adjacent States and Territories. Knowing the jealousy with which they

are regarded, the Chinese are disposed to understate their numbers, and it is probable that the true figures are nearer 100,000 than those given. Speaking roughly, they may be said to constitute at least one-fourth of the adult male population.
. . .

But it would be easier to recount the industries in which Chinamen are not yet to some extent engaged than to mention those in which they are, and every day their employment is extending, as employers in one branch of production after another, discover that they can avail themselves of this cheap labor. They are not only grading railways and opening roads (work for which they are now altogether relied on) cutting wood, picking fruit, tending stock, weaving cloth, and running sewing machines; but acting as firemen upon steamers, running stationary engines, painting carriages, upholstering furniture, making boots, shoes, clothing, cigars, tin and wooden-ware. . . .

The great characteristics of the Chinese as laborers are patience and economy—the first makes them efficient laborers, the second cheap laborers. As a rule they have not the physical strength of Europeans, but their steadiness makes up for this. They take less earth at a spadefull than an Irishman; but in a day's work take up more spadesfull. This patient steadiness peculiarly adapts the Chinese for tending machinery and for manufacturing. The tendency of modern production is to a greater and greater subdivision of labor—to confine the operative to one part of the process, and to require of him close attention, patience, and manual dexterity, rather than knowledge, judgment, and skill. It is in these qualities that the Chinese excel. . . .

CHEAPNESS OF CHINESE LABOR

But the great recommendation of Chinese labor is its cheapness. There are no people in the world who are such close economists as the Chinese. They will live, and live well, according to their notions, where an American or European would starve. A little rice suffices them for food, a little piece of pork cooked with it constitutes high living, an occasional chicken makes it luxurious. Their clothes cost but little and last for a long while. Go into a Chinese habitation and you will see that every inch of space is utilized. . . . Their standard of comfort is very much lower than that of our own people—very much lower than that of any European immigrants who come among us. This fact enables them to underbid all competitors in the labor market. Reduce wages to the starvation point for our mechanics, and the Chinaman will not merely be able to work for less, but to live better than at home, and to save money from his earnings. And thus in every case in which Chinese comes into fair competition with white labor, the whites must either retire from the field or come down to the Chinese standard of living. . . .

HOSTILITY TO THE CHINESE— UNEQUAL TAXATION

. . . But though the Chinese in many parts of the Pacific coast have been treated badly enough, a most exaggerated idea upon this subject prevails in the East. It is not true, as is sometimes asserted, that a Chinamen cannot walk the streets of a Pacific town without being insulted or assailed. One cannot walk half a block in these towns without meeting a Chinaman, and in any part of San Francisco, at any time, day or night, Chinamen (though boys occasionally shy stones at them) are much safer than are strangers in New-York.

As the competition of Chinese labor with white labor has become more general and threatening, the feeling against them has become correspondingly intense. But a counteracting feeling in their favor has also been developed. While making enemies of the workmen with whom they come into competition, they have made friends of the employers, who found a profit in their labor, and as they have become massed in the employ of great corporations, and in the cities, they are more easily protected.

There is now more reason for an anti-Chinese feeling in California than at any time before; and that feeling, though less general, may be more intense, but it certainly is not as powerful as it has been, and it is doubtful if it could at present secure the prohibition of Chinese immigration, even were there no Constitutional obstacles in the way. . . . There are too many interests becoming involved in the employment of Chinese labor to make this feasible, unless by some sudden awakening to their danger the working classes should be led to such thorough union as should make numbers count for more than capital. . . . A very large and powerful class, rapidly becoming larger and more powerful, is directly interested in maintaining their right to avail themselves of Chinese labor; and this class is further reinforced by those who will prospectively profit by the cheapening of wages, and those whom political sentiment has led to an acceptance in all its fullness of the doctrine of the equality of the races. . . .

CHARACTER OF THE CHINESE

. . . The Mongolians, who are now coming among us on the other side of the continent, differ from our own race by as strongly marked characteristics as do the negroes, while they will not as readily fall into our ways as the negroes. The difference between the two races in this respect is as the difference between an ignorant but docile child and a grown man, sharp but narrow-minded, opinionated and set in character. The negro when brought to this country was a simple barbarian with nothing to unlearn; the Chinese have a civilization and history of their own; a vanity which causes them to look down on all other races, habits of thought rendered permanent by being stamped upon countless generations. . . . A population born in China, reared in China, expecting to return to China, living while here in a little China of its own, and without the slightest attachment to this country—utter heathens, treacherous, sensual, cowardly, and cruel. They bring no women with them . . . except those intended for purposes of prostitution. . . .

WHAT SHALL WE DO WITH THEM?

Take it in any aspect, does not this Chinese question merit more attention than it has received? A little cloud now on the far Western horizon, does it not bid fair to overshadow the whole future of the Republic? . . . Give him fair play and this quality enables him to drive out stronger races. One hundred thousand Mongolians on the Pacific coast means so many less of our race now and hereafter to be. . . .

In truth it is not to be wondered at that Chinese immigration should find so many advocates in the Pacific States. With their unparalleled natural resources, an unlimited supply of this cheap labor will make them beyond all question the most remunerative field in the world for the employment of capital, where the rich will get richer with unexampled rapidity. California will not only become a great mining and a great agricultural State, but a great manufacturing State; controlling by virtue of her cheap labor the immense market opening in the heart of the continent, and competing successfully with New and Old England almost to their doors. Let but the introduction of Chinese labor go a little further and the same change which was wrought in Southern sentiment regarding Slavery by the invention of the cotton-gin will be completed on the Pacific in the feeling toward Chinese labor.

Henry George, "The Chinese in California," *New York Daily Tribune*, May 1, 1869.

ॐ

Chinese Immigrants Challenge Nativist Discrimination: California State Senate Investigation (1876)

As we might expect, the voices of Chinese immigrants never were heard as loudly in the public sphere as were the anti-immigration voices of native-born laborers. The docility of Chinese workers, however, was a myth that suited nativist aggression. When facing discrimination or exploitation, Chinese immigrants did rise up and resist, although with mixed results. In the spring of 1867, thousands of Chinese workers went on strike against the Central Pacific Railroad, demanding an eight-hour workday and wages of forty-five dollars a month. Charles Crocker flirted with the idea of transporting 10,000 black men from the South to replace the striking Chinese workers but instead settled on a plan of cutting off their food supplies and literally starving them back to work. In 1876, the California legislature initiated hearings on the problem of Chinese immigration. Although the legislature concluded that such immigration was "an unmitigated evil" and they successfully lobbied Congress to eventually pass the Chinese Exclusion Act in 1882, these hearings gave Chinese immigrants a chance to raise their voices against the daily discrimination they faced. Legislators tried to get most Chinese witnesses to confirm their presumed stereotypes (for example, that the Chinese were dirty or that they exploited women as prostitutes), but occasionally an independent immigrant would confound their efforts.

PROBLEMS TO CONSIDER

1. How did these immigrants challenge the hostile questioning they encountered from state legislators?
2. What do these testimonies reveal about the way Chinese immigrants understood the era's labor and citizenship issues? Compare their perspectives with Henry George's.

TESTIMONY OF HONG CHUNG (1876)

HONG CHUNG sworn.

Mr. Donovan—How long have you been in this country?

A.—Twenty-four years.

Q.—Are you in business here?

A.—I am Inspector for the Sam-yup Company.

Q.—Have you declared your intention of becoming an American citizen?

A.—Yes, sir. . . .

Q.—Are many other Chinamen going to become citizens?

A.—Yes, sir.

Q.—A great many?

A.—Yes, sir.

Q.—Will all become American citizens?

A.—Yes, sir.

Q.—And stay here?

A.—Yes, sir.

Q.—Will they become candidates for the office of Governor of the State as soon as they are citizens?

A.—May be; I don't know. They are going to become citizens. I like to be citizen. American man make no good laws for Chinaman. We make good laws for Chinaman citizens.

Q.—Would you like to be Governor of the State of California?

A.—Of course. I like the State of California a long time; I like a free country.

Q.—Would you like to be Governor?

A.—I cannot be Governor. I like the State of California, and I like to be a citizen of the American man's people.

Q.—Would you like to hold office under the free American Government?

A.—No, I wouldn't do it.

TESTIMONY OF LEM SCHAUM (1876)

LEM SCHAUM sworn.

Mr. Haymond—How long have you resided in California?

A.—About fourteen years, sir.

Q.—From what part of China did you come?

A.—One hundred and fifty miles from Canton. . . .

Q.—Are you a Christian Chinaman?

A.—Yes, sir.

Q.—How long since you believed in the Christian religion?

A.—Since about eighteen hundred and seventy.

Q.—Have you tried to make Christians out of your countrymen here?

A.—I tried that; but it is very hard work to do it.

Q.—Do some of them pretend to be Christians when they are not?

A.—Only those grown-up fellows; the young boys do not. Boys working around see the American customs, and we can instruct them in no time; but the old ones think Confucius' is the only good religion, and with them it is very hard work. . . .

Q.—How many Christian Chinamen do you think there are in California altogether?

A.—About four years ago we formed a Chinese Young Men's Christian Association at the Rev. Dr. Loomis' place. There were twenty-eight of us when we formed that society, but the number has grown up to about five hundred.

Q.—Do you think that many are Christians?

A.—I think about half are real Christians. . . .

Q.—You have seen the Chinese quarters? Do you think that it is good for the Chinese, or for the Americans, to have those people living as they do?

A.—I think it is very bad for both Chinese and Americans.

Q.—As a general rule, taking the one hundred and fifty thousand of them in California, they don't learn much good after they come here, do they? Don't they learn the vices of the country?

A.—That is your own fault. No Chinaman can take a walk up and down the street unless you find an Irishman or a Dutchman to strike them down. They struck one down and I told them I would have them arrested and put in the County Jail for six months. A great many Chinamen desire to learn to read and write English, and then also our methods of business, or any kind of work; perhaps the arts or sciences.

Q.—They live very cheaply, don't they?

A.—They must live cheaply, sir. They have got to live cheaply because they only get about fifteen dollars a month, or three or four dollars a week.

Q.—A great many live in the same house?

A.—Yes; a great many live together, because they have not got money enough to have rooms as you have. . . .

Q.—Suppose the mass of that immigration was stopped, do you think it would have any influence on our commercial relations with other parts of China?

A.—No. I think this immigration must stop. I say it is not only ruining Americans, but it ruins the Chinese. Their wages, we notice, come down every day. A short time ago Chinamen got thirty-six dollars a month working on the railroad. What do they get now? Twenty-six dollars per month—one dollar a day. This immigration must be stopped in some way. . . .

Q.—What is the general opinion of Christian Chinamen with whom you associate in this State as to the policy or impolicy of having this Chinese immigration continue without any limits?

A.—We think that this immigration must be stopped. It must be stopped in some way, and then we can look after those Christians educated in this country. We want to stretch forth our hand as far as we can so as instruct them about a better world than this. That is our object, and a good many of them are going back to preach at home. Looking at this thing from a Christian standpoint, I think that christianity is not advanced by this immigration, and I would give anything in the world to have it stopped.

Q.—In the Eastern States, when we proposed to check this immigration, or to limit it to the better class of Chinese, we were met with this proposition: that Chinese immigration to this country would have the result of christianizing China. I understand you to say that the immigration, such as is coming here now, don't tend to the advancement of christianity?

A.—It does not.

Q.—So it would be better, then, from your standpoint as a Chinaman, to stop it, for by stopping it you would make more Christians?

A.—Yes, sir.

———

Chinese Immigration: The Social, Moral, and Political Effect of Chinese Immigration. *Testimony Taken Before a Committee of the Senate of the State of California* (Sacramento: State Printing Office, 1876), 114, 135–39.

ஃ

Every Dog (No Distinction of Color) Has His Day (1879)
THOMAS NAST

Thomas Nast was the most prolific and best-known political cartoonist in nineteenth-century America. He was also a first-generation immigrant, born in Landau in the Rhineland (a region claimed at different times by Prussia, Bavaria, France, and Germany), and emigrated to the United States at age six. By the time he was fifteen, Nast had been hired as a cartoonist for the top illustrated newspaper in New York. He is responsible for the image of the Republican elephant and the Democratic donkey, icons that are still in use today. Nast was also a Radical Republican, and his editorial cartoons advocated civil rights for former slaves, although his images often reinforced rather than challenged American racial stereotypes. At the height of anti-Chinese politics in the 1870s, Nast produced the following cartoon for the cover of Harper's Weekly. *In it, he caricatures the slogans of postwar nativist politics, giving it the caption "Red Gentleman to Yellow Gentleman: 'Pale face 'fraid you crowd him out, as he did me.'" In the background is a freedman, sitting on a cotton bale, with the caption "My day is coming."*

PROBLEMS TO CONSIDER

1. What are the various messages embedded in Nast's cartoon?
2. Was Nast's cartoon directed at any particular group of Americans?

Thomas Nast, "Every Dog (No Distinction of Color) Has His Day," *Harper's Weekly*, February 8, 1879.

(The Granger Collection, New York.)

Fair Wages (1877)

A "STRIKER"

The Recent Strikes (1877)

THOMAS A. SCOTT

Railroad corporations were the vanguard of the rise of "big business" in the United States. They leaped to adopt modern management methods, stimulating additional manufacturing sectors such as the iron and coal industries and creating a national market for the products of American manufacturers. Yet despite tremendous industrial growth after the Civil War, in 1873 the nation entered the worst depression in its history, a four-year-long stagnation that left as many as a million workers unemployed. Railroad workers endured repeated wage reductions throughout the depression, prompting railroad strikes in 1873 and 1874, but none compared to the "Great Uprising" in 1877. In March 1877, the presidents of four railroads agreed to cut wages again. Workers had reached their breaking point. Simultaneous work stoppages occurred in fourteen states that July; and in Pittsburgh, the Pennsylvania state militia opened fire on strikers, killing forty people and prompting strikers to burn, loot, and destroy tracks, locomotives, and other railroad property. Railroad lines were disrupted throughout the Northeast and Midwest, and sympathetic strikes of other industrial workers broke out everywhere. In Chicago, 20,000 workers took to the streets. The 1877 railroad strike was the first nationwide strike in American history, and the first in which the federal government directed its considerable resources (the army) to support big business. Soon after the strike, the North American Review *published separately a letter from a striking railway worker and a letter from Thomas Scott, president of the Pennsylvania Railroad. Their statements illustrate the sharp differences between capital and labor during an era of unprecedented industrial expansion in America.*

PROBLEMS TO CONSIDER

1. How do the values and ideals of this railroad worker and the president of the Pennsylvania Railroad differ? Both men appear fearful for the future; what does each anticipate the future will bring?
2. What were the repercussions of using a slavery analogy to describe capital versus labor at the end of Reconstruction?

FAIR WAGES

Forty years ago my father came over to this country from Sweden. . . . He heard that North America was peopled and governed by working-men, and the care of the States was mainly engaged in the welfare and prosperity of labor. That moved him, and so I came to be born here.

He, and millions like him, made this country their home, and their homes have mainly made this country what it is. . . .

[Since the Civil War,] it seems to me, the power has got fixed so long in one set of hands that things are settling down into a condition like what my father left behind in Europe forty years ago, and what stands there still. I mean the slavery of labor. The landed aristocracy over there made the feudal system, just as the moneyed men of this continent are now making a ruling class. As the aristocracy used to make war on each other, so in our time the millionaires live on each other's ruin. As the feudal lords hired mercenary soldiers to garrison their strongholds and to prey on the common people, so the railway lords and stock-exchange barons hire a mercenary press to defend power, the object of both being the same: the spoils of labor. . . .

That government has been regarded by the laboring classes of Europe and by our people as the stronghold of the workingman, and in this our present difficulty we are referred to its Constitution which should afford us a remedy for our grievances, the ballot-box is the panacea for all and every complaint. It is not so; and those who point to the remedy know it to be a sham,—they know they can buy idlers and vagabonds enough to swell the ranks of wealth and run up a majority whenever a show of hands is required. They recruit the very men that wrecked Pittsburgh, and would pillage New York if they dared to face us, the workingmen, that fill the ranks of the militia.

We are sick of this game, we are soul-weary of looking around for some sympathy or spirit of justice, and, finding none, we turn to each other and form brotherhoods and unions, depots of the army of labor, officered by the skilled mechanic.

This organized force is now in process of formation, and prepared to meet the great questions of the age: Has labor any rights? If so, what are they? Our claim is simple. We demand *fair wages*.

We say that the man able and willing to work, and for whom there is work to do, is entitled to wages sufficient to provide him with enough food, shelter, and clothing to sustain and preserve his health and strength. We contend that the employer has no right to speculate on starvation when he reduces wages below a living figure, saying, if we refuse that remuneration, there are plenty of starving men out of work that will gladly accept half a loaf instead of no bread.

We contend that to regard the laboring class in this manner is to consider them as the captain of a slave-ship regards his cargo, who throws overboard those unable to stand their sufferings. Let those who knew the South before the war go now amongst the mining districts of Pennsylvania, and compare the home of the white laborer with the quarters of the slave; let them compare the fruits of freedom with the produce of slavery!

But we know the question is a difficult one to settle,—we do not want to force it on with threats. The late strike was not intended to break out as it did; things broke loose and took a direction we regretted. We find ourselves answerable for results we had no share in or control over. Nevertheless we accept the event as a symptom of the disorder that is consuming our body and pray the country to look to it,—it is not a passing complaint. . . .

When folks say that labor and capital must find, by the laws of demand and supply, their natural relations to each other in all commercial enterprises, and neither one has any rights it can enforce on the other, they take for granted that the labor "market" is like the produce market, liable to natural fluctuations. If that were so, we should not complain. But it is not. The labor market has got to be like the stock and share market; a few large capitalists control it and make what prices they please. This sort of game may ruin the gamblers in stocks, and injure those who invest, but the trouble is confined mostly to those who deserve to lose or those who can afford it.

But not so when the same practice operates in the labor market. The capitalist must not gamble with the bread of the workingman, or if he does, let him regard where that speculation led France one hundred years ago, when the financiers made a corner in flour, and the people broke the ring with the axe of the guillotine.

A "Striker"

A "Striker," "Fair Wages," *North American Review* 125 (September 1877): 322–25.

THE RECENT STRIKES

I do not wish, and happily it is not necessary, to fill your pages with the mere recital of the distressing cases of violence and outrage which marked the course of these riots unexampled in American history. Suffice it to say that the conduct of the rioters is entirely inconsistent with the idea that this movement could have been directed by serious, right-minded men bent on improving the condition of the laboring classes. How wages could be improved by destroying property, the existence of which alone made the payment of any wages at all possible, it is difficult to understand. Nothing but the insanity of passion, played upon by designing and mischievous leaders, can explain the destruction of vast quantities of railroad equipment absolutely necessary to the transaction of its business, by men whose complaint was that the business done by the full equipment in possession of the railways did not pay them sufficient compensation for their labor.

During the greater part of our century of national existence we have enjoyed such unbroken prosperity that we had perhaps come to expect exemption from many of the worst problems which perplex other and older civilizations. The vast area of public land open to cultivation and settlement had steadily drained off not only our own surplus population, but that of other countries, and the rapid extension of our railway system, by furnishing markets for the productions of all parts of the country, had increased the national wealth and built up a general prosperity. But for the Civil War *[followed by the panic of 1873]* this state of things might have continued to exist. . . . Every important industry in the country has been compelled to practise the closest and most rigid economies, in order to escape marketing its products at an absolute loss. . . . In every manufacturing State in the country it is perfectly well known that many establishments have been kept in operation simply that the men

might be employed. This has been done often without one iota of profit to the owners. . . .

With the falling off of revenue from traffic, the question was presented at once to railway managers, . . . whether it would not be both wiser and kinder to retain as many men as possible in the service, by so allotting the work as to permit all to earn a sum, smaller indeed than in the past, yet it was hoped sufficient to support themselves and their families during the severe period of depression. . . .

This insurrection, which extended through fourteen States, and in many cases successfully defied the local authorities, presents a state of acts almost as serious as that which prevailed at the outbreak of the Civil War. Unless our own experience is to differ entirely from other countries, — and it is not easy to see why it should, with the increasing population of our large cities and business centres, and the inevitable assemblage at such points of the vicious and evil-disposed, — the late troubles may be but the prelude to other manifestations of mob violence, with this added peril, that now, for the first time in American history, has an organized mob learned its power to terrorize the law-abiding citizens of great communities. . . .

If the government of the United States is to exercise its power of protection or of remedy, it perhaps can do so only through an adequate exhibition of the military force that may be given it for such purposes by Congress. The important question is to ascertain in what way the government can so exhibit its military force as to secure the utmost possible efficiency in the enforcement of law and order without jarring or disturbing the general framework of our institutions and our laws. It seems to be indispensable, in the light of recent events, that whatever force is to be used by the government in such emergencies should be so distributed and controlled that it may be concentrated upon any point or points that may be threatened within a few hours of any outbreak. . . .

The magnitude of the evil to be met and dealt with can hardly be overstated. The remedy to be provided should be equally prompt and effective. It must be discussed and adopted in the interest of the whole country, and not of any particular class; for the interests of all classes of our citizens are the same in the maintenance of domestic peace and civil order.

But to no one class in the community is an absolute assurance of peace so important as to the men who have no capital but their labor. When the accumulations of labor are put in peril by lawlessness, capital may always protect itself by suspending the enterprises which give labor its value and insure it its reward. Anarchy not only deprives the laboring man of his present subsistence, but puts in jeopardy all his hopes of improvement for his own future and the future of his family.

THOMAS A. SCOTT

Thomas A. Scott, "The Recent Strikes," *North American Review* 125 (September 1877): 352–62.

ᴈᴄ

CHAPTER 2

New and Old Frontiers: 1877–1900

In early 1890, William F. "Buffalo Bill" Cody, the former Indian scout turned theatrical showman, transported his Wild West extravaganza of cowboys, Indians, Texas steers, and Plains buffalo to Italy, where they played the major sites—Venice, Rome, Verona—of the cradle of Western civilization. Everywhere he went, the Italians hailed "Boofalo Beel" as "magnifico!" For the American press who followed the events, the sight of cowboys and Indians occupying the ruins of the Roman empire was full of comical juxtapositions. Watching the troupe's arrival at Verona's ancient amphitheater, a *New York Times* correspondent relished the irony of "cowboys with sombreros" strutting where "nude gladiators" had once clashed. Cody probably saw the humor, too. But for him, the pageant of the western frontier contained a serious history lesson about the arrival of a new world power and civilization. There was no joking, then, when one of the show's cowboys pulled his horse up to the gates of Verona's amphitheater and snapped to the Italian attendant, "Get a gait on yourself, there, Beardy, and come and open this here iron fence."

The teaching tools of Cody's Wild West history lesson—blazing gun battles between whooping natives and gallant cavalrymen, sensational stunts by buck-skinned sharpshooters and acrobatic horsemen—claimed to portray the nation's frontier past. But the organization, production, and distribution of the Wild West show, no less than the conflicts and struggles it dramatized, more accurately reflected and responded to the major social changes and conflicts of the late nineteenth century: the rapid shift to industrial manufacturing and the growth of big business, the massive immigration from southern and eastern Europe, the suppression of Native American resistance to white settlement of the trans-Mississippi interior, and the increasing popular support for imperialist adventures in the Caribbean and the Pacific. After all, with a labor force of more than six hundred, Cody's Wild West differed little from the big businesses that came to define the American economy in this period. Cody used modern managerial techniques to discipline his large work force, national railroad and transatlantic shipping networks to transport his product to markets throughout the United States and Europe, and telegraph systems to relay publicity information and financial transactions. Moreover, the Plains Indians who reenacted some of the crowd's favorite scenes—such as the 1876 battle at Little Bighorn, when a massive force of Cheyenne and Sioux annihilated Lieutenant Colonel George Custer and the Seventh Cavalry—were themselves immigrant laborers. They would not have gone east to work for Cody if their campaigns to maintain their lands had not ultimately been crushed by the U.S. Cavalry. In three performances a day, these Indians willingly assisted Buffalo Bill in telling his (presumably) reassuring story of the frontier struggles that marked American civilization's triumph over backward savagery.

How reassuring that story actually was is a problem worth examining. The participation of the losers in this struggle was supposed to lend authenticity to the performances. But every time the Indian actors wiped out Custer's forces in the Little Bighorn battle, they also reenacted their resistance to the expansion of the white nation and underscored the moral and social conflicts of the era's history. Such complicated perspectives and motivations were at play in all the major cultural encounters and social upheavals that marked the United States' emergence as a modern urban-industrial nation and leading world power in the late nineteenth century. This chapter examines the conflicts and encounters that shaped efforts in the United States to understand and guide the unanticipated circumstances of an era of big business and class conflict, of cultural confrontation and racial war, and of imperialist demands for global influence and power.

⌁ *Wealth and Commonwealth: Battles for Workplace Authority* ⌁

"The old nations of the earth creep on at a snail's pace," the industrialist Andrew Carnegie observed in 1885. But "the Republic thunders past with the rush of the express." The steel magnate's crowing exaggerated the velocity at which the New World was outpacing the Old and repressed his own and many Americans' unease with the speed of change (after all, he resided at times in a Scottish castle). But Carnegie's remarks succinctly represented the pervasive sense that industrial capitalism not only had wrought dramatic social and physical changes on the American landscape but also had ushered in a new system of meanings. Postwar industrialism in the United States was marked by manufacturing that was enormous in scale, continuously in operation, and massively productive. Dozens of workers hand-rolling a thousand cigarettes in several hours' work was the old order of business. A single person milling thousands an hour on a Bonsack cigarette-making machine (first patented in 1881) was "the rush of the express." Certainly, such features were visible in the antebellum period, but in the decades after the Civil War, they came to define the economy, reshaping American life far beyond the greatly enlarged and increasingly mechanized factories that changed the face of the nation's cities. The new industrialism altered not only how people labored but also how they interacted at the workplace; it changed not only how people procured what they needed but also the types of goods and services they regarded as essential. Late-nineteenth-century capitalism, in other words, launched a cultural upheaval, challenging older values and expectations with new arrangements and priorities. Who, for instance, accounted for America's greatness: the people who worked on the factory floor, or the men who owned the factory? Who mattered most: the people making goods, those selling or those buying them, or those profiting from their sale? Everyone recognized that industry was revolutionizing American life, but how Americans explained and assessed these disruptions differed, often violently. Defenders asserted that the ruthless competition of the emerging economic order was, to use the oil magnate John D. Rockefeller's words, "the working out of a law of nature and a law of God." In their view, Americans were living their freedom as individuals to the fullest. Others viewed with alarm the vast combinations of industrial and financial power and the social conflict that swept the nation. Instead of a republic of independent free men, they foresaw one of homeless beggars and tyrannical millionaires.

The Modern Corporation (1908)

GEORGE W. PERKINS

Many defenders of the new business order subscribed to the belief that individualism made American business great. As the financier Henry Clews explained in 1907, everyone "accomplishes more in a condition of freedom or Individualism, and the whole nation is richer, than if custom or a Socialistic community fettered and restricted men, and compelled them to work according to rule." However, one of the most important aspects of the new industrial culture was the widespread use of incorporation as a method of organizing businesses. In the largely unregulated and risk-filled marketplace of the late nineteenth century, corporations had many advantages over the partnerships or family ownership of firms that had characterized antebellum business. They were highly effective ways of pooling enormous capital through the public sale of stock; they also limited the financial liabilities of their owners, the stockholders, who stood to lose no more than they initially invested. In addition, corporations were well positioned to use decentralized forms of administration — tier upon subdivided tier of managers and assistant managers radiating from a central point — the only kind of organization capable of handling the vastly enlarged scale of the new businesses. What was the fate of individual freedom in a world dominated by mammoth bureaucratic organizations? The new corporate leaders had to justify the economic world they were designing. Such an argument was offered by George W. Perkins, a partner in the powerful banking house of J. P. Morgan and Company.

PROBLEMS TO CONSIDER

1. According to Perkins, what made the corporation a natural or a scientific phenomenon? What made cooperation more natural than competition?
2. Do you think Perkins also would have welcomed the cooperative ethic and organization of labor unions?

In the modern corporation we are confronted with a fact and not a theory. Whatever may be the individual attitude toward it, the corporation is here. What caused it, what it is doing, and what is to become of it are live questions, vital to all the people.

A corporation, in a way, is but another name for an organization. Broadly speaking, the first form of organization between human beings, of which we know, was the clan or tribe, in which the everyday conduct of the individuals was determined by the necessities of the group. This passed on into national organization, and then came the church as a growing and vast organization. Latest of all has come the organization of business.

But before all this, in the very beginning of things, the universe was organized; and all that man has done in society, in the church, in business, and all that he ever can do in the centuries to come, can never bring to pass so complete a form of organization, so vast a trust, so centralized a form of control, as passes before our eyes in each twenty-four hours of our lives as we contemplate that all-including system of perfect organization called the Universe. It does not require a very vivid imagination to picture the waste, the destruction, the chaos, that would follow if there were not perfect organization, perfect cooperation, perfect regulation, perfect control in the affairs of the universe. How could we live, for example, if there were constant competition between day and night or a constant struggle for supremacy between the seasons? Does any one, for a moment, think that he would prefer such a condition to the cooperation that now exists through all the affairs of the universe?

Organization being the all-permeating principle of the universe, the presumption is, therefore, in favor of organization wherever we find it or wherever it can be used. The corporation of to-day is entitled to that presumption; its underlying cause is not the greed of man for wealth and power, but the working of natural causes of evolution.

Business was originally done by individuals trading with one another; then by a firm of two or more individuals; then by a company; then by a corporation, and latterly by a giant corporation or what is commonly (though perhaps inaccurately) called a "trust." Each step was brought about by some great change that took place in the conditions under which the people of the world lived and worked; each step was, in fact, mainly determined by discoveries and inventions of the human mind. . . .

The days when business was a local affair of individual with individual were the days when people were scattered, knowing little of each other and having no dealings with each other outside the radius of a few miles. Then steam and, later, electricity came into man's service; and then, by leaps and bounds, the possibilities of trade became extended to a radius of hundreds of miles, even of thousands of miles. Vast possibilities of international trade loomed up. The corporation sprang into active being as an inevitable result of this expansion of trade; for no one man, no firm, no small company, could provide the capital or the organization to cope with such opportunities. The only bridge that can span the ocean is the corporation. The real cause of the corporation was not so much the selfish aims of a few men as the imperative necessities of all men. . . .

Perhaps the most useful achievement of the great corporation has been the saving of waste in its particular line of business. By assembling the best brains, the best genius, the best energy in a given line of trade, and coordinating these in work for a common end, great results have been attained in the prevention of waste, the utilizing of by-products, the economizing in the manufacture of the product, the expense of selling, and through better and more uniform service.

This same grouping of men has raised the standard of their efficiency. Nothing develops man like contact with other men. A dozen men working apart and for separate ends do not develop the facility, the ideas, the general effectiveness that will become the qualities of a dozen men working together in one cause. In such work emulation plays a useful part; it does all the good and none of the harm that the old method of destructive competition did: the old competition was wholly self-seeking and often ruinous, while the new rivalry, within the limits of the same organization, is constructive and uplifting. Thus the great corporation has developed men of a higher order of business ability than ever appeared under the old conditions; and what a value this has for the coming generation! The opportunity, the inducement it pro-

vides to become all-around larger men than those of earlier generations could become! . . .

The next period in corporation development should be a constructive one, constructive as to the relations of the corporation to its labor and to the public, and this can best be accomplished by the method of cooperation with supervision.

It is almost heresy to say that competition is no longer the life of trade. Yet this has come to be the fact, as applied to the old unreasoning and unreasonable competition, because of the conditions of our day. The spirit of cooperation is upon us. It must, of necessity, be the next great form of business development and progress. At this moment many people are looking askance upon the change, still believing in the old doctrine. They hold to it for several reasons: first, because they have inherited the belief; second, because they think that competition means lower prices for commodities to the public; third, because they think it provides the best incentive to make men work. This may have been the best-known method at one time, but it is not and cannot be true in the mechanical, electrical age in which we live. . . .

From every point of view the cooperative principle is to be preferred. It is more humane, more uplifting, and, with proper supervision, must provide a more orderly conduct of business—freer from failure and abuse, guaranteeing better wages and more steady employment to labor, with a more favorable average price to the consumer, one on which he can depend in calculating his living expenses or making his business plans.

George W. Perkins, "The Modern Corporation," in *The Currency Problem and the Present Financial Situation* (New York: Columbia University Press, 1908), 155–70.

ᔰ

The Works of the Cambria Iron Company (1878)
A. L. HOLLEY AND LENNOX SMITH

The Edgar Thomson Steel Works (1890)
CARNEGIE BROTHERS AND CO.

Industrialists and financiers such as George Perkins contended that modern capitalism was not an accident of history but rather a logical outcome of the laws of nature that the best scientific minds of the day were discovering. They frequently cited Darwinian evolutionary principles—the survival of the fittest, for example—to justify the triumph of increasingly large firms. On the ground level, a new category of business figure was more directly involved with allying science and industry to make companies competitive and profitable: industrial engineers, such as Alexander Lyman Holley, Carnegie Steel Corporation's master designer of steel plants. For Holley, engineering was not just an industrial occupation. It was the boldest force propelling civilization's "triumphal march"—splitting continents with canals, ripping iron ore from the earth's depths, and placing the "treasure-house of nature" at modern capitalism's disposal. Holley was less an inventor than an organizer, as his masterwork, the Edgar Thomson Steel Works near Pittsburgh, well illustrates. When completed in the mid-1870s, it was the most advanced facility in the world for mass-producing steel, most of it for the burgeoning railway industry. In his earlier projects (the Cambria ironworks in Johnstown, Pennsylvania, for instance), Holley modified existing plants. He organized the Thomson facility from the ground up. The result demonstrated the engineering imagination at work and showed how American industries were using new machinery and new ways of organizing production to control every dimension of manufacturing. Maps of the Cambria and Thomson works, reproduced here, allow a consideration of what Holley and the corporation he represented were trying to achieve in business, how they understood "nature" and technology, and how they measured the relative value and place of laboring men in the operation.

PROBLEMS TO CONSIDER

1. Compare the various elements of the two maps—the layout of buildings, their relation to transportation links. What differences and similarities strike you as the most important? Did the considerations that guided Holley's design at Edgar Thomson differ from the ones applied at Cambria?
2. Did the design of the Edgar Thomson plant resemble George Perkins's designs for the "modern corporation"?

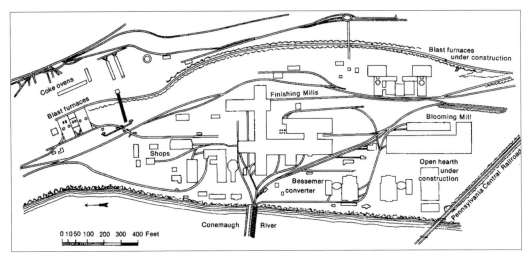

Map of Cambria ironworks.

(From A. L. Holley and Lennox Smith, "The Works of the Cambria Iron Company," *Engineering* 26 [July 12, 1878]: 22.)

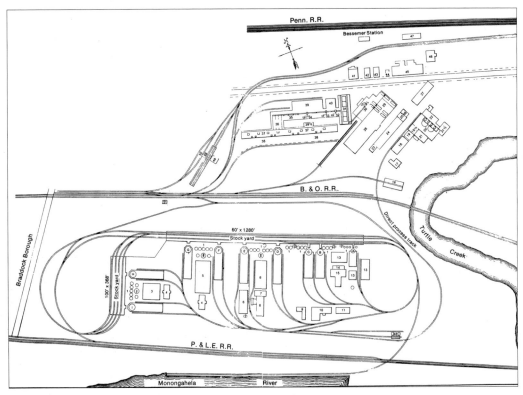

Map of Edgar Thomson steel plant.

(From Carnegie Brothers and Co., *The Edgar Thomson Steel Works and Blast Furnaces* [Pittsburgh: Joseph Eichbaum & Co., 1890], n.p.)

ॐ

The Principles of Scientific Management (1911)

FREDERICK W. TAYLOR

Frederick Winslow Taylor is often credited with formulating "scientific management." He tried to do with labor what Alexander Lyman Holley sought for plant design. Observing workingmen at a steel plant near Philadelphia, Taylor used what he called a scientific method to break down the component parts of each manufacturing task. His aim, he said, was to eliminate unnecessary steps and to organize workers and the work they performed for optimum efficiency. However, as Taylor well understood, this goal meant taking the control of labor away from workers and placing it in the hands of industrial engineers such as himself. Workers resisted the "Taylorization" of their jobs, and few companies adopted his principles until well into the twentieth century. But Taylor nevertheless insisted that his policies, because they were scientific, were consistent with the laws of nature and selfless. His system worked, not in the interests of any company's profit sheet or of any class of workers, but for the good of humanity. These claims can be evaluated in the following selection, in which he describes the ideal workingman.

PROBLEMS TO CONSIDER

1. Compare Taylor's conception of work with Holley's industrial designs (p. 50). Were their understandings of efficiency alike or different?
2. According to Taylor, what characteristics made an ideal workingman? What motivations were used to induce the worker Schmidt to work scientifically? Evaluate the equity of the arrangement. Who benefited more — Schmidt or his employer?

Our first step was the scientific selection of the workman. In dealing with workmen under this type of management, it is an inflexible rule to talk to and deal with only one man at a time, since each workman has his own special abilities and limitations, and since we are not dealing with men in masses, but are trying to develop each individual man to his highest state of efficiency and prosperity. Our first step was to find the proper workman to begin with. We therefore carefully watched and studied these 75 men for three or four days, at the end of which time we had picked out four men who appeared to be physically able to handle pig iron at the rate of 47 tons per day [*instead of the usual 12½ tons*]. A careful study was then made of each of these men.

We looked up their history as far back as practicable and thorough inquiries were made as to the character, habits, and the ambition of each of them. Finally we selected one from among the four as the most likely man to start with. He was a little Pennsylvania Dutchman who had been observed to trot back home for a mile or so after his work in the evening, about as fresh as he was when he came trotting down to work in the morning. We found that upon wages of $1.15 a day he had succeeded in buying a small plot of ground, and that he was engaged in putting up the walls of a little house for himself in the morning before starting to work and at night after leaving. He also had the reputation of being exceedingly "close," that is, of placing a very high value on a dollar. As one man whom we talked to about him said, "A penny looks about the size of a cart-wheel to him." This man we will call Schmidt. The task before us, then, narrowed itself down to getting Schmidt to handle 47 tons of pig iron per day and making him glad to do it. This was done as follows. Schmidt was called out from among the gang of pig-iron handlers and talked to somewhat in this way:

"Schmidt, are you a high-priced man?"

"Vell, I don't know vat you mean."

"Oh yes, you do. What I want to know is whether you are a high-priced man or not."

"Vell, I don't know vat you mean."

"Oh, come now, you answer my questions. What I want to find out is whether you are a high-priced man or one of these cheap fellows here. What I want to find out is whether you want to earn $1.85 a day or whether you are satisfied with $1.15, just the same as all those cheap fellows are getting."

"Did I vant $1.85 a day? Vas dot a high-priced man? Vell, yes, I vas a high-priced man."

"Oh, you're aggravating me. Of course you want $1.85 a day—every one wants it! You know perfectly well that that has very little to do with your being a high-priced man. For goodness' sake answer my questions, and don't waste any more of my time. Now come over here. You see that pile of pig iron?"

"Yes."

"You see that car?"

"Yes."

"Well, if you are a high-priced man, you will load that pig iron on that car tomorrow for $1.85. Now do wake up and answer my question. Tell me whether you are a high-priced man or not."

"Vell—did I got $1.85 for loading dot pig iron on dot car to-morrow?"

"Yes, of course you do, and you get $1.85 for loading a pile like that every day right through the year. That is what a high-priced man does, and you know it just as well as I do."

"Vell, dot's all right. I could load dot pig iron on the car to-morrow for $1.85, and I get it every day, don't I?"

"Certainly you do—certainly you do."

"Vell, den, I vas a high-priced man."

"Now, hold on, hold on. You know just as well as I do that a high-priced man has to do exactly as he's told from morning till night. You have seen this man here before, haven't you?"

"No, I never saw him."

"Well, if you are a high-priced man, you will do exactly as this man tells you to-morrow, from morning till night. When he tells you to pick up a pig and walk, you pick it up and you walk, and when he tells you to sit down and rest, you sit down. You do that right straight through the day. And what's more, no back talk. Now a high-priced man does just what he's told to do, and no back talk. Do you understand that?..."

This seems to be rather rough talk. And indeed it would be if applied to an educated mechanic, or even an intelligent laborer. With a man of the mentally sluggish type of Schmidt it is appropriate and not unkind, since it is effective in fixing his attention on the high wages which he wants and away from what, if it were called to his attention, he probably would consider impossibly hard work. . . .

Schmidt started to work, and all day long, and at regular intervals, was told by the man who stood over him with a watch, "Now pick up a pig and walk. Now sit down and rest. Now walk—now rest," etc. He worked when he was told to work, and rested when he was told to rest, and at half-past five in the afternoon had his $47\frac{1}{2}$ tons loaded on the car. And he practically never failed to work at this pace and do the task that was set him during the three years that the writer was at Bethlehem. And throughout this time he averaged a little more than $1.85 per day, whereas before he had never received over $1.15 per day.

———
Frederick W. Taylor, *The Principles of Scientific Management* (1911; repr., New York: Harper & Brothers, 1919), 43–47.

᠅

Knights of Labor Initiation (1886)

For Frederick Taylor, workers were in it for the money. But workingmen, when speaking for themselves, more often voiced their concern for the dignity and autonomy their work gave them as men—in their own eyes, but also in those of the brotherhood of their fellow workingmen and their communities as a whole. Mastering a skill, shouldering responsibility, and providing for their families were supposed to be qualities that any man—rich or poor—would view with respect. For them, labor was the noblest occupation for the individual man. Such ideals inspired a man to rise above narrow self-interests and to submit to the needs of his fellow workingmen. To do anything less was an unmanly violation of the worker's ethical code. The honest producer, in this view, was the foundation of national virtue; the prosperity he produced with his own hands ensured well-being not just for himself but also for the commonwealth. Many workingmen concluded that the changes industrialists advanced in the 1880s and 1890s were designed to make them economic, political, and social slaves to the businesses that employed them, or, as one ironworker protested, to "crush out the very manhood of the honest toiler." Workingmen responded with their own labor organizations or unions. The Noble and Holy Order of the Knights of Labor was the largest labor organization in the 1880s, with more than 700,000 members at its peak. Unlike craft unions, which excluded unskilled industrial laborers, the Knights urged all working people to join, including women and African Americans. Despite the internal disharmony such inclusiveness caused, the union grew larger with the economic downturn of the 1880s. New members took vows such as the one outlined in the following initiation rite.

PROBLEMS TO CONSIDER

1. What ideals and values shaped the organization and community that the Knights wished to foster? Why was the union so prone to strike?
2. What kind of world were the Knights trying to create? How did their values compare with those advanced by Perkins and Taylor?

U*nknown Knight*—Master Workman, our friend has satisfactorily answered all inquiries, and now desires to be covered with our shield, and admitted to fellowship in this Order.
. . .

Master Workman—Place our friend at the centre, and administer the pledge of honor. . . .

Obligation.
I do truly promise, on my honor, that I will never reveal to any person or persons whatsoever, any of the signs, or secret workings of the Order that may be now or hereafter confided to me, any acts done or objects intended, except in a lawful and authorized manner, or by special permission of the Order granted to me.

That I will not reveal to any employer or other person the name or person of any one a member of the Order without permission of the member.

That I will strictly obey all laws and lawful summons . . . and that . . . I will, to the best of my ability, defend the life, interest, reputation and family of all true members of this Order;

help and assist all employed and unemployed, unfortunate or distressed members to procure employ, and secure just remuneration; relieve their distress, and counsel others to aid them, so that they and theirs may receive and enjoy the just fruits of their labor and exercise of their art.

And I do further promise that I will, without reservation or evasion, consider the pledge of secrecy I have taken binding upon me until death. . . .

Unknown Knight—Worthy Foreman, . . . I present our friend for instruction.

Worthy Foreman—By labor is brought forth the kind fruits of the earth in rich abundance for our sustenance and comfort; by labor, (not exhaustive,) are promoted health of body and strength of mind; and labor garners the priceless stores of wisdom and knowledge. It is the "Philosopher's Stone,"—everything it touches turns to wealth. "Labor is noble and holy." To defend it from degradation, to divest it of the evils to body, mind, and estate, which ignorance and greed have imposed; to rescue the toiler from the grasp of the selfish is a work worthy of the noblest and best of our race. You have been selected from among your associates for that exalted purpose. Are you willing to accept the responsibility, and, trusting in the support of pledged true Knights, labor, with what ability you possess, for the triumph of these principles among men? . . .

Master Workman—On behalf of the toiling millions of earth, I welcome you to this Order, pledged to the service of humanity. Open and public associations having failed, after a struggle of centuries, to protect or advance the interest of labor, we have lawfully constituted this Assembly. Hid from public view, we are covered by a veil of secrecy, not to promote or shield wrongdoing, but to shield ourselves and you from persecution and wrong by men in our own sphere and calling, as well as others out of it, when we endeavor to secure the just reward of our toil. In using this power of organized effort and co-operation, we but imitate the example of capital heretofore set in numberless instances. In all the multifarious branches of trade, capital has its combinations; and whether intended or not, they crush the manly hopes of labor and trample poor humanity in the dust. We mean no conflict with legitimate enterprise, no antagonism to necessary capital; but men, in their haste and greed, blinded by self-interests, overlook the interests of others, and sometimes violate the rights of those they deem helpless. We mean to uphold the dignity of labor; to affirm the nobility of all who earn their bread by the sweat of their brow. . . . We shall, with all our strength, support laws made to harmonize the interests of labor and capital, for labor alone gives life and value to capital. . . . We shall use every lawful and honorable means to procure and retain employ for one another, coupled with just and fair remuneration; and should accident or misfortune befall any of our number, render such aid as lies within our power to give, without inquiring their country or creed, and without approving of general strikes among artisans; yet should it become justly necessary to enjoin an oppressor, we will protect and aid any of our members who thereby may suffer loss, and as opportunity offers, extend a helping hand to all branches of honorable toil.

Knights of Labor Illustrated (Chicago: Ezra A. Cook, 1886), 28–31.

☙

Editorials from the Locomotive Fireman's Magazine (1882–1888)

EUGENE V. DEBS

In the 1890s, Eugene V. Debs emerged as a national leader in the labor movement, spearheading the American Railway Union's failed strike against the Pullman Palace Car Company in 1894 and then helping to found the American Socialist Party in 1901. But in the early 1880s, he belonged to the Brotherhood of Locomotive Firemen in his native Terre Haute, Indiana. The brotherhood was a "lodge," not a union; unions assumed an antagonistic relationship between workers and owners. Debs did not initially think of himself as a radical or as working-class, and he believed that strikes unnecessarily stirred up bad feelings that prevented employers and employees from recognizing their common interests. He thought of himself, instead, as a citizen and a workingman, no less dignified or worthy of respect than his employer. In fact, he took pride in the success of American railroads, regarding them as engines of progress in American life.

Throughout the 1880s, as editor of the brotherhood's magazine, Debs penned editorials that addressed the pressing labor issues of the day. But the events of the decade—the severe economic depression, the era of trusts and monopolies launched by Standard Oil, the violence at Chicago's Haymarket Square, and defeats of strikes led by the Knights of Labor—pressed him to reassess his position on what or who was to blame for the conflict. Was capitalism itself to blame, or were greedy capitalists and unruly workers? Who should lead in harmonizing the parties—workers or their employers? The following editorials from three points in his career with the brotherhood—1882, 1885, and 1888— track the transformation of his outlook on the struggles between capital and labor.

PROBLEMS TO CONSIDER

1. In Debs's early views, what was the foundation of the basic harmony between the Brotherhood of Locomotive Firemen and the owners of the railways they worked for? What events and new ways of thinking caused Debs to change his views on the bonds joining workers and employers?
2. The words "manhood" and "manliness" were central to Debs's understanding of the harmonies and conflicts between workingmen and their employers. How did his understanding of what a "true man" would do change over time?

THE SQUARE MAN (1882)

While there is nothing meaner among men than the sneak, there is none grander or better than the square man. The sneak no one respects. The square man everybody honors. Riches and social position may belong to the former, but they will not bring him that mead of self-respect, that full measure of love from his fellows, which the square man enjoys as a result of his grandeur of character. Poverty and toil may be the lot in life of the latter, but he walks with his head amidst the stars. He is a king among his fellows.

The square man sympathises with his friends in distress. His is the kind heart to devise means of help for the downtrodden and the lowly. . . .

Everybody respects the square man. He may not wear good clothes; he may be a little ungrammatical in speech; he may even swear a little, and look rough and uncouth, but the good, honest, square man is there. If the square man grasps the throttle of an engine there will be no sleeping at that post. Lives are entrusted to him; all his faculties are on the alert for danger. No drink touches his lips while he is making his run. Clear-brained, keen-eyed, strong-armed he stands at his post, and if the hour of danger overtakes him while there, he will never desert it. Duty does not call to him in vain. . . . All who know him feel safe, for a square man is at the post of duty. . . . It makes no difference where you find him—on an engine or in a palace, homely, uncouth and poor, or rich, elegant and handsome, he is always the same undaunted, honorable, square man.

MASTERFUL MEN (1882)

Men confide in leaders. The bold man, the man of action, the man who grasps situations and masters them, he is the man whom his fellows love to honor; he is the man who becomes the standard-bearer in any great moral or political movement; he is the man who brings succor in the hour of danger, and upon him all hearts rely. Few men in moments of personal danger, or in days of national turmoil, act intelligently if left to their own resources. Some leader always springs to the front and assumes a command questioned by none. Such men are self-poised, heroic, calm. The swirl and clash of contending intellects, the mighty shock of arms, the hour fraught with fear and destruction, have no power to disturb that masterful balance of mind possessed by these leaders of men. . . .

There is something grand about the heroism of great warriors, who on the battlefield, amid smoke and carnage, remain the same stern, relentless, unstampedeable leaders. . . .

These are examples of great leaders, men whose names are upon the lips of all; there are others who deserve no less the world's honor. Men who risked life in the service of others. Men who saw the needs of the moment and grasped the golden opportunity. The engineman who stands by his engine in the hour of danger, going down with her in order that the lives entrusted to his care may be saved, is no less a hero, is no less a masterful man, than is the hero who dies for his country. To stand grandly at the post of duty, knowing the danger but flinching not, calm, alert, and active to avert destruction, is a picture of heroism.

ART THOU A MAN? (1885)

The question we have selected as a caption for this article has met our observation elsewhere. . . . It will be observed that the question is not, Art thou of the masculine gender? It goes deeper than the arts of the costumer. It ignores whiskers and mustache, size and weight. It regards with little concern, fortune or position, the plaudits of the crowd or self-glorification. The interrogatory, "Art thou a man?" demands for a satisfactory reply facts, in the presence of which subterfuge sits silent. Chicane [trickery] is at a discount and duplicity, unmasked, seeks refuge as best it may. There are thousands who, if they were asked, "Art thou a man?" would, indignant at what they would characterize as an insult, reply, "I am," and with pugilistic gesture add, "Try me." It is well-known they can hit hard with their "dukes," and it is equally well-known that mules are hard-hitters. As a consequence in their case the query, "Art thou a man?" is not satisfactorily answered. Something more than a superb development of muscle, prize-ring science and bulldog courage is required to constitute a man. There is a multitude of masculines who pass current in certain circles as men. Their outward appearance meets the exacting demands of Fashion. Inquire at the church and they are designated as "pillars." . . . But such things do not make a man. Is he a banker? Examine his accounts. To-morrow he closes his doors, and the world learns with amazement that he is a base hypocrite, a moral monstrosity, a social pestilence, a loathsome imposter, religious that he might the more successfully play the role of rascal. . . .

Observing people are quick to notice another type of individuals. They are conspicuous because they have money or can command money. They are money worshippers. They are often referred to as "financiers"—the progressive element. Those who keep the world in motion. It is said were it not for such men business would stagnate, and their operations and speculations are referred to in proof of the proposition. . . . To ask a representative of this class of citizens, "Art thou a man?" has a horrifying ring in the ears of their confreres and the fawning, degenerate lick-spittles, whose ambitions are parasitic, and they answer by asking, Why not a man? The reason why is found in the fact that they use their money, their opportunities and their influence to increase their gains by making life to the poor more perilous. They are the men who "corner" food, thereby reducing the buying power of the poor man's hard-earned dollars, a reduction which invites hunger pangs in the midst of abundance and shrouds many a home in gloom where otherwise would be joy and contentment. To call such persons men is to outrage the properties of speech and obliterate from the face of the earth those standards by which Christ measured men—venal, callous, heartless. Such people are men only because they are masculine. In all other regards they are so much less than men that were the destinies of mankind left to their control the wisdom of their Creator would be justly called in question.

Another type of men . . . so nearly allied to the class whose greed of gain renders them incapable of doing justice when their own interests are involved, blind to calamities which they create and deaf to appeals which their mercenary natures extort from their victims, are those who . . . by combinations seek to reduce the price of labor. They are known as "monopolists." They claim great credit for employing men, and would have it understood that but for them universal famine would visit the land. As a class, they profess to be animated by a profound desire to promote the welfare of laboring men, but in every instance, or with rare exceptions, laboring men find that those who are loudest in their avowals of sympathy are the quickest to reduce the dividends on the investments of toil. . . . The subject is susceptible of indefinite elaboration, and the more it is discussed the more ineffaceably becomes the impression in the public mind that when a representative of this class of individuals is asked, "Art thou a man?" the paving stones, if they had tongues, would cry out, "No." A MAN will not rob directly or indirectly. A MAN despises a lie, prevarication and subterfuge. A man is true to wife and home, to obligation and trust. . . . If when asked, Art thou a man? He responds, "I do unto others as I would have them do unto me. I seek no man's downfall that I may rise. I disdain to profit by the misfortune of others. . . ." Then a man is found, a man honest and true, who knows his rights, and knowing dare maintain them. . . .

WHERE STRIKES FLOURISH (1888)

The American idea is to resist oppression. Proverbial philosophy voices no sentiment more distinctly American, than that it is better to die free than to survive a slave, and when one man denies another man his rights, and the victim of the wrong is too abject, too cowardly to protest and resist, he is a craven, whom it were a monstrous calumny to call a man. . . .

The course the press is pursuing when discussing a strike is to place before the eyes of

American working men so many dollars, and then point out the sufferings in store for them if they reject the dollars. It goes without saying that to accept the dollars is to invite disgrace and degradation, that in accepting the dollars they invite the badge of servitude, surrender every prerogative of manhood, throw to the winds their independence, and trample upon the divine declaration "that all men are created equal," as pagans trample upon the cross. The dollar is to be everything—justice, right, principle, honor, manhood, citizenship, nothing. The corporation, in alliance with wind and water, is to rule, and working men, with their faces in the dust, are to serve, or, if they protest, if they demand their rights, if they aspire to the decencies of citizenship, if they demand for themselves, their wives and children something better than hovels for homes, something better than rags for clothing, and if from the fabulous abundance of food products which the Great God, who is no respector of persons, supplies, they ask for a sufficiency, they are denounced as the victims of demagogues, and are accorded less consideration than so many beasts of burden. [These] mandates, and millions of homes, now darkened by the insatiate greed of corporations, trusts and monopolies, would be emancipated from the ceas[e]less forebodings of calamities which the devilish ingenuity of soulless corporations have ready to hurl upon them if they dare to strike for fair pay for honest work.

The strike is the weapon of the oppressed, of men capable of appreciating justice and having the courage to resist wrong and contend for principle. The Nation had for its corner stone a strike. There were ingrates in 1776 who, like the press of the present, asked will you go to war for a contemptible "stamp tax" and an equally paltry "tea tax?" They asserted it were better to suffer in peace than go to war for principle. But the patriots of the times "that tried men's souls" were not built that way, and through eight years of gloom, of sacrifice and suffering they continued the strike. They fought and bled and died,

and still they fought on. The strike was never off for eight long years. There was a principle at stake. England was powerful, the strikers were weak in everything but courage, resolution and defiance. . . . To strike for right, for justice, for principle, is American, and when Americans submit to the wrong without protest, when they accept chains and degradation without a murmur the very name of American will be as odious as that of Helot, and when working men no longer resort to strikes as the last resort to maintain their manhood then their degradation beyond redemption has been secured and the corporations will have triumphed.

The corporation idea is to intimidate working men by showing them if they strike against flagrant wrongs when all other means fail to secure their rights, they will lose a certain amount of wages, and that being easily demonstrated they expect working men, regardless of conviction, will worship with pagan submissiveness the golden image they set up, fearing the ordeal through which they will have to pass if the nobility of their nature asserts itself and they strike rather than yield. All too often this Nebuchadnezzaran idea is correct. Men weak, effeminate, purposeless and spineless, yield. Yield like sheep and wear without shame the brand mark of their owner. But there are men, the "salt of the earth," who will not submit to wrong, who will wear no humiliating badge or brand. They will protest, and if need be they will strike, and like men who know their rights and knowing dare maintain, will accept with proud defiance the penalties in store for them.

The right never did succeed without a strike, and while arrogant injustice throws down the gauntlet and challenges the right to the conflict, strikes will come, come by virtue of irrevocable laws, destined to have a wider sweep and greater power as men advance in intelligence and independence.

Locomotive Firemen's Magazine, January 1882, 16; April 1882, 170–71; May 1885, 283–85; June 1888, 406–7.

❧

❧ *The Adventures of Buffalo Bill: William F. Cody's Wild West* ❧

To explain what makes their nation distinctive and their character unique, Americans often have relied on two different but related stories about the history of the West. The historian Frederick Jackson Turner outlined the "frontier thesis" in 1893. He described the historic conquest of the West as the crucible of *the* American character. Confronting nature renewed and democratized the American man by liberating him from the enfeebling social conventions of the East. The homesteading farmer, Turner argued, was the agent of civilization, and the plow his indispensable tool for bringing progress. The other story of the frontier also focuses on confrontation, but it was less between farmers and the land than between white men and "savages." In this story, the tool that brought order to a lawless wilderness was the gun. No one told this story more spectacularly or convincingly in the postwar era than the showman William F. "Buffalo Bill" Cody. In the late nineteenth century, these frontier theses commanded broad assent among Euro-Americans because they drew on an understanding of the past that made sense of the era's major problems, conflicts, and hopes.

Neither William F. Cody nor the story he symbolized conjured up images of a plow-pushing farmer. Clad in tasseled buckskin with gun in hand and wavy locks flowing from his sombrero, Cody was a natural-born showman. He projected his imposing masculinity not by civilizing the primitivism of the West, but by preserving and staging a spectacular version of it. Born in Iowa in 1846 and growing up poor, he made a name for himself in the post–Civil War period as a buffalo hunter and civilian scout, assisting the U.S. Cavalry in successful wars against the Plains tribes. He also guided parties of rich easterners on hunting expeditions, as the West, between periods of war, became a tourist destination for adventure-seeking businessmen. In all these capacities, Cody earned fame as an authentic westerner who not only looked the part but also lived the adventure. While his reputation was earned in many respects, Cody's fame was in large part manufactured. He was a fictional hero in cheap, mass-produced "dime novels," a stage character that actors portrayed in theaters, and an actor who performed himself in his own shows. Millions around the world learned what the Wild West was "really like" from reading about Buffalo Bill's exploits or by watching his show. For him as well as his fans, the historical and make-believe Buffalo Bills merged indistinguishably in practice and principle. His life seemed to be the story of the West, and the story of the West seemed to be his life.

Adventures of Buffalo Bill from Boyhood to Manhood (c. 1882)
COLONEL PRENTISS INGRAHAM

Cody acquired the name "Buffalo Bill" not from experience, but from Ned Buntline, the pen name of the dime novelist Edward Judson, who had gone on a hunting expedition with him. In Buntline's Buffalo Bill: King of the Border Men *(1869), Cody rode to the rescue of civilization against the familiar cast of frontier savages: bloodthirsty Indians and thieving rustlers. A popular stage production and many dime-novel imitations followed. At a time when Cody's virtuosity as a scout, hunter, and horseman was renowned west of the Mississippi, "Buffalo Bill" was a literary sensation in the East because of dime novels and "story papers." The dime novel was a popular form of literature that appealed to urban working-class men and boys. It was made possible by the forces of industrialization, mass production, and national distribution after the Civil War. Writers turned out stories with the speed and uniformity that factory workers turned out the actual finished books; moved by modern distribution systems, these books rapidly appeared on the shelves of rural and urban newsstands and dry-goods stores. Respectable middle-class parents sought to shield their sons from such bad influences. Besides pages filled with scenes of bloodshed and savages preying on white maidens, dime-novel heroes often were outlaws, such as "Deadwood Dick" or Jesse James. Historians have noted a working-class political perspective in such literature. Villainous "robber barons" or corrupt political figures met defeat by heroes who were democratic defenders of honest workingmen and defenseless women and children. Colonel Prentiss Ingraham's dime-novel biography of Cody, from the early 1880s, was an example of this genre.*

PROBLEMS TO CONSIDER

1. How did Ingraham establish Buffalo Bill's heroism? What made him a "civilizing" agent?
2. Did becoming an actor diminish or enhance the "truth" of Cody's story? Did Buffalo Bill's success on stage affect the credibility of the stories he told about the West?

CHAPTER I: PROLOGUE

That Truth is, by far, stranger than Fiction, the lessons of our daily lives teach us who dwell in the marts of civilization, and therefore we cannot wonder that those who live in scenes where the rifle, revolver and knife are in constant use, to protect and take life, can strange tales tell of thrilling perils met and subdued, and romantic incidents occurring that are far removed from the stern realities of existence.

The land of America is full of romance, and tales that stir the blood can be told over and over again of bold Privateers and reckless Buccaneers who have swept along the coasts; of fierce naval battles, sea chases, daring smugglers; and on shore of brave deeds in the saddle and afoot; of red trails followed to the bitter end and savage encounters in forest wilds.

And it is beyond the pale of civilization I find the hero of these pages which tell of thrilling adventures, fierce combats, deadly feuds and wild rides, that, one and all, are true to the letter, as hundreds now living can testify.

Who has not heard the name of Buffalo Bill—a magic name, seemingly, to every boy's heart?

And yet in the uttermost parts of the earth it is known among men.

A child of the prairie, as it were, Buffalo Bill will go down to history as one of America's strange heroes who has loved the trackless wilds, rolling plains and mountain solitudes of our land, far more than the bustle and turmoil, the busy life and joys of our cities, and who has stood as a barrier between civilization and savagery, risking his own life to save the lives of others.

Glancing back over the past, we recall a few names that have stood out in the boldest relief in frontier history, and they are Daniel Boone, Davy Crockett, Kit Carson and W. F. Cody, the last named being Buffalo Bill, the King of Bordermen. . . .

CHAPTER 29: BILL'S STORY OF HIS BECOMING AN ACTOR

". . . I was then Chief of Scouts in the Department of the Platte. And in January, 1872, just after the Grand Duke Alexis's hunt, which, by the way, I organized, I got a leave of absence, and for the first time in my life found myself east of the Mississippi river. . . .

"During my visit [to New York] I attended the performance at the Bowery Theater, in company with Colonel E. Z. C. Judson (Ned Buntline), and witnessed a dramatization of Judson's story, entitled 'Buffalo Bill, King of Border Men.' The part of 'Buffalo Bill' was impersonated by . . . an excellent actor, and I must say the fellow looked like me, as his make-up was a perfect picture of myself. I had not watched myself very long before the audience discovered that the original Buffalo Bill was in the private box, and they commenced cheering, which stopped the performance, and they would not cease until I had shown myself and spoken a few words.

"At that time I had no idea of going on the stage, such a thought having never entered my head. But some enterprising managers, believing there was money in me, offered me as high as $1,000 per week to go on the stage. I told them I would rather face 1,000 Indians than attempt to open my mouth before all those peo-

ple. I returned to my duties as a scout, and during the summer of 1872 Ned Buntline was constantly writing to me to come East and go on the stage, offering large inducements. As scouting business was a little dull, I concluded to try it for awhile. . . .

"Well, [opening] night came. The house was packed. Up went the curtain. Buntline appeared as Cale Durg, an old Trapper, and at a certain time Jack *[the western scout, "Texas Jack" Omohundro]* and I were to come on. But we were a little late, and when I made my appearance, facing 3,000 people, . . . it broke me all up and I could not remember a word. All that saved me was my answer to a question put by Buntline. He asked, 'What detained you?' I told him I had been on a hunt with Milligan. You see Milligan was a prominent Chicago gentleman who had been hunting with me a short time before on the plains, and had been chased by the Indians, and the papers had been full of his hunt for some time; Buntline saw that I was up a stump, for I had forgotten my lines, and he told me to tell him about the hunt. I told the story in a very funny way, and it took like wild-fire with the audience.

"While I was telling the story, Buntline had whispered to the stage manager that when I got through with my story to send on the Indians. Presently Buntline sung out: 'The Indians are upon us.' Now this was 'pie' for Jack and I, and we went at those bogus Indians red hot until we had killed the last one and the curtain went down amid a most tremendous applause, while the audience went wild. . . ."

Colonel Prentiss Ingraham, *Adventures of Buffalo Bill from Boyhood to Manhood* . . . (c. 1882), reprinted online in "Dime Novels and Penny Dreadfuls," Department of Special Collections, Green Library, Stanford University Libraries, http://www.sul.stanford.edu/depts/dp/pennies/texts/ingraham1_toc.html. © 1998, Academic Text Service, Stanford University Libraries/Academic Information Resources.

✒

The Indian War (1876)

Campaigning with Crook, and Stories of Army Life (1890)
CHARLES KING

Buffalo Bill: The Famous Scout Interviewed by an Eagle Representative . . . (1883)

Cody's most celebrated act of frontier violence occurred in July 1876, after *he had become a stage star. That spring, military commanders fighting the Sioux in the Dakota Territory had urged him to rejoin them as a scout. Cody closed his show season early in Wilmington, Delaware, and met up with the Fifth Cavalry shortly before a massive force of Sioux wiped out Colonel George A. Custer and his troops on June 25 at the battle at Little Bighorn. On July 17, while on patrol, Cody's unit spotted a small party of Indians preparing to ambush a pair of military couriers. The cavalry attacked, and in the skirmish Cody shot, killed, and scalped a young and comparatively undistinguished Cheyenne named Hay-o-wei. (Hay-o-wei, which means "Yellow Hair," was mistranslated as "Yellow Hand.") Thanks to Cody's own efforts before and after the fact, the encounter became legendary as an epic duel between Buffalo Bill and a mighty chieftain, resulting in "the first scalp for Custer." That morning, Cody had prepared for action by donning a flashy Mexican-style costume of black velvet highlighted in scarlet, with lace trim and silver buttons. Returning from the field, he collaborated with the* New York Herald *to publish the story. Later he shipped the proceeds of the encounter — his victim's war bonnet, shield, whip, and scalp — back east for public display. When the Wild West show got under way several years later, these souvenirs came in handy as advertisements for the feature reenactment, entitled "The Red Right Hand; or the First Scalp for Custer." For his part, Cody dressed in black velvet, supposedly the original costume. Anything Cody did seemed fit for the stage or the pages of popular fiction, and yet the killing of Hay-o-wei was not the "First Scalp for Custer" until Cody and others made the incident into a story of the West. The story-making process is apparent in these three versions of the incident: the* Herald's *dispatch; an historical account by Charles King, a cavalry lieutenant who witnessed the event and later authored many frontier adventure stories; and an 1883 newspaper interview with Cody during the Wild West show tour.*

PROBLEMS TO CONSIDER

1. Consider how Cody and others made this incident into a story. What similarities and differences do you see in the three accounts?
2. What was the story of the West told in these accounts? How did they explain the violence, and who the victims and the aggressors were? What made Cody's and the cavalry's actions heroic?

THE INDIAN WAR

At daybreak Monday morning Lieutenant [Charles] King, commanding the outposts to the southeast, sent in word that the war parties were coming over the ridge from the direction of the reservation. Joining him at the advanced post, General [Wesley] Merritt found the report correct. The command noiselessly mounted and was massed under the bluffs, a quarter of a mile to the rear, out of sight of the Indians. At the same time the wagon train was some six miles off to the southwest, slowly approaching, and the Indians were closely watching it, but keeping concealed from the view of its guard. The two companies of infantry with it were riding in the wagons. At six o'clock the Indians were swarming all along the ridge to the southeast, some three miles away. Suddenly a party of eight or ten warriors came dashing down a ravine which led directly under the hill where Lieutenant King, with his six men, were watching.

Waiting For Scalps

The object was as suddenly apparent. Two horsemen, unconscious of the proximity of the foe, had ventured out ahead of the train and were making rapidly for the creek. They were couriers with despatches to the command. The Indians, utterly ignorant of the rapid move of the Fifth [Cavalry], were simply bent on jumping on the couriers and getting their scalps. "Buffalo Bill," chief of the scouts, lay on the hill with King, and instantly sprang to his horse down off the hill.

"All you keep out of sight," said the General. "Mount now, and when the word is given[,] off with you."

Then, turning to the officer of the picket, he said: —

"Watch them, King. Give the word when you are ready."

Crouching behind the little butte, Bill and his party of two scouts and six soldiers were breathlessly waiting; half way up was the General. . . . The Lieutenant lay at the crest watching the rapidly advancing foe. Down they came nearer and nearer, the sun flashing from their brilliantly painted bodies and their polished ornaments. Then, just as they are dashing by the front of the hill, King shouts,

"Now, lads, in with you."

With a rush and yell the troopers are hurled upon the Indians' flank, not fifty yards away.

The First Redskin Shot

General Merritt springs up to see the attack just as a tall Indian reeled in his saddle, shot by Corporal Wilkinson, of K company. An answering bullet whistled by the General's head, when King — still on the watch — sung out,

"Here they come by the dozens."

The reserve Indians came swarming down from the ridge to the rescue. Company K was instantly ordered to the front. But before it appeared from behind the bluff the Indians, emboldened by the rush of their friends to the rescue, turned savagely on Buffalo Bill and the little party at the outpost.

Cody Kills Yellow Hand

The latter sprang from their horses and met the daring charge with a volley. Yellow Hand, a young Cheyenne brave, came foremost, singling Bill as a foeman worthy of his steel. Cody coolly knelt, and, taking deliberate aim, sent his bullet through the chief's leg and into his horse's head. Down went the two, and, before his friends could reach him, a second shot from Bill's rifle laid the redskin low.

"The Indian War," *New York Herald*, July 23, 1876, 7.

CAMPAIGNING WITH CROOK, AND STORIES OF ARMY LIFE

The little hill on which we are lying is steep, almost precipitous on its southern slope, washed away apparently by the torrent that in the rainy season must come tearing down the long ravine directly ahead of us; it leads down from the distant ridge and sweeps past us to our right, where it is crossed by the very trail on which we marched in, and along which, three miles away, the wagon train is now approaching. The two come together like a V, and we are at its point, while between them juts out a long spur of hills. The trail cannot be seen from the ravine, and *vice versa*, while we on our point see both. At the head of the ravine, a mile and a half away, a party of thirty or forty Indians are scurrying about in eager and excited motion. "What in thunder are those vagabonds fooling about?" says Buffalo Bill, who has joined us with Tait and Chips, two of his pet assistants. Even while we speculate, the answer is plain. Riding towards us, away ahead of the wagon train, two soldiers come loping along the trail. They bring despatches to the command. . . . They see no Indians; for it is only from them and the tram the wily foe is concealed, and all unsuspicious of their danger they come jauntily ahead. Now is the valiant red man's opportunity. Come on, Brothers Swift Bear, Two Bulls, Bloody Hand; come on, ten or a dozen of you, my braves — there are only two of the pale-faced dogs, and they shall feel the red man's vengeance forthwith. Come on, come on! We'll dash down this ravine, a dozen of us, and six to one we'll slay and scalp them without danger to ourselves; and a hundred to one we will brag about it the rest of our natural lives. Only a mile away come our couriers; only a mile and a half up the ravine a murderous party of Cheyennes lash their excited ponies into eager gallop, and down they come towards us.

"By Jove! general," says Buffalo Bill, sliding backwards down the hill, "now's our chance. Let our party mount here out of sight, and we'll cut those fellows off."

"Up with you, then!" is the answer. "Stay where you are, King. Watch them till they are close under you; then give the word. Come down, every other man of you!"

I am alone on the little mound. Glancing behind me, I see Cody, Tait, and Chips with five cavalrymen, eagerly bending forward in their saddles, grasping carbine and rifle, every eye bent upon me in breathless silence, watching for the signal. General Merritt and Lieutenants Forbush and Pardee are crouching below me. Sergeant Schreiber and Corporal Wilkinson, on all fours, are halfway down the northern slope. Not a horse or man of us visible to the Indians. . . . Half a mile away are our couriers, now rapidly approaching. Now, my Indian friends, what of you? Oh, what a stirring picture you make . . . ! Here, nearly four years after, my pulses bound as I recall the sight. Savage warfare was never more beautiful than in you. On you come, your swift, agile ponies springing down the winding ravine, the rising sun gleaming on your trailing war bonnets, on silver armlets, necklace, gorget; on brilliant painted shield and beaded legging; on naked body and beardless face, stained most vivid vermilion. On you come, lance and rifle, pennon and feather glistening in the rare morning light, swaying in the wild grace of your peerless horsemanship; nearer, till I mark the very ornament on your leader's shield. And on, too, all unsuspecting, come your helpless prey. I hold vengeance in my hand, but not yet to let it go. Five seconds too soon, and you can wheel about and escape us; one second too late, and my blue-coated couriers are dead men. On you come, savage, hungry-eyed, merciless. Two miles behind you are your scores of friends, eagerly, applaudingly watching your exploit. But five hundred yards ahead of you, coolly, vengefully awaiting you are your unseen foes, beating you at your own game; and you are running slap into them. Nearer and nearer — your leader, a gorgeous-looking fellow, on a bounding gray, signals "Close and follow." Three hundred yards more, my buck, and (you fancy) your gleaming knives will tear the scalps of our couriers. Twenty seconds, and you will dash round that point with your war-whoop ringing in their ears. Ha! Lances, is it? You don't want your shots heard back at the train. What will you think of ours? All ready, general?"

"All ready, King. Give the word when you like."

Not a man but myself knows how near they are. Two hundred yards now, and I can hear the panting of their wiry steeds. A hundred and fifty! That's right—close in, you beggars! Ten seconds more and you are on them! A hundred and twenty-five yards—a hundred—ninety—

"*Now*, lads, in with you!"

Crash go the hoofs! There's a rush, a wild, ringing cheer; then bang, bang, bang! And in a cloud of dust Cody and his men tumble in among them. . . . I jump for my horse, and the vagabond, excited by the shots and rush around us, plunges at his lariat and breaks to the left. As I catch him, I see Buffalo Bill closing on a superbly accoutred warrior. It is the work of a minute; the Indian has fired and missed. Cody's bullet tears through the rider's leg, into his pony's heart, and they tumble in confused heap on the prairie. The Cheyenne struggles to his feet for another shot, but Cody's second bullet crashes through his brain, and the young chief, Yellow Hand, drops lifeless in his tracks.

Charles King, *Campaigning with Crook, and Stories of Army Life* (New York: Harper & Bros., 1890), 34–38.

BUFFALO BILL: THE FAMOUS SCOUT INTERVIEWED

. . . Among the interesting stories to which the writer recently had the pleasure of listening was one about [Cody's] fight with Yellow Hand, a distinguished gentleman of the Cheyenne persuasion. For the first time after Custer's tragic death, the United States troops and the Cheyennes were face to face.

Yellow Hand had an excellent opinion of himself, and his fellow red men regarded him as the most accomplished scalper of the tribe.

Some negotiations were in progress and the Indian took advantage of the opportunity to challenge Mr. Cody to a duel. General Crook would not hear of it, but Buffalo Bill persisted, declaring that a refusal would destroy his standing with every painted warrior in the country. The encounter was witnessed by the troops on one side and the Cheyennes on the other, both sides being drawn up as if a general parade had been in order. Yellow Hand was a muscular savage and at little disadvantage with the white man in any physical respect. The two had been good friends for many years and Buffalo Bill's renown would have had a healthy influence with almost any other brave; but Yellow Hand was ambitious and as fearless as the most dauntless of his race. When he was told that the challenge had been accepted he leaped into his saddle with a war cry. He was on a powerful mustang which he handled to perfection, and he began at once the tactics known to Indian fighters generally, and particularly well known to his adversary. The adversaries did not leave their respective sides in a direct line. They described circles, which gradually grew smaller . . . until very dangerous shooting distance was established. The riders kept their bodies well concealed behind their horses, the animals understanding perfectly well what to do and needing little guidance. There was a simultaneous check on the reins, Buffalo Bill bringing up his horse the moment he saw his foe make a motion, which showed he was preparing for a shot. Under the neck of Yellow Hand's steed a rifle peered for a moment at the scout and there was a flash. A second report followed on the instant. Buffalo Bill was unhurt; Yellow Hand's horse dropped like a stone. The Indian was quick to disengage himself, and Bill was on the ground to meet him.

An appeal to bowie knives was the next thing on the programme, the men being within a stone's throw of each other. The bullet which had killed Yellow Hand's horse had passed through its owner's leg, but it did not seem to seriously disturb him. With a yell he rushed at

Cody. A keen blade flashed in the air and the arm which wielded it was caught as it came down with a vicious swoop. The curtain was rung down on Yellow Hand without delay. Buffalo Bill's knife entered his chest and cut its way across it from the left side in an almost horizontal line. The white man bent over the body of his prostrate and silent foe, ripped off a gory scalp and whirled it in the air, crying: "The first scalp for Custer!" . . .

"Buffalo Bill: The Famous Scout Interviewed by an Eagle Representative; Scenes in the 'Wild West' in Which William F. Cody Has Taken a Hand . . . Encounter with a Party of Custer's Murderers . . . ," *Brooklyn Eagle*, August 23, 1883, 1. *Brooklyn Daily Eagle* Online, 1841–1902, Brooklyn Collection, Brooklyn Public Library, Brooklyn, N.Y.

Buffalo Bill as an Educator (1886)

BRICK POMEROY

Cody did not regard himself as a showman; he never called his show a "show." Rather, he believed that presenting authentic scenes of western life made him more an educator than an entertainer; his audience seemed to agree with this assessment. The following editorial by a journalist, which was a regular feature of the souvenir program, outlines Cody's educational mission.

PROBLEMS TO CONSIDER

1. What was Cody trying to teach his audiences? According to Pomeroy, what were they learning?
2. How important was the extravaganza's apparent authenticity to its popularity?

One of the pronounced, positive, strong men of the West is Hon. Wm. F. Cody, of Nebraska, known quite generally the world over as "Buffalo Bill." A sturdy, generous, positive character, who as hunter, guide, scout, Government officer, member of the Legislature, and gentleman, rises to the equal of every emergency into which his way is opened or directed. Quick to think and to act, cool in all cases of pleasure or extreme danger; versatile in his genius; broad and liberal in his ideas; progressive in his mentality, he can no more keep still or settle down into a routine work incidental to office or farm life than an eagle can thrive in a cage.

The true Western man is free, fearless, generous and chivalrous. Of this class Hon. Wm. F. Cody, "Buffalo Bill," is a bright representative. As a part of his rushing career he has brought together material for what he correctly terms a Wild West Exhibition. I should call it a Wild West Reality. The idea is not merely to take in money from those who witness a very lively exhibition, but to give the people in the East a correct representation of life on the plains, and the incidental life of the hardy, brave, intelligent pioneers, who are the first to blaze the way to the future homes and greatness of America. He knows the worth and sturdiness of true Western character, and, as a lover of his country, wishes to present as many facts as possible to the public, so that those who will can see actual pictures of life in the West, brought to the East for the inspection of the public.

"Buffalo Bill" has brought the Wild West to the doors of the East. There is more of real life, of genuine interest, of positive education in this startling exhibition than I have ever before seen, and it is as true to nature and life as it really is with those who are smoothing the way for millions to follow. All of this imaginary Romeo and Juliet business sinks to utter insignificance in comparison to the drama of existence that is here so well enacted, and all the operas in the world appear like pretty playthings for emasculated children by the side of the setting of reality and the music of the frontier so faithfully and extensively presented and so cleverly managed by this incomparable representative of Western pluck, coolness, bravery, independence and generosity. I wish every person east of the Missouri River could see this true, graphic picture of Western life; they would know more and think better of the genuine men of the West.

I wish there were more progressive educators like Wm. F. Cody in this world.

He deserves well for his efforts to please and to instruct in matters important to America and incidents that are passing away *never more to return.* . . .

Since the railroad gave its aid to pioneering, America is making history faster than any other country in the world. *Her pioneers are fast passing away.* A few years more and the great struggle for possession will be ended, and generations will settle down to enjoy the homes their fathers located and fenced in for them. Then will come the picture maker — he who, with pen, pencil and panel, can tell the story as he understands it. Then millions will read and look at what the pioneer did and what the historian related, wishing on the whole that they could have been there to have seen the original. These are some of the thoughts to crowd in upon us as we view the great living picture that the HON. WM. F. CODY ("BUFFALO BILL") gives at the Wild West Exhibition, which every man, woman and child the world over should see and study as a realistic fact. . . .

We see "BUFFALO BILL," the last of the six greatest scouts this country has ever known, viz., BOONE, CROCKETT, CARSON, BRIDGER, "WILD BILL," and "BUFFALO BILL" — to our mind the greatest and most remarkable of all — a man whom this country will never duplicate. A none-such to the credit of Nature, the world and the mental and physical material of which he was formed, as one made to do a certain great work. A man in the prime of life, who, from the age of ten years, has fought fate and all adverse circumstances, and never to a loss. A man who is a man; as a scout; as a pioneer; as a Government officer; as an Indian fighter; as a mighty hunter; as a man of honor, and of more than ordinary skill and courage, commanding admiration — deserving of recognition as a great character in American history. A natural man of the highest order.

Brick Pomeroy, editorial, *New York Democrat* (1886). Reprinted in program (c. 1900) for the Wild West show, 8–10, author's copy.

ᴈ

ᴈ *The More Virile Virtues: Imperialism and the Fictions of Manhood* ᴈ

In an 1893 *Harper's Weekly* essay, the future "Rough Rider" and president Theodore Roosevelt joined an ongoing debate about the "Value of an Athletic Training" for the highly select category of young American men who attended college. Although outlining in detail the benefits of playing football to the player and the nation, Roosevelt saved his sharpest words for the game's critics, the "timid" men who "shrink from the exercise of manly and robust qualities if there is any chance of its being accompanied by physical pain." The best way to win an argument, it seemed, was to slander the manhood of one's opponents. But for Roosevelt and other men of his time, the debate about football was not simply about the value of sports; it also was about what they feared was the declining character of the nation's best and brightest, its leadership class of young white men. Some saw the violent (and occasionally deadly) sport as the nation's salvation; others saw it as part of the problem.

For generations, men who shared Roosevelt's privileged class and race had honored the man who demonstrated his strength of character by calmly exercising reason and independence in his public actions and wisdom in caring for his property and family. Rough and violent sports and occupations, they believed, were for brutish primitives, such as the Irish, who seemed unfit as men to govern a republic. But for growing numbers of Roosevelt's generation, civilized restraint in a man felt "over-civilized," timid, and weak. At a time when the West of Buffalo Bill and frontier Indian wars was fading fast, modern men were no longer forging frontiers, but instead settling into the bloodless comfort and ease of "a perfectly peaceful and commercial civilization." At the same time, icons of "the New Woman"—young, energetic, athletic, adventurous, even (some said) *virile*—became fixed in popular culture.

These complementary pictures of women glorying in their vitality as men fretted about theirs represented, at most, the experience of propertied, native-born, Protestant Victorians—the Americans able to agonize about losing or gaining the power to identify themselves as the Americans. At one level, such concerns suggest how the era's historical transformations affected women's and men's sense of themselves as "woman" or "man." At another level, though, anxieties about the problem of weak men infused the bitter debate about the need for American military intervention in the colonial conflicts that beset the outposts of European imperial powers. Many—such as Roosevelt or the imperialist U.S. senator from Indiana, Albert J. Beveridge—saw these conflicts as opportunities for the once heroic stock of the nation's finest men to recover the "virile virtues" needed to lead at home and abroad. The selections in this section explore how ideas about race, gender, and class shaped the conversation about the global destiny of the United States in the 1890s.

The Venezuelan Question (1896)

CARL SCHURZ

Letter to Henry Cabot Lodge (1896)

THEODORE ROOSEVELT

In the 1890s, the nation's expanding wealth and economic power coincided with the increasing shakiness of Spain's control of its colonial territories in the Caribbean and the Pacific. Imperialist and anti-imperialist forces in the United States went to battle in this decade over the unprecedented opportunities for the nation to acquire a foreign empire and to spread the benefits of American civilization to the backward regions of the world. In addressing questions that still trouble U.S. foreign policy today, the opposing sides argued not only about policy but also about the identity of the nation itself. Both sides used gender and race to stake out America's global boundaries and responsibilities. The following selections highlight two figures in this conversation: Carl Schurz, a German immigrant who had risen, in storied fashion, to the U.S. Senate as a reform Republican who championed antislavery in the antebellum years, civil service reform in the 1880s, and anti-imperialism at the end of his career; and Theodore Roosevelt, who would become president of the United States in 1901. In his speech, Schurz addresses the 1895 crisis over the border between Venezuela and colonial British Guiana. When American politicians contended that the Monroe Doctrine empowered them to settle the matter, Britain had the audacity to tell Uncle Sam to mind his own business—fighting words to figures such as Theodore Roosevelt, who were arguing for a strenuous expansion of American power around the world. Roosevelt's letter to his friend Henry Cabot Lodge addresses the anti-imperialism of Schurz and others.

PROBLEMS TO CONSIDER

1. In these arguments, what was the relevance of "manhood" to the merits of imperialism? Were Schurz and Roosevelt in agreement on any points?
2. "Savage" or uncivilized peoples served as object lessons for both Schurz and Roosevelt. What did references to "crazed" Malays and corrupt Chinese contribute to their arguments about America's role in the world?

THE VENEZUELAN QUESTION

I yield to no one in American feeling or pride; and, as an American, I maintain that international peace, kept in justice and honor, is an American principle and an American interest. As to the President's recent message on the Venezuela case, opinions differ. But I am sure that all good citizens, whether they approve or disapprove of it, and while they would faithfully stand by their country in time of need, sincerely and heartily wish that the pending controversy between the United States and Great Britain be brought to a peaceful issue.

I am well aware of the strange teachings put forth among us by some persons, that a war, from time to time, would by no means be a misfortune, but rather a healthy exercise to stir up our patriotism, and to keep us from becoming effeminate. Indeed, there are some of them busily looking round for somebody to fight as the crazed Malay runs amuck looking for somebody to kill. The idea that the stalwart and hard-working American people, engaged in subduing to civilization an immense continent,

need foreign wars to preserve their manhood from dropping into effeminacy, or that their love of country will flag unless stimulated by hatred of somebody else, or that they must have bloodshed and devastation as an outdoor exercise in the place of other sports—such an idea is as preposterous as it is disgraceful and abominable. . . .

What is the rule of honor to be observed by a Power so strong and so advantageously situated as this Republic is? Of course, I do not expect it meekly to pocket real insults if they should be offered to it. But surely, it should not, as our boyish jingoes wish it to do, swagger about among the nations of the world, with a chip on its shoulder, and shaking its fist in everybody's face. Of course, it should not tamely submit to real encroachments upon its rights. But, surely, it should not, whenever its own notions of right or interest collide with the notions of others, fall into hysterics and act as if it really feared for its own security and its very independence. As a true gentleman, conscious of his strength and his dignity, it should be slow to take offense. In its dealings with other nations it should have scrupulous regard, not only for their rights, but also for their self-respect. With all its latent resources for war, it should be the great peace Power of the world. It should never forget what a proud privilege and what an inestimable blessing it is not to need and not to have big armies or navies to support. It should seek to influence mankind, not by heavy artillery, but by good example and wise counsel. It should see its highest glory, not in battles won, but in wars prevented. It should be so invariably just and fair, so trustworthy, so good tempered, so conciliatory that other nations would instinctively turn to it as their mutual friend and the natural adjuster of their differences, thus making it the greatest preserver of the world's peace.

This is not a mere idealistic fancy. It is the natural position of this great Republic among the nations of the earth. It is its noblest vocation, and it will be a glorious day for the United States when the good sense and the self-respect of the American people see in this their "manifest destiny." It all rests upon peace. Is not this peace with honor? There has, of late, been much loose speech about "Americanism." Is not this good Americanism? It is surely to-day the Americanism of those who love their country most. And I fervently hope that it will be and ever remain the Americanism of our children and children's children.

Carl Schurz, "The Venezuelan Question," in *Speeches, Correspondence, and Political Papers of Carl Schurz*, 6 vols., edited by Frederic Bancroft (New York: G. P. Putnam's Sons, 1913), 5:250, 258–59.

LETTER FROM THEODORE ROOSEVELT TO HENRY CABOT LODGE

I see that [Harvard University's] President Eliot attacked you and myself as "degenerated sons of Harvard." It is a fine alliance, that between the anglo-maniac mugwumps, the socialist working men, and corrupt politicians . . . to prevent the increase of our Navy and coast defenses. The moneyed and semi-cultivated classes, especially of the Northeast, are doing their best to bring this country down to the Chinese level. If we ever come to nothing as a nation it will be because the teaching of Carl Schurz, President Eliot, the *Evening Post* and the futile sentimentalists of the international arbitration type, bears its legitimate fruit in producing a flabby, timid type of character, which eats away the great fighting features of our race. Hand in hand with the Chinese timidity and inefficiency of such a character would go the Chinese corruption; for men of such a stamp are utterly unable to war against the Tammany *[New York City's Democratic political machine]* stripe of politicians. There is nothing that provokes me more than the unintelligent, cowardly chatter for "peace at any price" in which all of those gentlemen indulge.

Selections from the Correspondence of Theodore Roosevelt and Henry Cabot Lodge, 1884–1918, 2 vols., edited by Henry Cabot Lodge (New York: Scribner's, 1925), 1:218–19.

⁊

Speech Before the House of Representatives (1898)
JAMES R. MANN

The destiny of Spain's imperial possessions in the Caribbean and Pacific provoked the most divisive debate of the era. Many Americans responded with sympathy for the victims of the atrocities committed by Spanish colonial authorities as they attempted to crush indigenous uprisings in Cuba. Anti-Spanish hostility was further fueled by pro-imperialist newspapers in the United States. The shrillest were in New York City: Joseph Pulitzer's World *and William Randolph Hearst's* Journal. *They beefed up circulation with exaggerated accounts of Spanish crimes and demanded war to answer alleged insults to American honor—such as the mysterious explosion that sank the American battleship* Maine *in Havana harbor in February 1898. Newspapers held Spain responsible and castigated Republican president William McKinley for not immediately declaring war. (The* Journal *and other papers made much of the fact that, in the Civil War, McKinley had served for a time as a commissary agent charged with supplying food rations to the troops.) The war against Spain came in April 1898, lasted three months, and cost the lives of more than 5,000 Americans, most of whom died from disease, not in actual combat. Despite McKinley's promises to grant independence to Spain's empire, only Cuba achieved sovereignty, which was qualified by a provision in its constitution that granted the United States the right to intervene militarily in Cuban affairs. The Spanish-American War rewarded the United States with military and political control of the Philippines and Puerto Rico, among other lands. It also seemed to vindicate the policies that imperialists had advocated. Certainly, as imperialists commonly argued, the war had freed colonial peoples from Spanish rule. But what had it done for America? The following selection, a speech in Congress by Representative James R. Mann, a Republican from Illinois, explains the meaning of the recently declared war against Spain.*

PROBLEMS TO CONSIDER

1. Why, according to Mann, were Americans waging war against Spain? What did the war accomplish for the nation?
2. What factors accounted for the superiority of America's fighting men?

Mr. Chairman, the spirit of commercialism has been subordinated to the spirit of humanity. Patriotism is again supreme in our hearts. Greed and the love of gold have yielded to the touch of sympathetic nature. No nobler offering to humanity, no greater sacrifice of self-interest, no loftier example of human kinship has ever been made. A mighty nation, wholly devoted to the arts of peace, absorbed in trade and gain, permeated with the desire for wealth and comforts, without a powerful army and with only a moderate navy, goes to war with a determined, cruel, and revengeful people because it dares to fight for the right and is determined to stop forever the despotic and cold-blooded cruelty to and robbery of the island of Cuba by the nation of Spain.

To our shame be it said that there are still those in our country who are unmoved by the piteous pleadings of the starving thousands in Cuba and whose eyes do not moisten or hearts swell when they read of the starving babes endeavoring vainly to draw sustenance from the breasts of dead and starved mothers.

Some of these have hypocritically preached tenderness and honor for years, and now their fear of suffering or their greed for gain overcomes all other emotions. But they are few in number. . . .

A short time ago we engaged in a political contest in our land which many of us believed vitally involved the sacred honor of our country. The lesson of that campaign would have been lost if it had not taught our citizens that the honor of a country is above gain, above gold and silver, above ideas of currency or tariff, and that the honor of our country can only be sustained and upheld by the inner consciousness that we have done that which we believe to be right and sacred, whether it means war or peace; whether it means the beating of the sword into the plowshare or the plowshare into the sword. [Applause.]

We do not fight for a fancied slight; we do not fight for a commercial wrong; we do not fight for an increase of territory; we do not fight because our commercial spirit has been outraged; we do not fight because our land has been invaded; we fight because it has become necessary to fight if we would uphold our manhood; because the leader of nations on our continent can not stand idly by while Spain is, with cold blood and cruelty, slaughtering and starving our next-door neighbors to death; because unless we are willing to fight we must abandon our vaunted pretensions of enlightened humanity and civilization; because we can not "pass by on the other side." . . .

It has been said that war was terrible; that war is hell. Let it be so! . . .

Has war grown so terrible that we now are afraid of it? Shall we muffle our ears and blind our eyes and pluck out our hearts to the piteous moanings and pleadings of the starving thousands in Cuba because we are afraid to spill our blood? Thank God, the American people have red blood instead of ice water running in their veins! . . .

Have we grown so rich, so enervated, so attached to the unholy dollar, that we are afraid to fight for freedom? . . .

No, Mr. Chairman, we have taken our stand. We insist that no nation on this continent shall have the liberty to torture and starve her subjects deliberately and coldly to death, and that position we are willing to defend with our fortunes and our lives.

Representative James R. Mann, "Patriotism Is Again Supreme in Our Hearts," speech before the House of Representatives, on April 28, 1898, *Congressional Record* 31, pt. 5: 4362.

ꙮ

The Spanish-American War in Song (1898)

Union and Confederate Veterans Reunite to Free Little Cuba (c. 1898)

FRITZ GUERIN

When Congress declared war against Spain, a band played both "Dixie" and "Battle Hymn of the Republic" to commemorate the moment. Those performances, like the previous document, indicate how contemporaries believed that the war was a nationalizing endeavor that would heal the internal divisions afflicting the nation. Such arguments often were the subject of the many patriotic war songs that American newspapers commissioned and published to show their support for the war and to galvanize national unity. The songs and the photographic tableau reproduced here suggest how new technologies — inexpensive newspaper printing, photographic reproduction — were enlisted in the imperialism debate. The following documents reflect on two of the most anxiety-provoking subjects at the heart of this debate: the sense that the United States remained a nation divided by the Civil War, and the questionable patriotism of the sons of America's richest families.

PROBLEMS TO CONSIDER

1. How did the first pair of songs (from the *Minneapolis Journal*) and the photographic tableau establish the national brotherhood of northerners and southerners? What concerns about the rich were dispelled by the third song about "dudes" (from the *Cleveland Leader*)?

2. How effective do you think songs and images such as these were in uniting the nation or defining the meaning of the war with Spain?

I. THE SOUTHERN VOLUNTEER

Yes, sir, we fought with Stonewall,
    And faced the fight with Lee;
But if this here Union goes to war
    Make one more gun for me!
I didn't shrink from Sherman,
    As he galloped to the sea;
But if this here Union goes to war
    Make one more gun for me!

I was with 'em at Manassas—
    The bully boys in gray;
I heard the thunderers roarin'
    Round Stonewall Jackson's way;
And many a time this sword of mine
    Has blazed the way for Lee;
But if this old Nation goes to war
    Make one more gun for me.

I'm not so full o' fightin',
    Nor half so full o' fun,
As I was back in the sixties
    When I shouldered my old gun;
It may be that my hair is white—
    Sich things, ye know, must be,
But if this old Union's in for war
    Make one more gun for me!

I hain't forgot my raisin'—
    Nor how in sixty-two,
Or thereabouts, with battle shouts,
    I charged the boys in blue;
And I say: I fought with Stonewall
    And blazed the way for Lee,
But if this old Union's in for war
    Make one more gun for me!

II. HIS NORTHERN BROTHER

Just make it two, old fellows;
    I want to stand once more
Beneath the old flag with you,
    As in the days of yore.
Our fathers stood together,
    And fought on land and sea
The battles fierce that made us
    A Nation of the free.

I licked you down at Vicksburg,
    You licked me at Bull Run;
On many a field we struggled,
    When neither victory won.
You wore the gray of Southland,
    I wore the Northern blue;
Like men we did our duty
    When screaming bullets flew.

Four years we fought like devils,
    But when the war was done
Your hand met mine in friendly clasp,
    Our two hearts beat [as] one.
And now when danger threatens
    No North, no South, we know,
Once more we stand together
    To fight the common foe.

My head, like yours, is frosty—
    Old age is creeping on;
Life's sun is lower sinking,
    My day will soon be gone.
But if our country's honor
    Needs once again her son,
I'm ready, too, old fellow—
    So get another gun.

DUDES BEFORE SANTIAGO

They scoffed when we lined up with Teddy,
    They said we were dudes and all that;
They imagined that "Cholly" and "Fweddie"
    Would faint at the drop of a hat!
But let them look there in the ditches,
    Blood-stained by the swells in the van,
And know that a chap may have riches
    And still be a man.

They said that we'd wilt under fire,
    And run if the foeman said "Boo!"

But a fellow may have a rich sire
    And still be a patriot, too!
Look there where we met twice our number,
    Where the life-blood of dudes drenched
    the earth!

"The Southern Volunteer" (pp. 8–9), "His Northern Brother" (pp. 9–10), and "Dudes Before Santiago" (p. 31), reprinted in *Spanish-American War Songs: A Complete Collection of Newspaper Verse During the Recent War with Spain*, edited by Sidney A. Witherbee (Detroit: Sidney A. Witherbee, 1898), 8–10, 31.

Union and Confederate Veterans Reunite to Free Little Cuba, by Fritz Guerin (c. 1898).

(© Corbis.)

Uncle Sam's New Class in the Art of Self-Government (1898)

W. A. ROGERS

Answering the question of what the war had done for America and Americans required addressing, in part, the fate of former Spanish colonials who now found themselves under the dominion of the United States. What was to become of such persons? Were they capable of becoming American citizens? These questions took on added meaning at a time of rising opposition to the immigration of southern and eastern Europeans, who were coming to the United States in record numbers. The following editorial cartoon from Harper's Weekly *engages the questions about the fate of Spanish colonials. The figure in the dunce cap is the Philippine patriot leader Emilio Aguinaldo. The two boys undergoing Uncle Sam's discipline are a "Cuban ex-patriot" and a "guerrilla." The Cuban revolutionary leader Maximo Gomez is reading "his book." On the far right, Hawaii and Puerto Rico are reading their lessons. The map of the globe in the background is labeled "Map of the United States and Neighboring Countries."*

PROBLEMS TO CONSIDER

1. Was the cartoon an argument for or against imperialism? What story was being told here about the Filipinos' and other former colonials' prospects for American citizenship?
2. What did the schoolhouse represent in the debate about America's potential empire?

UNCLE SAM'S NEW CLASS IN THE ART OF SELF-GOVERNMENT.

W. A. Rogers, "Uncle Sam's New Class in the Art of Self-Government" from *Harper's Weekly*, August 27, 1898.

(The Granger Collection, New York.)

❧

The Sultan of Sulu; An Original Satire in Two Acts (1902)

GEORGE ADE

The anti-imperialism literature was practically an industry in itself throughout the 1890s and into the new century. Among the most widely read or listened-to critics were America's foremost humorists. Mark Twain, Finley Peter Dunne, George Ade, and others attacked the imperialists with merciless satire, especially once U.S. forces sought to subdue the native uprising against American rule in the Philippines with a brutal military campaign. The Spanish Philippines had hardly been a concern in the nation's run-up to war over Cuba. Once the United States won control of the islands and their 5 million inhabitants, business and political leaders argued that vital national interests were at stake in keeping them under American control. Moreover, they argued, the primitive Filipino people deserved the benefits of American civilization. In the eyes of anti-imperialists such as George Ade, American claims were ripe for satire. A native of Indiana, Ade made his name as a writer for the Chicago Record *newspaper, which sent him to cover the U.S. campaign in the Philippines. Ade doubted the benevolence of American aims and satirized missionaries and politicians, first, in a series for the* Record *called "Stories of Benevolent Assimilation." Then, in 1902, he produced a musical comedy,* The Sultan of Sulu, *which was one of the year's great stage hits in Chicago and New York. A critic for the* New York Times *called it "reasonably, intelligently, philosophically laughable." Ade based the plot on an actual series of events from America's colonial venture in the Philippines: the U.S. treaty with a native tribal ruler, and the civilization program that American Protestant missionaries sought to enact on the sultan's subjects. The following scene occurs early in the production as the Filipino natives spot the arrival of the U.S. fleet and experience American benevolence for the first time. Dingbat is captain of the Sultan Ki-Ram's guard, and Hadji is his private secretary.*

PROBLEMS TO CONSIDER

1. What was Ade's anti-imperialist message in this scene? What did Ade's comic use of exotic native maidens, a polygamous sultan, and his hapless cronies suggest about why he opposed imperialism?
2. How effective is humor as a political weapon? What are the advantages of political satire, as demonstrated in this example?

DINGBAT: A large white ship has come into the harbor.

HADJI: A ship—in the harbor?

DINGBAT: It is crowded with soldiers.

HADJI: Soldiers?

DINGBAT: The flag is one of red, white, and blue, spangled with stars.

HADJI: Never heard of such a flag.

DINGBAT: What's more, sir, they're coming ashore.

HADJI: . . . How glad I am that I am merely a private secretary! [*Distant boom of cannon.*] Aha! That seems friendly. They are firing a salute.

[*Shell, with fuse sputtering, rolls on from left and disappears behind palace. Sound of explosion.* Hadji *disappears headlong into the palace, followed by* Dingbat. *The broken volleys of musketry become louder and louder. In the incidental music there is a suggestion of "A Hot Time in the Old Town." Sharp yells are heard off left, and then a body of United States Volunteers in khaki and marines in white pours on the stage in pell-mell confusion.* Lieutenant William Hardy, *in a white uniform of the Regulars, comes down through the centre of the charging squad. He has his sword drawn.*]

LIEUTENANT WILLIAM HARDY AND CHORUS OF SOLDIERS:

"Hike"

We haven't the appearance, goodness knows,
    Of plain commercial men;
From a hasty glance, you might suppose
    We are fractious now and then.
But though we come in warlike guise
    And battle-front arrayed,
It's all a business enterprise;
    We're seeking foreign trade.

Refrain

We're as mild as any turtle-dove
    When we see the foe a-coming,
Our thoughts are set on human love
    When we hear the bullets humming.
We teach the native population
    What the golden rule is like,
And we scatter public education
    On ev'ry blasted hike!

We want to assimilate, if we can,
    Our brother who is brown;
We love our dusky fellow-man
    And we hate to hunt him down.
So, when we perforate his frame,
    We want him to be good.
We shoot at him to make him tame,
    If he but understood.

Refrain

We're as mild, etc.

[*During the second verse, the wives and native women return timidly, drawn by curiosity. They gather about the soldiers and study them carefully, more or less frightened but not altogether displeased.* Lieutenant Hardy *addresses the company of natives.*]

HARDY: I am here to demand an audience with the Sultan.

CHIQUITA: [*Stepping forth.*] *Indeed!* And who are you that presumes to demand an audience with the Bright Morning Light of the Orient?

HARDY: Why, how do you do? I am Lieutenant Hardy—a modest representative of the U.S.A.

[Hadji *cautiously emerges from the palace.*]

HADJI: [*Overhearing.*] The U.S.A.? Where is *that* on the map?

HARDY: Just now it is spread all over the map. Perhaps you don't know it, but we are the owners of this island. We paid twenty millions of dollars for you. [*All whistle.*] At first it did seem a large price, but now that I have seen you [*indicating wives*] I am convinced it was a bargain. [Chiquita *has lighted a native cigarette and is serenely puffing it.* Lieutenant Hardy *addresses her chidingly.*] You don't mean to say you smoke?

CHIQUITA: Don't the ladies of your country smoke?

HARDY: The *ladies* do—the women *don't*.

[Hadji *observes the confidential chat between the officer and the principal wife, and he is disturbed in spirit.*]

HADJI: Lieutenant! [*More loudly.*] *Lieutenant!* Did you come ashore to talk business or to break into the harem?

HARDY: Beg pardon. [*Stepping back into a stiff, military attitude.*] Does the Sultan surrender?

HADJI: He says he will *die* first.

HARDY: *That* can be arranged. We are here as emissaries of peace, but we never object to a skirmish—eh, boys?

[*The soldiers respond with a warlike shout, which frightens the native women. The lieutenant reassures them.*]

HARDY: Young ladies, don't be alarmed. We may slaughter all the others, but you will be spared. Meet us here after the battle. . . .

[Colonel Jefferson Budd, Henrietta Budd, Wakeful M. Jones, Pamela Frances Jackson . . . *enter.* . . . Henrietta *is a very attractive girl, in a stunning summer gown.* Colonel Budd *is large and imposing, somewhat overburdened with conscious dignity. He wears a colonel's service uniform.* Wakeful M. Jones *is a brisk young man in flannels.* Miss Jackson *is a sedate and rigid spinster. . . .*]

PAMELA: [*Inquiringly.*] The Sultan?

CHIQUITA: He is within—making his will.

HENRIETTA: His will?

CHIQUITA: He expects to be captured. They are going to do something dreadful to him.

BUDD: [*Impressively.*] We are going to assimilate him.

CHIQUITA: Yes, that's why he's making his will.
. . .

[*Later, the Sultan enters.*]

KI-RAM: Now, then,
for a farewell speech that will look well in the school histories. I die—I die that Sulu may—

BUDD: Why, your Majesty, you are not expected to die.

KI-RAM: No? [*With an expression of glad surprise.*]

BUDD: We are your friends. We have come to take possession of the island and teach your benighted people the advantages of free government. We hold that all government derives its just powers from the consent of the governed.

ALL: Hear! Hear!

BUDD: Now, the question is, do you consent to this benevolent plan?

[*The soldiers bring their guns to "charge bayonets."* Ki-Ram *looks right and left and finds himself walled in by threatening weapons. He hesitates.*]

KI-RAM: Are all the guns loaded?

BUDD: They *are.*

KI-RAM: I consent.

BUDD: Good! The education of your neglected race will begin at once under the direction of these young ladies.

George Ade, *The Sultan of Sulu; An Original Satire in Two Acts* (New York: R. H. Russell, 1903), 10–14, 16, 25–26.

৵

∽ CHAPTER 3 ∾

Order and Disorder:
1890–1920

IN 1913, Florence Kelley, secretary of the National Consumers' League (NCL), told the women of New York's Smith College Club exactly what went into the cheap candy that their social improvement societies handed out to poor children each Christmas season. Manufacturers, who cut corners to keep their goods cheap *and* profitable, swept up the bits and pieces of candy from the kitchen floors and tossed everything collected—including chewing gum discarded by the factory women and whatever the workingmen had spat onto the floor—back into the kettle. In addition, when the big seasonal orders flooded in at the last minute, factory owners kept their working women into the early morning hours wrapping sweets. This, she said, was the "candy you feed to the children of the poor." The Smith women could choose not to buy cheap sweets, but that, Kelley said, addressed only part of the problem. They also needed to remember *who* made the candy, their sisters among the poor who labored under inhumane conditions because wealthy women neglected to order holiday bonbons on time. If they placed their orders in a timely manner, these clubwomen could actually make a difference in the lives of the children who ate the candy and the working people who made it.

The efforts of Kelley and the NCL to unite the separate worlds of women shoppers and women workers through links of sympathy and reform said much about the swiftly changing political culture of the Progressive Era. In the period between 1890 and 1920, a tide of intense reform agitation swept the United States. President Theodore Roosevelt applauded its "fierce discontent with evil" and its "firm determination to punish the authors of evil, whether in industry or politics." Progressives—most of whom were native-born and middle-class—responded to the social transformations and upheavals described in the previous chapter. They became convinced that they had to reform the world around them, if they wanted to protect themselves and their children. They had to go into the slums and change the people who lived there. They had to surrender their traditional antiregulatory bias for more active institutional authorities—local, state, and federal governments; research universities; and reform organizations staffed by trained professionals. Such authorities were needed to safeguard the public good against irresponsible business practices, political corruption, and the poverty, disease, and immorality spawned by the social dislocations of a rapidly urbanizing and industrializing nation. Building public playgrounds, restricting immigration, marking off public lands as national parks, regulating (and finally outlawing) saloons, redesigning municipal governments, prosecuting unfair and anticompetitive business practices, battling cholera with improved urban sewage and water systems—all of these reforms reflected Progressives' reinvention of what could and should be done by public authorities.

The NCL encouraged these reforms. But what placed it among the era's major reform organizations was its recognition of how the market transformations described in chapter 2 fundamentally reorganized the patterns and habits of urban and rural life. In the nineteenth-century household economy, production and consumption were integrated in families and local communities, which made their own goods and organized their time away from work in informal gatherings. By the early twentieth century, Americans relied instead on new commercial institutions—mail-order houses, specialty and department stores, hotels and vacation resorts, amusement parks, dance halls. In American society, Florence Kelley said, "every person is a consumer," and in the United States most shoppers were women. They might not be able to vote or hold office as men could, but formal political privileges mattered little in comparison to the enormous influence of women who were organized and disciplined to make rational and "righteous" purchases.

Consumer capitalism, like industrialization, challenged expectations about the power of business in a democratic society, the relation of the market to public and private life, the distinctions between social classes, the gender boundaries regulating the sexes, and the moral implications of an economy oriented toward consumer goods and having fun. The documents in this chapter explore the fervent social and cultural agitation in the Progressive Era and focus on Americans' responses to a world increasingly driven by the need and demand for manufactured consumer goods and pleasures.

❧ *Mothering Modernity:*
Women and Progressive Reform ❧

In 1918, a cartoon in the *New York Telegram* showed an attractive, middle-class homemaker (her apron identified her as "Mother America") hanging out her freshly washed laundry of Progressive reform initiatives for cleaning up the nation. Suspended from the clothesline were socks labeled "eight-hour workday" and "equal pay for women," a pair of underwear marked "child labor laws," and towels tagged as "the minimum wage," "universal suffrage," and "municipal playgrounds." In the matter of reforming a nation as afflicted with corruption as the United States, the caption explained, "A Woman's Work Is Never Done." The cartoon is an effective reminder of the vital leadership that countless reform-minded women contributed to Progressive campaigns to cleanse the nation of its evils. Progressivism brought women into areas of business and politics that historically were exclusively male territories. Whether women were working for a living, studying for a college degree, or organizing public service programs, their growing presence in such arenas challenged assumptions about their tenderness and frailty, which suited them to domesticity and motherhood. Whether as workers or as reformers, such women redefined the meaning of public space, which historically had derived its significance from their absence.

Some historians describe the projection of women's influence to the world outside the home as "maternalist politics." This agenda profoundly influenced the direction of Progressive Era reform and shaped the scope of social welfare programs that we regard today as government's most basic concerns. But did scouring the filth from the face of American society alter conventional understandings of womanhood and its fundamental difference from manhood? In the minds even of many reformers, women's assertive "mothering" of America threatened to weaken men's political and social authority and to erode the differences between the sexes, with men *and* the nation the losers in the outcome. This section allows an exploration into the ways Progressive women and men advanced or resisted the pervasive social and cultural changes that were reshaping their lives and expectations at the turn of the twentieth century.

The Future of the Woman's Club (1904)
WINNIFRED HARPER COOLEY

As the tainted-candy example demonstrates, Progressives transformed the scope of political concerns and participation in American life. Clubwomen were leaders in the expansive project of maternalist politics. They actually called their agenda "municipal housekeeping." The "woman's club" movement dates from the late 1860s through the 1890s, when hundreds of thousands of middle-class and wealthy women, unsatisfied with the rewards of a comfortable home life, sought to expand their horizons by forming literary or arts clubs for members of their sex and class. Clubwomen presumably were concerned merely with self-improvement and cultural and feminine matters — learning to appreciate Shakespeare and poets such as Robert Browning. But extraordinary figures such as Jane Cunningham Croly, the founder of the Sorosis club in 1868, pushed their organizations in directions less politely cultural and individualistic and more aggressively political, culminating with the formation of the General Federation of Women's Clubs in 1890. "We prefer Doing to Dante, Being to Browning," one clubwoman declared. The federation was a highly centralized organization that mirrored the combinations businesses were forming to enhance their leverage. By consolidating its power, the federation could better apply women's moral qualifications as mothers and wives to the broad array of social problems—especially those such as child labor and pure food—that involved women, children, and families but which men were neglecting. Such affairs, as the title of a club movement book put it, were The Business of Being a Club Woman. *With its coast-to-coast organization and high-profile leadership, the federation had an "upper-crust" tone that frequently made headlines in newspaper society pages. At the same time, clubwomen also sought to establish the "sisterhood" of wealthy and working-class women on the basis of their common oppression and their shared womanhood, the universal application of which was critical to the fate of humanity. In the following speech, clubwoman Winnifred Harper Cooley reflects on the historical importance of this businesslike movement.*

PROBLEMS TO CONSIDER

1. What were the aims of the woman's clubs? How did these aims accord with traditional understandings of womanhood? Did describing governance as "housekeeping upon a large scale" affect the understanding of public space as male?
2. What were Cooley's beliefs about motherhood? Would you say that she adhered to or redefined conventional understandings of women's natures?

The amazing fact is that women's clubs ever came into being! Civilization awaits the first daring path-breaker, and those who follow in the beaten road marvel that it took so long for the first dauntless one to mark it out.

That woman—the weak, the despised, the priest-ridden, believed to be the original sinner, the ruin of the human race, an unclean thing, a beast of burden, unworthy of education, forbidden the perusal of the scriptures, veiled in a harem, burned on her husband's funeral pyre, considered cursed in giving birth to mankind (or, in mediæval times, respected for maternity, yet still man's inferior, his chattel, his toy), at best and last, esteemed solely for motherhood—that this being should timidly venture forth into the arena of intellectual and civil life, gently wrest from man, one by one, his pre-empted prerogatives, and persuasively, serenely assume

"his" education and professions, this is the marvel of the ages! . . .

One sometimes speculates as to the result of the psychological action of the club upon the individual woman, in the past and the future. We have only to review what the *club idea* has done for women, in order to foretell its infinite possibilities. It has made them more democratic—less narrow and exclusive. It has heightened their plane of thinking; it has taught them habits of concentrated study; it has multiplied their available topics of conversation and eliminated the constant personal note therefrom; it has lifted them bodily from the pettiness and restraint of domestic drudgery. No one can question the benefit to the home and to society of broadening and deepening the life and experiences of the "home maker." Women, through club work, are learning the value of cooperation, the sacredness of friendship, the necessity for tolerance and charity, of magnanimity and considerateness. The club develops not merely a clever and versatile, but an expansive and harmonious, a well-rounded individual.

. . . We naturally speculate upon the *destination* of this mighty new current that has swept aside all former conservative estimates of feminine possibilities—enlarging woman's "sphere" until it is co-existent with the globe that limits the activities of mankind—and we venture to prophesy optimistically of the work of women in the twentieth century. . . .

It is true . . . that clubs have fulfilled their mission in the peculiar lines formerly followed. But there is still the gigantic problem of a semi-barbarous world crying to be civilized. The poor we have always with us; likewise the criminal (in and *out* of jail). Our morals still spring largely from policy, our religion from superstition. Our social system is a rough compromise, blocked out by our ancestors, who groped for wisdom, and settled upon the highest plane at the time accessible—but one inadequate to our growing needs. Our government is the best yet attempted, but it is even now feeling "the growing-pains of evolution," and our politics, thus young, is seriously diseased.

Organization is one of the highest achievements of modern life. Organization is effectiveness. It is the secret of success. It made the Catholic Church a world-force; it has given the Standard Oil Company and the Steel Trust their Titanic power. Women now are more or less perfectly organized throughout the world. *Organization implies responsibility*. The machinery is awaiting women; it would be immoral waste to allow it to rust. Through it must be worked out many of the social and industrial problems of the future.

The woman's club will be in the broadest sense a civic club, because civic life is only less vital than home life, which is its foundation. City government is only housekeeping upon a large scale. *Economy*, from the Greek, means "law of the house," and political economy is the law of the household carried into the community. Women have the training of the ages back of them in domestic economics; what class is better fitted to undertake the problems of our cities?

Of course, women never can work with absolute effectiveness until they are enfranchised. A person can do some things with his hands tied, but is better able to work when free. The eternal feminine has expressed itself through indirect channels long enough. . . . But in democratic times and countries we believe in expressing ourselves frankly and honestly, with each individual free to act and to choose for the good of the whole. Women desire no vicarious labor or sacrifices. Political and industrial freedom is but a means to an end—*the perfecting of human society through the individual*; and for this alone do the schools, the churches, and the clubs exist. . . .

Winnifred Harper Cooley, "The Future of the Woman's Club," in *The New Womanhood* (New York: Broadway Publishing Co., 1904), 94, 97–99, 101–3.

๖

Woman's Mission and Woman's Clubs (1905)
GROVER CLEVELAND

Their social pedigrees, wealth, and defense of motherhood did not shield clubwomen from charges of nation-wrecking insubordination. Many men of the time were willing to concede, in theory, that women were entitled as fellow human beings to the same rights they enjoyed. Yet most men also agreed there was something unnatural, unlovely, even coarse about a woman moving freely in public among crowds of men and daring to tell legislators how to make the world a better place. Moreover, clubwomen, like their sisters in the suffrage and temperance movements, were highly successful in organizing and exercising power to colonize and civilize the province of activities that men ruled. In 1905, former president Grover Cleveland, who regretted the day twenty-five years earlier when he had given money to a woman's club, took to the pages of the nation's leading women's magazine to bring clubwomen to their senses.

PROBLEMS TO CONSIDER

1. According to Cleveland, what was harmful about the woman's club movement? In what ways were his criticisms founded on expectations about how "woman" was supposed to be? Why was there no place for maternalist politics in Cleveland's view of public life?
2. On the subject of true womanhood, were Cleveland and Cooley in agreement? Why would their respective understandings of women's natural duties and responsibilities have led Cleveland to condemn the woman's clubs and Cooley to celebrate them?

One who can remember a mother's love . . . and a mother's care in childhood, or who has known in later days the joys a devoted wife brings to the life of man, ought to be able to calculate upon general experience so largely tallying with his own that he need not fear protest or dissent in treating of the scope and character of woman's mission. It is a melancholy fact, however, that our subject is actually one of difficult approach; and it is a more melancholy fact that this approach is made difficult by a dislocation of ideas and by false prospectives on the part of women themselves. To those of us who suffer periods of social pessimism, but who, in the midst of it all, cling to our faith in the saving grace of simple and unadulterated womanhood, any discontent on the part of woman with her ordained lot, or a restless desire on her part to be and to do something not within the sphere of her appointed ministrations, cannot appear otherwise than as perversions of a gift of God to the human race . . .

The real difficulty and delicacy of our topic becomes most apparent when we come to speak of the less virulent and differently directed club movements that have crossed the even tenor of the way of womanhood. . . .

We certainly ought not to be too swift in charging the tendency toward club affiliation on the part of our women to a deliberate willingness to forget or neglect their transcendent mission or home duties. Unquestionably this tendency is partly due to the widespread and contagious fever for change or rearrangement which seems to leave no phase of our people's life untouched. I believe it has also been largely provoked and intensified by the increase of club life among the husbands and fathers of our land, and by their surrender to such business preoccupation or the madness of inordinate accumulation, as results in the neglect of wives and those to whom, under all rules of duty and decency, they owe attention and companionship—thus creating a condition of man's guilt which tempts retaliation in kind. . . .

No woman who enters upon such a retaliatory course can be sure that the man she seeks to punish will be otherwise affected than to be made more indifferent to home, and more determined to enlarge the area of his selfish pleasures. She can be sure, however, that cheerlessness will invade her home, and that if children are there they will be irredeemably deprived of the mysterious wholesomeness and delight of an atmosphere which can only be created by a mother's loving presence and absorbing care. She can also be certain that, growing out of the influence which her behavior and example are sure to have upon the conduct of the wives and mothers within the range of her companionship, she may be directly responsible for marred happiness in other households, and that as an aider and abettor of woman's clubs she must bear her share of liability for the injury they may inflict upon the domestic life of our land. It must be abundantly evident that, as agencies for retaliation or man's punishment, woman's clubs are horribly misplaced and miserably vicious. . . .

I am persuaded that without exaggeration of statement we may assume that there are woman's clubs whose objects and intents are not only harmful, but harmful in a way that directly menaces the integrity of our homes and the benign disposition and character of our wifehood and motherhood. . . . I believe that it should be boldly declared that the best and safest club for a woman to patronize is her home. American wives and American mothers, as surely as "the hand that rocks the cradle is the hand that rules the world," have, through their nurture of children and their influence over men, the destinies of our Nation in their keeping to a greater extent than any other single agency. . . .

For the sake of our country, for the sake of our homes, and for the sake of our children, I would have our wives and mothers loving and devoted, though all others may be sordid and heedless; I would have them disinterested and trusting, though all others may be selfish and cunning; I would have them happy and contented in following the Divinely appointed path of true womanhood, though all others may grope in the darkness of their own devices.

———

Grover Cleveland, "Woman's Mission and Woman's Clubs," *Ladies' Home Journal*, May 1905, 3–4.

ᴥ

Southern Women and Racial Adjustment (1917)
LILY HARDY HAMMOND

The maternalist politics of the club movement also took deep root in southern cities and towns among white and black women, with important implications for the history of a region where the gender ideal of genteel femininity and the racial ideal of white supremacy were presumed sacrosanct. Beginning in the 1890s, white men had sought to reinforce their patriarchal authority in southern politics and society through legal and extralegal maneuvers designed to make white domination an unquestioned fact of life. Disfranchising black men to expel "the Negro" from politics was the first order of business. Jim Crow (segregation) laws and restrictions further imposed a new and especially dehumanizing exile of African Americans from the mainstream of life. The architects of the new racial and gender order explained that these measures were necessary to preserve civilization, the bedrock of which was the purity of southern white womanhood. Only a powerful white manhood, willing and able to use extreme measures to protect this order, could safeguard white women against the alleged sexual desire that black men harbored for them.

For all the talk of segregation as the natural order, middle-class and wealthy whites depended for their way of life on poor black southerners — to perform the menial tasks of collecting garbage or cleaning buildings, to do their housekeeping and cooking, to tend their children, to perform the role of their inferiors. The paradox was that whites' contempt for blacks and their fears of racial mixing worked side by side with the essential connections between the two social groups. The public health campaigns of Progressive Era southern clubwomen demonstrate the complicated ways in which these paradoxical circumstances affected political and social life in the era of disfranchisement, Jim Crow, and lynch justice. The following two documents examine maternalist politics in the South from different racial perspectives. The first, a pamphlet authored by the white clubwoman Lily Hardy Hammond, explains what happened when white women discovered that their homes were only as germ-free as the homes and neighborhoods of their African American maids.

PROBLEMS TO CONSIDER

1. According to Hammond, what factors enabled white women and black women to overcome their differences and work together? Was Hammond challenging the racial, gender, and class hierarchies that dominated southern society?
2. What did Hammond's frequent use of words like "discovery" suggest about white women's perspectives on African American life? Did acquiring new insights into the lives of black women affect white women's assumptions of their own superiority?

The manners and morals of every community reflect the standards sanctioned or permitted by its privileged women. Individuals stand above this common level, blazing ethical trails into the unmoral wilderness of our wider human associations, and draw after them, here and there, adventurous groups; but there can be no mass advance until the individual impulse toward righteousness, which is justice in its finest sense, is reinforced by a common standard embodying a force greater than the individual.

These common standards are furnished, actively or passively, by the privileged women, from whose homes they spread into the community. Racial adjustment, like many other moral issues, waits on the leadership of these women. Their attitude toward it is thus of both sectional and national importance; and their increasing development of broad humanitarian standards in racial relations is worthy of note. . . .

Material progress waits on moral progress; and the full prosperity of Southern industry and commerce waits in a most vital sense upon the moral status of the Negro home. It is the privileged white women who alone can fix this status for the entire community, building it up in white

respect, and helping the better class of colored women to build it up in colored life.

The purpose of this pamphlet is to show our women's entrance upon this great humanitarian and patriotic service. To perform it they are adventuring into the unknown, discovering their cooks and washerwomen as women beset by womanhood's clamorous demands and utterly unable to meet them without help and sympathy. It is out of this thought of privileged white women for these handicapped mothers, children, and homes that the eventual adjustment of our bi-racial Southern life will come. . . .

**THE DEMOCRACY
OF THE MICROBE**

Any one who will follow common sense far enough will land up to their eyes in Christianity; the two refuse to accept divorcement. The club women came upon Christian principles of racial adjustment without realizing that they were dealing with racial problems at all. They simply started out with common sense as their guide and cleanliness as their goal.

Their clean-up campaigns, confined at first to the white part of town, were pronounced by common sense to be only fifty per cent efficient; so the cooperation of colored women was sought. The club of Charlotte, N.C., was one of the pioneers—and less than a decade ago. They invited the women of the colored missionary societies to a meeting at which the mayor, the health officer, the white and the colored women all spoke; and the result . . . was that the white women were put on their mettle to keep up with the colored ones in the cleaning that followed. The city's health record and the babies flourished in consequence.

In this way, in several pioneer towns, a common meeting ground was discovered for the women of the two races—the need of human homes for cleanliness and health. The meeting of human needs never endangers the preservation of true racial lines; this the women clearly sensed, and went to their new work joyously. Common sense, prodded by the microbe, had prompted the first step; but some of the women glimpsed a background of religious teaching and motive with which the experiment fitted in, and from which it drew high sanction.

In a few years this cooperation for community health has spread throughout the South, leavening popular thought with a consciousness of a common need, which must be met for both races or for neither. And while that leaven works the women have been making further discoveries.

THE NEGRO HOME

. . . Some club women, two or three years ago, as a result of one of these clean-up campaigns, began to visit occasionally a colored Mothers' Club to talk about some of the problems common to all mothers. Thus they learned that in the hitherto respectable section in which most of these women lived three houses of vice had been opened, all owned by white men, though one was run by a colored woman. They had made short work of her case after a fashion of their own: she had simply developed an insuperable objection to the neighborhood, and had forced her employer to let her move. But against the white women they were helpless. An appeal to the police would have closed the houses in that city, but they feared the vengeance of the proprietors and their women—a thing the police could take no cognizance of until it became an accomplished fact. Most of them owned, or were buying, their homes; they could not leave, or risk being burned out.

The club's Department of Civics took the matter up at once, and without involving the colored women. The houses were closed, and the sense of the common needs of human homes was broadened in that community. . . .

The bond of a common womanhood, deeper than all racial separateness, asserted itself, as it will when such an emergency is understood. . . .

THE EDUCATED COLORED WOMAN

This discovery of the educated colored woman is of deep significance. It is she who must lift her people, but she can do so little without our help! The experience of one club woman is typical here. She seized upon a friend in the street one day to share her recent discovery.

"You know I'm on the committee to meet the colored teachers in the clean-up campaign," she began. "—— is the chairman of their committee"—naming the head of a local school. "You know she's a college graduate; I've heard about her for years. I thought she'd be a sort of spoiled cook, you know—forward, and all that. Well, she's perfectly *fine*! I didn't know there were any Negroes like that. That committee will work like it was greased. It means everything to the Negroes—and a lot to us, too—to have a woman like that at work among all these colored people here."

Her face was alight with the interest of her discovery—a feeling a number of women are coming to understand as they make similar discoveries in their own communities. . . .

The outstanding feature of her experience, however, and that of many others, was the finding, in these uncharted regions, the same old landmarks of human need. They are common to all races and all time, and a realization of this fact is one of the things which is helping us to broaden out of a sectional into a world life.

Lily Hardy Hammond, *Southern Women and Racial Adjustment* (Lynchburg, Va.: J. P. Bell, 1917), 5–6, 16–19.

ᔓ

The Negro Home and the Future of the Race (1918)

MRS. BOOKER T. (MARGARET MURRAY) WASHINGTON

As Hammond made clear, one of the discoveries of white women was that middle-class black women already had their own network of woman's clubs that addressed the same concerns, although from a different perspective. When white clubwomen asserted themselves politically, they violated the gender order. For black clubwomen, activism was far more dangerous. They were black women tampering with the dictates of white supremacy. Margaret Murray Washington, who was married to the African American educator Booker T. Washington, understood this difference. A leading reformer in her own right, she worked to make certain that members of her own race achieved some of the benefits of social services that white Progressives sought to reserve for whites. Washington also represented "the better class" of black womanhood that Hammond admired. The following address, which was delivered at an interracial sociological conference, allows us to evaluate whether her maternalist politics urged African Americans to adjust to white supremacy—the charge of accommodation usually leveled against her husband's reforms—or to resist white domination.

PROBLEMS TO CONSIDER

1. Did Washington suggest that the interests and agendas of black clubwomen and white clubwomen were the same or different? Did she understand the potential for interracial alliance in the same way that Hammond understood it?
2. Consider Washington's reference to the "needs" of the South and the democratic tendencies of germs. Did conceding the inferiority of black homes bow to white supremacy, or manipulate whites' assumptions of their superiority to get what she wanted?

In the cities of the South the colored people . . . own 217,942 homes; for the entire South the colored people own one home to every twenty persons. It is poor taste to boast ever, . . . but this is not a poor showing for a people who started out not more than fifty years ago with no homes at all. The colored man and his family living in the country districts must be encouraged to buy more land, to build larger and better homes, to understand that it is a mistake to attempt to rear his children in a home without pictures, without music, without papers, magazines, with little or no consideration for the number of children in his family to be accounted for as to room, place at the table, and the conveniences necessary in building up a happy and substantial family. . . .

To be sure there are many well-to-do colored families all over the South who live in and own well furnished homes sufficiently large and comfortable, but these are the select few. A larger number of our people in the cities live in neighborhoods unprotected by police supervision, on streets poorly lighted, in houses with only two or three rooms. . . . If the authorities of our Southern cities would take into consideration the fact that we are really a part of the body politic and that, although we are a distinct race with perhaps some distinct traits and characteristics, we have many things in common with all the other citizens of the community, and one of these is a love of family life, a desire and yearning to bring our children up in a wholesome and clean atmosphere, a growing desire to create for ourselves an ideal which expresses itself more and more in decent living, our homes and the future of our race and of both races would be happier.

Colored people of the Southern cities should be encouraged to build and furnish their homes. Is this quite enough? No, they should be encouraged to build beautiful homes. We are not likely to do this if we know that the sewage will stop just before it reaches the corner of the neighborhood in which we live; . . . [or] if we know that in our neighborhood women of ill fame of our own race are permitted to live and flaunt themselves at will either day or night and that white women of ill fame are forced to remain at our next door. . . . The lack of these

conditions brings about unrest, discontent, lack of cooperation, lack of confidence, and finally bitterness and hatred which often end in crime.

There is another reason, which may be considered selfish; but it is better to do some things from a selfish standpoint than not to do them at all. Where the homes of colored people are comfortable and clean, there is less disease, less sickness, less death, and less danger to others. Disease knows no color line; we meet each other necessarily daily in the kitchen, in the nurseries, on the streets, in the stores, and often in more intimate ways, as trained nurses, chauffeurs, coachmen, etc.; and whatever disease attaches itself to a colored person because of lack of decent surroundings is not unlikely to transfer itself to a white person, even though his surroundings may be clean and more comfortable or luxurious.

There is still another side to this question of having decent homes by colored people. Is not the South in need to-day of a larger number of industrious and well-lived people more than ever before in the history of its development? Every year 225,000 colored people die in the South; 100,000 of these deaths could be prevented if there were better homes, cleaner streets, proper sewerage, better bathing facilities. Does the South not need these men and women to build its roads, to cultivate its fields, to increase and develop its wealth and citizenship?

————

Mrs. Booker T. (Margaret Murray) Washington, "The Negro Home and the Future of the Race," in *Democracy in Earnest*, edited by James E. McCulloch (Washington, D.C.: Southern Sociological Congress, 1918), 335, 338–40.

ᘒ

Brochures and Broadsides Campaigning For and Against Women's Suffrage (c. 1915-1920)

Questions of difference arose most keenly and passionately in the Progressive Era because reformers frequently sought to change social practices and relations that had been justified by the presumably natural and necessary distinctions between women and men, white and nonwhite, poor and middle class, fit and unfit. For aroused passions, no issue could compare with the debates surrounding the Nineteenth Amendment, which, when ratified in 1920, guaranteed women the right to vote. Opponents of women's suffrage, female as well as male, insisted that social disorder would follow if women violated their natural province (the home) and social role (motherhood) by voting. Supporters, however, insisted that voting would not change American womanhood but rather would extend the reach of motherhood's benevolent influence and counteract the destructive tendencies of men. The pro- and antisuffrage literature featured here illustrate various positions in the debate.

PROBLEMS TO CONSIDER

1. How did these documents use "difference" to stake out their position on women's suffrage? What differences were illustrated here?
2. Were there any points of agreement in the anti- and prosuffrage positions? What were their most fundamental points of disagreement?

WOMEN IN THE HOME

The place of the Woman is in the Home. But merely to stay in the Home is not enough. She must care for the health and welfare, moral as well as physical, of her family.

SHE is responsible for the cleanliness of the house.

SHE is responsible for the wholesomeness of the food.

SHE is responsible for the children's health.

SHE is responsible above all for their morals.

How far can the mother control these things?

She can clean her own rooms and care for her own plumbing and refuse, BUT if the building is unsanitary, the streets filthy, and the garbage allowed to accumulate, she cannot protect her children from the sickness that will result.

She can cook her food well, BUT if dealers are permitted to sell adulterated food, unclean milk, or short weight or measure, she cannot provide either wholesome or sufficient feeding for her family. . . .

She can send her children out for exercise, BUT if the conditions on the streets are immoral and degrading, she cannot shield them from these dangers.

It is the government of the town or city that controls these things and the officials are controlled by the men who elect them.

Women do not elect these officials, yet we hold the women responsible for the results of—

Unclean Houses, Defective Sewerage, Unwholesome Food, Fire Risks, Danger of Infection, Immoral Influence on the Streets. If women are responsible for the results, let them have something to say as to what the conditions shall be. There is one simple way to do this. GIVE THEM THE VOTE.

Women are by nature and training housekeepers. Let them help in the city housekeeping. They will introduce an occasional spring cleaning.

———

"Women in the Home," prosuffrage broadside, Equal Suffrage Association of North Carolina, c. 1915–1920, North Carolina Collection, University of North Carolina at Chapel Hill, Chapel Hill, N.C.

(Carrie Chapman Catt Papers, Tennessee State Library and Archives, Nashville, Tenn. Courtesy of the Tennessee State Library and Archives.)

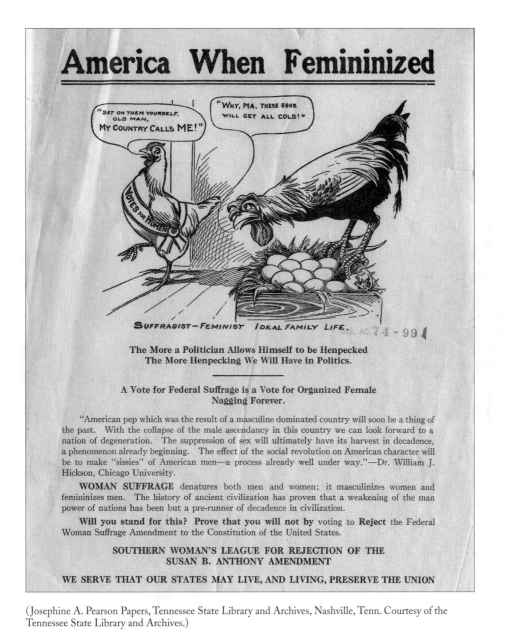

(Josephine A. Pearson Papers, Tennessee State Library and Archives, Nashville, Tenn. Courtesy of the Tennessee State Library and Archives.)

Woman to the Rescue (1916)

The Crisis *was the official publication of the National Association for the Advancement of Colored People (NAACP), a civil rights organization. The NAACP supported the suffrage amendment and published the following cartoon in* The Crisis *in 1916. The image of a black woman using the club of the "Federal Constitution" to defeat racial disfranchisement and segregation laws in the South also shows a black man fleeing the scene and muttering, "I don't believe in agitating and fighting. My policy is to pursue the line of least resistance. To h — with Citizenship Rights. I want money. I think the white folk will let me stay on my land as long as* I stay in my place. *— (Shades of [the race riot against blacks in]* WILMINGTON, N.C.*) The good whites ain't responsible for bad administration of the law and lynching and peonage — let me think awhile, er —." This cartoon's history did not end in* The Crisis. *It later reappeared as an argument against women's suffrage in a brochure published by white southerners.*

PROBLEMS TO CONSIDER

1. In the opinion of *The Crisis*, what made black women a progressive force in the movement for race equality? In the opinion of southern whites, what made them a force of disorder?
2. What aspects of this cartoon enabled it to serve as an argument both for and against women's suffrage? How did the image connect gender order and racial order?

(The Houghton Mifflin Company wishes to thank the Crisis Publishing Co., Inc., the publisher of the magazine of the National Association for the Advancement of Colored People, for use of this image first published in the May 1916 issue of *The Crisis*.)

↝ An Enchantment and a Snare: The Modern Department Store ↝

The promise of "abundance" has been a selling point for the idea of America since the earliest European settlements. Nature itself was the New World's cornucopia ("horn of plenty"), spilling forth shafts of wheat, timber, fur, fish and game, adventure, riches—everything that seemed scarce in Europe. By the late nineteenth century, America's glory was less its natural setting than the bounty its modern industrial economy produced. In a society deeply stratified by wealth, race, sex, and ethnicity, all could not enjoy this bounty equally. Americans nevertheless embraced this vision of plenty. They wanted factory-made clothing and phonographs, the excitement of dance halls, the pleasure of meals at restaurants or beer gardens, the leisure of vacation time at the seashore or an outing to watch moving pictures. These desires for the new and the modern altered the boundaries of American culture in visible ways, introducing far-reaching changes in behavior, outlook, and attitude. Besides mail-order houses, the most important institution generating visions of plenty was the department store. By 1900, such stores operated in small and large cities, where they had so taken root in Americans' consciousness that people regarded them as vital elements of their everyday lives. Department stores in the Progressive Era were not parts of "chains," as we know them today. Usually they were independent businesses. But in terms of size and scope, nothing like them had existed in the United States prior to 1880.

The leading merchants—Marshall Field in Chicago, Joseph L. Hudson in Detroit, Morris Rich in Atlanta, Rowland H. Macy in New York, John Wanamaker in Philadelphia—prospered by exploiting the core features of modern city life: rising urban populations, new sources of investment capital, mass transit systems, and economies of scale from industrial manufacturing. Department stores, like their counterparts in industry, were big businesses that combined into single operations the goods and services that separate merchants had traditionally offered. But the leading and more upscale department stores did more than just mass selling. They also transformed the methods of retailing to change how people thought about goods. Marshall Field described his store as "a vast repository of possibilities to the individual customer." Stores mounted spectacular pageants and decorative schemes featuring Turkish harems and gardens of paradise to excite desires and wishes rather than to cater to needs. The new "modern" merchants also regarded themselves as progressive businessmen who placed the customer's interests first. The creed of Marshall Field was emblematic of the spirit of modern merchandising: "Give the lady what she wants." Still, no merchant could afford to let customers decide for themselves what they wanted or what store they would patronize. When the journalist Hartley Davis called the department store an "enchantment and a snare," he more accurately described the often adversarial interactions among merchants, store clerks, and customers in the new world of consumption. For all their agreement over the desirability of consumer goods, however, Americans were divided over the meaning of and access to abundance in the Progressive Era.

The Promotive Education of Modern Advertising (1903)

The most influential department store merchant was John Wanamaker, whose stores in Philadelphia and New York made the phrase "the customer is always right" the guiding ethos of American retailing. Wanamaker began operations in the 1870s; his Philadelphia business grew enormously and in 1910 moved into a landmark facility, which a journalist described as "the largest and costliest building ever devoted to retail merchandizing — a veritable seventh wonder of the modern world." Wanamaker asserted that his enterprise was not a "capitalist" or "Wanamaker store" conducting business for his profit alone, but a "people's store" attending to the public good. The following editorial, which appeared in a 1903 newspaper ad for his New York store, explains how Wanamaker's advertising provided a public service.

PROBLEMS TO CONSIDER

1. How did Wanamaker distinguish between "bad" and "good" advertising? How did advertising serve the "public good"?
2. Wanamaker asserted that advertising "educates desire." How did this phrasing distinguish the sale of goods from salesmanship?

Advertising plays a part in the world of trade that does not appear upon superficial reading.

True, there is much advertising that contains nothing beyond screams of alleged bargains and rhetorical rhodomontade *[pretentious boasting]*. But there is advertising with a deeper purpose, which while written with the expectation of sufficiently remunerative immediate response, also serves a deeper and broader usefulness to the store that exploits it, as well as conserving to broad public good.

You probably think of advertising as confining its efforts to winning your interest in the store's merchandise, and impressing you with the fact that a certain store is a good one to trade with.

But advertising of the higher sort aims at ever so much more. It does not confine its efforts to telling you where to buy things of which you feel the need —

It Educates Desire
Following its larger purpose of stimulating the industries of the world, it tells you what new things the genius of the world has contrived, for the comfort or beautifying of the person or the home.

It tells the world what the rest of the world is wearing, or using in the home. It tells all the beauty or benefits of the articles. It also tells how easy it is to possess these things.

It teaches the public that there are better things to eat than they have used before. It tells them of garments that perhaps they have neglected to possess until advertising exploited the necessity. It tells them of things that add character and distinction to the home; and homes grow more beautiful.

The successful writer of advertising has a keen sense of the philosophy of human nature. He knows what inconveniences and discomforts exist in everyday life. He knows the personal ambitions, the housekeeping ambitions, of people. Then he tells just how the various kinds of merchandise may meet the perhaps unvoiced wishes of the reader.

The consumer is glad to receive the suggestion which betters his condition; and industry is stimulated by increased demand.

Perhaps Pianos will illustrate the theory, as the theory has been abundantly proven through Piano selling, since being exploited by WANAMAKER advertising.

Here is a home that enjoys music, yet not possessing a piano. The members of the family are always delighted when they hear the piano played in homes of friends, but the desire is cut short by the thought of the cost, and the matter drops.

But advertising presents the great plea for music — its benefits, its refining influences, the immeasurable and lasting benefits to the home. Then desire grows. Other advertising continues the argument, and tells how easy it is to possess a piano, despite its seemingly large cost. At length desire ripens. And where desire is earnest, the means can always be found.

The selfish effort of the advertising has taught the purchaser first, the benefit of possession, then the means; and the home secures a thing of never-ending delight; which can easily be paid for when the effort is made. And by reason of the multiplication of such instances, the great piano industry grows into new life, bringing prosperity to skilled artisans, and infinite enjoyment to an ever-increasing number of piano-possessing homes.

The same principle applies to a thousand kinds of merchandise of which people would never learn the full significance, and so never be instilled with the potential desire for possession without the insistence of proper advertising.

The recognition of this larger usefulness of advertising has contributed to the broad influence possessed and disseminated by WANAMAKER advertising.

"The Promotive Education of Modern Advertising," Wanamaker store advertisement, *New York Times*, February 18, 1903.

↝

The Department Store at Close Range (1907)
HARTLEY DAVIS

Was the modern merchandising as practiced by department stores as egalitarian and public-spirited as Wanamaker contended? In today's stores, a tag shows the price you will pay for the item you purchase. This convention, which is little more than a century old, was introduced by the new generation of department store merchants. In the old system, buying cloth or flour or any other product resembled purchasing an automobile today; everyone knew that the final price had to be negotiated. The new merchants prided themselves on eliminating the adversarial relationship of seller and buyer haggling over price. They touted one-price selling as a progressive innovation that served the public interest. In this account, the journalist Hartley Davis examines how the pricing of goods contributed to the complicated social world of the stores where three groups — store owners and managers (mostly men), salesclerks (mostly women), and customers (again, predominantly women), each with their own interests — intersected in every transaction.

PROBLEMS TO CONSIDER

1. Did this close-up view of the department store describe a social setting of harmony and common interest, or one of political and economic conflict?
2. Consider the three parties involved in a sale: merchant, salesclerk, shopper. Who lost or gained power in the new pricing system?

Resolutely the Shopper from the Suburbs turned her eyes away from the enticing displays in the windows of the big department store as she made for the main entrance with the briskness of set purpose. But inside, temptation was inescapable, for one may not walk through a department store with one's eyes fixed on the floor nor turned toward the ceiling, unless one wishes to be made a shuttlecock. And straightway the Shopper was checked by certain dainty articles seductively displayed at the jewelry counter. For ever so long she had craved one of those fan-chains and here they were offered at the bargain she had been waiting for—a ridiculously low price, just half what—

Hardening her lips and her resolution, the Shopper from the Suburbs passed on—with a gratulatory sense of virtue mingled with regret, a not unusual concomitant of temptation resisted. . . . But really she must have one of those belts. . . . And that aigrette *[a feathered hair ornament]* was just what she needed to wear with her new gown at the dinner on Thursday. She paused guiltily for a second and then hurried on. The material in that shirt-waist must have cost more than the price asked, and it was stunning. Really, it would be saving money to buy it—just like putting it in the bank. One never can have too many shirt-waists. And those stockings—The Shopper from the Suburbs felt her determination oozing from her at the sight of each bargain table, and in self-defense she hurried toward the rear.

She bought the paper of hooks and eyes for which she had come to the store, paid five cents for it, and asked to have it delivered at her home in Orange, New Jersey. The saleswoman diplomatically asked if the lady couldn't take the little package with her—they didn't like to deliver parcels so easily portable. But the Shopper from the Suburbs really couldn't think of carrying the package, because her purse was full and she was going to make some calls. Besides, she couldn't see that it made any difference to the store; their delivery wagon passed her house every day. So the saleswoman said that the hooks and eyes would be delivered. . . .

The hooks and eyes were sold to her at a price perhaps a little less than the store actually paid the manufacturer for them—nearly all the staples at the notion counter are sold at cost, or below. The cost of selling them was at least two cents and the cost of suburban delivery was twenty-five cents, so the net loss to the store on the transaction was twenty-seven cents.

How can department stores afford to make this sort of sale?

They couldn't if all shoppers resisted the alluring displays in the windows, on the counters and tables. . . .

The popular idea is that a department store is merely the grouping together of a large number of separate businesses under one roof. But the experiment of assembling businesses in one store to minimize the cost of rent and other fixed charges has been tried and discontinued as a failure. The success of the department store rests upon an entirely different principle—upon standardization. The departments are not independent, but highly specialized activities conforming to certain fixed laws that govern the whole establishment.

The old way of doing business was simple and the methods were highly elastic. The proprietor bought as cheaply as he could, usually in quantities that were measured only by his capacity to sell and by his credit. He marked the goods in cipher, sometimes giving the actual cost and the minimum selling price, sometimes only the latter, and left it to his clerk to get as large a profit as could be wheedled from the customer. The proprietor was therefore absolutely dependent upon the cleverness of his clerks for his profit; the clerk who imposed most upon the customer was the best salesman and commanded a relatively high salary. The percentage of selling cost was thus enormous. Relying considerably on his own personality to win business, the proprietor usually stationed himself at the entrance of the store to greet customers and to settle disputes.

Now the difference between the old way and the new is the difference between the old-time workshop, where everything was made by hand, and the factory, where machinery does the work. The machine makes articles exactly alike in standard sizes and the cost of production is enormously reduced, as every one knows. The modern methods of conducting a department store represent the introduction into mercantile life of this factory idea, in so far as it stands for uniformity, automatism, and cheapened production. Like the factory, the department store is itself a huge, extremely complicated machine, and the store that most nearly approaches automatic perfection in its operation is the most successful.

Probably the most important factor in the development of the department-store machine is the idea of "one-price articles marked in plain figures." This makes it possible for the goods practically to sell themselves. The element of bargaining, the most important feature of the old system, is almost wholly eliminated. The chief function of the clerk is to see that the machine works properly. He has no more to do with fixing the selling price than has the purchaser.

Hartley Davis, "The Department Store at Close Range," *Everybody's*, September 1907, 312–14.

ॐ

Christmas from Behind the Counter (1907)
RHETA CHILDE DORR

Why Don't More Women Trade with Me? (1917)
ARCHER WALL DOUGLAS

Women's role as purchasers and sellers of goods had expanded throughout the nineteenth century until shopping and retail sales were commonly regarded as female occupations. By the 1920s, women accounted for 80 to 85 percent of consumer purchasing, yet modern shopping and selling in a service-oriented consumer economy still raised questions about the natures of the people involved (men as well as women) and of the goods themselves. For instance, who was the shopping woman? Was she an easily manipulated victim of enticing advertisements and her own changeable and insatiable desires? Or was she a rational decision maker who managed her household and, through her purchases, shaped her home for the better? In the era of one-price selling, was the salesclerk a mere unskilled tender of goods that, as Hartley indicated, practically sold themselves, or was selling a craft? The following articles examine how both shoppers and sellers sought to manipulate the sales environment to their advantage. The first piece, on Christmas season working conditions, was compiled by a middle-class reformer who took a position as a department store salesclerk. Reformers in this era often disguised themselves to penetrate the world of industry and labor in order to discover and expose the real conditions operating in those arenas. The second document, examining the "woman shopper," was published in a magazine for business managers.

PROBLEMS TO CONSIDER

1. How did the writers represent the relationship between clerks and customers? Would you describe their encounters as political?
2. What do these articles tell us about the social and cultural context of shopping? Did class differences disappear in department stores?

CHRISTMAS FROM BEHIND THE COUNTER

It is not difficult to get a job in a department store at the Christmas season. You must apply in good time, that is, before the 15th of December; you must look strong enough to live thru the experience, or, at least, not to die on the premises before the end of the holiday week; you must be neat in appearance and fairly intelligent; you must present proof of respectability. In only a very few stores is previous experience required.

I did not venture to apply at the more fashionable shops . . . I modestly chose a great establishment patronized by the rank and file of people, who buy for cash, and have no illusions that they are materially influencing store management. I believe that this kind of store is more typical of the general run of department stores thruout the country . . .

Having been accepted as an extra clerk, I . . . meekly followed my guide to the office of the store instructor. In this room I found about thirty other candidates, girls and men . . . One girl was entering the Christmas mill because her father, an ironworker, had fallen from a skyscraper and broken both legs. . . . Another worked in a trade which was dead during the winter months. . . . None of us, you may be sure, were engaging to work fifteen hours a day for sheer amusement. . . .

My first day in the shop passed rapidly. The novelty and excitement of the scene was so stimulating that I was hardly conscious of fatigue, or even of the flight of time. About half past five in the afternoon the head of the department came around distributing supper money. She carried a cigar box full of small silver, and each girl was given 35 cents. The extra clerks, who worked only during the holiday season, were paid at a somewhat higher rate than the regular force. I was receiving $7 a week, which was a dollar more than the average. . . .

At first the allowance struck me as rather meager, but . . . I learned . . . that in a very splendid Broadway shop . . . overtime money amounting to a little more than enough to pay for one's supper was given, but always with a great flourish of trumpets, as a manifestation of rare benevolence. The clerks had to sign little circulars, acknowledging their gratitude, a thing they greatly disliked to do. . . .

The shop patronized by the rank and file has other advantages, from the clerks' point of view. In our establishment they were allowed to go upstairs in the regular elevators and eat a comfortable meal in the store restaurant. In the fashionable shop the clerks are obliged to take time from their hour to don street wraps, walk down several flights of stairs, unless they are lucky enough to catch the freight elevator, and seek a restaurant outside.

The explanation lies in the relative social difference between the customer and the clerk in the two establishments. In the fashionable shop a great gulf divides the two, and the customer would not tolerate association in elevator or restaurant with the humble saleswoman.

In the other shop the social position of the customer and that of the clerk are not far removed. The two are in the same class and are likely to meet outside the shop. Hence there is no objection on the part of the customer if a tired figure in black sits opposite her in the restaurant. . . .

In all my life I never faced anything more reluctantly than the necessity of getting up at half past six the next morning. I ached all over from the unaccustomed standing. A dismal rain beat on the window panes, the house was dark and still, and my bed was an alluring thing. It seemed to me that my case was a hard one — unique, in fact — but . . . [I found] that I was far from being the only early riser in New York. The street was fairly thronged with a hurrying crowd, in which women and girls predominated — a great army of neat, black-gowned feminine figures, which you will never see unless you take a walk in the business quarter between seven and eight in the morning.

Rheta Childe Dorr, "Christmas from Behind the Counter," *Independent*, December 5, 1907, 1340–43.

WHY DON'T MORE WOMEN TRADE WITH ME?

It is obvious that the retail merchant who expects to make a success of his job must usually appeal to the woman shopper. For women do most of the shopping today, and the amount they do promises to increase as women become more and more economically independent.

In the beginning, how to get and hold a woman's trade is not so much strictly a matter of business as a study in psychology. The rules of trade that obtain with men do not always "go" with women, a fact that some merchants fail to understand. . . .

The difficulty in keeping a woman's trade is that sooner or later her personality becomes involved, often in most unexpected ways. In the final analysis every proposition in a woman's life ultimately becomes personal; and she is likely to trade at a store or pass it by, depending on whether she does or does not like the people there who serve her. Freshness, flippancy, or indifference to her wishes are discourtesies she can hardly forgive. For shopping is serious with her, not only because it is a recreation, and possibly an adventure, but likewise because it calls for the exercise of her best judgment in spending whatever money she has in her possession.

I once knew a young wife whose husband gave her $25 as a birthday present. They were in moderate circumstances so the amount seemed to her a small fortune. She decided to spend it all on a shopping trip. She went to a large department store, much frequented by rich people, and attempted to buy a modest piece of silverware. The salesman was visibly bored by a customer who wanted something worth only about $10, and like the poor salesman that he was, told her of the costly purchases made recently by some of his customers, whose names she recognized from the society columns.

The young wife was not only impressed, but she was irritated at the snobbery of the salesman; and, worse, her pride was hurt at the implication of the slight value placed upon her trade. So she returned to a less pretentious store where she commonly did most of her buying, and to a favorite young saleswoman, who rejoiced with her over her birthday present, sympathetically suggested various ways of spending it, and even more sympathetically listened to the story of the indifferent salesman. So they had a beautiful time together, and in the end the $25 remained in the till of the less pretentious store.

You can never afford to be in a hurry with the woman shopper. If she has much to say, and she sometimes has, in the way of irrelevant information, you must listen with patience and sympathy if you want to hold her trade. Nor can you afford to be too familiar. . . .

Most of all, perhaps, does [the woman shopper] appreciate square treatment and a delicate flattery that may be expressed through little acts of consideration and courtesy. I know of a successful clothing merchant . . . who holds the trade of his women customers by his fair dealing. Everything is exactly as he represents it, and he diplomatically impressed upon the women who trade with him that they are evidently the kind who carry sincerity and good taste into every phase of their lives; and that for them to buy shoddy or cheap merchandise would be foreign to their real natures.

On the other hand, it is undeniably true that there is nothing the average woman shopper appreciates so readily as a bargain. Even more than a man she will chase the delusion of getting something for nothing. The merchant who caters to the average woman shopper will usually make bargain sales part of his policy. . . .

Now the sum of the argument is that the woman shopper is attracted by those things which appeal to her sense of justice and fairness, to her ease and convenience, to the necessity of making her allowance cover a multitude of wants, and most of all to her respect and confidence. Also she has a long memory, both ways.

Archer Wall Douglas, "Why Don't More Women Trade with Me?" *System* 32 (December 1917): 906–8.

৯৶

ॐ *Progressive Playgrounds:* *Amusement Parks and Dance Halls* ॐ

One of the hit songs of 1911 was Irving Berlin's "Everybody's Doin' It." The lyrics sound (and were) risqué, but they actually referred to the dance craze that swept the nation after 1910 and set off equal parts joy and anxiety about the overheated hugs that the wild sounds of ragtime aroused between women and men on the dance floor. But it was not just dancing that everybody was doing. It was "going out," having a good time, escaping from the everyday. Entertainment entrepreneurs in the Progressive Era transformed American cities and towns into playgrounds for adults, featuring popularly priced theaters, vaudeville and melodrama houses, dance halls, amusement parks, beach resorts and bathhouses, baseball parks, restaurants, beer gardens, casinos, nickelodeons (nickel-priced movie theaters), and eventually movie palaces.

This flourishing economy, which one showman described as "the billion-dollar smile," was a national and a nationalizing development. Americans "from Seattle to New York, from Bangor to the Gulf," as he put it, were pursuing pleasure in much the same way. The growth of this economy contributed to the democratization of leisure in this period. The wealthy elite had always had time for recreation and resorts that catered to their pursuits. Working- and middle-class Americans had had free time, too, but their activities were informally organized and integrated into the larger life of work, family, neighborhood, and community. By 1890, however, growing numbers of Americans were thinking of leisure as "time off" from work and were using that time and spending their money in ways that we would recognize today: going out to eat or dance or see a moving picture, shopping for pleasure, taking a vacation. In one sense, going to work in a corporate and industrial economy seemed less meaningful in itself, and more valuable for what it enabled men and growing numbers of working women to do or buy. For many, too, going out meant leaving the private sphere and entering a new kind of public space where women and men could seek out intense feelings and exuberant pleasures free from the supervision of family and neighborhood. Finally, the leisure economy raised questions about "culture" and class in American life. At a time when American millionaires were donating fortunes to build cultural sanctuaries for high artistic expression in music, sculpture, painting, and drama, the general population was flocking to the cheap commercial offerings of jazz, moving-picture shows, and amusement-park spectacles.

As "having fun" gravitated to the center of twentieth-century life and commerce, Americans struggled to locate the rapidly shifting boundary between high culture and popular culture, healthy pleasure and disorderly conduct, savage and civilized entertainments. Did a night out on the town refresh the hard-working man to be more productive on the job, or did it make him wish never to work again? Did jazz stir the soul or pollute it? Did dancing invigorate the body or turn women into vulnerable sexual objects? Did the ruddiness that sunshine left on beachgoers' bare shoulders rejuvenate overcivilized white bodies with savage energy, or did it compromise the social and cultural privileges of white skin? Such questions and anxieties, which were a continuous aspect of twentieth-century history, indicated that going out also meant breaking out of the confinements and expectations of gender, race, sexuality, and class.

Amusing People (1910)
FREDERIC THOMPSON

Frederic Thompson was one of the early twentieth century's master showmen and an influential architect of the national leisure economy. In 1903, he opened a spectacular amusement park of his own design, Luna Park, at New York's Coney Island. With millions of visitors passing through its gates the very first summer, the resort almost immediately became a national sensation, inspiring hundreds of imitators across the United States and eventually around the world. In this article, Thompson explains the "psychology" of his amusements.

PROBLEMS TO CONSIDER

1. How did Thompson explain Luna Park's success? Why did amusement parks usually feature buildings that looked like Turkish mosques and Japanese temples?
2. What was Thompson's psychology of amusement? Compare his notions of human desires to the views of department store merchants.

When I say summer amusement, I mean, of course, what you mean: that thing which draws millions of people to hundreds of places, in scores of cities, over the very broad acres of our land. I mean those places which cause railroad terminals to be choked on hot evenings, and decent Saturdays and almost any sort of Sundays, and crowd and delay trolley-cars, and make much worry for the traffic authorities. If you really want to be more specific: Picture many white steeples, and numerous minarets, and innumerable highly-decorated buildings of every conceivable architecture, from the prototype of a Turkish mosque to the styles obtaining among the more imaginative of the Japanese, with a strain of the architectural fashions which are creditably supposed to obtain in fairyland; imagine swirling things, and tortuous things, and very quickly moving things, and gentlemen with rather bright clothes and (unfortunately) somewhat hoarse

voices who make vigorous announcements of activities within; imagine countless crowds of women in white and quite as many men in many colors, strolling, waiting, peering, laughing; being borne off in curious contrivances that rush and dash; being carried again by other curious contrivances that jump and dance—imagine the sounds of distant bands and present chatter; above all, imagine movement, movement, movement, movement everywhere—and you have a tolerable idea of summer amusement to-day, as people understand summer amusement. . . .

Think . . . of the cellar door . . . of childhood. For that door was the first step in the evolutionary process of that white house, or all those white houses, of minarets and towers and elaborate ornateness which I've been telling you about. That little door was the protoplasmic germ—if you want to be scientific—of modern American summer amusement. For summer amusement was evolved from it, just as man was evolved from that little speck which scientists talk so scientifically about. Because that little door had within it the mystery, the thrill, the glamorous uncertainty which is the foundation of all success in the corridors of summer amusements.

You remember—they opened that little door and there was blackness there. They closed it on you and you trembled, trembled deliciously. You wondered what would happen if they forgot about you. You shivered for a little while there in the black—and then you issued forth again with a strange exultancy. Your little nerves had cried to be thrilled—and they were thrilled. Henceforth, you regarded that little cellar door with a strange reverence, a joyous fear. And it was a versatile thing, too, because when the thrill of the dark wore off you could slide down its slippery surface and that was another thrill— a thrill that never ceases.

It was not until you grew up and got beyond it that you craved the thrill of something else. And that craving to thrill, that undeniable, universal craving to thrill which possesses every man or woman, boy or girl—is the objective point at which all summer amusement providers aim. . . .

Later sprang up the white palaces, first at Coney Island, and afterward throughout the country. That was but nine years ago. Now the Luna Parks and the Dreamlands and the Won-derlands and the various extraordinary lands of amusement parks represent this investment of the fifty millions. . . . I may now properly come to the psychology of summer amusement.

And the first thing which the summer amuse-ment provider has to recognize is that men and women are not really men and women at all, but only children grown up. He comes to recognize that the average mature human is not the com-plex thing which he had previously imagined. He comes to learn that all people are primitive in their tastes and pleasures. . . . Suspense, thrill and—grateful satisfaction—this is the body and the spirit of all amusement . . .

This child-nature is the first thing which you must sedulously follow, and study and refuse to be parted from it if you would be a successful promoter of summer amusement. . . . You will find that the most popular appeals are those which are the most starkly primal—and blood-related to some children's game. Taking a ride, for instance. Only this must be a longer ride, a steeper ride, a more thrilling ride than that which the other children—the children not grown up—demand. The cellar door must be enlarged.

And now begin the problems to be solved when you cater to these children long since grown. Their nature, it is true, undergoes no change. But their tendencies do. And their ten-dencies make up for their nature. . . ."A newer one, a newer one" is continually being borne to you. . . . These grown-up children want new toys all the time . . . Each season the grown children become more insatiable. They are thrill-hungry. They ask a new thought; they demand a new laugh; they clamor for a new sensation. . . .

You watch your successful devices as a cat watches a mouse. You are open to any sugges-tion or complexity of variation which could pos-sibly grow out of it.

You become a hunter for ideas, a stalker for suggestions. You become a sort of humanized sponge for ideas, ideas, ideas for those millions of insatiable ones. . . .

Finally, and in brief, you must imagine your public . . . as a great clock which your experi-ence and intuition enables you to wind up. The average man lives very largely the creature of conventions, the tragic victim of set and settled circumstances. Custom and habit force him to take life solemnly. This is your problem if you are going to be successful as a summer amuse-ment promoter. You must wind that man up. . . .

Frederic Thompson, "Amusing People," *Metropolitan*, August 1910, 601–5, 610.

᠀

Scene from Coney Island (1917)

In this scene from a 1917 silent short comedy, the era's famous funnyman, Roscoe "Fatty" Arbuckle, and his companions are shown having fun on "The Whip," a ride at America's best-known amusement park, Coney Island's Luna Park. The new popular entertainment form of movies often addressed the social and moral order of commercial amusements. In this comedy, for instance, Arbuckle ditches his unattractive and overbearing wife and picks up more appealing female playmates to enjoy the island's pleasures.

PROBLEMS TO CONSIDER

1. How did the scene shown here demonstrate the meaning of fun in the Progressive Era's commercialized playgrounds of amusement?
2. What patterns of interaction between women and men were licensed in these new public spaces?

(*Coney Island*, produced by Paramount Pictures, 1917.)

The Way of the Girl (1909)

BELLE LINDNER ISRAELS

Women and men "going out" where they could do as they pleased was one of the most durable innovations fostered by the Progressive Era leisure economy. Earlier generations of American women and men went through the social rituals of romance and courting in or near the home, where parents or neighbors kept an eye on them. In the city as commercial playground, however, going out became the way that young women and men met and enjoyed the pleasures of nightlife. Some historians call this mixing of the sexes "heterosociality," to distinguish it from earlier organizations of public space in which women and men socialized separately. The most striking—and for many, the most troubling— signs of heterosociality were the young, laboring women who worked in offices, retail establishments, and urban factories and spent their time off looking for a good time. This pleasure-seeking woman, whose poverty necessitated relying on men to "treat" her to the city's nightlife, became one of the prominent symbols of the shifting cultural boundaries of modernity and of the New Woman discussed earlier in this chapter. Was she immoral to begin with, or did nightlife corrupt her? Was she a self-actualizing agent, or a vulnerable victim? Was she a rational actor, or a frivolous girl? The following article, which appeared in The Survey, *a publication for Progressive social reformers, attempted to make sense of this woman and of "treating," from a non-working-class perspective.*

PROBLEMS TO CONSIDER

1. How did the author evaluate "treating" and commercial leisure? Was she sympathetic to working women?
2. Is there any way to read this document for evidence of how working women understood themselves and what they were doing? Would they have agreed with Israels's assessment?

The amusement resources of the working girl run the gamut from innocent and innocuous vacation homes and settlement dancing schools, sparsely furnished for those "well recommended," to the plentiful allurements of the day boat, with its easily rented rooms, the beach, the picnic ground, with its ill-lighted grove and "hotel," to numberless places where one may dance and find partners, with none too scrupulous a supervision. . . .

It is an industrial fact that the summer months find thousands of working girls either in the position of compulsive idleness through slack season in the trades with which they are familiar, or attempting "to kill time" through one or two weeks of a vacation, unwelcome because it bears no definite recreative fruit. The general aspects of the amusement problem of the working girl bear certain undetermined relation to the undercurrents besetting society in a large city, in proportion as opportunities for healthful outlet for social desire are adequate or inadequate. Industrial activity demands diversion. Industrial idleness cries out for rational recreation. As these are provided wisely and freely, the population of the underworld decreases. As they are neglected, the tide rises. . . . The recreative desire of the young girl [is unable] . . . to content itself with a comparatively expensive and therefore infrequent visit to the theater. Her aspirations demand attention from the other sex. No amusement is complete in which "he" is not a factor. The distinction between the working woman and her more carefully guarded sister of the less driven class is one of standards, opportunities, and a chaperone. Three rooms in a tenement, overcrowded with the younger children, make the street a private apartment. The public resort, similarly overcrowded but with those who are not inquisitive, answers as her reception room. . . .

Coney Island—the people's playground—where each year "everything is new but the ocean" is the most gigantic of the efforts to amuse.

A dancing master said: "If you haven't got the girls, you can't do business! Keep attracting 'em. The fellows will come if the girls are there."

Coney Island does attract them. It only costs fare down and back, and for the rest of it the boys you "pick up," "treat."

When the girl is both lucky and clever, she frees herself from her self-selected escort before home-going time, and finds a feminine companion in his place for the midnight ride in the trolley. When she is not clever, some one of her partners of the evening may exact tribute for "standing treat." Then the day's outing costs more than carfare. With due recognition of the simpler amusement places on the island—such as Steeplechase Park, where no liquor is sold, and also of the innocent pleasure along the beach front, not even belittling the fact that "nice" people dance in the Dreamland ball room, the fact remains that the average girl has small powers of discrimination. So many hundred places abound on the island to counterbalance the few safe ones, that "careers" without number find their initial stage . . . at this resort.

The danger is not in the big places on the island, where orderly shows and dance halls are run, and where young persons may go unattended. But the greatest number of music halls and dance resorts are along the side streets of the Bowery, and, with the exception of one or two semi-respectable places, are thoroughly disreputable. On Saturday and Sunday nights many young working girls are attracted to these places. They know the bad reputation of some of them, but the dancing floor is good, there are always plenty of men, and there are laughter and liberty galore. . . .

The "treats" the girls seem to want and care for, are not so much the amusement enterprises of shows and carrousels, but things to drink. "He treated," is the acme of achievement in retailing experiences with the other sex, and the account that begins with, "They followed us, and then they tipped" (meaning they raised their hats) goes through the stages, "They asked us to give them a dance" to, "They treated—She had beer and I had a lemon soda." For it is a characteristic that all the hunting, masculine and feminine, is done in couples. You are always sure of company then should you fail to so dire an extent as not to "catch on," and consequently not be "treated." . . .

While the Committee on Amusements and Vacation Resources was prepared to find [alternative amusement outlets offered by settlement houses and other organizations] for idle girls meager, it has been astounded to find how very small and insufficient the provision is. . . . The ordinary average working girl, earning five or six dollars a week, cannot possibly get away from her greatest enemy,—the summer period of nothing to do. Girls are so eager to find occupation for these idle days that they will offer to do almost anything. . . . The girls with days and weeks to pass, haunt the public roof gardens, recreation piers, and other outdoor places . . . The money earned by the average girl is an absolute necessity in her home. Such part of it as is given to her for her weekly expenses is all expended, and when the summer months come, there is nothing put away. How could there be on six dollars a week . . .? Going about these summer amusement places, one is struck by the absence of the settlement girl. Of many hundreds of girls spoken to only nine had ever heard of a settlement or a church society. . . . Perhaps the [settlement's] vacation home is "dull" in comparison with the fascinations of the outdoor resorts. Would it be possible to effect some sort of combination? Future summer homes to be established would find shore locations give the most satisfaction to a clientèle of working girls. The water offers so many things that are altogether different from the girl's daily run of life that she would not miss the society of men . . . The beach offers so much that makes for healthy tiredness at night. Dancing among themselves or a few simple games would pass away the very short evening hours, before the girl felt that her bed was the most inviting place to go to. . . . The week end from Saturday noon to Sunday night shows a great gap in the life of the girl. She is driven to the beaches and the amusement parks and the picnic places, and driven to the worst of them, because she has choice or knowledge of all too few good ones. Some amusement parks of the right sort and a real "people's playground" at the seashore would help the situation immensely. . . .

We must recover from the idea that the public is intrinsically bad. It needs instruction in the fine art of using, not abusing its privileges, and a little faith in the great American proletariat will develop a marvelous return.

Let us frankly recognize that youth demands amusement. When the cities begin to see their duties to the little ones, playgrounds come. Youth plays too. Instead of sand-piles give them dance platforms; instead of slides and seesaws, theaters; instead of teachers of manual occupations, give them the socializing force of contact with good supervising men and women. Replace the playground, or more properly, progress from the playground to the rational amusement park.

Denial of these privileges peoples the underworld; furnishing them is modern preventive work and should be an integral part of any social program.

Belle Lindner Israels, "The Way of the Girl," *The Survey*, July 1908, 486–89, 492–94, 496–97.

ꝏ

The Angle-Worm Wiggle (c. 1910)
MAYNARD SCHWARTZ (LYRICS) AND HARRY S. LORCH (MUSIC)

"The town is dance mad," Belle Israels observed of New York City in "The Way of the Girl." Dancing to ragtime music was the amusement that young people demanded above all others. The craze hit the United States after 1905. By 1912, Kansas City already had forty-nine dance halls, and 12,000 to 13,000 Milwaukeans were counted dancing in that city each night. Dance madness disclosed the roots of twentieth-century American popular culture in marginalized racial and working-class communities. The music (ragtime) as well as the dance styles (the turkey trot, the bunny hug, and other steps named for libidinous animals) originated with African American entertainers who had developed their styles playing in the tenderloin districts of New Orleans and other southern cities. Migrating north, these musicians found work initially in working-class saloons and music halls, but by 1915 they were playing the same tunes in the posh cabarets of the smart set.

To hear moral reformers talk, Americans of all classes were "tough dancing"—gyrating and hugging in a way that mimicked heterosexual intercourse to the syncopated rhythms and "most blatant and vulgar" lyrics of ragtime music. Although segregated by race and often by class, commercial amusements and especially dancing confused the boundaries of race, gender, and class and signaled the rise of a new sexual order. Whether they loved or hated ragtime, most white Americans regarded it as dirty black music. However, many of the most popular songs of the dance craze years were adapted by Jewish songwriters working in New York's Tin Pan Alley music publishing business. The most famous "rag" of them all was Irving Berlin's "Alexander's Ragtime Band," which sold millions of copies in sheet music. "The Angle-Worm Wiggle" also came out of Tin Pan Alley.

PROBLEMS TO CONSIDER

1. What made songs such as these—and the dances they described—so popular? What boundaries or limits of the dominant cultural order did they defy? What aspects did they affirm or reinforce?
2. Women were much more likely than men to know how to dance. Would songs like these appeal especially to women? How did they depict female sexuality?

I'll slide that Cubanola Glide,
But that's no ecstasy,—
I'm getting tired of dancing to that Men-
  dolssohn strain,
It has lost its charm for me.
Out in San Francisco there's the "Grizzly bear,"
They dance it ev'rywhere that's true,
But there's a little movement, honey,
I will show to you.

Chorus:
Oh, babe, tell it to me,
Can you do the angle-worm wiggle with me?
When I dance that wiggling dance,
I simply have to giggle with glee.
So hold me tight, don't you let me fall;
Sway me round the hall, to that angle-worm
  crawl.

Oh, babe, tell it to me,
Can you do that angle-worm wiggle with me?

Don't tease I like to hug and squeeze
But not just now my hon',
Oh please don't kiss me like you would your
  mother, no more;
Kissing that way is no fun.
When we're out in 'Frisco we will have the
  "Bear"
But I don't care to swing it now.
Oh there's that little movement, honey,
Let me show you how.
(Chorus)

"The Angle-Worm Wiggle," lyrics by Maynard Schwartz, music by Harry S. Lorch (Chicago: Victor Kremer, 1910).

ᔕ

Investigators' Reports, Committee of Fourteen, New York City (1912)

How did pleasure-seeking women and men understand their dance madness? Most evidence of what went on inside dance halls came from figures who saw themselves as outsiders, principally moral reformers and middle- and upper-class slummers. In many American cities, commissions were formed, in good Progressive fashion, to gather reliable evidence on commercialized vice, especially the "social evil" of prostitution. In New York City, the Committee of Fourteen, an association of some of the city's wealthiest and most influential citizens, hired investigators, usually operating in disguise, to infiltrate the new forms of commercial leisure. Reformers assumed that these businesses both harbored prostitutes and actively lured unsuspecting women into the trade. The following reports by the committee's undercover agents describe the dancing at a New York club in 1912. Such investigations were predicated on the expectation that the facts about these businesses would indict them for the behavior they encouraged. If read with more detachment, the reports reveal much, not just about the attitudes of reformers but also about the value that young people attached to commercial amusements.

PROBLEMS TO CONSIDER

1. What behaviors were the agents on the lookout for? They describe the dances as unrestrained. Was that an accurate reading of what they saw?
2. If we set aside the investigators' moral condemnation of what they saw, what can we learn about the behavior and interactions of working women and men who patronized dance halls?

Kennedy, cor. 38 street and Broadway

Mr. S. and I went into the above place on November 9, at midnight. The entrance was well lit. We went in and took a seat not far from the door. Between the dances was a cabaret show; three different women sang, walking up to different tables. These women sat among the audience.

The dancing was tough. Men and women held each other in a tight grasp, the women putting their arms right around the men. Almost all walked the two step in a combination bunny hug and nigger. Several couples danced the shivers and some of the dipping varieties which are danced in the dance halls. One couple had a distinct houchi kouchi movement. Women danced together, and were speedily separated by men whom they joined at tables after the dance.

Near us sat three women and two men. Two of these women sang, and danced together. They quickly picked up partners and one of them left this party and remained some time with the man she had picked up. Then after this party had broken up and only one man remained she again joined him at his table, and they sat talking together in a rather intimate way. At another table were two men, who were evidently alone, but about ten minutes after our entrance they had two women with them. Another of the singers changed her place several times from one table to another. All these women whom I mention and

all the other women whom I saw in this place were undoubted prostitutes. I did not see one woman who looked respectable. . . .

In the matter of Murray's

All summer reports have been received from friend that the dancing permitted on the roof of Murray's was "The Limit." This came from various sources; Kent, Mrs. I. etc. I personally visited the place on the evening of August 22nd, being there from about 11:30 to 12:30 A.M. I was accompanied by a [m]ale friend (W.T.A.). We met there male friends including a state office holder.

The dancing was being done in a cleared space between the front and rear room; at the east end of the middle room. Some of the music was waltz time and the dancing was decent, [b]ut just as soon as the turkey trot tune was played the dancing became immodest, indecent and disgustingly sexual. That it was exceptional was shown by the fact that many of the guests left their tables and gathered around the [cleared] space to [watch] the disgusting exhibition.

Recommendation: Compel the taking out of a Dance Hall license and the cutting out of Turkey trot tunes and all indecent dancing. . . .

Committee of Fourteen Investigators' Reports, Committee of Fourteen Papers, New York Public Library, New York, N.Y.

Investigators' Reports, Committee of Fourteen, New York City (1918)

Young working women, who flocked to the sounds of excitement and glamour at dance halls, especially alarmed middle-class observers who disapproved of women and men mingling together outside the restraints of family, home, and neighborhood. As evidence, they cited "charity girls," young working women who, too poor to pay their own way, let men pick them up in exchange for the "treat" of a night on the town. For reformers, women who were "treated" were swapping sexual favors for a good time and thus wandering dangerously close to prostitution. But the vice reports on "treating" allow us to examine the patterns of sociability in public amusements and how gender and class expectations shaped reformers' interpretations of the interactions of women and men. The reports also allow us to consider how "charity girls" imagined themselves and what they were doing.

PROBLEMS TO CONSIDER

1. Why were women not allowed to approach a man's table? Did this restriction protect women or increase their vulnerability? Compare how investigators and male supervisors and bartenders of dance halls viewed female patrons.
2. Do these documents help us understand working women's enthusiasm for dance halls?

Bronx Park Casino (dance hall), March 9, 1918
State conditions found in the back room, or other connecting rooms. In dance hall, about 50 unescorted women, 200 unaccompanied men, 200 couples, some of the women appeared to be professional prostitutes, more than half of the women seemed to be game. No active soliciting but quite a few pickups. . . .

Remarks. This dance hall catering to loafers and girls of questionable characters. A few professional prostitutes here, Saw no active soliciting but saw men leave their tables and take unescorted women for dance then join these women at [their] tables after the dance, Saw women dance alone on the floor but did not see any of these men break the women while on the floor, Management will not stand for this. Saw a few couples hugging, also saw women speaking to men and calling them from different tables. Also noticed a few of the men partly under the influence of liquor. . . . Saw no women smoking,

no suggestive dancing or any other disorderly actions. Goldstein [owner] on the lookout all the time, apparently trying to run this place right but don't think he'll succeed, patronized by too many undesirable men and charity girls. Is known around this neighborhood as a place where a man can pick up a woman. Got into conversation with Georgie Dunn, the waiter, he asked me why I didn't show up last week, said he was off and would have got a couple of girls here and we could have gone out together, told him I had no time, Said we'll do it some night this week, make a regular party, said he didn't think he'd be able to do it this week, is broke. . . . He said there's loads of gash comes in here, easy to get them too. I can always stake a guy to a piece of gash, I said why don't you stake me, he said stick around, I'll get something for you, do you see those two girls there, they are 2 sisters, both of them gash, if you were here a few minutes earlier, I'd have put you next to them, they were here alone and these 2 men just grabbed them a couple of minutes before you came in. (he was referring to 2 young girls sitting with 2 men at different table) He said he is a little busy now but if I would stick around he would get me something before I left. . . . Also sat at Boston, the waiters station, asked him if there wasn't anything on his station, they are all regular tots, they all gash, are a lot of good fellows, but wont' give you a tumble if they don't know you. Also told me to stick around and said if theres anything he could put me next to he would. . . . No active soliciting but plenty of pickups and waiters will stake man to woman if [they] know him. Patronized by a lot of charity girls.

Bronx Park Casino, July 27th, 1918
Still patronized by the same crowd of charity girls and loafers but saw no professional looking prostitutes here. Saw men take unescorted women for a dance and then join them at their tables after the dance, also leave the premises with them. Saw women dance alone on floor but did not see any men break these women while on floor. Also saw men leave their tables and join unescorted women at their tables and order drinks for them. Saw no women smoking cigarettes, no couples kissing or hugging, no suggestive dances. A few of the men appeared to be under the influence of liquor and were pretty noisy but were not acting disorderly. There seems to be quite an improvement here but this is still a place where a man can pick up a charity girl. I asked Boston the waiter if there wasn't anything around that he could put me next to, he said there was a few around before that he knew were there but there aint any around now. I asked him what about those 2 girls there (there was 2 girls sitting a few tables away from me) he said I wouldn't advise you to have anything to with them, they will drink with you and pull your leg for all your worth and then bid you good night, said they are only a couple of——teasers, he knows them, they stung a couple of his friends. Told me if I was around earlier in the evening, he would have put me next to something. [The manager Leopold said] in a place like this there are always some women around that you can make, Told me the comm [of 14] refused to give them their license because some of the women on their way to the toilet would stop and talk with men at some of the tables claimed they were soliciting. He said men are allowed to go to womens tables but women are not allowed to go to mens tables. . . .

Committee of Fourteen Investigators' Reports, Committee of Fourteen Papers, New York Public Library, New York, N.Y.

ᴈ

Modern Dancing (1914)
MR. AND MRS. VERNON CASTLE

Reformers in various American cities sought, usually without success, to outlaw or ban the turkey trot, tango, and other dances. Vernon and Irene Castle had greater success in the endeavor to cleanse and reform popular dancing, rather than to ban it outright. The Castles were the elegant and tasteful masters of modern dancing and instructors and companions to America's wealthiest trendsetters. In the following selection from their guidebook Modern Dancing, *they and their wealthy patron Elizabeth Marbury describe what the Castles and modern dance had contributed to contemporary life.*

PROBLEMS TO CONSIDER

1. What did it mean for the Castles to reform modern dance? Should they be regarded as Progressive reformers?
2. Vernon Castle believed that ragtime music was essential to dancing (his favorite performers were James Reese Europe's Negro band). What was achieved by keeping the music but modifying the dance steps?

We feel that this book will serve a double purpose. In the first place, it aims to explain in a clear and simple manner the fundamentals of modern dancing. In the second place, it shows that dancing, properly executed, is neither vulgar nor immodest, but, on the contrary, the personification of refinement, grace, and modesty.

Our aim is to uplift dancing, purify it, and place it before the public in its proper light. When this has been done, we feel convinced that no objection can possibly be urged against it on the grounds of impropriety, but rather that social reformers will join with the medical profession in the view that dancing is not only a rejuvenator of good health and spirits, but a means of preserving youth, prolonging life, and acquiring grace, elegance, and beauty.

INTRODUCTION
[BY ELIZABETH MARBURY]

In a recent address by the poet Jean Richepin before the members of the French Academy the evolution of modern dances was convincingly traced from the tombs of Thebes, from Orient to Occident, and down through ancient Rome. M. Richepin protested against the vulgarization of these dances when performed by inartistic and ignorant exponents, but argued that centers should promptly be established in every capital of the world where the grace and beauty and classic rhythm to which the modern dance so naturally lends itself should be developed and emphasized.

With this aim in view Castle House in New York was started, and the services of Mr. and Mrs. Vernon Castle were secured by me to conduct and superintend the dancing there. Mr. and Mrs. Castle stand pre-eminent to-day as the best exponents of modern dancing. In Europe as well as in America it has been universally conceded that as teachers they are unequaled. Refinement is the keynote of their method; under their direction Castle House became the model school of modern dancing, and through its influence the spirit of beauty and of art is allied to the legitimate physical need of healthy exercise and of honest enjoyment.

The One Step as taught at Castle House eliminates all hoppings, all contortions of the body, all flouncing of the elbows, all twisting of the arms, and, above everything else, all fantastic dips. This One Step bears no relation or resemblance to the once popular Turkey Trot, Bunny Hug, or Grizzly Bear. In it is introduced the sliding and poetical Castle Walk. The Hesitation Waltz is a charming and stately glide, measured and modest.

The much-misunderstood Tango becomes an evolution of the eighteenth-century Minuet. There is in it no strenuous clasping of partners, no hideous gyrations of the limbs, no abnormal twistings, no vicious angles. Mr. Castle affirms that when the Tango degenerates into an acrobatic display or into salacious suggestion it is the fault of the dancers and not of the dance. The Castle Tango is courtly and artistic, and this is the only Tango taught by the Castle House instructors.

Mr. and Mrs. Vernon Castle, *Modern Dancing* (New York: Harper & Bros., 1914), 17, 19–20.

ᢌᢇ

~: CHAPTER 4 :~

The Profits and Perils of Prosperity: 1915–1934

IMAGINE TAKING THE FOLLOWING TEST. Each sentence offers four choices to complete it. Only one of them is correct. Draw a line under that word or term. If you are unsure, guess.

1. Isaac Pitman was most famous in
   physics   shorthand   railroading   electricity.
2. Velvet Joe appears in advertisements of
   tooth powder   dry goods   tobacco   soap.
3. The Battle of Gettysburg was fought in
   1863   1813   1778   1812.
4. The Wyandotte is a kind of
   horse   fowl   cattle   granite.
5. The dictaphone is a kind of
   typewriter   multigraph   phonograph   adding machine.
6. Marguerite Clark is known as a
   suffragist   singer   movie actress   writer.
7. The stanchion is used in
   fishing   hunting   farming   motoring.
8. "Hasn't scratched yet" is used in advertising a
   duster   flour   brush   cleanser.
9. The number of a Zulu's legs is
   two   four   six   eight.
10. The Knight engine is used in the
    Packard   Lozier   Stearns   Pierce Arrow.*

---

*The correct answers: 1. shorthand; 2. tobacco; 3. 1863; 4. fowl; 5. phonograph; 6. movie actress; 7. farming; 8. cleanser; 9. two; 10. Stearns.

These questions were a fraction of the intelligence-measuring "alpha" tests to which the U.S Army subjected hundreds of thousands of its most promising recruits and draftees during World War I (illiterates were given the visual "beta" version). In other words, the army presumed that this test provided a measurement of IQ.

The scientists who designed these examinations were engaged in one of the broadest experiments in social engineering in U.S. history. The presumed benefits of finding men with "typically American" intelligence were easily stated. By measuring their inborn, rather than their acquired, intelligence, the army could enhance the efficiency of its operations, matching manpower with appropriate occupations, filtering out the "feeble-minded," and identifying the highly intelligent for the command positions to which they were suited. Scientists saw the test as Progressive democracy in action, with science serving the public good. Such claims for the test (as your experience with it probably attests) can hardly stand up to scrutiny. Would it matter whether the examinee were a woman or a man? middle-class, working-class, or poor? rural or urban? native-born or foreign-born? To perform well would require a familiarity with barnyard animals, the icons and vocabulary of consumer capitalism, and the tools and techniques of modern office management. A typical American would know that Velvet Joe sells tobacco and that a Knight engine powers a Stearns motorcar. In other words, intelligence — which is to say American identity — amounted to a working familiarity with the signs, vocabulary, and systems of a mass urban, corporate, and consumer society. Such a hybrid intelligence could not have existed fifty years earlier (or fifty years later).

What the alpha exam sketched was not so much a coherent ideal but rather an unstable composite of the cultural signs and signals of the widespread changes in the years before, during, and after the Great War. Along with the urbanization of what recently had been a predominantly agricultural and rural society came startling social and cultural changes: apparent advances in science and technology that, for some, promised a more enlightened society and, for others, a less humane and democratic America; the growth of national markets for nationally advertised brand-name commodities, from household goods to the heroes of the baseball diamond and the "wild" sounds of African American blues singers; and the massive internal and foreign immigrations that continued to challenge the equation of "civilization" with northern European whiteness. The artifacts collected in this chapter delve into the cultural turmoil of the Great War and beyond.

❧ *The Great War and Beyond* ❧

By November 1918—nineteen months after President Wilson had asked for and received from Congress a declaration of war against Germany and its allies—more than 2 million American troops had been sent into what a U.S. senator had described as "that vortex of blood and passion and woe." American troops, however, were not drawn into a vortex. Instead they brought a decisive end to the slaughter that Europeans had inflicted on themselves for more than four years. By the time of the armistice that same November, the war had claimed 116,000 American lives (53,000 in combat), a fraction of the number of Russian and French deaths (1.7 million and 1.35 million respectively). Although the outlooks of many Europeans were fundamentally altered by their participation in the systematic killing, American soldiers were more likely to be witnesses to than victims of that horror. When the war ended, many felt they were returning home with reasons to celebrate, reinvigorated by the fight "Over There."

The celebrations were, in many respects, short-lived. Even if the losses inflicted on American fighting men were small in comparison, the international conflict brought important changes at home. The mobilization stimulated the domestic economy, increasing both wages and the demand for labor just as workingmen were drawn into military service. Contributing to these conditions was the virtual cessation of European immigration once the conflict started in 1914, an effect that gave new strength to the anti-immigration movement. The severe labor shortages that resulted created favorable conditions for the labor movement. Union membership, which industrial capitalists had fought for the last four decades, doubled between the outbreak of war and 1920. In many areas, women temporarily shifted into men's jobs. More important, the favorable conditions spurred the first mass migration of African Americans out of the Deep South in pursuit of better work and wages in northern cities. In many cases, working and living conditions were worth the journey, but deadly race riots broke out in cities where whites resisted the unwanted "invasion" of their communities. These signs of division and conflict emerged at the same time that a revived spirit of national unity and self-sacrifice boosted efforts for Progressive social engineering, furthering the causes of two constitutional amendments: prohibition (1919) and women's suffrage (1920). The war, from which most American men returned home alive and well, significantly altered the class, racial, and gender landscape of the United States.

Images of War (1915–1919)

From the start of the European war in 1914, Americans debated the meaning of the conflict, the righteousness of the various combatants, and what their nation's role should be. Pro-interventionists insisted that a manly civilization would not stand on the sidelines of the conflict, whereas the anti-interventionists who founded the Woman's Peace Party targeted men as the innately bellicose enemies of civilization. In 1915, two Tin Pan Alley songwriters penned a number that tapped into the prevalent antiwar feelings: "There'd be no war today, If mothers all would say, 'I didn't raise my boy to be a soldier.'" By early 1917, the bottom had fallen out of the musical market for such sentiments. With "100 percent Americanism" the standard for supporting the war, many Americans came to regard son-hugging mothers as themselves a problem.

The images (posters, broadsides, sheet music covers, photographs) that were used to sell or to discredit American involvement in the European conflict underscore how effectively the techniques and talents of commercial advertising and magazine illustration were enlisted in the war debate. The depth of these resources had not been available during any earlier war. The following samples of war-era propaganda — the cover illustration of the antiwar song quoted in the previous paragraph, a poster urging Americans to buy war bonds, and two enlistment posters for the U.S. military — reveal the symbiotic relationship between political debate and popular culture. They also show how illustrators and ad copywriters (in the case of the "Serve on the Rhine" poster) used representations of manhood and womanhood to argue why Americans should or should not join the fight in Europe.

PROBLEMS TO CONSIDER

1. Compare how young manhood was defined in relation to womanhood and motherhood to explain why Americans should or should not fight. How did these relationships establish the nature of the enemy and argue a position on American intervention in the war?
2. Would you describe these posters as advertisements? If so, what techniques did they employ to sell the war?

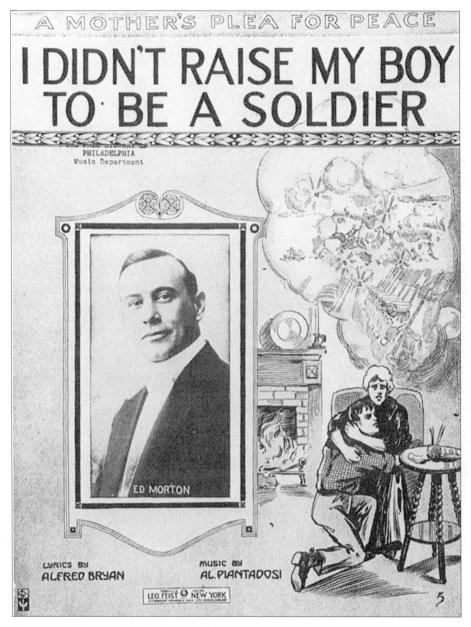

(The Granger Collection, New York.)

(The Granger Collection, New York.)

(HIP/Art Resource, New York.)

SERVE ON THE RHINE—NOW, IN THE A.E.F.

Here is Opportunity—Are YOU the Man?

My boy—your Uncle Sam is sending 50,000 men like you, right now, to serve in France and on the Rhine. The flag floats in many parts of the world, and Uncle Sam will maintain an efficient, patriotic army to guard it. So besides the contingents for Europe, many other red-blooded men are invited to volunteer and choose what part of the world they will serve in.

Will *You* Go?

In Panama, Alaska, Hawaii, the Philippines, China [etc.] . . . opportunity is offered clean, ambitious, intelligent young men. The choice is yours! . . .

Good Pay, Enjoyable, Inspiring Work, Recreation and Man-Building

Food, clothing, living quarters, medical and dental attention—all of the very best —absolutely FREE. The present rate of pay is $30 a month or more. In other words, *the soldier now has a net profit of about a dollar a day!*

Can you pay all your living expenses from your present income and have a dollar a day left over? Probably not.

Military Life is Outdoor Life

It inculcates self-control, quick-thinking, alertness, regularity, exactness, bodily fitness. It makes you hard as nails; a trained, co-ordinated unit of clean bone and muscle. *Most men gain weight as a result of army life!*

Free Vocational Training in the Army Fits You for Success

Suppose you are a young man looking about you for a trade as a *stepping stone to success in life*—Uncle Sam offers many educational opportunities, and pays you *while you study*. . . .

Liberty and Recreation

The soldier off duty writes letters, smokes, plays baseball, pool, football or most any other game he likes; goes to the movies, or theatres; in fact, does about as he pleases. . . . He meets agreeable people, including lots of nice girls. . . . In fact, he *usually has a better time than a civilian.* . . .

What else do you want to know? This advertisement tells only a part of the story. Get the rest today. Don't delay. Act now!

(U.S. American Expeditionary Recruiting Poster, original in the Minnesota Historical Society Poster Collection, St. Paul, Minn.)

෴

Selected Letters (1917–1918)

PAUL ELIOT GREEN

In April 1917, twenty-three-year-old Paul Green, a student at the University of North Carolina, responded to the president's declaration of war by enlisting in the armed forces. He was assigned to an engineering division responsible for support services (building roads, notifying families of casualties) and eventually was sent to Europe. He had grown up on his father's North Carolina farm and knew little of the world other than the polite and comfortable circumstances of his youth in the rural South. The letters he sent home to his father, sister Mary, and girlfriend Erma while stationed at training camps in North and South Carolina and in the war zones of France describe his motivations and ideals, his adjustment to the "rough set of fellows" who were in his unit, and the course of how he grew as a "man." After the war, Green returned to North Carolina and became a celebrated playwright, winning the Pulitzer Prize for drama in 1927 for In Abraham's Bosom.

PROBLEMS TO CONSIDER

1. Examine these letters to measure how Green was changed by the war. What happened to his idealism about the war's aims over the course of the conflict?
2. How important were gender and class to Green's descriptions of those changes? In what circumstances did Green refer to himself or fellow soldiers as "men" or as "boys"?

[Summer 1917?], Goldsboro, N.C.
Dear Mary:

Possibly you think I don't care about writing to all of you. If you do think that, you almost think the truth. Everything seems so far removed and foreign to the things around home that a reminder of home affairs isn't so very pleasant as one might think. . . .

We are leaving here for Charlotte to-morrow morning—a trip of 231 miles. We shall have to travel all to-morrow afternoon and night. You may know I dread it—all. Our job will be to aid in constructing the camp for the northern troops. So far as I know we shall have to dig trenches for the water pipes, put in sewage, etc. But we needn't care. . . . While we eat like hogs and as much, we needn't dread anything. The boys remind us every day that nothing matters at all. . . .

When I was at Chapel Hill, I thought that was a rough place; but this is the roughest place on earth. The profanity of the soldiers is awful.

Co. B. is a roaring, rough set of fellows. There is an old blacksmith that sleeps in our tent who is the roughest man, I know, that ever saw daylight. But the truth is, every one of those pirates has a good streak in him. If you strike them in the right way, each is your friend. . . .

[P.S.] The swear words were used to give you a touch of camp life. For my part, I never am going to curse. I'm going to stay straight. It will not be hard for me to do it, for all profanity and vulgarity sickens me.

Camp Sevier, Greenville, S.C.
[18 September 1917]
Dear Papa:

. . . As I mentioned in my last letter, I am liking this life as well as I could like it. Grumbling is not in my line of business, and I find that the only wise method in the army is to take whatever comes along. One must throw away his own likes and dislikes, and become a part of the big whole. Of course, it is reasonable to think that the only way for any army to be effective is to have each individual lose his individuality and become, like the atoms in a driving wheel, only a part of the machinery. But I can tell you it goes against the grain for a man to have to give himself free-heartedly and unreservedly to the Government. The only thing that keeps me sound and with a healthy point of view towards the army is a knowledge of the fact that we are fighting a great fight, and for the principles of right living. I believe there is more of sorrow than bitterness among the men in uniform because we are compelled to fight the Germans. These boys in camp are brave, and when the time comes they will not be found wanting. I often hear them, and talk, myself, talking about the chances of getting out of the melée alive. Most of them think we are facing certain death, tho' a long ways ahead. But despite this belief they go ahead and drill and play ball, also sing their foolish songs as if all the world was sunshine and everything was a spring morning in their lives. I don't care if most of our soldiers are rough and brutal in regard to the delicacies of life; they can't help it. Even tho' such is the case they deserve the respect and admiration of the rest of the world. I know that when I am mustered out I shall not be so refined nor so easy-going as once I was. But what I lack in those things doubtless will be made up in a power to push ahead, and to push strongly, although such a life as I am now living is not exactly to my liking. But I argue this way, that what the god of circumstances thrusts upon a man, that will he have to endure, and on that account I am growing to like the army. . . .

Camp Sevier, S.C., May 13, 1918
My dear Father, —

Perhaps you have been thinking that both your boys were on their way to France. I have hesitated to write during the last few days, owing to the fact that everything connected with the Engineers is so uncertain—as far as the enlisted man is concerned at the present. Even tho' I am writing now, we are still in the same state of uncertainty. None of us knows when we are to leave. . . .

But I'm not miserable. There is too much to be done. I have 53 men to look after at all times—their clothing, boots, equipment—all rests upon my shoulders. The last ten days have been the hardest of my life. I have been trying to get these 53 men equipped for over-sea service. I can't stick my head out of the tent without someone's calling, "Sgt. Greene, have you got me any leggin laces?" or shoe laces, or tent pins, as the case may be. But I like it all. I love the hardness of this life. I love to stick my chest out and call the men to attention. You'd laugh if you could see me one of these *early* mornings standing on the drill field, making my voice crack like a whip, and bellowing, "Squads, Right! March"—and the like. . . .

And [my brother] Hugh loves a soldier's life, too. I went to see him—I slipped away—the last night he was here. He was so excited over going that he couldn't be still. It was a sight to see him dressed up in his paraphernalia. . . . I shall never forget this last night I spent with Hugh. He seemed nearer to me then than ever before. I looked at him and thought of all he was to go thru—the dangers of the sea, the firing-line, the charge of the bayonets and a hundred other things. For myself I'm glad to meet these dangers, but he seems so slender and small—and yet you can't kill him. He's tough as steel. Somehow I know he's going to get thru, and in many ways I'm glad he's getting his share of life, but perhaps I was a little sentimental that night. . . .

Belgium, August 25, 1918
Dearest Erma:

. . . Honey, it's hard to tell you exactly what I am doing. At the present I'm a sort of bookkeeper for the whole regiment of engineers. . . . The most unpleasant thing of all is the casualty list. Reporting the killed and wounded is my job also. And alas! I've marked up several friends whose mothers today are speaking to God about the eternal *Why?* But withal our losses are extremely light, it appears to me, compared to those of Germany. . . .

Yes, and I've learned another thing I was forgetting: the poor tired earth has drunk enough blood within the last four years as to be offensive in the sight of God. Not long ago I was on an old battlefield. We were digging trenches. One could hardly push his spade into the ground without striking a bone of somebody's boy. Yes, horrible; but war. And a few days ago I was at another place where 54,000 men "went west" in one day. Awful! Yes, but war. Oh, I tell you the people in America never dreamed of what our brave allies endured for three long years. They were content to slide around in noiseless automobiles . . . while thousands of boys who loved the fields of England or the skies of France went down into the Valley, and went without a rod or staff to comfort them. . . .

I have seen only Hugh since I came over—saw him once a few weeks ago. *But remember he is on the line with all his Green's blood crying for a German to come and face him.* If the worst should happen to him, which God forbid!—you will agree with me in saying, "He was a man. He could not have died more gloriously. It is well." . . .

Engineer Purchasing Office
Paris, France, A.P.O. 702.
May 16, 1919
Dear Papa—

To-night I've been thinking of home, and so, I must write a note. Whenever I feel the desire strongly to see everybody back there, I usually write, and then I'm reconciled to "Gay Paree" and everything she means.

As I've told you before, my work consists of helping to pay French Government bills. During these last days, business has been slowing up, and . . . it appears that we shall have finished everything before the fall. Now don't worry; Hugh and I will be there before the old China tree turns yellow in September. Anyway, aren't you just a little pleased with us—that we had grit enough to play the game through; that though we both wanted to go home, we realized that this was an opportunity of learning and experiencing things that would never come again? Really after every A.E.F. man has left France you can say, "Well, my boys went into it, and they stayed (*of their own free will*) and saw the last inning played. One helped settle the thousand and one accounts; the other helped keep the peace of the country. Yes, they saw the whole thing through, and the pain of a few months of separation was over-balanced by the knowledge of the world they gained. Yes, as the Greens ought, they played to the last hole." Can't you say that? Thank God, neither of us is so babyish that he dreams nightly of his bottle and nipple on the mantel-shelf back home. We wanted to see something of the world, and we're seeing it, believe me. No. I'm not praising ourselves, I hope, but I want you to let bother pass when you see the boys coming home. . . .

Selected Letters, Paul Eliot Green (1917–18), Paul Eliot Green Papers (#3693), Manuscripts Department, Southern Historical Collection, University of North Carolina, Chapel Hill, N.C. Transcriptions from http://docsouth.unc.edu/wwi.greenletters/greenletters.html.

ᢒ

"Over There" (c. 1917)

GEORGE M. COHAN

By 1917, George M. Cohan and Irving Berlin (see chapter 3) were Tin Pan Alley's leading composers—or, better, "songsters"—and had begun to establish their styles of music on the Broadway stage. Cohan had started a musical revolution in American professional theater in 1904 with Little Johnny Jones. *He introduced the still-popular hits "Yankee Doodle Boy" ("I'm a Yankee Doodle Dandy / A Yankee Doodle do or die") and "Give My*

Regards to Broadway." He also led an insurrection against American theater's deference to the diction and melodies of European-style operettas. Cohan's memorable tunes were enlivened with ragtime rhythms and thumping nativist sentiments delivered in the colloquial tongue of ordinary American men. Berlin continued the domestication of American music. His "Alexander's Ragtime Band" (1911), one of the most popular songs in American musical history, fueled the popular dance craze and served as a prelude to his Broadway fame.

Better than anyone in their day, Cohan and Berlin knew what made music both popular and American. With war fever on the rise in 1917 and afterward, they rallied to the higher cause of intervention, introducing the only "war songs" to survive the conflict: Cohan's "Over There" and Berlin's "Oh! How I Hate to Get Up in the Morning." Cohan's popular anthem has become a kind of shorthand for the fevered war enthusiasm of 1917. To get a sense of why the song worked so well, it should be heard (or even sung), rather than simply read. Still, the words themselves are useful for the way in which they express a widely popular conception of America's role in the conflict and demonstrate Cohan's skills as a popular lyricist.

PROBLEMS TO CONSIDER

1. Compare Cohan's song with those written for the Spanish-American War (see chapter 2). Was there anything about the lyrics of "Over There" that made it more "American" or popular than the earlier examples?
2. How does the song establish Johnnie's identity? How might Paul Green have responded to this song?

Johnnie, get your gun, get your gun, get your gun,
Take it on the run, on the run, on the run,
Hear them calling you and me;
Ev'ry son of liberty.

Hurry right away, no delay, go today,
Make your daddy glad, to have had such a lad,
Tell your sweetheart not to pine,
To be proud her boy's in line.

Chorus:
Over there, over there,
Send the word, send the word over there,
That the Yanks are coming, the Yanks are coming,
The drums rum-tumming ev'rywhere.
So prepare, say a pray'r,
Send the word, send the word to beware,

We'll be over, we're coming over,
And we won't come back till it's over over there.

Johnnie, get your gun, get your gun, get your gun,
Johnnie show the Hun, you're a son-of-a-gun,
Hoist the flag and let her fly,
Like true heroes do or die.
Pack your little kit, show your grit, do your bit,
Soldiers to the ranks from the towns and the tanks,
Make your mother proud of you,
And to liberty be true.

(Chorus)

───────
"Over There," lyrics and music by George M. Cohan (New York: L. Feist, c. 1917).

⚬

New York Cheers "Yip, Yip, Yaphank" (1918)

"Oh! How I Hate to Get Up in the Morning" (1918)

IRVING BERLIN

Upon induction in the army, Irving Berlin was sent to Camp Upton near New York City. At the time, Berlin was the toast of the theatrical world, a very wealthy man who was accustomed to doing things his way. He was infamous, for instance, for working all night and sleeping the day away. Army life was an unwelcome change for Berlin. To ease his own pain and boost troop morale, he helped organize a camp musical, which rapidly evolved into a full-scale theatrical production called Yip, Yip, Yaphank. *The show, with its all-soldier cast, eventually worked its way to a sensational run on Broadway. As the following review shows,* Yip, Yip, Yaphank *incorporated the standard features of the day's most popular musical entertainments. Berlin's performance of "Oh! How I Hate to Get Up in the Morning" was the hit of the show.*

PROBLEMS TO CONSIDER

1. What made *Yip, Yip, Yaphank* an "American" show? Why did Berlin include a minstrel show in the production?
2. Compare Berlin's song with that of Cohan. Were they popular for different or similar reasons? Did they have similar estimations of war's effects on fighting men?

NEW YORK CHEERS "YIP, YIP, YAPHANK"

Imagine this — the Century Theater jammed to the doors . . . and ringing with a wild, friendly clamor of "Berlin! Three cheers for Berlin! . . ."

No, it wasn't a triumph of German propaganda, in fact, the whole occasion was part of the plan to take Berlin off the map. Every man on the stage carried a gun that he hopes to aim direct at the Kaiser. The cheers were for a boyish-looking little man in a soldier's uniform who stood before the curtain — Sergeant Irving Berlin, who was the first to go over the top with the syncopated rag, when he wrote *"Alexander's Ragtime Band."* . . .

Berlin made "Yip, Yip, Yaphank" distinctly a man's show. There was real illusion to the "feminine" cast of "Biff Bang," the earlier naval success at the Century [Theatre], the "girls" were

actually dainty and graceful. But the Yaphank chorus was frankly masquerading.

Of course, the reason is that Camp Upton is a melting pot, and offered entirely different material to work with. . . .

So the Yaphank ensemble was more to be commended for brawn than beauty, although they disarmed criticism by each admitting their former occupations and habits in pithy couplets — one said he "was a packer, and ate plug tobaccer." The rest were quite as evidently intended for anything but show girls, but, oh, what soldiers they will make! . . .

After the opening chorus, which developed into a minstrel show with only the endmen in blackface and the rest in the conventional khaki, Captain McAllister told the men that there was a hard, seasoned enemy on the other side of the footlights, and, although it was completely surrounded and pocketed, it would have to be riddled with riddles, bombed with jokes, and vanquished with songs before it could be annihilated. . . .

The enthusiasm and vigor of the boys on the stage and the stimulus of the songs swept everyone irresistibly into the spirit of the evening. It was more like the last inning of a world-series ball game than anything else.

The minstrel finale, a Darktown wedding, introduced the only real lady in the cast, a colored baby-vampire, who acted as flower-girl, and fairly stopped proceedings with a pair of eyes that would be worth a million dollars in the movies if they were topped with Pickford curls instead of Topsy pigtails.

―――――

"New York Cheers 'Yip, Yip, Yaphank,'" *Theatre*, October 1918, 222.

"OH! HOW I HATE TO GET UP IN THE MORNING"

The other day I chanced to meet a soldier
   friend of mine,
He'd been in camp for sev'ral weeks and he
   was looking fine;
His muscles had developed and his cheeks
   were rosy red,
I asked him how he liked the life, and this is
   what he said:

"Oh! How I hate to get up in the morning,
Oh! How I'd love to remain in bed;

For the hardest blow of all, is to hear the
   bugler call:
You've got to get up, you've got to get up,
You've got to get up this morning!'"

Some day I'm going to murder the bugler,
Some day they're going to find him dead;
I'll amputate his reveille and step upon it
   heavily,
And spend the rest of my life in bed.

A bugler in the army is the luckiest of men,
He wakes the boys at five and then goes back
   to bed again;
He doesn't have to blow again until the
   afternoon,
If ev'rything goes well with me I'll be a bugler
   soon.

"Oh! How I hate to get up in the morning,
Oh! How I'd love to remain in bed,
For the hardest blow of all is to hear the
   bugler call:
You've got to get up, you've got to get up,
You've got to get up this morning!'"

Oh! boy the minute the battle is over,
Oh! boy the minute the foe is dead;
I'll put my uniform away, and move to
   Philadelphia,
And spend the rest of my life in bed.

―――――

"Oh! How I Hate to Get Up in the Morning," lyrics and music by Irving Berlin (New York: Waterson, Berlin & Snyder Co., 1918).

ᣟ

ᣟ *Rural Values: Debating the Destiny of Modern American Culture* ᣟ

In early December 1915, an ad in the *Atlanta Constitution* announced, "The Conqueror is Coming!" The exclamation was not warning about an invading force, but declaring a reason to celebrate. Despite black ministers' pleas to keep D. W. Griffith's *The Birth of a Nation* out of local movie houses, Atlantans were going to get to see the cinematic wonder that was conquering audiences around the nation. Griffith's landmark movie depicts the glorious rise of the Ku Klux Klan in the dark days of Reconstruction, when "Negro rule" had disrupted civilization's natural racial order and left white women at the mercy of savage black men. In the film, northern and southern white men, once enemies, recognize the disaster of Reconstruction's racial egalitarianism and join forces to restore white men to power. In doing so, they make the world safe again for civilized womanhood and give birth to an American nation unified, once and for all, by the whiteness of its citizenry.

The ability of Griffith's film to conquer all regions of the United States with a profoundly racist and partisan cinematic "history" of the American nation signaled the unusual importance that ideas about the character of the rural South, its peoples, and their bloody transition to modernity through civil war and the abolition of slavery would assume in American culture in the twentieth century. Much as they have with the West, Americans of all races have relished telling and listening to the "story" of the South, in various and often conflicting forms, in order to understand and explain the character of the nation and its peoples. This section examines two important historical controversies that were rooted in the rural South but which seemed to shed light on the most pressing social, political, and cultural issues of 1920s America: the evolution debate that erupted in a small Tennessee town in 1925, and the debates about the "blues," the music that southern black performers popularized when they migrated to northern cities during and after World War I. In both cases, the roots of southern culture provided the subject for Americans to argue over the modern nation's identity and destiny.

⌇ OF WHAT VALUE IS EVOLUTION? THE SCOPES TRIAL AND 1920s AMERICAN CULTURE

In May 1925, a group of enterprising men in Dayton, Tennessee, a small hill-town between Chattanooga and Knoxville, read that the American Civil Liberties Union was searching for a "test case" to challenge the constitutionality of a recently passed Tennessee statute, which made it a misdemeanor criminal offense to teach Darwinian evolution in that state's public schools. Dayton's boosters were less concerned about the effects of exposing students to Darwinism than they were eager to put their town in the limelight of publicity. The well-rehearsed arrest and trial of John T. Scopes — an amiable twenty-four-year-old who was filling in for the usual biology teacher at the local high school — got them what they wanted. In July 1925, reporters and writers from across the United States and Europe and a number of the nation's leading scientists and lawyers briefly occupied the town for the trial.

The legal issue was whether Scopes had taught evolution (he admitted that he had). Newspapers heralded it as the "Scopes Monkey Trial," presuming that it would answer a question unrelated to the defendant's guilt or innocence: whether human beings were descended from apes, as Charles Darwin had claimed, or whether they were the special creation of the Christian God, as most Americans agreed the book of Genesis in the King James Bible described. The lead defense attorney, Clarence Darrow, was the nation's most famous trial lawyer, a fearless defender of unpopular radicals, and a defiant agnostic. The assisting prosecutor was the

"Great Commoner," William Jennings Bryan, three times the unsuccessful Democratic Party presidential nominee. After the war, he was a leading anti-evolutionist, defending the American majority's opinion that "man" was the object of God's original design. The jury convicted Scopes as expected; the Tennessee Supreme Court then overturned the conviction on a technicality.

Designed as a publicity stunt, the trial was both a symptom and a product of the growing presence and power of popular culture in the 1920s. Newsreel footage was made for distribution in movie houses; the new technology of radio broadcast the trial. The event's pitting of modern science against the backwardness of rural American life was manufactured and consumed as a national (and even nationalizing) event and entertainment. But the picture produced was not a one-dimensional defense of the unbiased and progressive methods of science. Alternative images and voices also issued from Dayton. Together these contending views demonstrated that "man's" origin or nature was never a narrowly religious or scientific matter, but one central to the dominant social issues of the day, from anti-immigration laws to the charged discourse on the benefits and dangers of "civilization" to the white race.

A Civic Biology Presented in Problems (1914)
GEORGE WILLIAM HUNTER

Many Progressives believed that science provided a set of tools and a new language that could harmonize the nation's warring interests—labor and capital; native-born and foreign-born; city dwellers and rural folk; white and nonwhite; rich, middle-class, and working-class. The key element was the scientific method of inductive reasoning: general conclusions were to be reached only after the observer had impartially considered the data and then thoroughly tested his hypotheses through experimentation and experience. Applying such an approach to the physical universe seemed straightforward enough, but many people believed that science could and should be applied to the political problems of the day. Science, they presumed, provided resolutions that only the unreasonable, self-interested, or superstitious could object to. A Civic Biology Presented in Problems— *the textbook that Scopes actually taught—was written by George William Hunter, a high school biology teacher. At the time of the crime,* A Civic Biology *actually was state-approved for use in all Tennessee public high schools; it also was the most widely taught biology text in the United States. Like the Scopes trial, Hunter's textbook is a revealing record of Progressive hopes for mass education in science and scientific problem solving. In the following passages from* A Civic Biology, *Hunter explains the aims of his textbook and why studying biology is "vital" to American youth.*

PROBLEMS TO CONSIDER

1. Why was Hunter's plan of study "presented in problems"?
2. Why was this book called *A Civic Biology*? According to the author, what is the relation of science to democratic political institutions and practices? What lessons from biology create better citizens?

FOREWORD TO TEACHERS

A course in biology given to beginners in the secondary school should have certain aims. These aims must be determined to a degree, first, by the capabilities of the pupils, second, by their native interests, and, third, by the environment of the pupils.

The boy or girl of average ability upon admission to the secondary school is not a thinking individual. The training given up to this time, with but rare exceptions, has been in the forming of simple concepts. These concepts have been reached didactically and empirically. Drill and memory work have been the pedagogic vehicles. . . . The first science of the secondary school, elementary biology, should be primarily the vehicle by which the child is taught to solve problems and to think straight in so doing. No other subject is more capable of logical development. No subject is more vital because of its relation to the vital things in the life of the child. A series of experiments and demonstrations, discussed and applied as definite concrete problems which have arisen within the child's horizon, will develop power in thinking more surely than any other subject in the first year of the secondary school.

But in our eagerness to develop the power of logical thinking we must not lose sight of the previous training of our pupil. Up to this time the method of induction, that handmaiden of logical thought, has been almost unknown. Concepts have been formed deductively by a series of comparisons. All concepts have been handed down by the authority of the teacher or the text; the inductive search for the unknown is as yet a closed book. It is unwise, then, to directly introduce the pupil to the method of induction with a series of printed directions which, though definite in the mind of the teacher because of his wider horizon, mean little or nothing as a definite problem to the pupil. The child must be brought to the appreciation of the problem through the deductive method, by a comparison of the future problem with some definite concrete experience within his own field of vision. Then by the inductive experiment, still led by a series of oral questions, he comes to the real end of the experiment, the conclusion, with the true spirit of the investigator. The result is tested in the light of past experiment and a generalization is formed which means something to the pupil. . . .

As would be expected, boys have different biological interests from girls, and children in rural schools wish to study different topics from those in congested districts in large communities. The time has come when we must frankly recognize these interests and adapt the content of our courses in biology to interpret the *immediate* world of the pupil.

With this end in view the following pages have been written. This book shows boys and girls living in an urban community how they may best live within their own environment and how they may cooperate with the civic authorities for the betterment of their environment. A logical course is built up around the topics which appeal to the average normal boy or girl, topics given in a logical sequence so as to work out the solution of problems bearing on the ultimate problem of the entire course, that of preparation for citizenship in the largest sense. . . .

The author believes that he has made a selection of the topics most vital in a well-rounded course in elementary biology directed toward civic betterment. The physiological functions of plants and animals, the hygiene of the individual within the community, conservation and the betterment of existing plant and animal products, the big underlying biological concepts on which society is built, have all been used to the end that the pupil will become a better, stronger and more unselfish citizen. . . .

Biology in its Relation to Society. — Again, the study of biology should be part of the education of every boy and girl, because society itself is founded upon the principles which biology teaches. Plants and animals are living things, taking what they can from their surroundings;

they enter into competition with one another, and those which are the best fitted for life outstrip the others. Animals and plants tend to vary each from its nearest relative in all details of structure. The strong may thus hand down to their offspring the characteristics which make them the winners. Health and strength of body and mind are factors which tell in winning.

Man has made use of this message of nature, and has developed improved breeds of horses, cattle, and other domestic animals. Plant breeders have likewise selected the plants or seeds that have varied toward better plants, and thus have stocked the earth with hardier and more fruitful domesticated plants. Man's dominion over the living things of the earth is tremendous. This is due to his understanding the principles which underlie the science of biology.

Finally the study of biology ought to make us better men and women by teaching us that unselfishness exists in the natural world as well as among the highest members of society. Animals, lowly and complex, sacrifice their comfort and their very lives for their young. In the insect communities the welfare of the individual is given up for the best interests of the community. The law of mutual give and take, of sacrifice for the common good, is seen everywhere. This should teach us, as we come to take our places in society, to be willing to give up our individual pleasure or selfish gain for the good of the community in which we live. Thus the application of biological principles will benefit society.

George William Hunter, *A Civic Biology Presented in Problems* (New York: American Book Co., 1914), 7–11, 18.

❧

Mr. [William Jennings] Bryan's Last Speech (1925)

William Jennings Bryan's attack on evolutionism and his defense of Genesis illustrate the familiar conflicts of the 1910s and 1920s: the clash between rural and metropolitan values in an urbanizing corporate society; the bold confidence in science and the outrages underwritten by technologies in the Great War; modernist Christians' willingness to accommodate scientific and medical authority and antimodern fundamentalists' defending folkways and customs; majoritarian politics and individual freedom. Present throughout this discussion, too, was a debate about the nature of civilization and of civilized men and women. Central to Bryan's conception of a "civilized man" was his view of and respect for Jesus Christ as the "prince of peace." All of these issues can be detected in the address Bryan prepared as a closing argument to the jury in the Scopes trial. He never delivered it because the case went to the jury without argument; he revised it for publication immediately before he died, just five days after the jury returned a verdict against Scopes.

PROBLEMS TO CONSIDER

1. What is a "civilized" society, according to Bryan? Why does the teaching of evolution threaten civilization?
2. Aside from the question of "truth," what did Bryan consider to be the main conflict between evolutionary science and Christian religion? On what major points did Bryan and Hunter disagree?

Christianity welcomes truth from whatever source it comes, and is not afraid that any real truth from any source can interfere with the divine truth that comes by inspiration from God Himself. It is not scientific truth to which Christians object, for true science is classified knowledge, and nothing therefore can be scientific unless it is true.

Evolution is not truth; it is merely an hypothesis—it is millions of guesses strung together. It had not been proven in the days of Darwin; he expressed astonishment that with two or three million species it had been impossible to trace any species to any other species. . . . But of what value is evolution if it cannot explain the origin of species? . . .

There is no more reason to believe that man descended from some inferior animal than there is to believe that a stately mansion has descended from a small cottage. Resemblances are not proof—they simply put us on inquiry. . . . The inability of science to trace any one of the millions of species to another species, outweighs all the resemblances upon which evolutionists rely to establish man's blood relationship with the brutes.

But while the wisest scientists cannot prove a pushing power, such as evolution is supposed to be, there is a *lifting* power that any child can understand. The plant lifts the mineral up into a higher world, and the animal lifts the plant up into a world still higher. So, it has been reasoned by analogy, man rises, not by a power within him, but only when drawn upward by a higher power. There is a spiritual gravitation that draws all souls toward heaven, just as surely as there is a physical force that draws all matter on the surface of the earth towards the earth's center. Christ is our drawing power. . . .

It must be remembered that the law under consideration in this case does not prohibit the teaching of evolution up to the line that separates man from the lower forms of animal life. The law might well have gone farther than it does and prohibit the teaching of evolution in lower forms of life; the law is a very conservative statement of the people's opposition to an anti-Biblical hypothesis.

The defendant was not content to teach what the law permitted; he, for reasons of his own, persisted in teaching that which was forbidden for reasons entirely satisfactory to the law-makers. . . .

Darwin reveals the barbarous sentiment that runs through evolution and dwarfs the moral nature of those who become obsessed with it. . . . Darwin speaks with approval of the savage custom of eliminating the weak so that only the strong will survive and complains that "we civilized men do our utmost to check the process of elimination." How inhuman such a doctrine as this! He thinks it injurious to "build asylums for the imbecile, the maimed, and the sick," or to care for the poor. Even the medical men come in for criticism because they "exert their utmost skill to save the life of everyone to the last moment." And then note his hostility to *vaccination* because it has "preserved thousands who, from a weak constitution would, but for vaccination, have succumbed to smallpox"! All of the sympathetic activities of civilized society are condemned because they enable "the weak members to propagate their kind." Then he drags mankind down to the level of the brute and compares the freedom given to man unfavorably with the restraint that we put on barnyard beasts. . . .

Could any doctrine be more destructive of civilization? And what a commentary on evolution! He wants us to believe that evolution develops a human sympathy that finally becomes so tender that it repudiates the law that created it and thus invites a return to a level where the extinguishing of pity and sympathy will permit the brutal instincts to again do their progressive (?) work. . . .

Can any Christian remain indifferent? Science needs religion to direct its energies and to inspire with lofty purpose those who employ the forces that are unloosed by science. Evolution is at war with religion because religion is supernatural; it is, therefore, the relentless foe of Christianity, which is a revealed religion.

Let us, then, hear the conclusion of the whole matter. Science is a magnificent material force, but it is not a teacher of morals. It can perfect machinery, but it adds no moral restraints to protect society from the misuse of the machine. It can also build gigantic intellectual ships, but it constructs no moral rudders for the control of storm-tossed human vessels. It not only fails to supply the spiritual element needed but some of its unproven hypotheses rob the ship of its *compass* and thus endanger its cargo.

In war, science has proven itself an evil genius; it has made war more terrible than it ever was before. Man used to be content to slaughter his fellowmen on a single plain — the earth's surface. Science has taught him to go down into the water and shoot up from below, and to go up into the clouds and shoot down from above, thus making the battlefield three times as bloody as it was before; but science does *not* teach brotherly

love. Science has made war so hellish that civilization was about to commit suicide. . . . If civilization is to be saved from the wreckage threatened by intelligence not consecrated by love, it must be saved by the moral code of the meek and lowly Nazarene. His teachings, and His teachings alone, can solve the problems that vex the heart and perplex the world. . . .

Again force and love meet face to face, and the question, "What shall I do with Jesus?" must be answered. A bloody, brutal doctrine — Evolution — demands, as the rabble did nineteen hundred years ago, that He be crucified. . . .

_____

"Mr. [William Jennings] Bryan's Last Speech," in William Jennings Bryan and Mary Baird Bryan, *The Memoirs of William Jennings Bryan* (Philadelphia: United Publishers, 1925), 532–34, 550–51, 554–55.

ᴥ

The New Decalogue of Science (1923)
ALBERT EDWARD WIGGAM

To make his case against evolution, Bryan quoted at length from Albert Edward Wiggam's The New Decalogue of Science. *Wiggam was a prominent evolutionist and eugenicist. Eugenicists believed that genetic makeup at birth determines the kind of physical and moral being that an individual can become. They also believed that the individual is part of a genetic race; each race possesses genetic character traits, and no amount of education can alter the predetermined pattern. Eugenicists favored the white races. Nordics, they said, were natural rulers who built modern civilization; the colored races of Africa and Asia were primitives. As reformers, supporters of eugenics encouraged the state to regulate the biological design of the nation's citizenry by halting the immigration of people they regarded as inferior racial stock. Their lasting achievement was the federal Johnson-Reed Immigration Act of 1924, which established a quota system for determining who could enter the United States. The limits were set at 2 percent of the European nationalities recorded in the 1890 census — the accounting immediately prior to the massive immigrations from eastern and southern Europe and Russia. Wiggam was an important popularizer of these ideas.*

PROBLEMS TO CONSIDER

1. What made Wiggam's ideas useful to Bryan's argument against the teaching of evolution?
2. How did Wiggam defend evolution as a moral system and condemn his antievolutionist adversaries?

The first warning which biology gives to statesmanship is that the advanced races of mankind are going backward; that the civilized races of the world are, biologically, plunging downward; that civilization, as you have so far administered it, is self-destructive; that civilization always destroys the man that builds it; that your vast efforts to improve man's lot instead of improving man are hastening the hour of his destruction; that the brain of man is not growing; that man as a breed of organic beings is not advancing; that microbial diseases are chiefly the by-products of our civilizations; that these microbial diseases are apparently decreasing, while at the same time man's incapacity to resist them is probably increasing; that the great physiological diseases of man's body—heart disease, Bright's disease, diabetes, cancer, degenerative diseases of the arteries, liver and central organs— are increasing; that the functional neuroses, the diseases that affect man's mind and behavior—neurasthenia, hysteria, epilepsy, insanity and the multi-form minor mental and nervous derangements of function—are probably all increasing; that weaklings, paupers, hoboes and imbeciles are increasing; that leadership and genius—great men and first-class workmen— are decreasing. . . .

I am not at this moment concerned primarily with whether our intelligence is high or low but with its prospective, indeed by your present methods, its certain decline. The danger to this country is not from its seventy or eighty or ninety million who may have little or no brains, but from its five or ten millions who have. It may be that to-morrow some necromancy of education or some ectoplasmic injection will transform our twenty or thirty or forty per cent. of social and political dunces into geniuses. But pending that possibility, the psychologist has spread here before you the main materials of democracy. If our estimate of these materials be too high or too low it does not greatly matter.

No nation was ever overthrown by its imbeciles. Nature abhors a vacuum and for that reason weeds out the heads of fools. The significant thing is that the fools are increasing and those responsible for their welfare are decreasing.

For you defy nature with your civilization. As [American psychologist G.] Stanley Hall has said: "Man has not yet demonstrated that he can remain permanently civilized." Or as Sir E. Ray Lankester, the British biologist, has warned you, you have taken evolution out of the mighty hand of nature into your own feeble one. And unless you have the courage and intelligence to go on and complete the task, nature will periodically hurl you back into savagery—the red sea of natural selection—where as he says, she "will wreak upon you the vengeance which she always has in store for the half-hearted meddler in great affairs." Man dare not be a half-hearted meddler in this great affair of his own evolution. He has egotistically taken it into his own hands, and yet so far has used scarcely more intelligence than would a babe who had had placed in his tiny fingers the cosmic engine that guides the stars.

Evolution is a bloody business, but civilization tries to make it a pink tea. Barbarism is the only process by which man has ever organically progressed, and civilization is the only process by which he has ever organically declined. Civilization is the most dangerous enterprise upon which man ever set out. For when you take man out of the bloody, brutal but beneficent hand of natural selection you place him at once in the soft, perfumed, daintily gloved but far more dangerous hand of artificial selection. And, unless you call science to your aid and make this artificial selection as efficient as the rude methods of nature, you bungle the whole task. And you are doing this on a colossal scale in industrial America.

Albert Edward Wiggam, *The New Decalogue of Science* (Indianapolis: Bobbs-Merrill, 1923), 25–26, 32–34.

✍

"The Battle Hymn of Tennessee" (1925)

MRS. E. P. BLAIR

"He's a Variety of the 'Species'!" (1925)

What kind of men and women opposed the teaching of evolution? Reflecting on the verdict, the journalist H. L. Mencken cited the "simian imbecility" of the anti-evolution law and warned his sophisticated national readership to look out: "Neanderthal man is organizing in these forlorn backwaters of the land, led by a fanatic, rid of sense and devoid of conscience." Although such unflattering images have persisted in popular culture, the organized anti-evolution cause in Tennessee actually was led by educated, middle-class people, a disproportionate number of whom were women. The following sources, published at the time of the trial in two of Tennessee's leading daily newspapers, indicate how the anti-evolutionists defined themselves as well as their enemies. Mrs. E. P. Blair, author of the poem published by the Nashville Tennessean *newspaper, was a leader in the state's anti-evolution movement. The cartoon appeared on the front page of the* Memphis Commercial Appeal, *which used its news reporters, editorial writers, and staff cartoonist to carry the standard of anti-evolutionism.*

PROBLEMS TO CONSIDER

1. Does the poem help us understand why the anti-evolution cause appealed to so many women like Blair?
2. How did the images of men in the cartoon define the menace of evolution and defend the credentials of anti-evolutionists? Do these two sources suggest there was general agreement on the gender politics of anti-evolution?

"THE BATTLE HYMN OF TENNESSEE"

Between Truth and Error, Right and Wrong,
   The fight is on.
For country, God, and mother's song
   It must be won!
Go sound the alarm, go gather your forces,
   Oh Tennessee!
Land of the pioneer, home of the volunteer,
   The daring, the free. . . .

Now Error, the monster, calls forth her cohorts
   From sea to sea.
They come from earth's four corners down
   To Tennessee.
They challenge your power to rule your own
   Your rights deny.
They scoff at you, ridicule you,
   Your laws defy.

Their forces are clad in garments great,
   Of science and law.
With the camouflage cloak of knowledge
   To hide their claw.
Go look at the havoc and heartache of nations
   Where they have passed through.
Their blasting breath has meant instant death
   To the noble and true.

God made this His battleground, for you've
   Been wise and true.
Earth's unborn, its children, mothers and nations
   Are calling to you.
So Tennessee, light your candle of wisdom!
   Your altar of prayer!
And the God of Truth fire and inspire you
   To do and to dare!

Mrs. E. P. Blair, "The Battle Hymn of Tennessee," *Nashville Tennessean,* June 29, 1925, 2.

"He's a Variety of the 'Species'!" *Memphis Commercial Appeal*, July 9, 1925.

(Courtesy of *The Commercial Appeal*, Memphis, Tennessee.)

"The John T. Scopes Trial" (1925)
CARLOS B. McAFEE (CARSON J. ROBISON)

Just four months after the end of the Scopes trial, Nashville's WSM radio station—itself only a year old—broadcast the Grand Ole Opry country music show for the first time. Americans already owned more than 2 million radios, and many were able to tune in to this signal cultural event. With such changes occurring at the time, it should come as no surprise that on the very day the Scopes trial began, the singer Vernon Dalhart teamed up with the songwriter Carson J. Robison (using the pseudonym Carlos B. McAfee) to record the following "hillbilly" song in a New York City studio. Just one of many written to exploit the trial's publicity, McAfee's song found a ready audience in the South and wherever William Jennings Bryan was admired. Its popularity reflected two important social and cultural changes in the 1920s and afterward: the growing audience of radio listeners and the expanding, highly mobile, and increasingly national audience for country, hillbilly, and cowboy songs.

PROBLEMS TO CONSIDER

1. What is the conflict described here? What does the song (and its popularity) suggest about the power of popular culture to shape or reflect an understanding of the trial?
2. Compare this song to the sentiments in "The Battle Hymn of Tennessee" and the newspaper cartoon. Do they discredit the critics of anti-evolution in similar or different ways?

All the folks in Tennessee are as faithful as
    can be,
And they know the Bible teaches what is right;
They believe in God above and his great
    undying love,
And they know they are protected by his might.

Then to Dayton came a man with his new
    ideas so grand
And he said, "We came from monkeys long
    ago";
But in teaching his belief Mister Scopes found
    only grief,
For they would not let their old religion go.

Chorus:
You may find a new belief, it will only bring you
    grief,
For a house that's built on sand will surely fall;
And wherever you may turn there's a lesson you
    will learn

That the old religion's better after all.

Then the folks throughout the land saw his
    house was built on sand,
And they said, "We will not listen anymore";
So they told him he was wrong and it wasn't
    very long,
Till he found that he was barred from ev'ry
    door.

Oh, you must not doubt the word that is
    written by the Lord,
For if you do your house will surely fall;
And Mister Scopes will learn wherever he may
    turn,
That the old religion's better after all.
(Chorus)

———

Vernon Dalhart, "The John T. Scopes Trial" (1925), lyrics transcribed from Columbia Phonograph Co. recording 15037-D (140680), guitar and violin by Carlos B. McAfee, sung by Vernon Dalhart.

ᴥ WILD WOMEN: THE BLUES IN 1920s AMERICA

Between 1916 and 1921, more than half a million African Americans moved out of the Deep South and into the industrial centers of the Northeast and Midwest. Most were responding to the dire labor shortage created by diminished foreign immigration and the escalating demand for workers in the booming war economy. In addition, many were hoping to escape the degrading working and living conditions in the South. This first Great Migration changed the demographic face of an already multicultural and divided urban America. It also fundamentally altered and shaped American culture as those migrants brought the blues with them. This peculiar rural and southern form of vocal music had its roots in the call-and-response songs of antebellum slavery, but by 1900 the blues was the folk music of the rural black southern working class. The blues also was a commercial entertainment form, produced by professionals performing for segregated audiences of African Americans across the rural South. By 1920, the blues artists who moved north had linked up with the urban jazz performers who had ignited the dance craze among urban middle- and upper-class whites.

The original demand for blues "race records" came from African Americans, many of them new to northern and southern cities. But white urban Americans also passionately consumed blues records and performances. The most celebrated jazz orchestras and the most famous blues singers were more likely to be heard by whites-only audiences. For such fans, tramping to nightclubs in Harlem or Chicago to hear the blues was an act of cultural resistance, a way of demonstrating their sense of adventure, disregard for respectability, youthful exuberance, and defiance of prohibition. The African American writer James Weldon Johnson recalled watching white audiences trying to "throw off the crusts and layers of inhibitions laid on by sophisticated civilization" and to "recapture a state of primitive joy in life and living" by "doing their best to be colored."

The artists whose voices introduced white audiences to "primitive joy" were usually working-class African American women such as Ma Rainey, Bessie Smith, Victoria Spivey, and Ethel Waters. These women were able to foment a rebellion of their own by voicing an alternative perspective on the racial, gender, and class expectations of whites and blacks alike. In doing so, they were part of the larger cultural ferment stimulated by the rural-to-urban migrations of the war era. The dramatic and (to some) unsettling new voices shouting for attention and demanding the authority of self-definition were unmistakable in the phonograph recordings of early blues performers.

"When Will I Get to Be Called a Man?" (1928)

BIG BILL BROONZY

"Wild Women Don't Have the Blues" (1924)

IDA COX

Blues singers often sang of what it meant to be a black man or black woman in a world dominated by whites, as can be seen in the following verses. The first is by the early blues performer and writer "Big Bill" Broonzy. Born in Mississippi, a World War I veteran, Broonzy lived in Chicago in the 1920s, working in menial day jobs while also recording and performing his blues. The second is by the famous blueswoman Ida Cox. Born in Georgia in 1896, Cox ran away as a child to join a traveling minstrel show. In 1923 she signed a recording contract with Paramount and played the part of the independent, sexually commanding blueswoman to the max, with songs like "One Hour Mama" ("I want a slow and easy man, He needn't ever take the lead"). "Wild Women Don't Have the Blues" is her best-known song.

PROBLEMS TO CONSIDER

1. What do these singers suggest about the difficulties that black women and men faced: Were they the same or different? What different strategies did they use to earn their identity as "woman" or "man"?
2. What would sophisticated white audiences in the 1920s have heard in these songs? Would they have regarded these songs as reflections on the human condition in general, or on the condition of blacks in the United States?

"WHEN WILL I GET TO BE CALLED
A MAN?"

When I was born in the world, this is what
    happened to me:
I was never called a man and now I'm fifty-three

I wonder when will I be called a man
Or do I have to wait 'till I get ninety-three?

When Uncle Sam called me I knew I would be
    called the real McCoy
But when I got in the army they called me
    soldier boy

I wonder when will I be called a man
Or do I have to wait 'till I get ninety-three?

When I got back from overseas, that night we
    had a ball
I met the boss the next day, he told me "Boy get
    you some overall"

I wonder when will I be called a man
Or do I have to wait 'till I get ninety-three?

I worked on a levee camp and a chain gang too
A black man is a boy to a white, don't care what
    he can do

I wonder when will I be called a man
Or do I have to wait 'till I get ninety-three?

They said I was undereducated, my clothes was
    dirty and torn
Now I got a little education, but I'm a boy right
    on

I wonder when will I be called a man
Or do I have to wait 'till I get ninety-three?

Big Bill Broonzy, "When Will I Get to Be Called a Man?"
lyrics printed in Yannick Bruynoghe, *Big Bill Blues: William
Broonzy's Story* (New York: Oak Publications, 1964), 70.

"WILD WOMEN DON'T HAVE THE BLUES"

I hear these women raving 'bout their monkey
  men
About their trifling husbands and their no good
  friends
These poor women sit around all day and moan
Wondering why their wandering papas don't
  come home
But wild women don't worry, wild women don't
  have no blues

Now when you've got a man, don't never be on
  the square
'Cause if you do he'll have a woman everywhere
I never was known to treat no one man right
I keep 'em working hard both day and night
'Cause wild women don't worry, wild women
  don't have their blues

I've got a disposition and a way of my own
When my man starts kicking I let him find
  another home
I get full of good liquor, walk the streets all night
Go home and put my man out if he don't act
  right
Wild women don't worry, wild women don't
  have their blues

You never get nothing by being an angel child
You better change your ways and get real wild
I wanna tell you something, I wouldn't tell you
  a lie
Wild women are the only kind that really get by
'Cause wild women don't worry, wild women
  don't have their blues

<hr>

Ida Cox, "Wild Women Don't Have the Blues," transcribed
from *Ida Cox Complete Recorded Works 1923–1938, Volume 2:
c. March 1924 to April 1925*, Document Records DOCD-
5323. Written by Ida Cox, 1924.

ᴈ

"Mistreatin' Daddy" (DATE UNKNOWN)

BESSIE SMITH

Blues audiences seemed especially fond of numbers that fantasized about women violently evening the score with abusive men. The newspaper ads for such songs, which appeared in urban black weeklies such as the Chicago Defender *and the* Pittsburgh Courier, *were among the most sensational ads used to sell records. Okeh, Paramount, and Columbia, the major "race record" labels, were owned by white businessmen who hired white advertising firms to write the ads. Bessie Smith's rendition of "Mistreatin' Daddy" was a popular version of this genre.*

PROBLEMS TO CONSIDER

1. Consider how this song uses violence to establish the singer's identity. Compare it to how Cox used sexual agency in "Wild Women." Were they songs of protest?
2. Black (and sometimes white) men often wrote the songs that black blueswomen performed. Which matters more in determining a song's meaning: who wrote it, who sang it, or who was listening to it?

Daddy, can't you plainly see, I'm through
    with you as I can be
Don't want you hangin' around, because you
    threw me down
When you made me go away, then I knew you'd
    want me back someday,
Like old "Billy" Shakespeare I don't never re-
    peat, that is all I've got to say

Mistreatin' daddy, mistreatin' mama all the time
(Just because she would let you)
Mistreatin' daddy, mama's drawed a danger line
(If you cross it, I'll get you)

If you see me sittin' on another daddy's knee
Don't you interrupt me 'cause I'm mean as I
    can be
I'm like the butcher right down the street,
I could chop you all to pieces like you was a
    chunk of meat

Mistreatin' daddy, you used to knock your
    mama down
(Then you knew I fell for you)
Had me so nervous, I would start to duckin'
    around
(Yes! Ev'ry time I saw you)
But now I've got you off my mind,
and found another daddy who is just my kind,
Mistreatin' daddy, I've got another papa now

Mistreatin' daddy, mistreatin' mama all the time
(Just because she would let you)
Mistreatin' daddy, mama's drawed a danger line
(If you cross it, I'll get you)

If you see me sittin' on another daddy's knee
Don't you interrupt me 'cause I'm mean as can
    be
I've got a temper folks talk about,
I will grab you and I'll very nearly turn you
    wrong side out

Mistreatin' daddy, you used to knock your
    mama down
(Then you knew I fell for you)
Had me so nervous, I would start to duckin'
    around
(Yes! Ev'ry time I saw you)

You nearly caused my heart to break,
And now I'd soon to see you as a rattlesnake,
Mistreatin' daddy I've got another papa now,
And he's mistreatin' me too
Daddy like you used to do

"Mistreatin' Daddy," words and music by Porter Grainger and Bob Ricketts. © 1923 by Bourne Co. Copyright renewed. All rights reserved. International copyright secured. ASCAP.

↝

Toward a Critique of Negro Music (1934)

ALAIN LOCKE

The Harlem Renaissance was the creative enterprise of "the New Negro"—typified by urban, usually college-educated African American men—in the fifteen years after World War I. It took as its starting point an observation that the African American intellectual W. E. B. Du Bois made in 1903: "until the art of the black folk compels recognition they will not be rated as human." But recognition by whom and according to what standards of elite achievement? Such questions had divided African Americans since emancipation. Du Bois encouraged the cultivation of a "Talented Tenth" among black Americans, a cultural vanguard who would compel attention and respect by the force of their talents. Some, especially among the striving middle class, endeavored to assimilate into the dominant white culture by showing their equal mastery of the ideals of "civilization," but

others were suspicious of what they saw as race-based hierarchies of taste and value em-
bedded in those ideas. Determined to speak for a consciously African American identity,
they regarded success on those terms as a surrender to white domination. In light of this
complicated array of aspirations, the blues queens presented thorny problems with their
assertively unfeminine, self-consciously black, blatantly sexual performances and identi-
ties. At the center of the debate was Alain Locke, a Harvard graduate, the first African
American Rhodes Scholar, a professor of philosophy at Howard University, and an influ-
ential figure in channeling the wealth of white patrons to talented black (mostly male)
artists in the 1920s. Locke praised the intrinsic beauty of black spirituals and embraced
the originality of jazz, but he regretted the vulgar popular expression that these musical
forms usually took. He passionately believed that the New Negro would be the vanguard
of cultural excellence and progress in the twentieth century. The "highest intellectual
duty" of any artist, Locke lectured his students and followers, "is the duty to be cultured."

PROBLEMS TO CONSIDER

1. What are the standards of cultural excellence that Locke applied to "Negro music"? Why did he think there had been no "great [Negro] musicians"?
2. What were Locke's objections to popular blues and jazz performers such as Bessie Smith?

I have read nearly all that has been written on the subject [of Negro music], and do not hesitate to rate most of it as platitudinous piffle — repetitious bosh; the pounds of praise being, if anything, more hurtful and damning than the ounces of disparagement. For from the enthusiasts about Negro music comes little else than extravagant superlatives and endless variations on certain half-true commonplaces about our inborn racial musicality, our supposed gift of spontaneous harmony, the uniqueness of our music idioms and the infectious power and glory of our transmuted suffering.

True — or rather half-true as these things undoubtedly are, the fact remains that it does Negro music no constructive service to have them endlessly repeated by dilettante *[uninformed amateur]* enthusiasts, especially without the sound correctives of their complementary truths. The state of Negro music, and especially the state of mind of Negro musicians needs the bitter tonic of criticism more than unctuous praise and the soothing syrups of flattery. While the Negro

musician sleeps on his much-extolled heritage, the commercial musical world, reveling in its prostitution, gets rich by exploiting it popularly, while the serious musical world tries only half-successfully to imitate and develop a fundamentally alien idiom. Nothing of course can stop this but the exhaustion of the vogue upon which it thrives; still the sound progress of our music depends more upon the independent development of its finer and deeper values than upon the curtailing of the popular and spurious output. The real damage of the popular vogue rests in the corruption and misguidance of the few rare talents that might otherwise make heroic and lasting contributions. For their sake and guidance, constructive criticism and discriminating appreciation must raise a standard far above the curbstone values of the market-place and far more exacting than the easy favor of the multitude.

Indeed for the sound promotion of its future, we must turn from the self-satisfying glorification of the past of Negro music to consider for their salutary effect the present short-comings of Negro music and musicians. It is time to realize that though we may be a musical people, we have produced few if any great musicians,—that though we may have evolved a folk music of power and potentiality, it has not yet been integrated into a musical tradition,—that our creativeness and originality on the folk level has not yet been matched on the level of instrumental mastery or that of creative composition,—and that with a few exceptions, the masters of Negro musical idiom so far are not Negro. . . .

These shortcomings . . . are due primarily to external influences. Those Negro musicians who are in vital touch with the folk traditions of Negro music are the very ones who are in commercial slavery to Tin Pan Alley and subject to the corruption and tyranny of the ready cash of our dance halls and the vaudeville stage. On the other hand, our musicians with formal training are divorced from the people and their vital inspiration by the cloister-walls of the conservatory and the taboos of musical respectability. . . .

Indeed the whole field is full of paradoxes, for after all the most original and pioneering creative use of Negro musical idioms still goes to the credit of white composers from Dvorak down to Aaron Copeland, Alden Carpenter, George Gershwin, Paul Whiteman, and Sesana.

What does this mean? Primarily that Negro musicians have not been first to realize the most genuine values of Negro music, and that the Negro audience has not pioneered in the recognition and intelligent appreciation of the same. . . . But lest we charge all of this to outside factors, let us remember that much has also fallen upon our own stony ground of shallow appreciation or been choked by the hostile thorns of a false and blighting academic tradition. No musical idiom that has arisen from the people can flourish entirely cut off from the ground soil of its origin. . . .

I ask the reader's patience with these negative but incontestable statements. Encouragingly enough at certain historical stages this same state of affairs has existed with other musical traditions,—with Russian music before Glinka, with Hungarian music before Liszt and Brahms, and with Bohemian music before Dvorak and Smetana.

However, if we would draw consolation from these parallels, we must remember that it took revolutionary originality and native genius to transform the situation, lift the level and break the path to the main-stream for each of these musical traditions. It is inevitable that this should eventually happen with Negro folk-music for it is not only the most vivid and vital and universally appealing body of folk-music in America, there is little in fact that can compete with it. Yet it is far from being much more as yet than the raw material of a racial or national tradition in music. . . . Mr. W. J. Henderson is right in a recent article, "Why No Great American Music," when he says,—"Where there is no unification of race, as in this country, the folk idiom does not exist except as that of some fraction of the people." He is equally right in saying,—"the potent spell of the Negro spiritual is a deep-rooted, almost desperate grasp of religious belief. It is the song of the Negro soul. It not only interests, but even arouses, the white man because of its innate eloquence," but,—he continues, "the Negro spiritual tells no secret of the wide American soul; it is the creation of black humans crushed under slavery and looking to eternity for their only joy." For the present, this is quite true. But the very remedy that Mr. Henderson prescribes for the creation of a great national music is the same for the proper universalization of the spirituals and other Negro folk-music. What is needed is genius, as he says, and still more genius. That is to say, the same transforming originality that in the instances cited above widened the localisms of Russian, Hungarian and Czech music to a universal language, but in breaking the dialect succeeded in preserving the rare raciness and unique flavor. Certainly the Negro idioms will never become great music nor representative national music over the least common denominators of popular jazz or popular ballads. And perhaps there is more vital originality and power in our secular folk music than even in our religious folk music. It remains for real constructive genius to develop both in the direction which Dvorak clairvoyantly saw.

But [Dvorak's] *New World Symphony* stands there a largely unheeded musical sign-post pointing the correct way to Parnassus, while the main procession has followed the lowly but well-paved jazz road. Not that the jazz-road cannot lead to Parnassus; it can and has,—for the persistent few. But the producers of good jazz still produce far too much bad jazz, and the distinc-tion between them is blurred to all but the most discriminating. Jazz must be definitely rid of its shoddy superficiality and its repetitive vulgar gymnastics. . . . Only true genius and almost consecrated devotion can properly fuse art-music and folk-music. . . . Only rare examples of this have appeared as yet, and there is just as much promise of it in Louis Armstrong's and Ellington's best, perhaps more—than in the la-bored fusions of Carpenter, Gruenberg, Gersh-win and Grofe. . . .

Alain Locke, "Toward a Critique of Negro Music," *Opportunity*, November 1934, 328–31.

ᔢ

The Negro Artist and the Racial Mountain (1926)
LANGSTON HUGHES

The poet, novelist, and essayist Langston Hughes was one of the great figures of the Harlem Renaissance and of American art as a whole in the 1920s and 1930s. He also was among the very few African American artists who embraced the blues and jazz as "true Negro art," integrating it into his own verse.

PROBLEMS TO CONSIDER

1. According to Hughes, why do "respectable" blacks reject expressive arts such as the blues and jazz? What factors make the blues "black" and not "white"?
2. Did Hughes and Locke understand "blackness" and "art" in the same way?

One of the most promising of the young Negro poets said to me once, "I want to be a poet—not a Negro poet," meaning, I believe, "I want to write like a white poet"; meaning subconsciously, "I would like to be a white poet"; meaning behind that, "I would like to be white." And I was sorry the young man said that, for no great poet has ever been afraid of being himself. And I doubted then that, with his desire to run away spiritually from his race, this boy would ever be a great poet. But this is the mountain standing in the way of any true Negro art in America—this urge within the race to-ward whiteness, the desire to pour racial indi-viduality into the mold of American standardi-zation, and to be as little Negro and as much American as possible.

But let us look at the immediate background of this young poet. His family is of what I suppose one would call the Negro middle class: people who are by no means rich yet never uncomfort-able nor hungry—smug, contented, respectable folk, members of the Baptist church. The father goes to work every morning. He is a chief steward at a large white club. The mother sometimes does fancy sewing or supervises parties for the rich families of the town. The children go to a mixed school. In the home they read white papers and magazines. And the mother often says "Don't be like niggers" when the children are bad. A frequent phrase from the father is, "Look how well a white man does things." And so the word white comes to be unconsciously a symbol of all virtues. It holds for the children beauty, morality, and money. The whisper of "I want to be white" runs silently through their minds. This young poet's home is, I believe, a fairly typical home of the colored middle class. One sees immediately how difficult it would be for an artist born in such a home to interest himself in interpreting the beauty of his own people. He is never taught to see that beauty. He is taught rather not to see it, or if he does, to be ashamed of it when it is not according to Caucasian patterns.

For racial culture the home of a self-styled "high-class" Negro has nothing better to offer. Instead there will perhaps be more aping of things white than in a less cultured or less wealthy home. . . . Nordic manners, Nordic faces, Nordic hair, Nordic art (if any), and an Episcopal heaven. A very high mountain indeed for the would-be racial artist to climb in order to discover himself and his people.

But then there are the low-down folks, the so-called common element, and they are the majority — may the Lord be praised! The people who have their hip of gin on Saturday nights and are not too important to themselves or the community, or too well fed, or too learned to watch the lazy world go round. They live on Seventh Street in Washington or State Street in Chicago and they do not particularly care whether they are like white folks or anybody else. Their joy runs, bang! into ecstasy. Their religion soars to a shout. Work maybe a little today, rest a little tomorrow. Play awhile. Sing awhile. O, let's dance! These common people are not afraid of spirituals, as for a long time their more intellectual brethren were, and jazz is their child. They furnish a wealth of colorful, distinctive material for any artist because they still hold their own individuality in the face of American

standardizations. And perhaps these common people will give to the world its truly great Negro artist, the one who is not afraid to be himself. Whereas the better-class Negro would tell the artist what to do, the people at least let him alone when he does appear. And they are not ashamed of him — if they know he exists at all. And they accept what beauty is their own without question.

Certainly there is, for the American Negro artist who can escape the restrictions the more advanced among his own group would put upon him, a great field of unused material ready for his art. . . . And when he chooses to touch on the relations between Negroes and whites in this country with their innumerable overtones and undertones surely, . . . there is an inexhaustible supply of themes at hand. To these the Negro artist can give his racial individuality, his heritage of rhythm and warmth, and his incongruous humor that so often, as in the Blues, becomes ironic laughter mixed with tears. But let us look again at the mountain.

A prominent Negro clubwoman in Philadelphia paid eleven dollars to hear Raquel Meller sing Andalusian popular songs. But she told me a few weeks before she would not think of going to hear "that woman," Clara Smith, a great black artist, sing Negro folksongs. . . .

The Negro artist works against an undertow of sharp criticism and misunderstanding from his own group and unintentional bribes from the whites. "Oh, be respectable, write about nice people, show how good we are," say the Negroes. "Be stereotyped, don't go too far, don't shatter our illusions about you, don't amuse us too seriously. We will pay you," say the whites. . . .

Most of my own poems are racial in theme and treatment, derived from the life I know. In many of them I try to grasp and hold some of the meanings and rhythms of jazz. I am as sincere as I know how to be in these poems and yet after every reading I answer questions like these from my own people: Do you think Negroes should always write about Negroes? I wish you wouldn't read some of your poems to white folks.

How do you find anything interesting in a place like a cabaret? Why do you write about black people? You aren't black. What makes you do so many jazz poems?

But jazz to me is one of the inherent expressions of Negro life in America; the eternal tom-tom beating in the Negro soul—the tom-tom of revolt against weariness in a white world, a world of subway trains, and work, work, work; the tom-tom of joy and laughter, and pain swallowed in a smile. Yet the Philadelphia club-woman is ashamed to say that her race created it and she does not like me to write about it. The old subconscious "white is best" runs through her mind. . . . But, to my mind, it is the duty of the younger Negro artist, if he accepts any duties at all from outsiders, to change through the force of his art that old whispering "I want to be white," hidden in the aspirations of his people, to "Why should I want to be white? I am a Negro—and beautiful!" . . .

Let the blare of Negro jazz bands and the bellowing voice of Bessie Smith singing Blues penetrate the closed ears of the colored near-intellectuals until they listen and perhaps understand. Let Paul Robeson singing "Water Boy," and Rudolph Fisher writing about the streets of Harlem, and Jean Toomer holding the heart of Georgia in his hands, and Aaron Douglas drawing strange black fantasies cause the smug Negro middle class to turn from their white, respectable, ordinary books and papers to catch a glimmer of their own beauty. We younger Negro artists who create now intend to express our individual dark-skinned selves without fear or shame. If white people are pleased we are glad. If they are not, it doesn't matter. We know we are beautiful. And ugly too. The tom-tom cries and the tom-tom laughs. If colored people are pleased we are glad. If they are not, their displeasure doesn't matter either. We build our temples for tomorrow, strong as we know how, and we stand on top of the mountain, free within ourselves.

———
Langston Hughes, "The Negro Artist and the Racial Mountain," *The Nation*, June 23, 1926, 692–94.

ᴧ

ᴧ *The Most Advertised Athlete in the Game: Babe Ruth and Baseball in the 1920s* ᴧ

Professional baseball was reborn in the 1920s as the all-American sport of clean living and keen competition. In the 1910s, even those who knew nothing about the sport knew that baseball was not a wholesome, respectable leisure-time activity. In addition to the usual game-time action of spitballs, beaned batters, and brawls, players' fondness for saloons, brothels, and gambling underscored the rough, antidomestic origins of the sport in the urban working-class male culture of the nineteenth century. By the time of World War I, though, baseball's owners were refurbishing the sport in ways comparable to the Progressive attacks on dance halls. They were building new parks, superintending their players' behavior, and encouraging the fiction that playing the game renewed the nation's lost pastoral past. Attendance was on the rise when members of the Chicago White Sox, conspiring with gamblers, threw the 1919 World Series to the Cincinnati Reds. Not even the "Black Sox" scandal, however, could dim the big news in baseball in 1920. George Herman "Babe" Ruth, in his first season after being traded from the Boston Red Sox to the New York Yankees, hit fifty-four home runs—more than anyone had dreamed possible.

The home-run-hitting Ruth became the dominant figure in baseball in the 1920s and America's most famous citizen. He redefined the style of play with his seemingly superhuman ability to knock the ball far beyond the fences. "I swing every time with all the force I have," he explained, and though often striking out, "when I hit the ball, I *hit* it." That prodigious swing made the spectacle of power the most revered element of the game. But Ruth was as famous for his fame as he was for his sports achievements. His well-timed arrival in New York City—the emerging publishing, advertising, publicity, and radio-broadcasting center of the United States—was fortuitous. Ruth's unique body and mind powered his baseball feats, but the new technologies and media of American consumer culture produced his celebrity. His slum origins and the rowdy masculine pleasures that he favored linked Ruth to baseball's unrestrained past. In his hands, though, disorderly behavior had an irresistible, colorful charm when combined with his celebrated love of children, especially boys. Ruth seemed a new kind of man for his day, powerful yet exuberantly boyish—a combination that both confounded and delighted those who watched him. To be sure, Ruth was more than a reflection of his age. Nonetheless, while his careers as athlete and celebrity plot the Progressive renovation and cleansing of baseball, they also indicate the changing cultural boundaries and gender ideals that governed and promoted professional sports in the 1920s.

News Accounts of Babe Ruth's "Misconduct" (1925)

Ruth's initial contract with the Yankees made him one of the better-paid players in professional baseball. It also bound him to "refrain and abstain entirely from the use of intoxicating liquors" and to abide by the team's curfew. Contract or no, Ruth would not be kept from enjoying the masculine pleasures that came through the fruits of his wealth and fame. His undisciplined carousing most famously reached a peak in 1925, when he missed the first part of the season with a dire case of syphilis, which was poetically disguised for public consumption as the "stomach ache heard 'round the world." Once Ruth returned, he was not himself on the field, although his zest for nightlife seemed undiminished. Toward the end of the season, the Yankee organization tried to rein him in.

PROBLEMS TO CONSIDER

1. How did the following accounts explain Ruth's behavior? What did "growing up" have to do with being a man, or a hero?
2. Did the Yankees and the newspaper editorialist comprehend the nature of Ruth's fame?

RUTH FINED $5,000; COSTLY STAR BANNED FOR ACTS OFF FIELD

ST. LOUIS, Aug. 29 (AP).—George Herman (Babe) Ruth, baseball's premier slugger, today was fined $5,000 and suspended indefinitely by Manager Miller Huggins of the Yankees for "general misconduct." Ruth made no comment when Huggins told him to pack up and leave St. Louis for New York. The home-run king checked out of his hotel immediately, ostensibly to follow Huggins's orders.

Later Huggins said Ruth had been penalized for "misconduct off the field." . . .

"Does 'misconduct of[f] the field' mean drinking?" Huggins was asked.

"Of course it means drinking," said Huggins, "and it means a lot of other things besides. There are various kinds of misconduct. Patience has ceased to be a virtue. I have tried to overlook Ruth's behavior for a while, but I have decided to take summary action to bring the big fellow to his senses.

"I am disciplin[in]g him for general misconduct off the ball field, detrimental to the best interests of the club during this present road trip. I am not saying anything about his actions on the ball field.

"Every one knows he has been having an off year and his weak batting has been excused on account of his illness this Spring.

"When he started playing the first of June he was on probation more or less, bound to take care of himself physically and live up to the rules of club discipline.

"He has forgotten all about these restrictions on this trip, hence the fine and suspension."

"Ruth Fined $5,000; Costly Star Banned for Acts Off Field," *New York Times*, August 30, 1925, 1. Copyright © 1925 by The New York Times Co. Reprinted with permission.

JOHNSON UPHOLDS HUGGINS

CHICAGO, Aug. 30 (AP).—President Ban Johnson of the American League is "heartily in accord with the pun[i]shment meted to Babe Ruth by Manager Miller Huggins of the New York Yanks."

"Ruth has the mind of a 15-year-old boy and must be made to understand where he belongs," President Johnson said today. "The American League is no place for a player who dissipates and misbehaves. The matter of disciplining Ruth has been under consideration for some time and I am heartily in accord with Manager Huggins's action.

"For a player receiving $52,000 a year, Ruth ought to have made himself a hero instead of reflecting discredit on himself, his team and the game. He has been on probation to observe training rules, and this he hasn't done. Misconduct, drinking and staying out all night are things that will not be tolerated."

"Johnson Upholds Huggins," *New York Times*, August 31, 1925, 11. Copyright © 1925 by The New York Times Co. Reprinted with permission.

TWO HEROES

On one and the same day "TY" COBB was hailed as First Citizen of Detroit after twenty years of professional baseball in that city, and "BABE" RUTH was fined $5,000 and indefinitely suspended. In the phrase of O. HENRY, "sic rapid transit" the glory of the diamond. On it national heroes are created with more rapidity and louder acclaim than anywhere else in the country, yet how precarious their position, how fickle the popular favor on which they live! The roar of applause in the bleachers turns with incredible ease into howls of disapproval. And hands that one year are waved in greeting to a mighty man of the baseball field, the next will show their thumbs turned down on him. It requires more than skill at the game, more than physical prowess, for one of these heroes to prevent his head being turned by easily won and glamorous success. Where most of them fail is in remaining modest, in properly judging the fleeting nature of their fame, in seeing the necessity of keeping in good bodily trim and of saving something for the rainy days certain to come after the fair weather. But this means that a professional baseball player of the highest eminence ought to have a strong character as well as keen eyes and perfectly coordinate muscles. That, however, as the run of them go, would be asking too much.

"Two Heroes," editorial, *New York Times*, August 31, 1925, 14. Copyright © 1925 by The New York Times Co. Reprinted with permission.

ᴕ

What Draws the Crowds? (1925)

GRANTLAND RICE

One of the new consumer items of the 1910s and 1920s was sports reporting. Newspaper coverage of sporting events had expanded rapidly since the early twentieth century, reflecting the growing taste for vigorous, athletic manhood so admired by middle-class male readers. The New York Daily News, *a tabloid newspaper founded in 1919, assigned a reporter to follow Ruth's antics year-round. The best-known practitioners of the trade developed an aesthetic that is identified today with the Golden Age of sports reporting. Heywood Broun, W. O. "Bill" McGeehan (author of the "stomach ache" deceit), Grantland Rice, and others working for the leading city papers did not describe in spare tones what happened in sporting events so much as shape them into highly literate narratives of masculine contest and display. Ruth was tailor-made for such reporting, according to Grantland Rice, who compared him in the following article with the great bare-knuckle prize fighter John L. Sullivan.*

PROBLEMS TO CONSIDER

1. How did Rice explain Ruth's "appeal to the millions"? Why did Ruth stand above other men of comparable talents? What advantages did Ruth enjoy because of his boyishness?
2. Rice placed Ruth in two categories: "skilled artisans" and "dramatists of high degree." Were these classifications compatible or at odds with each other?

W̱ho have been the two greatest drawing cards, the two most popular figures in the history of sport? . . .

For drawing-card value and personal appeal the two names that head the cast must be John L. Sullivan and Babe Ruth. Their glory began in Boston. John L. was born there and Babe Ruth began his major league career in the same city.

The study of crowd-drawing psychology is interesting. Sullivan and Ruth, great in their respective lines, did not appeal to the millions for this reason alone. They live, in action or in memory, as something more than great competitors. Each had an appeal to great multitudes far beyond his abilities with fist or bat. . . .

What are the attributes that made these two men the greatest drawing cards ever known to sport?

Both were big, bluff, boisterous or in a fashion roistering types. Neither was the world's strictest adherer to training or discipline. The language of neither was ever intended for the fashionable chit-chat of a ballroom. They will be remembered as given to straight talk, without compromise or diplomacy. They will both be remembered as models in the raw, rather than as smooth and polished specimens. Neither made any attempt to conceal rough edges, to cover up such edges with a cloak of any polite sort.

But their names have always carried a thrill, dating back to the time that each came to his glory.

In the first they were both, at their heights, Apostles of the Punch. They were wallopers—each a record maker of prodigious punching power—and the multitudes have always esteemed the roar or thud of the wallop as the sweetest of all melodies. . . .

Both John L. and Ruth violated all the common-sense rules of economy and thrift, and this also added a few sprigs to their laurel wreaths, possibly as being further proof that money to them was unimportant, that it was only the game and the glory of the game that counted. . . .

The same has always been true of Ruth, who still in spirit is only a kid of fourteen or fifteen. You might think the kids would stand aside in awe of the home-run kid. But once let upon the field they are all over him, climbing his vast body, pulling him down to play with him as if he were some big pet, sent there for a frolic and a romp. And Ruth in the meanwhile has spent innumerable hours going out of his way to help youngsters singly and in groups, to take them autographed baseballs, to help pay their doctors' bills, to prove that he is still one of them in every manner of life.

Above all else, both were on the level in this sense: each gave to his game all he had, at every start, with a deep appreciation of the great public that brought him fame and fortune. The usual method of the champion is to despise this public. Few champions have liked crowds. To John L. Sullivan and to Babe Ruth these crowds stood as sponsors of their greatness, as makers of their greatness, audiences entitled to the finest work of the artist at every move. Neither ever faked, neither ever shirked, and with all their crudities both, in addition to being skilled artisans at their trade, were dramatists of high degree with peculiar qualities of crowd attraction that no one else in the game has known. They were the architects of personal destinies that no mere skill alone could ever hope to reach.

Grantland Rice, "What Draws the Crowds?" *Collier's*, June 20, 1925, 10, 44.

ᴔ

When "Babe" Ruth Was Beaten by John J. McGraw (1922)

H. D. SALSINGER

There was an alternative model of sports heroism to that embodied by Ruth, described here in this account of the 1922 World Series between Ruth's Yankees and the cross-town rivals, the New York Giants. The Giants' John J. McGraw, who is celebrated here, was neither a player nor an owner, but the manager *of the team. The author of this article credited the Giants' triumph to McGraw's managerial "system."*

PROBLEMS TO CONSIDER

1. What was the model of baseball skill embodied here by McGraw? How did he differ from Ruth?
2. Could McGraw's system have been applied as effectively to managing a business or an industry? Were the Giants a team or an organization?

. . . Ruth was in perfect playing condition [in the 1922 World Series against the cross-town rivals, the Giants]. He had reached his top form and he was in position to lead the attack. Ruth's condition was expected to give the Yan-kees the confidence that they lacked in the preceding year and, being in shape, Ruth was expected to kill the confidence in the Giants. Before the series it seemed much as if Ruth would be the deciding factor.

National League adherents feared that Ruth was too great an obstacle for the Giants to overcome both from a physical and psychological standpoint. He towered ominously in the advance dope. Ruth was McGraw's problem.

Of all the strategy that McGraw showed in the series his best was probably in connection with Ruth. Here he made a master move. Ruth was at bat in the first inning of the first game. Two out and none on. Ruth strutted to the plate menacingly. Here he expected to find Nehf, the pitcher prepared to work on him. Ruth was certain that Nehf would pitch him only bad balls and try to make him swing at a bad one. But Nehf did nothing of the kind. Nehf, instead of working on Ruth, pitched to him. Not alone that, but he pitched him slow curve strikes, just above the knee. Before Ruth could recover from the shock he struck out, and in that strikeout was one of the turning-points of the game.

McGraw, in ordering his pitchers to pitch to Ruth, took into consideration the psychology of Ruth. He knew what Ruth expected. He knew that Ruth would never look for anything but bad balls, and if he could upset Ruth by pitching to him, he would beat him; and beating Ruth went a long way toward beating the Yankees. When his usefulness was destroyed, their attack was shattered. . . .

Ruth was an utter failure in the series. He became a failure from the first time at bat, and the Giants' pitchers showed all too plainly that Ruth can easily be handled at bat. They did not pitch him a fast ball and they kept a slow ball low on him, curving it frequently. Ruth wilted and faded.

Never was McGraw baseball better illustrated than in the World's Series. There is nothing orthodox about the McGraw system. He believes in doing the unorthodox. He finds high strategy in doing the unexpected, in crossing up his opponents.

McGraw plays baseball as the great masters of chess play. He has in mind the moves to come. Some of his thrusts may fail, but only in the physical failure of the moment. He probably did not count heavily upon the success of the play, but his object was the effect. . . .

McGraw plays the McGraw system. This system is distinctive. The McGraw plan of play is not alone the best in baseball, but it is the best in sport. Using the McGraw method the physical superiority of an opponent is readily discounted and, on analysis, the McGraw system is simple. . . . It is the only method that assures success. It is the system that discounts superior strength and numbers. And all it is can be summed up in one word—unity.

The Giants against the Yankees was a matter of inferior units, perfectly combined and harmonizing, against superior units disconnected. In other words, team-play against individual effort.

McGraw does not so much want ballplayers who can play ball as he wants players that can do what McGraw asks them to do. This has been the McGraw rule, and he has made it absolute. McGraw is the Czar of play, the dominant autocrat. McGraw orders and demands absolute obedience. The men that play ball for McGraw must do what McGraw asks; if they do not, they cease to play for him. His success has been in getting men to do his bidding without question, to obey instructions implicitly, to become part of the whole instead of being individuals. That is the foundation upon which McGraw has built his success. . . .

McGraw is probably the greatest strategist of baseball. He knows more baseball than any other man in his own league. He is a psychologist. And he is a born leader. But all of McGraw's knowledge of the game, all his craft and cunning, all his deft strategy would not bring him to the top if he did not demand and secure united action.

McGraw's greatest achievement was in the World's Series of 1922. In this series McGraw rose to new heights, to borrow a worn expression. He gave a demonstration that must be regarded as the greatest ever furnished in the game and he set a goal that managers will find it hard to reach. Never in the history of the sport was the work of a team so completely dominated, so absolutely controlled by a single individual as was the play of the Giants against the Yankees.

McGraw, sitting in the dugout in the corner nearest the home plate, directed nine men on the field. He shifted his infielders and outfielders for the batsman; he signaled his catcher on every pitched ball; he told his batsmen whether to hit, bunt or wait.

But, McGraw did not plan his attack and defense with the start of each game. It was not on the spur of the moment. He was simply applying the McGraw system of attack and defense to the situations—on pitched balls. Before the series he had everything planned, his entire line of play. He held one meeting with his players at which the coming series was discust, and McGraw outlined to them what he expected them to do. But players are apt to forget in the exciting moments of play, and therefore McGraw reminded them before each pitch.

H. D. Salsinger, "When Babe Ruth Was Beaten by John J. McGraw," *Baseball*. Reprinted in *Literary Digest*, December 2, 1922, 57–60.

૱

CHAPTER 5

Bad Times and Good Times: The Era of the Depression: 1929–1942

IN 1932, with national unemployment approaching 25 percent, banks failing in record numbers, and personal incomes dropping at a dizzying rate, the newspaper columnist Walter Lippmann rhetorically asked, "From what source come these unmanly fears that prevail among us? . . . This despairing impotence? What is it that shakes the nerves of so many?" The very way in which Lippmann questioned the nation's manhood in the midst of the economic crisis and social upheaval of the day adds a dimension to our understanding of the far-reaching effects of the Depression. Severe economic depressions had staggered the United States before, but no earlier recession or depression matched the length and depth of the 1930s disaster or challenged Americans from so many directions. Never had the nation's working and white-collar classes been so reliant on impersonal corporations and the expansion of industrial and consumer capitalism. Never had farmers been so thoroughly integrated into and subject to fluctuations in national and international commodities markets. Never had domestic economic growth been so determined by consumer spending. When such businesses and markets shrank dramatically and personal incomes declined with them, the millions sent into unemployment or financial uncertainty had difficulty understanding how and why. Individual character still seemed the bedrock of America's greatness, yet the Depression was a worldwide disaster that no single nation could correct on its own. The economy's collapse profoundly shook Americans' assumptions about their individual and national independence from the problems that supposedly beset only lesser nations and people.

In the 1930s, most Americans did not face starvation or homelessness during even the hardest times; malnutrition, wretched health care, temporary dislocation, and diminished or poorer living conditions were more common for the vast numbers who were most severely affected. What the greater population was most likely to experience was the sense of cultural dislocation and the impotence, fear, and shaky nerves that Lippmann described as "unmanly." When married women were able to find factory work more easily than their laid-off husbands, or sons and daughters were more readily hired at low wages than their fortysomething or, worse, fiftysomething fathers, the security of home and family was offered at the price of upsetting the dominant gender hierarchies and ideals. Franklin D. Roosevelt's New Deal programs constructed a corporate and bureaucratic government to match the corporate economy. When government stepped in to help because ordinary men could not support their families, long-standing assumptions about individual self-reliance and limited government lost some of their power. Such premises retained their hold, but the new circumstances now begged the question: which was worse, being afraid or allaying those fears by relying on public relief?

The documents and images in this chapter explore the social, political, and economic hard times of the Depression era as a broad field of conflicting and consensual cultural experience. Whether in the form of New Deal guidelines, published "success" stories, or radio comedies, Americans drew on and used ideals of gender, race, class, and sexuality to shore up the walls of their cultural houses, making sense of, preserving, changing, and coping with the Depression.

❧ *Coping with the Depression: Popular Advice Literature in the 1930s* ❧

Throughout the 1930s, there was no shortage of advice on how men and women could and *should* respond to the Depression. Radicals, many of them Marxists operating in industrial unions and highbrow journals, urged working-class Americans to unite in the defeat of capitalism. With the electoral expulsion of Republican president Herbert Hoover in 1932, New Deal Democrats sought to reassure Americans that hard times were a temporary condition that the federal government would help them survive. Most Americans, however, were unconvinced that the dire conditions of the Depression demanded either a radical overhauling of political and economic practices or a permanent national welfare state infrastructure. They believed, instead, that while people might need a little help at times, in general they should be able to take care of themselves. "In those days, everybody accepted his . . . responsibility for his own fate," a psychiatrist recalled about the Depression era. If a man was unemployed, it was "your own fault, your own indolence, your own lack of ability."

Two of the era's most influential guidance counselors—the flamboyant health guru, bodybuilder, and publisher Bernarr Macfadden, whose magazines sold more than 7 million copies monthly by 1935; and the writer Dale Carnegie, author of the 1936 bestseller

How to Win Friends and Influence People—encouraged and exploited this diagnosis of the Depression by examining its causes and effects, especially in regard to the ideal of the breadwinning man. Both men claimed to be mere gatherers of homegrown folk wisdom, the ageless truths that had assisted ordinary Americans in overcoming trials and defeats and that had helped them make something of themselves. Macfadden's magazines and Carnegie's how-to manual were part of the vast literature of the Depression, and their appeal came in large part from the "true stories" they told about how Americans got themselves into and out of hard times.

Hard Times Made a Man of Me; An Actual Experience (1933)
PHYSICAL CULTURE

The Wife Who Stood Still . . . Was It Jealousy or Fear That Made Her Fight Her Husband's Ambition? (1931)
TRUE STORY

"This business of living is always a test of manhood," Bernarr Macfadden explained, in characteristic fashion, to his Depression-era readers in 1933. But there was a bright side: "Sometimes it takes hard times to put a man on his toes . . . make him fight and give him back his strength." The lessons of such adversity were outlined at great length in the pages of the numerous magazines he published in the 1930s. Macfadden's True Story *was probably the most widely read national publication in the United States. He and his wife started it in 1919 as a spinoff of their popular health and fitness magazine* Physical Culture. *Part of* True Story's *appeal was its alleged realism, which was captured in the publication's slogan: "Truth is stranger than fiction." Macfadden stocked* Physical Culture *and especially* True Story *with submissions from his readers, whose personal stories were solicited and then substantially edited by the magazine. The confessional stories of weak or depraved women and men teased readers with lurid titles and cinematic photos depicting the heartbreak and thrill of the personal corruption and illicit romances they exposed.*

From the beginning, the professional middle class—ministers, secular reformers, and college-educated readers—denounced and ridiculed the "pulp" tabloid for peddling its sensationalist tales of women and men who had gone wrong. Macfadden countered that his magazines were instructive and served the public good by exposing "the influences . . . that destroy character." By the end of the 1920s and through the Depression years, True Story *was a powerful force in American culture, with an audience composed largely of young working-class women, who purchased 2 million newsstand copies each month. It had become, in a sense, a popular literature, the paper counterpart to the emerging radio genre of the soap opera. Two examples of Macfadden's style of journalism are presented here: in the first, from* Physical Culture, *a man explains how he recovered from the Depression; in the second, from* True Story, *a woman ("Karen") confesses how she destroyed her husband.*

PROBLEMS TO CONSIDER

1. Were the stories in Macfadden's magazines suited to Depression-era audiences, or would they have appealed to readers in any time period? How did they explain why the Depression occurred and how it could be overcome?
2. Consider the gender perspectives of these personal narratives. What did they say a "woman" or a "man" should be? How did they account for a man's success and failure?

HARD TIMES MADE A MAN OF ME

A new type of invalid is with us—the depression victim. Among us today is an astonishingly large number of men and women who are unknowingly heading toward physical ruin. Their plight is not due to malignant ailments, or malformations. They are not losing their health because of prolonged physical illness. They are becoming physically unfit because, unknowingly, they have long been mentally ill.

The most crushing blow that can be dealt you is . . . "to see the things you gave your life to broken." Today there are multitudes of men and women who, having devoted their lives to service, in the arts, sciences, and business, now see their work swept away, and, often, the results of their years of efforts entirely destroyed. Appalled by their own plight, they frequently lose hope. Their nerves become shaken. Their digestion upset. Privation, dread of the future, and sleepless nights "sow the wind" of physical sickness.

They are far from craven. They have always been determined people. All of their lives they have faced facts. Silently, and with self-reliance, they have faced their obstacles, and overcome them. Therein lies the cause of their dilemma—heretofore, they conquered.

They must be active. Tuned to achievement, they must do something. It is this multitude of silent sufferers that should turn to physical culture, and rebuild their lives on the foundation of health, if they would escape "reaping the whirlwind."

I know. I am one of them.

It is with the hope that my personal experience may act as an incentive to other men and women, that they may take heart and begin once more to construct useful, purposeful lives, that I am reciting it.

Now I am happy, purposeful, and manfully prepared to face the facts of life that lie before me, and fight them. One year ago I was reaching that dreadful stage of listlessness known to the utterly doomed. . . .

I am a typical American . . .

After my discharge from the army, I secured a modest job in a large organization. During the following six years, I was most lucky. Opportunities came to me to do interesting work of enlarged importance.

Then occurred a merger of several companies. I came to New York. My work fascinated me. There was lots of it to do. . . .

For five years prior to the big smash I kept at it. No vacations during that time. And often, on my way home for a little rest, I greeted the rising sun, after working twenty hours. . . .

Then the "smash." The realization that the work of dreaming and building was about to be destroyed. . . . I lost my job. All these events filled me with despair. The mental agony of those months have left everlasting scars on me. . . .

Then my health failed. The will to live and achieve almost burned out. It seemed like the end. . . .

My first problem was decidedly physical. Neuritis tortured me. Even my eyes and my teeth contributed their bit to the general debacle. . . .

Seeking for a method that would teach me how to correct the thoughtlessness of years, I came across a book on fasting. . . .

Until this time I had never willingly fasted. The plan I followed called for a ten-day fast. I ate at noon every other day. On the fast day I took copious internal baths. My plan called for exercise, exercise, and more exercise. . . .

That was less than one year ago. . . . My fears have long since vanished. My heart is filled with the joy of living. I am in better condition physically than I have been at any time in my life. . . .

I feel younger, and look it—I am told, than I did ten years ago. My mind is keener, more alive than I believed it possible to be. . . .

Truly, these are unusual times. I believe that we can make the future a healthful, purposeful, happy period of years. We must adjust ourselves. If you are one of "my gang," get busy physically. It costs only an effort—though it be a fortune to the downhearted.

By physical activity, undaunted by weakness in body and will, I am building a foundation of physical power on which I shall rear my future life. . . .

<hr>

"Hard Times Made a Man of Me; An Actual Experience," *Physical Culture*, March 1933, 21, 100–101.

THE WIFE WHO STOOD STILL

Though I am American born, my parents came of European peasant stock. My dear mother brought up her brood in the highest standards she knew. Two virtues, in particular, she lost no opportunity to instill into us. One was contentment with one's station in life. The other was thrift. And because I learned her lessons well— too well!—my life lies in ruins about me now.

Understand me. These two qualities *are* virtues, and it was not their fault that I came to shipwreck. The fault lay in my own narrow, literal interpretation of them. Didn't the great Apostle tell us, "The letter killeth, but the spirit giveth life?" Well, so it was with me.

I grew up on a truck farm in the Middle West, just outside the thriving town of Graham. A big packing house had recently opened a branch cannery in Graham, and I often drove in with father to deliver a load of produce at the factory.

It was thus that I met Stephen Brent. He was one of the cannery foremen. He was an orphan, and boarded in the town. He had been employed at the main plant. I loved him, I think, from the moment our first glances met. Father went into the office to see the superintendent, and after Stephen had weighed the tomatoes, he lingered outside to talk to me. . . .

If ever two people were made for each other, and knew it, it was Stephen Brent and myself on that August day. Before we drove away, he asked if he might call.

Two months later we were married.

It had been a delightful courtship, but one which made me vaguely uneasy. Stephen was a generous lover, and the presents and attentions he showered upon me were simply overwhelming. Secretly I promised myself that my first task as a wife would be to curb what I called his wasteful extravagance. . . .

The months sped by. To me, at least, our first year was one of perfect happiness. I was busy every minute, for I did my own laundry work and sewing, in addition to the everyday housework. It always amazed Stephen to see me take a bargain counter length of cheap material and turn it into a frock. True, I never had the knack of putting style into my work, but I sewed very neatly and the dresses I made were quite fashionable enough for me. As I said to Stephen, people like us couldn't expect to dress like millionaires.

"People like us!" It was not until long afterward that I realized how my frequent use of that phrase grated on him. I used it in all good faith. With my Old Country notions, it never occurred to me that a factory worker should hope or expect to be anything but a factory worker. . . .

I have said that my story is not a record of sin, but of foolish mistakes. In that first happy year I unknowingly sowed the seeds of all unhappiness.

Thrift. Contentment. Precious virtues these were, surely? Ah, but "the letter killeth!"

My first child, Dora, was born on our first wedding anniversary. Born at home, for I had heard frightening tales of hospital charges.

I was strong and young, and recovered from my ordeal with amazing quickness. I was on my feet on the fourth day, and on the seventh I put my washing on the line. Stephen begged me to take it easy for awhile, but I laughed at him. I would show him that he had not married a lazy, self-coddling wife.

The next year, Donald, our son came. He was also born at home and I was up at work within a week.

A few weeks after Donald's birth, my mother came to me with a welcome proposal. The young daughter of one of her neighbors wanted to come to town to take a shorthand course. If I would take her in, Gerda would earn her keep by helping me with the housework.

I did not feel the need of help and suggested, instead, that Gerda's father pay a reasonable sum for her board. This was arranged and I was very glad, for we had an extra room and it was like finding money to me.

Gerda Jensen was a queer, quiet girl, a year younger than myself. I had known her from childhood, though we had never been intimate. I can remember her at six years old, passionately proclaiming, "When I grow up, I'm going to be a *lady*!"

She made very little trouble, for she was busy with her books. . . .

Only one thing bothered me in those days. Stephen was changing. Oh, it was nothing I could put a finger on! But his boyish laugh rang out less frequently nowadays, and there was a puzzled, considering look in his blue eyes. Every now and then he would make some suggestion that I considered childishly impractical. . . .

One step my husband did take, without even telling me until it was done. I was furious when I found that he had sent in a magazine coupon and enrolled for a correspondence course in factory management. I could see no excuse for it, and I bitterly resented the evenings when he sat at the dining room table, absorbed in his books and writing busily. Gerda would go in and talk to him sometimes, quite as if she knew what it was all about. I coldly ignored the whole thing.

I look back now on that fourth year of my marriage and wonder at the blind, self-righteous little fool I was. It was not quite so happy as the previous years, but I saw no portent in it; no hint of disaster to come. But it was there, writ large for any one with eyes to see!

One night Stephen came home all excitement. The moment we sat down at the table, he announced his big news. Mr. Parker, the cannery superintendent, was being transferred to another branch.

I could see nothing startling in that, but I tried to show an interest. "That means a new boss for you, doesn't it, dear?" I asked dutifully.

"Maybe not." His blue eyes were shining, and there was a curious ring of exultation in his voice. "Maybe it means — well, it's all just in the air, and I expect I'm setting my hopes too high. But there's a chance that I may be the new boss myself!"

"Oh, Steve, how splendid!" It was Gerda who spoke first, and her eyes were shining too.

"Stephen, that's just silly," I said impatiently. "What do you know about running a factory? You'd simply make a mess of it if they let you try, which, of course, they won't. Why you're just a common workman, and that's an *office* job!"

"And what if it is?" Gerda put in quickly. "Steve knows the business from the ground up, on the practical side. He's read and studied till he knows all there is to know about the management part of it. The men like him. I don't see any reason in the world why he shouldn't make a wonderful success as superintendent."

"Gee, Gerda, you're great!" Stephen leaned eagerly toward her. . . .

I was completely forgotten, sitting there with my two babies. Stephen was telling, not us, but *her*, pouring out his hopes and plans, while she listened with a face as glowing as his own.

I was not jealous of her, then. No, let me be honest. I did not know that I was jealous. My chief emotion was anger; anger with Stephen for what I considered his childish rainbow-chasing; anger with Gerda for encouraging it. Why, Stephen hadn't even finished high school; his father had been a day laborer. Of course they wouldn't give him charge of the factory; it was ridiculous.

But at the root of my anger was certainly the thought, "*She* put him up to it! This whole thing is *her* doing!" . . .

For ten days the appointment hung fire. My attitude on that first night had stung Stephen to resentment, I suppose. He said nothing more of it to me, but every night he and Gerda would sit out on the front porch, eagerly talking it over. . . .

On the tenth day I could stand it no longer. I was in the midst of my weekly washing when the thought suddenly came to me that there was a way to put a stop to this foolishness. Stephen was acting like a child, I told myself. Like a child, he must be taught a lesson. . . .

I dried my reddened hands, loaded the babies into their carriage and set off down the long, dusty street toward Mr. Parker's house. I did not stop to change my spattered house frock or pin up my straggling hair. I was only a workingman's wife. Why bother to appear what I was not? . . .

The trim little maid who answered my ring seemed surprised at my appearance, but when I told her who I was, she said that Mr. and Mrs. Parker were in the rose arbor at the side of the house, and she supposed I could go around there, if I liked. . . .

Fumbling for words, I poured out my mission [to Mr Parker]. I had come to ask Mr. Parker to talk to my husband. He wouldn't listen to me, and he was making my life miserable with this silly bee in his bonnet.

I realized . . . that Stephen hadn't a chance in the world of becoming superintendent; that he wasn't fitted for it in any way. But I couldn't make him see it. I wanted Mr. Parker to tell him, not simply that he needn't hope for this particular job, but that it was foolish and wrong for a working-man to give way to such crazy dreams. . . .

I gained my end. I left with Mr. Parker's thanks, and his grave assurance that Stephen would not receive the appointment.

Stephen came home the next day with a stricken look in his eyes, his shoulders sagging.

Mr. Parker had not betrayed my confidence. He had simply announced that the company was sending down a man from Chicago to take his place.

I had thought that, now the blow had fallen, it would be my place to comfort Stephen. I felt toward him much as I felt to little Donald when I corrected him for some childish fault. He had erred and he had learned his lesson. My heart was overflowing with forgiveness and tender pity. I wanted only to kiss away the sting of the just punishment.

How little we can foresee the results of the events we set in motion! . . .

Stephen wanted no comfort of me. He carried his wounds to Gerda, and she poured balm into them. To me he said only, "Well, come on with the I-told-you-so's, why don't you?"

To her he said—I know not what. As before, I tossed wearily on my bed, listening to the murmur of voices from the porch below. His sullen and despairing now, hers tender and consoling.

The night came when I could endure it no longer. I went down to them and, with harsh, ugly accusations, drove her from my home. . . .

Surely, I told myself, we could settle back into our old life, when we were so loving and so happy. . . .

But something had come over my husband; something I had not the wit to understand or cope with.

Our industrial town, thoroughly and peaceably unionized, had been free of labor troubles until quite recently. Stephen had always been a union man, of course, and was respected and liked by his fellow members.

It was with a shock that I heard . . . that Stephen was "getting mixed up" with a crew of Red agitators who had recently descended upon the town. He attended their meetings and brought home books and queer newspapers whose contents filled me with dismay. Worse, he was aiding in spreading their doctrines among the wilder spirits in his own union. . . .

He was sullen and irritable all the time now, and it was with some timidity that I told him what [I had heard]. I was shocked at the violence with which he answered me.

"Plugging for the capitalists now, are you?" he sneered. "Say, that's funny—coming from you! Why, it's you, Karen, that's been trying all these years to make me class-conscious." . . .

"But Stephen, I didn't say that," I protested, dismayed. "At least, I didn't mean—Oh, Stephen, you know I didn't mean anything like that Bolshevik talk. I—I think it's just terrible!"

"Say, you don't know what you mean," he answered contemptuously. "But it's all right, kid, you did me a favor at that. I used to fall for that stuff about every man having his chance here in America—thought I was as good as any of 'em, and could go right up to the top if I'd just study and try." . . .

The blue eyes that had looked love into mine were positively blazing now with insane excitement, and I drew back, frightened, from his fierce clutch on my arm. . . .

There was more to come. For suddenly he began to speak of money, the comfortable balance we had in the bank. The *cause* needed funds, it seemed. You could only fight fire with fire; money with money. He had told the comrades that all he had he would willingly throw into the common pot, for the good of all.

"Oh, Stephen, you didn't!" I protested, sick at heart. "Why, that's *our* money! We've worked and saved and done without for it—surely you don't mean to—"

He laughed, that jeering laugh that was not quite sane. "Another place you were right, little comrade! *You* were the one who preached thrift, who piled up the money in the bank. Money wrung from the capitalists! Ha, it'll go back to them in a form they won't welcome! I must not forget to tell Rykoff what the cause owes to my dear little communist wife."

"Stephen," I said, trying hard to steady my voice, "if you do this—if you throw in your lot with those—those traitors; if you give them the little fund we've saved for our home, for our babies, then this is the end. You and I are through." . . .

"I'm going now, Karen," he said abruptly. "You said yourself we were through. And I hope to heaven I never see you again so long as I live."

I have never seen him since that day. . . .

"The Wife Who Stood Still . . . Was It Jealousy or Fear That Made Her Fight Her Husband's Ambition?" *True Story*, January 1931, 36–37, 106–9.

ꕚ

The Big Secret of Dealing with People (1936)
DALE CARNEGIE

Dale Carnegie's How to Win Friends and Influence People *was and remains one of the great publishing sensations of the twentieth century. The cover of a recent edition claims "Over 15,000,000 Copies Sold." As popular as it still is, the book and its enthusiastic reception were very much products of the Depression era, although the crisis was never mentioned in its pages. Carnegie successfully aimed his book at middle-class businessmen and young men measuring their future prospects in a time of limited job or career opportunities. Such men probably were not penniless, but they likely had suffered the indignities of diminished income and status in the contracted economy. Carnegie made his strategies for enhancing "inter-personal relations" into a set of "rules" applicable to all aspects of middle-class life. "They work like magic," Carnegie promised. "I have seen the application of these principles literally revolutionize the lives of many people."*

*The following selection, from the section "Fundamental Techniques in Handling People,"
is from the 1936 edition.*

PROBLEMS TO CONSIDER

1. Examine how Carnegie defined "success." What was it that men didn't have but wanted? How were they to get it? What accounted for their sense of failure?
2. How did Carnegie's diagnoses of human "frailties" and formulas for personal achievement compare with those in Macfadden's publications? Did Carnegie's techniques build the same kind of "man"?

There is only one way under high Heaven to get anybody to do anything. Did you ever stop to think of that? Yes, just one way. And that is by making the other person want to do it.

Remember, there is no other way.

Of course, you can make a man want to give you his watch by sticking a revolver in his ribs. You can make an employee give you co-operation—until your back is turned—by threatening to fire him. You can make a child do what you want it to do by a whip or a threat. But these crude methods have sharply undesirable repercussions.

The only way I can get you to do anything is by giving you what you want.

What do you want?

The famous Dr. Sigmund Freud of Vienna, one of the most distinguished psychologists of the twentieth century, says that everything you and I do springs from two motives: the sex urge and the desire to be great.

Professor John Dewey, America's most profound philosopher, phrases it a bit differently. Dr. Dewey says the deepest urge in human nature is "the desire to be important." Remember that phrase: "the desire to be important." It is significant. You are going to hear a lot about it in this book.

What do you want? Not many things, but the few things that you do wish, you crave with an insistence that will not be denied. Almost every normal adult wants—

1. Health and the preservation of life.
2. Food.
3. Sleep.
4. Money and the things money will buy.
5. Life in the hereafter.
6. Sexual gratification.
7. The well-being of our children.
8. A feeling of importance.

Almost all these wants are gratified—all except one. But there is one longing almost as deep, almost as imperious, as the desire for food or sleep which is seldom gratified. It is what Freud calls "the desire to be great." It is what John Dewey calls the "desire to be important."

Abe Lincoln once began a letter by saying: "Every body likes a compliment." Yes, we all crave honest appreciation. We all long for sincere praise. And we seldom get either.

Here is a gnawing and unfaltering human hunger; and the rare individual who honestly satisfies this heart-hunger will hold people in the palm of his hand and "even the undertaker will be sorry when he dies."

The desire for a feeling of importance is one of the chief distinguishing differences between mankind and the animals. To illustrate: When I was a farm boy out in Missouri, my father bred fine Duroc-Jersey hogs and pedigreed white-faced cattle. We used to exhibit our hogs and white-faced cattle at the county fairs and livestock shows throughout the Middle West. We won first prizes by the score. My father pinned his blue ribbons on a sheet of white muslin, and when friends or visitors came to the house, he would get out the long sheet of muslin. He would hold one end and I would hold the other while he exhibited the blue ribbons.

The hogs didn't care about the ribbons they had won. But Father did. These prizes gave him a feeling of importance.

If our ancestors hadn't had this flaming urge for a feeling of importance, civilization would have been impossible. Without it, we should have been just about like the animals.

It was this desire for a feeling of importance that led an uneducated, poverty-stricken grocery clerk to study some law books that he found in the bottom of a barrel of household plunder that he had bought for fifty cents. You have probably heard of this grocery clerk. His name was Lincoln. . . .

This desire makes you want to wear the latest styles, drive the latest car, and talk about your brilliant children.

It is this desire which lures many boys into becoming gangsters and gunmen. "The average young criminal of today," says E. P. Mulrooney, former Police Commissioner of New York, "is filled with ego, and his first request after arrest is for those lurid newspapers that make him out a hero. The disagreeable prospect of taking a 'hot squat' in the electric chair seems remote, so long as he can gloat over his likeness sharing space with pictures of Babe Ruth, LaGuardia, Einstein, Lindbergh, Toscanini, or Roosevelt."

If you tell me how you get your feeling of importance, I'll tell you what you are. That determines your character. That is the most significant thing about you. For example, John D. Rockefeller gets his feeling of importance by giving money to erect a modern hospital in Peking, China, to care for millions of poor people whom he has never seen and never will see. Dillinger, on the other hand, got his feeling of importance by being a bandit, a bank robber and killer.

When the G-men were hunting him, he dashed into a farmhouse up in Minnesota and said, "I'm Dillinger!" He was proud of the fact that he was Public Enemy Number One. "I'm not going to hurt you, but I'm Dillinger!" he said.

Yes, the one significant difference between Dillinger and Rockefeller is how they got their feeling of importance.

History sparkles with amusing examples of famous people struggling for a feeling of importance. Even George Washington wanted to be called "His Mightiness, the President of the United States"; . . . and Mrs. Lincoln, in the White House, turned upon Mrs. Grant like a tigress and shouted, "How dare you be seated in my presence until I invite you!" . . .

Some authorities declare that people may actually go insane in order to find, in the dreamland of insanity, the feeling of importance that has been denied them in the harsh world of reality. . . .

If some people are so hungry for a feeling of importance that they actually go insane to get it, imagine what miracles you and I can achieve by giving people honest appreciation.

There is only one man in the world who has ever been given a salary of a million dollars a year, so far as I know; and in spite of all the Scotch jokes, he was paid that staggering sum by a Scotsman.

Andrew Carnegie paid Charles Schwab a million dollars a year. Because Schwab is a genius? No. Because he knew more about the manufacture of steel than other people? Nonsense. Charles Schwab told me himself that he had many men working for him who knew more about the manufacture of steel than he did. Schwab truly responded to people. He knew instinctively that they hungered for recognition; so he gave them praise and appreciation.

Schwab says that he was paid this salary largely because of his ability to deal with people. And what is his secret? Here it is in his own words—words that ought to be cast in eternal bronze and hung in every home and school, every shop and office in the land—words that children ought to memorize instead of wasting their time memorizing the conjugation of Latin verbs or the amount of the annual rainfall in Brazil—words that will all but transform your life and mine if we will only live them:

"I consider my ability to arouse enthusiasm among the men," said Schwab, "the greatest asset I possess, and the way to develop the best that is in a man is by appreciation and encouragement. . . ."

We nourish the bodies of our children and friends and employees; but how seldom do we nourish their self-esteem. We provide them with roast beef and potatoes to build energy; but we neglect to give them kind words of appreciation that would sing in their memories for years like the music of the morning stars.

Some readers are saying right now as they read these lines: "Old stuff! Soft soap! Bear oil! Flattery! I've tried that stuff. It doesn't work—not with intelligent people."

Of course, flattery seldom works with discerning people. It is shallow, selfish, and insincere. It ought to fail and it usually does. . . .

In the long run, flattery will do you more harm than good. Flattery is from the teeth out. Sincere appreciation is from the heart out. No! No! No! I am not suggesting flattery! Far from it. I'm talking about a new way of life. Let me repeat. *I am talking about a new way of life.* . . .

Let's cease thinking of our accomplishments, our wants. Let's try to figure out the other man's good points. Then forget flattery. Give honest, sincere appreciation. Be "hearty in your approbation and lavish in your praise," and people will cherish your words and treasure them and repeat them over a lifetime—repeat them years after you have forgotten them.

———

Dale Carnegie, "The Big Secret of Dealing with People," in *How to Win Friends and Influence People* (1936; repr., New York: Simon & Schuster, 1937), 43–55.

ꝶ

ꝶ *"I Hope You Can Help Me": Americans Appeal to Their President and the First Lady* ꝶ

Why were people in America poor? The Depression raised this question as never before. Economic hardship was an ordinary aspect of American life from the nation's beginnings, but the scale of the Depression's long-term unemployment and deprivation made poverty a national crisis. Prior to that time, the poor had been the concern of municipal and community-based private and public relief agencies. The length and depth of the Depression overwhelmed the existing welfare structure. Roosevelt's New Deal social welfare programs, in 1933 and afterward, brought wide-scale federal assistance to individual Americans for the first time. The president, however, saw his programs as emergency actions to alleviate the immediate distress. He and his advisers further worried that social welfare was potentially dangerous to the health of the nation.

The letters that American citizens addressed to Franklin Roosevelt or to his wife, Eleanor, suggest how ordinary people reacted to federal responses to the problems of unemployment and poverty. They reveal Americans' perceptions of their condition, the Great Depression, and other Americans better or worse off than themselves. The letters also show how the New Deal amounted to more than an array of experimental social welfare programs. The Roosevelts and many administration officials were savvy about the political importance of the new technologies of mass communication in radio, movies, magazines, and newspapers. From the beginning, they used these technologies, as no politicians had before, to dramatize that the institutions of government were not coldly formal and impersonal but were actually extensions of their socially engaged, radiantly friendly, stubbornly optimistic, and generously caring personalities. "Never before have we had leaders in the White House to whom we felt we could go with our problems," observed an Alabama woman. This sense of connection between ordinary people and the Roosevelts comes across in the unprecedented volume of mail sent to them in the 1930s (450,000 letters in the week after the 1933 inauguration alone). According to official policy, all letters were answered, although only in the rarest instances by the Roosevelts themselves.

State of the Union Address (1935)
FRANKLIN D. ROOSEVELT

In his 1935 State of the Union address, President Roosevelt outlined the justification for and aims of the Works Progress Administration (WPA), which soon became the New Deal's main program of direct relief from the severe poverty of the Depression. In its simplest terms, the WPA substituted federally paid jobs for preexisting local and federal cash relief payments (provided by the Federal Emergency Relief Administration, or FERA). Between mid-1935 and mid-1940, the WPA supported about 30 percent of the 8 to 10.7 million Americans who were out of work at any time. With millions on its payrolls, the agency represented an unprecedented scale of federal welfare assistance, although most unemployed Americans (six to seven of every ten) always remained unassisted by its aid.

PROBLEMS TO CONSIDER

1. How did Roosevelt define the problem of poverty in the United States during the Depression era? Why were people poor or unemployed? What effects did poverty have on people?
2. Roosevelt referred to the "lessons of history" to support his views on how welfare affects individuals. Would his views have applied to women as well as to men? to nonwhites as well as to whites? to the long-term poor as well as to those thrown out of prosperity and into poverty by the Depression?

I recall to your attention my message to the Congress last June in which I said, "Among our objectives I place the security of the men, women, and children of the Nation first." That remains our first and continuing task: and in a very real sense every major legislative enactment of this Congress should be a component part of it. . . .

More than two billions of dollars have also been expended in direct relief to the destitute. Local agencies, of necessity, determined the recipients of this form of relief. With inevitable exceptions, the funds were spent by them with reasonable efficiency, and as a result actual want of food and clothing in the great majority of cases has been overcome.

But the stark fact before us is that great numbers still remain unemployed.

A large proportion of these unemployed and their dependents have been forced on the relief rolls. The burden on the Federal Government has grown with great rapidity. We have here a human as well as an economic problem. When humane considerations are concerned Americans give them precedence. The lessons of history, confirmed by the evidence immediately before me, show conclusively that continued dependence upon relief induces a spiritual and moral disintegration fundamentally destructive to the national fiber. To dole out relief in this way is to administer a narcotic, a subtle destroyer of the human spirit. It is inimical to the dictates of a sound policy. It is in violation of the traditions of America. Work must be found for able-bodied but destitute workers.

The Federal Government must and shall quit this business of relief.

I am not willing that the vitality of our people be further sapped by the giving of cash, of market baskets, of a few hours of weekly work cutting grass, raking leaves, or picking up papers in the public parks. We must preserve not only the bodies of the unemployed from destitution but also their self-respect, their self-reliance, and courage and determination. . . .

There are . . . three and one-half million employable people who are on relief. . . . This group was the victim of a Nation-wide depression caused by conditions which were not local but national. The Federal Government is the only governmental agency with sufficient power and credit to meet this situation. We have assumed this task and we shall not shrink from it in the future. It is a duty dictated by every intelligent consideration of national policy to ask you to make it possible for the United States to give employment to all of these three and one-half million employable people now on relief, pending their absorption in a rising tide of private employment.

It is my thought that, with the exception of certain of the normal public-building operations of the Government, all emergency public works shall be united in a single new and greatly enlarged plan.

With the establishment of this new system we can supersede the Federal Emergency Relief Administration with a coordinated authority which will be charged with the orderly liquidation of our present relief activities and the substitution of a national chart for the giving of work.

This new program of emergency public employment should be governed by a number of practical principles:

(1) All work undertaken should be useful, not just for a day or a year, but useful in the sense that it affords permanent improvement in living conditions or that it creates future new wealth for the Nation.

(2) Compensation on emergency public projects should be in the form of security payments, which should be larger than the amount now received as a relief dole, but at the same time not so large as to encourage the rejection of opportunities for private employment or the leaving of private employment to engage in Government work.

(3) Projects should be undertaken on which a large percentage of direct labor can be used.

(4) Preference should be given to those projects which will be self-liquidating in the sense that there is a reasonable expectation that the Government will get its money back at some future time.

(5) The projects undertaken should be selected and planned so as to compete as little as possible with private enterprises. . . .

(6) The planning of projects would seek to assure work during the coming fiscal year to the individuals now on relief or until such time as private employment is available. . . .

Franklin D. Roosevelt, State of the Union address, January 4, 1935, *Congressional Record* 79, pt. 1:95–96.

⤳

Letters About WPA Aid to the Poor (1935–1936)

The first set of letters to the Roosevelts presented here, which concern WPA matters, address subjects central to the history of the Depression and New Deal and also under-score Americans' changing perceptions of their relation to the federal government. From the WPA's inception, Americans' attitudes were defined by expectations of what such an agency should achieve and what they, from their own experience as recipients of relief or observers of its operation, believed it actually accomplished. At the same time, the pro-grams themselves did not aim simply to provide "relief" through jobs; they also incorpo-rated policies designed to preserve (or at least not to undermine) the gender order of the "family wage" system of the working (breadwinning) father and homemaker mother. For instance, only one member of a family could hold a WPA job; this policy presumed that only the male head of household would need and get work. If any member of a family held a private-sector job, the family would be taken off federal relief, a rule that quashed wives' and older children's incentive to seek work, even though they generally were more employable than mature men. Finally, WPA wages were set locally — wages in Chicago, for instance, were greater than those in rural Texas — and did not vary, no matter if the worker was the sole support of a household of two or of twenty-two.

PROBLEMS TO CONSIDER

1. Think about these letters as "stories" about the Depression. What did these narratives say about the various perspectives on the causes and effects of poverty? on what the WPA should achieve? on who did and did not deserve assistance?
2. What factors might have accounted for the different views? What did these let-ters suggest about how the writers understood their relationship to the federal government (particularly to the Roosevelts) and what that government should do for them?

LETTER TO THE ROOSEVELTS FROM MRS. GOLDIE GIBLER (1935)

Mr & Mrs F D. Roosevelt—

I am the Mother of 9. children the oldest is 17. the youngest 7 mo. I have 5 children are in school and I want to ask a favor of you if you will be kind enugh to help me it will be more than apprecated.

what I want to know is this. could you please tell me how to make $35. per month go around. I cant seem to have any luck bying food & clothing & have money left for shoes & school suplies. and with Xmas coming on. they are helthy normal children & exspect some thing for Xmas & I cant find a way out. my oldest girl is 17 years old she is married and a way from home. that leaves 8 at home all the time now. my age is 38 Mr Giblers is 38. we have been married 18 years

And all we have is our *children*
Ivan is 15 years.
Leslie is 14 years
bettie is 11 years
arleta is 9 years
Robert is 7 years
Leona is 5 years
Harriett is 2 years
Charlette is 7 mo.

if you can help me in any way I will be very happy

I wish you would visit Laurence Kansas some time. We are for you and the presedent 100 per cent. and think that you both have been wonderful. please keep the good work going on.

I am yours with respect
Mrs Goldie Gibler

. . . please answer this letter.

Maby I am foolish to bother you with my troubles but I trust that you can help me find a way out.

LETTER TO FRANKLIN ROOSEVELT FROM MRS. VIOLA ASHBY (1935)

Dear Mr Franklin D. Roosevelt

Please find time to read this letter of plea to you a doer of good & right. You have & are doing all you can for the unemployed people whilst through no fault of your some of the head of the administration offices here in Wichita certainly are treating some of us unemployed unfair now since the switch over from P.W.A. *[Public Works Administration]* to W.P.A. They are hiring wemon of the city that never has applied or appealed to the relief work because they are self suporting with their nice homes & Cars Radio Telephones money in the Banks and snubs us poor wemons that had to apply for relief work because we had no good homes & every thing that goes with it with money in the banks.

I will quote you a few names not all just a few of the women that has been put to work of the above named class. . . .

Mrs Lula Hill a Farm owner a beautiful home in the city also a beauty culturist. . . .

Mrs Daisy Grinsted Beautiful home and at the time quit a job of work for to except work that is a possision in the Sewing room. . . .

I mention thease to let you know how unfair the relief bosses here are doing so many worthy poor unfortionate wemon.

Now my self concerning the sewing group I worked in . . . practly from the beginning. . . . My case worker closed my card for no just or leagel cause and kept promising me that she'd reopen my card and let it run that way untill to day which is the 18th of Nov. My Regeration *[registration]* shows Sewing all the time and to day when I received my card they had Sewing stricken out and Inserted maid. . . .

The trouble here is they do things here under cover and in a thing I wish that you could know how a lot of things is being conducted and gobbling of money that has been [un]justly appropiated and never reach where it was intended to go only in a measly mite. . . .

Society women . . . suck up the money and leve us in want. I wish some times that you had Goverment Special investigators and my self and many other could put them wise to a plenty facts In a manner the way so many of us Colored women are being treated Mr President I voted for you & your adminstation in good faith and a host of my women friends I had faith & confidence in you from the begining you told your followers & suppoters that you would see that no one starved, nor suffer to much that you would stand by us yes sir I am still staying with you with all the votes I can bring with me and that will be no small amount. And I hope that your action in my case will go out as a beacon light for right Justice to all the unemployed people.

I do not want you worried with to long a letter so I close my letter but not my faith I await your eraily reply yours Very Respt.

Mrs Viola Ashby

LETTER TO FRANKLIN ROOSEVELT FROM CLIFFORD CROCKETT (1935)

Dear Sir;

I am the father of five children, the oldest is seven and the youngest two. I have been transferred from the releif, to the W.P.A. work project, at fifty-five dollars a month. With sum of money I am told, I must buy clothes for a family of seven, feed them, pay rent, buy coal, and pay others bill that are necessary, I have figured every possible way, but I find it impossible to do so on fifty-five dollars a month. Please explain to me why I am expected to do the impossible. I am a painter by trade. I have been learning shoe making for the last two months, but had to give it up when assigned to this work. I am not allowed to make enough for my family to live on, and not allowed to learn a tread which will guarantee proper support for my family in the future. I have been on the releif for four years—I do not wish to be on it all my life—I would like to be a man again, and not a begger, please advise what actions to take concerning this letter.

Thanking you in advance for any consideration you can give me

Sincerely,
Clifford Crockett

LETTER TO FRANKLIN ROOSEVELT FROM LUCILLE A. EISENDRATH (1936)

Dear President Roosevelt:—

I want to ask you a question—a question the answer to which is deeply significant to me and to that large group of inarticulate Americans of whom I am one.

We experienced your election almost four years ago with a glorious and exquisite joy which was capable of expressing itself only in tears. You were the realization of our great dream for a socially-minded administration. You had gaily and gallantly articulated our philosophy—the obligation of government to all its citizens. With high hopes we watched you not only shoulder that responsibility, but proceed to act directly and courageously upon it. Our faith in the philosophy and sincere idealism of the New Deal remains unshaken. We would defend it with all that is within us.

Yet now, almost four years later, I am in doubt. I am baffled and afraid before the tech-

nique which was to make of our dream a glorious reality. Hence I ask you:

Is the expenditure of our money for non-wealth producing projects now contemptuously called "boondoggling" to continue?

I see before me in my own city large groups of men going about raking leaves and transporting dirt from one place to another. To continue to support this type of relief which returns nothing to our government directly or indirectly can only lead inevitably to the specter of national bankruptcy with the wiping out of my savings and my husband's. Even in my position as a housewife, I see great work to be done right here in my city. Actual slum clearance, not the building of high-priced apartments on vacant land which is now in progress, or perhaps the building of a subway, or many other crying needs of a large municipality, which you men of government know so much better than do I, are examples. Intelligent, well-conceived plans, I believe, would amortize themselves either directly or through increased wealth to be paid back in the form of income taxes.

To clarify my question: Is this haphazard employment of men and expenditure of our funds a temporary thing, an emergency measure, a stop-gap until plans for useful, and, at least, self-sustaining projects can be completed? Or is the expenditure of our monies to continue unchecked on non-productive projects with the resultant increasing debt which can only be wiped out by crushing taxes or repudiation?

I am afraid, not only for myself, but for my children. I look to you for an answer, while I give fervent thanks that as an American citizen, I still have the perogative to doubt and to ask.

Respectfully Yours,
Lucille A. Eisendrath

Letters to Franklin and Eleanor Roosevelt, Works Progress Administration Records, National Archives and Records Administration, College Park, Md.

⁊

Letters Asking Mrs. Roosevelt for Help with Adoption

Even the briefest survey of the millions of letters written to the president and First Lady reveals that the Roosevelts succeeded in convincing many Americans of their sincere, humane concern for their welfare. People were willing to share the most private details of their lives with the Roosevelts in hopes of gaining their help. This implied intimacy was especially evident in letters addressed (usually) to Eleanor Roosevelt, seeking her help in locating children who could be adopted. The federal government had no direct role in child adoptions, which were state matters; the letters were referred to the Children's Bureau. That federal agency dealt with health and welfare matters affecting children and provided general information on adoption procedures. Nonetheless, the letters contain a wealth of insight—into women's images of the First Lady, into their attitudes toward childbearing and child rearing and what constituted a "family," and how those attitudes were affected by the Depression.

PROBLEMS TO CONSIDER

1. What do these letters say about how some Americans were reevaluating the state's relationship to the family? What generalizations can be made about how the Depression reoriented Americans' understanding of the role of government in assuring the public welfare?
2. Examine how the difficulties these people faced in having or adopting children forced them to articulate a definition of family. How did the Depression figure in their understanding of what a family is?

LETTER TO ELEANOR ROOSEVELT FROM MRS. PRICE BREWER (1941)

Dear Madam:—

My husband and I would like to know if there is any chance of us adopting a war refugee or any baby of the white race. We can't find out where to get this information. We knew if anyone could help us it would be you. We are thirty-four and thirty-one years of age. Have a grammar school education, but believe every one should have a higher one. We are financially poor but in good health. We have been on relief and may be again, who knows. Some times it seems our hearts will burst with longing for a baby. Although poor, we believe some babies would be better off with us than where they now are. We could give a baby an abundance of love, and that counts a lot. We are natives of Oklahoma, but are registered voters of California, having been here six years. We were both raised by good families. Mr. Brewer's was comfortably fixed, mine were poor—

Hoping to get an early reply.

I remain
Sincerely Yours,
Mrs. Price Brewer

P.S. We have been married fifteen years. A doctor told us it be impossible for us to ever have a baby.

LETTER FROM THE CHILDREN'S BUREAU (1941)

My dear Mrs. Brewer:

Mrs. Roosevelt has asked us to answer your letter telling of your wish to adopt a small child.

None of the refugee children are available for adoption since it is planned to unite them with their families when the hostilities end.

It is usually wise for those considering the adoption of a child to consult authorized child-placing agencies in their own State. In California there are two agencies that are authorized to place children for adoption. . . .

We are wondering, however, if in view of your present circumstances, it would not be desirable for you and your husband to defer your application for a child until your own future is more secure. Although child-placing agencies recognize the importance of the warmth of parental affection and care in a child's life, they take great pains to place children where it is likely that the child's future will be economically secure as well.

You and Mr. Brewer may like to read the little folder on adoption which is enclosed.

Sincerely yours,
Mary E. Milburn,
Research Assistant,
Social Service Division.

LETTER TO ELEANOR ROOSEVELT FROM
MRS. HELENE B. CHANDLER (1943)

Dear Mrs. Roosevelt,

I am writing in regards of a matter in which I hope you can help me in. I have been married five years. During this time I have not been bless with a baby, as I had hope I would. I have went to docters, tried different medicine, but all this has fail, So I went to the Children Aid & ask to have a child. I fill some papers out, my husband and I sign them, Everything went alright. Until yesterday Dec 13th when I call the worker about the baby. I was inform that I could not have a baby of 4 mos because I lived in a basement, Altho the flat is very well heated, plenty of sunshine, I see no reason why they won't let me have the baby. Why is it, that I who wants a baby very much, can't have one? When women who don't want them, have them and have them on door steps, in alleys, My marriage is going on the rocks because of this, I am writing to you because I think you can help me. But if you can't I don't, and can't go on living. I am colored, age 21, with a hi school education. My husband has a very good job at the City Hall. So I am pleading, begging you to help me. You are my last hope, my last ray of light.

Hoping to hear from you very soon. I remain.

Yours Truly
Mrs Helene B. Chandler

Letters to Franklin and Eleanor Roosevelt, Children's Bureau Records, National Archives and Records Administration, College Park, Md.

✌

✌ Tuning In: Resistance and Reassurance in Popular Culture ✌

In 1920, virtually no American homes possessed the consumer appliance recognizable today as the radio. Even if they had, there was little to listen to besides amateurs talking or playing phonograph recordings in the makeshift broadcasting facilities of their garages or attics. By 1930, everything had changed. As many as 12 million American homes (about 40 percent of the total number of households) already owned consumer radio sets, most of them in modest packaging, but some stylishly set in expensive cabinetry. Americans listened to regular and often nationally distributed programming (westerns, soap operas, musical variety shows) broadcast from the early-morning hours to late at night by more than six hundred radio stations nationwide. In about a decade, commercial broadcasting, with the advertising revenues it generated, had become a major American industry. It also was highly professionalized and centralized, dominated by a handful of companies—General Electric, RCA, Westinghouse—that manufactured the hardware, produced the programs that generated advertising, and distributed the product on the airwaves.

The excitement of the "Golden Age of Radio" in the 1930s was in the programming. Listening to the radio became a basic way that Americans centered and organized their private lives and understood themselves in relation to their fellow citizens who were tuning in to the same programs. Radio was not the only entertainment mania that made the 1930s an unusual era of sight and sound in American history. Movies, too, were a powerful cultural force and common social experience, attracting 80 million viewers weekly in 1930 (the nation's population was about 123 million). These media combined with mass-circulation newspapers and magazines such as *True Story* to organize and tap into national audiences that were larger in number and geographically more widespread than ever before in American history. Radio stars joined movie stars in occupying public attention in the pages of fan magazines. When President Roosevelt designed his "fireside chats" to be broadcast via radio, he showed his appreciation of the power of the new communications and entertainment culture. With all of these developments, it is easy to overstate the unifying effect of popular culture. Even when millions listened to the same show, they were not necessarily hearing the same message. This section, which examines the most beloved radio show of the Depression as well as popular songs from the era, explores how audiences "tuned in" to this new cultural form during the period of the greatest social and economic crisis in the nation's history.

ᜆ THE PROBLEMS OF *AMOS 'N' ANDY*

In mid-March 1928, a Chicago radio station aired the first episode of *Amos 'n' Andy*, which quickly became the most popular and influential radio program in America. The story followed two black men from Georgia who, like tens of thousands of real-life southerners at the time, had made their way north to Chicago (and later New York) for a better life. "Dis job we got now aint no good," Andy explained to Amos in the first broadcast. "If we git up to Chicago, son, we kin make some big money." But they never do strike it rich, and listeners found much of the humor in their determination to defy their predestined limitations.

Like the songs of the blues performers of the 1920s, *Amos 'n' Andy* struck many of its African American fans as drawn from the authentic experience of migration from the South and the gap between high hopes and often-disappointing realities. In truth, however, two white men with long careers in blackface minstrelsy invented *Amos 'n' Andy* and played the parts of the hapless entrepreneurs behind the Fresh Air Taxicab Company. Charles Correll of Peoria, Illinois, was the voice of the industrious, well-meaning, but infallibly naive Amos. Freeman Gosden, a native of Richmond, Virginia, played his credulous companion, the big-talking, self-important buffoon Andy. In some ways, *Amos 'n' Andy* seems dependent on a century of minstrelsy adjusted to the perennial theme of America as a nation of opportunity-seeking immigrant men, forever starting their lives anew—yet theirs was no success story. In other ways, *Amos 'n' Andy* was unlike any popular entertainment of its day or before. In the 1930s novel and movie *Gone with the Wind*, Mammy and Miss Prissy inhabited an essentially white world. Amos and his pretentious compatriot were fully developed characterizations, the central figures in a drama of their own making and set in an imagined African American social world. The fact that they appealed to audiences on both sides of the color line that historically has divided the United States underscores the enduring fascination of African American culture, then as today.

Amos 'n' Andy (1930)

Amos 'n' Andy was a radio serial—a continuous story line, broken into fifteen-minute episodes, delivered six nights a week, and "sponsored" by a major national brand-name commodity (Pepsodent toothpaste). Like popular television serials today—such as HBO's The Sopranos *or the CW Network's* One Tree Hill *—the show teased audiences by prolonging suspenseful plot lines over weeks or months and leaving listeners hanging at the end of each episode. During the peak season of 1930–1931, the most talked-about series of episodes followed the misbegotten engagement of Andy and Madam Queen, who owned a beauty shop near the taxi company. Andy's hot-then-cold pursuit of Madam Queen, his schemes to wriggle out of the marriage commitment, and Madam Queen's breach-of-promise lawsuit against him—a variation on the ancient convention of the henpecked man—lured an estimated 40 million listeners each night for several months. Correll and Gosden were the show's only actors; female characters such as Madam Queen were only spoken about, as in these two scenes from the "Breach of Promise" series.*

PROBLEMS TO CONSIDER

1. How important was race to the humor presented in these scenes? Did these episodes exploit particular expectations about black manhood and womanhood, or did they rely on expectations about gender relationships that apply to all people?
2. Consider how important dialect was to the humor of the stories. What kind of men would speak in this manner? Which audiences would find their gibberish funny, and which would find it offensive? Would all listeners find it funny for the same reasons?

EPISODE NO. 862

Andy's thoughts have turned to his proposed marriage to Madam Queen. Amos, realizing Andy's mental strain, has been very lenient with him on that account. Andy is down in the dumps. He spent the entire day in the taxicab office and now as the scene opens we find him sitting on the side of his bed at the rooming house. He has two large pieces of paper on a chair directly in front of him and a pencil in his hand as Amos enters. Here they are: —

AMOS: (fading in) Well, hello dere, Andy. Whut yo' doin' home so early tonight?

ANDY: Oh, I don't know, I kind-a left Madam Queen's a little early. Thought I'd come home an' git some rest — think oveh ev'ything.

AMOS: Whut is yo' got dere on de paper?

ANDY: I'ss 'splain it to yo' in a minute — I aint finished wid it yet. Dey is sta-stusticks.

AMOS: Dey is whut?

ANDY: Oh — figgehs an' things like dat — sta-stu-sticks.

AMOS: Well son, you is on de road to gittin' married.

ANDY: I might be on de road, but I ain't walkin' down de road myself — somebody's pushin' me down dere.

AMOS: Anything wrong?

ANDY: No, it just look like I git in deepeh all de time, though. I almost made up my mind to ast Madam Queen to put off de weddin'.

AMOS: Yo' did huh?

ANDY: Yeh, I had it all 'ranged to ast her to put it off 'cause I was goin' tell her dat my mama ast me neveh to git married on a odd yeah like 31, but if I'd ast her dat now, we'd git married Decembeh de 31st — so dat wouldn't he'p none.

AMOS: Is you told her dat you is all ready to git married?

ANDY: I ain't told her nuthin'. All I do is go places wid her an' sign things.

AMOS: Whut is yo' done signed now?

ANDY: Well — las' night she told me dat she wanted me to go out wid her tonight an' look at a flat, so I went oveh an' we picked out one. I give de man two dollahs an' signed some kind o' papeh. I don't know whut 'twas. Signed up fo' a yeah.

AMOS: Well, whut is you doin' rentin' a flat if you don't know if you goin' git married or not?

ANDY: Well, whut is yo' goin' do when two people is workin' on yo'? I put my hands in my pocket knowin' dat if I keep in dere I would sign nuthin' wid 'em.

AMOS: Well, how'd yo' happen to sign it?

ANDY: Dat's whut I'se tellin' yo'. Madam Queen was workin' on me, an' so was de salesman. I went to shake hands wid de man, an' he had a fountain pen in his hand — fust thing I know I had it in MY hand — Madam Queen had hold o' my wrist, put it down on de papeh an' de fust thing I know I was writin' my name.

AMOS: 'Fore yo' knowed it huh?

ANDY: I don't think that it means nuthin' though 'cause he said to me "How 'bout signin' on de dotted line" — Madam Queen said "Alright" but when I signed de line wasn't dotted, it was a straight line.

AMOS: Straight line?

ANDY: Yeh, he calls me de tenant — an' I KNOW I ain't dat. But I give him two dollahs to git out of it. I'll straighten DAT out.

AMOS: You said it — you is gittin' in deeper all de time.

ANDY: An' de funny part of it is, I don't wanna do none o' dis stuff. I just find myself goin' an' signin'. Monday we pick out wall papeh. I'll have to make a reposit on dat.

AMOS: If you could git all de money dat you don't put up fo' reposits, you could git along fo' 'bout a month on dat money.

ANDY: Don't I know it? I ought to git me a reposit collector.

AMOS: Whut kind o' wall papeh yo' gonna pick out?

ANDY: I ain't goin' pick out none. SHE do de pickin'. All I do is argue wid de man—try to tell him I don't want it—see how little I kin put up fo' a reposit, 'cause I figgeh I lose it anyway.

AMOS: You cert'ny is handlin' dis good.

ANDY: Whut yo' mean?

AMOS: Well, you just go places, an' sign things, an' you don't know whether yo' want 'em or not?

ANDY: SHE makes up my mind in HER head. I figgeh dat if I kin git out o' dis mess by sign-in' a few papehs an' givin' a few dollahs heah an' a few dollahs dere, I is betteh off dan I IS been.

AMOS: Well, whut is you goin' do on yo' weddin' day?

ANDY: I don't know—I was just thinkin'—How far is Mexico—dey can't git yo' dere, kin dey?

AMOS: Oh, dey kin git yo' *anywhere*. She'll git yo'.

ANDY: I know SHE would—I ain't ast yo' dat—I ast if de Police kin git yo'.

AMOS: Well, I don't know. . . . You wanna git out of it alright.

ANDY: WANNA git out of it? Whut you think I arguin' fo' an' givin' ev'ybody two dollahs?

AMOS: Look like to me you just doin' de wrong thing.

ANDY: Well, I'll show yo' whut I been figgerin' heah today. I got 2 sheets o' papeh heah.

AMOS: Whut is dey?

ANDY: Well, one of 'em is new rules dat I is goin' make afteh de fust o' de yeah. De otheh one is rescuses I kin tell Madam Queen to git out o' dis weddin'.

AMOS: Read me some o' dem rescuses.

ANDY: Well, de fust one dat popped in my head don't mean nuthin' but I put it down. No. 1— "I don't feel like gittin' married."

AMOS: Yeh, dat's great. Dat ought to be enough right dere. You must-a strained yo'self think-in' o' dat one, didn't yo'?

ANDY: Don't git sarcrastic now, or I won't read yo' nuthin'.

AMOS: Go on, read 'em to me. If dey ain't no better dan dat one though you might as well tear up de list.

ANDY: No. 2— "De repression is on, an' it's gonna git bettah 'round March."

AMOS: Whut else yo' got?

ANDY: Den I got dis one down heah dat I told yo', "Mama told me neveh to git married on a odd yeah."

AMOS: She don't care nuthin' 'bout whut yo' mama told yo'.

ANDY: Den I got anotheh one down heah. "Would we be happy?" Dat's goin' make her mad an' I can't show her dat one. Den de next one is "Is it right fo' a man to marry a girl 10 yeahs oldeh dan he is?"

AMOS: Is she dat much olden dan you is?

ANDY: She is 12 yeahs oldeh dan I is, I think. But I'se lettin' her off easy wid 10, an' even dat's goin' make her mad.

AMOS: How you know she's dat old?

ANDY: Well—I remembeh her tellin' me once sumpin' 'bout de world's fair in Chicago, an' she kind-a slipped an' said sumpin' 'bout she had her pitcheh took dere, an' den again she say she had her pitcheh took when she was

10 yeahs old, an' I saw de pitcheh an' on de back of down in de corneh I saw "World's Fair Chicago 1892," an' I got hold of a bookkeepeh, an' he figgehed it out fo' me — she's 'bout 48 yeahs old.

AMOS: Boy, I didn't know she was dat old.

ANDY: She got so much o' dat beauty cream oveh dere, she rub dat on her face all de time, keep her lookin' good.

———

Amos 'n' Andy, Episode No. 862 (December 27, 1930), Manuscript Division, Library of Congress.

EPISODE NO. 865

AMOS: . . . Whut in de world did yo' say to Madam Queen?

ANDY: Well — somebody says it's a minute to 12 — I stahted thinkin'. 'Fore I knowed it I heerd some bells ringin' — ev'ybody was hollerin' "Goodbye 1930, hello 1931 — Happy New Year," so I whispered in Madam Queen's ear, I say "Sweetheart, come oveh heah in de corneh, I wanna tell yo' sumpin'."

AMOS: Of all de tricks you done ever pulled, dat was de worst one.

ANDY: Den I say to her — I fo'git zackly whut I DID say, I was kind-a nervous, but I remem-beh sayin' sumpin' like "Honey I don't see how we goin' git married tomorrow." She say "Whut yo' mean?" I say "Honey we goin' have to put off de weddin' 'cause mama told me neveh to git married on a odd year like 1931," an' I looked at her an' her eyes was gittin' as big as saucehs. She ast me again if I was foolin' an' I said "Honey to tell you de truth, I just can't git married tomorrow." Den I wished her a happy New Yeah.

AMOS: I looked over in de corner an' saw yo' talkin'.

ANDY: Den she kind-a backed up lookin' at me, an' while she was lookin' at me I heard her call fo' her sisteh. Dat's when I left.

AMOS: Well, whut did yo' run away fo'?

ANDY: Well, I wasn't goin' git in no argument wid *both* of 'em, 'cause if both of 'em jump on me, it was goin' be too bad.

———

Amos 'n' Andy, Episode No. 865 (December 31, 1930), Manuscript Division, Library of Congress.

ༀ

Charles Correll and Freeman Gosden as "Amos" and "Andy" (1929)

What did Amos and Andy look like? The actors faced unusual problems of representation. Because they were unseen, Correll's and Gosden's impersonations struck many listeners — including African Americans — as authentically black, not as caricature. Nevertheless, their radio performances drew on minstrel traditions of whites performing blackness. Gosden and Correll did not "black up" for the radio, but they did for publicity shots. In the program's first year, photos show them in the conventional white-lips/black-face minstrel makeup. After 1929, they stopped whitening their lips to achieve a more realistic style of racial impersonation, such as that seen in their 1930 movie Check and Double Check. *The two men also frequently appeared before admiring audiences without any makeup. The problems of representing the characters are presented by two examples of* Amos 'n' Andy *publicity images, both from 1929. The first photograph shows them in traditional blackface (they are behind the bars of a gate, not a jail); the second shows African American boys and men sharing a laugh with Correll and Gosden.*

PROBLEMS TO CONSIDER

1. Examine the efforts to picture *Amos 'n' Andy*. How did each image use race to convey the identity of the two characters?
2. What did the images suggest about Correll and Gosden's authority to represent African American characters?

Charles Correll and Freeman Gosden as "Amos" and "Andy," *Chicago Daily News* (1929).
(Chicago Daily News Collection, Chicago History Museum/Chicago Historical Society, DN-0088828.)

Charles Correll and Freeman Gosden visit with African American boys and men, *Chicago Daily News* (1929).

(Chicago Daily News Collection, Chicago History Museum/Chicago Historical Society, DN-0088835.)

❧

Protests Against Amos 'n' Andy (1930–1931)

One indication of Amos 'n' Andy's *large following among African Americans was its endorsement by the* Chicago Defender, *a black weekly. Each week its editorial page was emblazoned with the creed "American Race Prejudice Must Be Destroyed!" In August 1931, the* Defender *invited Gosden and Correll to Chicago—the destination of their famous characters' original migration—to join the jazz orchestra leader Duke Ellington as celebrity guests at the paper's annual summer picnic and parade. Appearing without makeup, the radio stars and the "wild ovation" they received from the tens of thousands of black Chicagoans were testimony to African Americans' own complicated attitudes about race. Such fanfare as the* Defender *picnic fueled a debate among leaders in the African American civil rights movement about the meaning and value of* Amos 'n' Andy *to the image of the successful and respectable "New Negro," which was central to black middle-class efforts to win greater opportunities, freedoms, and legal protections for African Americans. Some praised the figures as symbols of the promise of black industry; others rejected them as vulgar stereotypes of hopeless racial ineptitude. The following exchange of letters, which was published in Baltimore's* The Afro-American *newspaper, suggests how the show raised issues that had divided black Americans since the postslavery era: the relations between poor and middle-class African Americans, the effectiveness of hard work in overturning prejudices against black men, and whether black men must earn or demand the respect of white men. The first letter, from Clarence LeRoy Mitchell, a Howard University student, provoked a bitter response from the young newspaper reporter Roy Wilkins, who later headed the National Association for the Advancement of Colored People. Following the letters is an announcement of a petition drive in 1931 sponsored by the* Pittsburgh Courier, *an African American weekly with a national circulation. The* Courier *was the most persistent foe of* Amos 'n' Andy. *Robert L. Vann, the paper's editor, led the campaign to gather a million signatures on a petition to make federal regulatory authorities ban the show from the airwaves. Vann did not succeed in getting either a million signatures or the ban.*

PROBLEMS TO CONSIDER

1. What were the basic disagreements about how African Americans should be represented in popular culture? Why was there concern with the *image* of black Americans? What importance did class concerns assume in the denunciations and defenses of *Amos 'n' Andy*?
2. Did the writers agree on any points? For instance, how did they evaluate the power of popular culture? Why did the *Courier*'s campaign fail?

LETTER TO THE EDITOR FROM CLARENCE LEROY MITCHELL (1930)

To the Editor:

William S. Hedges, white, writing in the Washington Post, Sunday, February 2, had much to say in a complimentary way of Mr. Gosden and Mr. Correll, who play the role of Amos 'n Andy . . .

We are not surprised at what Mr. Hedges thinks of the average Negro, for we know that there are thousands of white persons who would go into the office of any Negro enterprise and expect to find Amos 'n Andy; to any Negro church and see and hear "Hallelujah" *[a 1929 Hollywood movie]*; to any section of a city inhabited by colored people and expect to find the "Two Black Crows" *[a blackface vaudeville duo]*; in every enterprise or to any Negro home and see Roy Cohen's short stories in action *[a white writer of stories featuring comical African Americans]*.

Speaking of Amos 'n Andy, "So fair," says Mr. Hedges, "have they been in their depicting a pair of Southern Negroes in Northern cities that, not only have they brought amusement to millions of whites, but they have brought amusement and are especial favorites among colored people in the radio audience. In fact, there has never been a protest from a Negro regarding the broadcast."

I wonder do we really care? Mr. Gosden, Mr. Correll, and others have a come-back when they remind us of our own people who carry such acts upon the stages and even a little bit of free clowning by bell boys, porters and waiters for their white spectators.

Not so very long ago, I said to an old white man, who had used the word "nigger" too frequently for my comfort, "I beg your pardon, sir— I must correct you." "Why," he said, "I didn't think you would object to that when I hear the word so much among your own people."

As a matter of fact, when we are thrilled at seeing "Hallelujah"; when we buy all the records of the "Two Black Crows," because "they are so funny," and are particularly impressed with Roy Cohen's short stories in the Saturday Evening Post, and enjoy hearing Amos 'n Andy tell us how ignorant we are, we are not only as "patient as a jackass," but just about as sensible.

It is quite noticeable now that the Jews, Irish and even the Chinese have almost put an end to belittling jokes about the less fortunate in their groups.

If one really finds amusement in ignorance, he could go to any Southern town, or Northern one for that matter, and find among the unfortunate whites plenty of "funny" ignorance just as realistic as Amos 'n Andy. But what thinking person would dare poke fun at the darker side of life of his people?

There is one big reason why we should protest Amos 'n Andy, and all other ridiculous portrayals of Negro life. The average white person does not know as much about our finer qualities as we think he does, and the logical conclusion is that he is more likely to judge the whole group by what comes to him in the way of amusement, which he is forced to believe because of his lack of knowledge of our achievements.

For instance, a leading business man of Washington did not know that Dr. Emmett J.

Scott *[a Howard University administrator]* was colored; another did not know that Howard University had a colored president; a leading Philadelphia physician had never heard of Howard at all. He thought that Lincoln was the only Negro university in the country.

A white girl engaged in social work in a small western town, had never heard of a colored physician; in fact, she admitted she had never thought about it. A member of the staff of the Cook County (Illinois) Hospital had never heard of an exclusively Negro medical school. These are a few of many examples that illustrate the white man's lack of knowledge of our better selves.

If we care, there will be no more Amos 'n Andy.

Clarence LeRoy Mitchell, letter to the editor, *The Afro-American*, February 15, 1930, 6.

LETTER TO THE EDITOR FROM ROY WILKINS (1930)

To the Editor:

In your issue of February 15 I see a letter signed Clarence LeRoy Mitchell, who is evidently a student at Howard University, which bemoans Amos 'n Andy, Octavius Roy Cohen, and the "Two Black Crows." This young writer is afflicted with the same kind of reasoning which has held the race up to more ridicule and prevented more rapid progress than anything a black-faced comedy team, or a burlesque writer could ever broadcast. I submit that if we grant that Amos 'n Andy and the rest are giving an inaccurate picture of Negro life, is it not the duty of the "better element" (of which Mr. Mitchell obviously considers himself a part) to present, "publicize" and propagandize what he calls "our better selves"?

I ask you if the suppression of Amos 'n Andy will make Emmett Scott known to any greater number of people in Washington, D.C., or Peoria, Illinois? If, in all the years of its existence,

Howard University has not been able to attract the attention of a lone physician in Philadelphia, or Walla Walla, will the stopping of the sale of records of "the Two Black Crows" help the situation any?

If Negroes turn their dials, boycott the Black Crow records and read the New Republic instead of the Saturday Evening Post, would the "better selves" be any more prominent or of any more use than they are now?

Obviously not. Nor, in turn, would white people be more informed regarding them.

It seems to me that Mr. Mitchell has fastened on the development of appearances as an objective rather than on the development of intrinsic worth. If Amos 'n Andy, the Two Black Crows and Roy Cohen's stories are true and typical, then no amount of glossing over, rarin' and pitching, by Mr. Mitchell or anyone else will be able to suppress them; if they are not true and typical, but only burlesques and humor, then they do no harm.

Amos 'n Andy, now, if the feature be carefully analyzed, will be found to contain absolutely no offensive matter at all—no offensive words or titles, not a single "coon," "nigger," "darky," "spade," "inky," or "blackie."

In this respect, I'll wager it is far cleaner than any campus group which may be got together at Howard University or any other College. The feature is clean fun from beginning to end. It has all the pathos, humor, vanity, glory, problems and solutions that beset ordinary mortals and therein lies its universal appeal.

How would Mr. Mitchell like to have Amos 'n Andy? In plug hats, with morning coats, striped trousers, glassined hair, spats, patent leather shoes and an Oxford accent? Instead of having them struggling with the immediate and universal problem of how to get and keep a decent and usable spare tire for the taxicab, would he have them prating of mergers, mortgages, international loans and foreign trade balances?

All this, if you please, for the purpose of demonstrating that Negroes are not like Amos 'n Andy, but like Owen D. Young *[the prominent white businessman]* or W. E. B. DuBois *[the African American intellectual]*?

Absurd, of course. What Mr. Mitchell and all the so-called "better element" need to do is stop straining after the appearance of what they are not, and give some attention to being a wholesome, genuine edition of what they really are. Rest assured that if Howard University does its work well, its products will make it known to the far corners of the land, let alone the neighboring city of Philadelphia; that if Emmett Scott be known as a useful citizen, it does not matter what his racial identity may be; and if Negro doctors give up congregating in large centers for social purposes and devote themselves to medicine where they are needed, any moderately informed social worker in any town big enough to boast a social agency will know about them.

Remember also that while we have been sniffing about with our heads in the clouds, Mr. Gosden and Mr. Correll have a $100,000 a year contract; Mr. Cohen sojourns in Palm Beach; and Mr. Moran and Mr. Mack travel about the country in a specially-built Packard with (of all the irony) a Negro chauffeur . . . all off material which we, if we had more wit and less false pride, might have set down in much better fashion.

No, we do not need a can for the innocent fun and harmless burlesques, but we do need one for the articulate, but non-performing pretenders in the so-called "better element."

Roy Wilkins, letter to the editor, *The Afro-American*, March 22, 1930, 6.

↝

PROTEST PETITION AGAINST
AMOS 'N' ANDY (1931)

WANTED!
One Million Signers
A Nation-wide Protest Against
"Amos 'n' Andy"

WHEREAS, For more than a year, two white men, known as "Amos 'n' Andy" to the radio world, have been exploiting certain types of American Negro for purely commercial gain for themselves and their employer; and

WHEREAS, The references made to the Negro are of such character as to prove detrimental to the self respect and general advancement of the Negro in the United States and elsewhere; and

WHEREAS, Already Negro womanhood has been broadcast to the world as indulging in bigamy, lawyers as schemers and crooks and Negro Secret Orders as organizations where money is filched from its members by dishonest methods, thereby placing all these activities among Negroes in a most harmful and degrading light; and

WHEREAS, The Pittsburgh Courier has inaugurated a nation-wide protest against the further practices of these white men who are commercializing certain types of American Negroes at a reputed salary of Six Thousand Dollars per week;

THEREFORE, We, the undersigned, do most solemnly join the protest of The Pittsburgh Courier and ask that the comedians so exploiting our group be driven from the air as a menace to our self respect, our professional, fraternal and economic progress, and to that end do sign our names and addresses hereto. We authorize The Pittsburgh Courier and other like agencies to present this protest to whatever authorities may have the power to make this protest most effective and conclusive.

Protest petition against *Amos 'n' Andy, Pittsburgh Courier*, September 12, 1931, 2.

᧞

᧞ THE SOUNDS OF THE DEPRESSION

Radio programming, of course, featured music, not just serialized comedy and drama. The music business had boomed in the 1910s and early 1920s when middle-class urban and suburban Americans bought blues and jazz recordings to dance to. By the mid-1920s, radio sales were cutting into the demand, a trend that the Depression made far worse. Even though record sales did not recover until the end of the 1930s, the broad access to radios in that decade actually extended the reach of commercially produced music to new mass audiences, many of them comparatively poor and rural Americans. The national popularity of pillow-soft ballads sung by Bing Crosby or the many versions of 1931's devil-may-care hit, "Life Is Just a Bowl of Cherries," reflected radio's ability to manufacture hit songs and spread metropolitan musical tastes and styles well beyond the nation's cities. These sounds competed and cross-pollinated with other influences, such as blues, jazz, gospel, hillbilly, and western music. Nashville's Grand Ole Opry, broadcast nationally, built huge radio followings for the rural sounds of country and western artists such as Jimmie Rodgers and the Carter Family singers, but their songs incorporated diverse influences, from Tin Pan Alley to the blues. Thus, the songs of the era reflected not only the growing power of the broadcasting industry but also the diversity of audiences' preferences and experiences. Many of the hit songs were attuned to the various ways in which Americans saw or encountered the social and economic crisis of the Depression.

Who's Afraid of the Big Bad Wolf? (1934)

FRANK CHURCHILL

In late May 1933, Walt Disney's cartoon The Three Little Pigs *debuted at Radio City Music Hall in New York City and quickly became a nationwide sensation, playing to enthusiastic audiences of children* and *adults. The story was an old one, but the Disney production mixed in some new and topical ingredients—from the highly colorful and antic action of the animation itself to the patched-up costume of the wolf at the door—to create a fable for the worst days of the Depression. The following ditty is the cartoon short's opening anthem, which itself became a radio hit. Pigs 1 and 2, who shortsightedly choose to build flimsy houses of straw and sticks, were dressed in the conventional Victorian fancy suits for little rich boys, and they sang in a high, piping soprano. Pig 3, on the other hand, wore a workingman's overalls and delivered his song in a sturdy bass voice.*

PROBLEMS TO CONSIDER

1. What explains the extraordinary popularity of this song? How would you evaluate the effectiveness of the song's messages as advice on how to cope with the Depression?
2. How did the gender and class symbols of the little pigs work with the lyrics of "Who's Afraid of the Big Bad Wolf?" to deliver a commentary on the causes and effects of the Depression?

Pig number 1:
I build my house of straw,
I build my house of hay,
I toot my flute,
I don't give a hoot
And play around all day.

Pig number 2:
I build my house of sticks,
I build my house of twigs,
With a hey-diddle-diddle,
I play my fiddle,
And dance myself a jig.

Pigs 1 and 2:
Who's afraid of the big, bad wolf,
The big, bad wolf, the big, bad wolf?
Who's afraid of the big, bad wolf?

Pig number 3:
I build my house of stone,
I build my house of bricks,
I have no chance
To sing and dance
'Cause work and play don't mix.

Pigs 1 and 2:
He don't take no time to play,
Time to play, time to play.
All he does is work all day.

Pig number 3:
You can play and laugh and fiddle.
Don't think you can make me sore.
I'll be safe and you'll be sorry
When the wolf comes to your door.

Pigs 1 and 2:
Who's afraid of the big, bad wolf,
The big, bad wolf, the big, bad wolf?
Who's afraid of the big, bad wolf?

————

∿

"Love for Sale" (1930)
COLE PORTER

"I Went to a Marvellous Party" (1939)
NOËL COWARD

Not all responses to the social and political climate of the 1930s embraced the success formulas of the bricklaying pig. In fact, two of the era's most celebrated writers for musical theater and image-conscious urban sophisticates, Cole Porter and the English-born Noël Coward, prospered in the Depression decade by declaring their utter immunity to the claims of the work ethic. In a time when most Americans worried about tomorrow, they were unabashed hedonists who possessed more than sufficient wealth to play the part. Contemptuous of middle-class morality, Coward and Porter were famous for their appetites for pleasure, which they conveyed in their witty, suave, and sexually provocative song lyrics. With their sly, ironic observations on (to use Porter's phrase) "this thing called love," such songs seem well suited to a time of social and psychological uncertainty.

Their lifestyles and artistic styles also mirrored their sexual preferences. Although their songs ordinarily were performed by presumably heterosexual women and men, both writers were discreetly but actively gay, at least among their high-society heterosexual cronies and other homosexual men who enthusiastically patronized their shows. Porter and Coward participated in and exploited the new "double life" of gay invisible visibility in the 1930s. In the 1920s, the styles and performances of gay subcultures had been both tolerated and highly visible in American cities. In the 1930s, however, municipal authorities waged intensive campaigns to clamp down on behaviors newly categorized as sexual "deviance," especially in their public commercial forms. At a time when the economic and social upheavals of the Depression undermined the family wage system and made mockeries of men who had to rely on public relief or their wives' wages, the spectacles of "fairy" public performances could hardly be tolerated. Still, despite the successful police efforts at repression, urban gay life did not disappear. In many respects, it flourished, although less visibly and often more distantly from the centers of urban culture. At a time when some theater chains forbade the words "fairy" or "pansy" to be uttered on their stages, Porter's and Coward's stock-in-trade was double entendre —*or double meaning. Even when ardently masculine crooners like Frank Sinatra voiced them, their songs contained the potential for alternative meanings that registered with gays even as they sailed over the heads of the dominant sexual culture that stigmatized homosexual men as "deviant."*

The first song here, Porter's "Love for Sale," was part of the 1930 Broadway musical The New Yorkers. *Coward's "I Went to a Marvellous Party" was from his 1939 revue* Set to Music. *It describes the fashionable world of which the songwriter was emblematic. Inspired by a party thrown by the lesbian socialite Elsa Maxwell, it was written to be sung by Beatrice Lillie, a theatrical star with a large gay following and one of the few in her day to publicly condone homosexuality.*

PROBLEMS TO CONSIDER

1. How did these songs relate to the writers' and the audience's sexuality? What enabled them to communicate different messages to different members of their audience?
2. Were these songs in any way about the Depression?

"LOVE FOR SALE"

When the only sound in the empty street
Is the heavy tread of the heavy feet
That belong to a lonesome cop,
I open shop.

When the moon so long has been gazing down
On the wayward ways of this wayward town
That her smile becomes a smirk,
I go to work.

Love for sale,
Appetizing young love for sale.
Love that's fresh and still unspoiled,
Love that's only slightly soiled,
Love for sale.
Who will buy?
Who would like to sample my supply?
Who's prepared to pay the price
For a trip to paradise?
Love for sale.

Let the poets pipe of love
In their childish way,
I know ev'ry type of love
Better far than, they.

If you want the thrill of love,
I've been thru the mill of love;
Old love, new love,
Ev'ry love but true love.

Love for sale,
Appetizing young love for sale.
If you want to buy my wares,
Follow me and climb the stairs,
Love for sale.
Love for sale.

———————

Cole Porter, "Love for Sale," in *Music and Lyrics by Cole Porter: A Treasury of Cole Porter* (New York: Chappell & Co., 1974), 20–23. Copyright © 1930 by Harms Inc., reprinted by permission of Warner Bros. Music.

"I WENT TO A MARVELLOUS PARTY"

Quite for no reason
I'm here for the season,
And high as a kite.
Living in error
With Maude at Cap Ferrat
Which couldn't be right.

Everyone's here and frightfully gay,
Nobody cares what people say,
Tho' the Riviera
Seems really much queerer
Than Rome at its height.
Yesterday night.

I went to a marvellous party
I must say the fun was intense,
We all had to do what the people we knew
Would be doing a hundred years hence.
Dear Cecil arrived wearing armour

Some shells and a black feather boa.
Poor Millicent wore a surrealist comb
Made of bits of
Mosaic from St. Peter's in Rome,
But the weight was so great that she had to go
    home,
I couldn't have liked it more!

————

Noël Coward, "I Went to a Marvellous Party," in *Noël Coward Song Book* (London and New York: Methuen, 1984), 188–90. Copyright © the Estate of the late Noël Coward.

ॐ

"No Depression (in Heaven)" (RECORDED 1936)
THE CARTER FAMILY

Scholars of American music often credit the Carter Family from Virginia's Appalachia— A.P.; his wife, Sara (the lead vocalist); and the gifted guitarist Maybelle (Sara's sister, A.P.'s sister-in-law)—with inventing commercial country music, starting with their first records in 1927 and continuing through the Depression years. Playing rhythmic acoustic guitars and singing in three-part harmony, the Carters compiled a massive recording output of blues, gospel, and folk ballads, including many tragic "event" songs, such as those inspired by the Scopes trial. The trio also is commonly celebrated today as influential figures linking American folk traditions practiced by generations of singing and guitar-picking rural amateurs to the post-1920 era of commercial radio and the music recording industry. However, no matter how unsophisticated their music may sound today, the Carters were hardly backwoods primitives. They were talented and highly inventive adapters and interpreters of the broad market of American musical styles dating from the nineteenth century: blues, ragtime, gospel, jazz, as well as the parlor and saloon songs that were staple wares of the sheet music business in the late nineteenth century. Their music was both popular and, for its time, "pop" music, making them ideally suited to reflect on the meaning of the greatest event of the 1930s—the Depression. "No Depression (in Heaven)" dates from about 1930, but the Carters recorded a version adapted by A.P. in 1936 in a New York studio. Unlike Disney's lighthearted hit or the self-consciously sophisticated compositions of Coward and Porter, the Carters' song called the Depression by name.

PROBLEMS TO CONSIDER

1. Compare "No Depression (in Heaven)" to the diagnoses of the social crisis in the other songs in this section. The differences may be obvious in how they explain the Depression, but what similarities do you detect?
2. The self-reliance doctrine expressed by the pigs in "Who's Afraid of the Big Bad Wolf?" is often cited as a traditional American response to social change or disruption. Was the Carters' song a traditional response, too?

For fear the hearts of men are failing,
For these are latter days we know.
The Great Depression now is spreading,
God's word declared it would be so.

Chorus: I'm going where there's no depression,
To the lovely land that's free from care.
I'll leave this world of toil and trouble,
My home's in heaven, I'm going there.

In that bright land, there'll be no hunger,
No orphan children cryin' for bread,

No weeping widows, toil or struggle,
No shrouds, no coffins, and no death. (*chorus*)

This dark hour of midnight nearing
Tribulation time will come.
The storm will hurl the midnight fears
And sweep lost millions to their doom. (*chorus*)

———

The Carter Family, "No Depression (in Heaven)," lyrics transcribed from *The Carter Family: The Later Years of the First Family of American Music, 1935–1941*, Disc C (New York City, 1936–1937), JSP Records JSP7708C.

∿

CHAPTER 6

"Why We Fight": World War II and American Culture: 1941–1945

NOT LONG AFTER the Japanese surprise attack on the American fleet at Pearl Harbor, the U.S. Army Chief of Staff George C. Marshall enlisted the popular Hollywood filmmaker Frank Capra for an unusual mission. At the time, Capra was known for stirring movie fables such as *Mr. Smith Goes to Washington* (1939). Marshall put him to work on a different species of moviemaking—a series of military instructional films explaining America's war and postwar aims to army recruits. Capra's *Why We Fight* series used film footage captured from America's enemies, animated maps, and arresting narration by veteran actors to "let the enemy prove to our soldiers the enormity of his cause—and the justness of ours." The first installment on the Nazi menace, *Prelude to War* (1943), made such an impression that it won an Academy Award for Best Documentary. It and its successors were commercially released. The theatrical trailer promised "55 minutes of Democracy's Dynamite! . . . the greatest gangster movie ever filmed . . . more diabolical . . . than any horror-movie you ever saw!" America's going to war, it seemed, was not so unfamiliar at all. It was a lot like what was playing at the movies.

The perceived need for such sensational assertions of "why we fight" may seem surprising. Recent movies such as *Saving Private Ryan* have emphasized that Americans today have forgotten how their present freedoms were purchased by the enormous sacrifices of World War II. Such concerns, however, are not new. Throughout the 1930s and until the attack on Pearl Harbor, the majority of Americans felt that the United States should remain neutral despite the expansionist aggression of the militarist-fascist powers of Germany and Italy in Europe and Japan in eastern Asia and the Pacific. At the time of the United States' entry into the war, the nation's military forces were small and unprepared for any major conflict, much less a global confrontation with the world's most powerful militaries. Japan's actions instantly reversed isolationist public opinion and eased President Roosevelt's case for the universal mobilization of the U.S. economy and government for war. Despite public support, public officials and private citizens alike worried that with the fighting occurring so far away, Americans on the home front would experience little real deprivation or sense of involvement. Softened by the comparative comfort of everyday life, they would lose the enthusiasm and willingness to sacrifice provoked by Pearl Harbor. The war might be lost, not on the battlefield, but on the home front.

The preoccupation with "why we fight" indicates the ways in which World War II focused attention on how Americans not only imagined the meanings of citizenship, freedom, and civic obligation but also relied on ideas about race, gender, and sexuality to explain the conflict and its relation to their lives. Although few realized or expected it at the time, Americans were collectively involved in the most disruptive and transformative years in twentieth-century American history. As this chapter shows, most Americans agreed that the war had to be won. Conflict often arose, though, when they tried to explain why they fought and what they fought for.

〜 Something Bigger Than a War Poster: The Four Freedoms 〜

Perhaps the most powerful and enduring images addressing the issue of "why we fight" are the paintings of the "Four Freedoms" that the artist Norman Rockwell published in the *Saturday Evening Post* in early 1943. Rockwell did not invent the freedoms from fear and want and of speech and religion. He drew them from President Franklin D. Roosevelt's internationally publicized State of the Union address in January 1941. In that speech, the president had explained the crisis facing the United States, its stake in the international conflict, and the ideals that guided his vision of the postwar world. At the time, the United States was not yet at war, and Roosevelt had won a commanding reelection in 1940 based on his promise never to "send an American boy to fight in a European war." But in the months before the attack on Pearl Harbor, the president intensified his campaign for the necessity of directly involving Americans in the conflict. Meanwhile, the United States was expanding its military buildup and its support to Great Britain.

Rockwell's work emerged two years after the president's speech, with American forces already fully engaged in combat. Rockwell originally had offered his images to the War Department's Office of War Information (OWI), but the officials there showed little interest in them. When Rockwell went to the *Post*, the magazine jumped at the opportunity, and the illustrations were met with great and unanticipated acclaim. Instantly famous, the original paintings were put on a national tour in major department stores, and the OWI, now on board, printed millions of poster reproductions to promote the sale of war bonds. An official letter from the president hailed Rockwell's "superb job in bringing home the plain, everyday truths behind" the Four Freedoms.

State of the Union Address (1941)
FRANKLIN D. ROOSEVELT

In November 1940, 55 percent of the voters reelected Roosevelt to an unprecedented third term as president. Despite his campaigning on the promise of American neutrality in the war that had already swept around the globe, the large margin of victory enabled Roosevelt to push the United States more directly in support of France and Great Britain against Germany. His State of the Union speech explained the "freedoms" to which Americans were committed.

PROBLEMS TO CONSIDER

1. In defining the "four essential human freedoms," was Roosevelt defining American values or universal human values? Would the denial of these freedoms at home or in foreign nations obligate Americans to take action?
2. Would you describe Roosevelt's prescriptions as politically radical, conservative, or neutral?

In the future days, which we seek to make secure, we look forward to a world founded upon four essential human freedoms.

The first is freedom of speech and expression everywhere in the world.

The second is freedom of every person to worship God in his own way everywhere in the world.

The third is freedom from want, which, translated into world terms, means economic understandings which will secure to every nation a healthy peacetime life for its inhabitants everywhere in the world.

The fourth is freedom from fear—which, translated into world terms, means a worldwide reduction of armaments to such a point and in such a thorough fashion that no nation will be in a position to commit an act of physical aggression against any neighbor—anywhere in the world.

That is no vision of a distant millennium. It is a definite basis for a kind of world attainable in our own time and generation. That kind of world is the very antithesis of the so-called new order of tyranny which the dictators seek to create with the crash of a bomb.

To that new order we oppose the greater conceptions—the moral order. A good society is able to face schemes of world domination and foreign revolutions alike without fear.

Since the beginning of our American history we have been engaged in change—in a perpetual, peaceful revolution—a revolution which goes on steadily, quietly adjusting itself to changing conditions—without the concentration camp or the quicklime in the ditch. The world order which we seek is the cooperation of free countries, working together in a friendly, civilized society.

This Nation has placed its destiny in the hands and heads and hearts of its millions of free men and women; and its faith in freedom under the guidance of God. Freedom means the supremacy of human rights everywhere. Our support goes to those who struggle to gain those rights or keep them. Our strength is in our unity of purpose.

To that high concept there can be no end save victory.

———

Franklin D. Roosevelt, State of the Union address, January 6, 1941, *Congressional Record* 87, pt. 1:46–47.

ᘒ

Norman Rockwell: My Adventures as an Illustrator (1960)
NORMAN ROCKWELL

Norman Rockwell has the popular reputation today as the twentieth century's foremost celebrant of an essential "American identity" that is rooted in the humorous simplicity and ethnic uniformity of rural and small-town New England life. Rockwell was not a native to such scenery, however. He was born in New York City and lived either there or in its suburbs until his mid-forties, when he relocated to rural Vermont. Moreover, he earned his fame and wealth supplying cover illustrations for the Saturday Evening Post, *the era's foremost mass-circulation magazine and a product itself of fully industrialized processes of manufacturing and distribution. All of this is to suggest that Rockwell's images — their apparent meanings and their reception by audiences — are anything but simple nostalgia. Rather, they are richly imagined texts that addressed the primary social and political issues of their day. Their value as historical sources is especially apparent in the Four Freedoms images. In the following excerpt from his autobiography, the artist explains how he turned Roosevelt's words into pictures.*

PROBLEMS TO CONSIDER

1. How did the symbols Rockwell chose to illustrate the Four Freedoms shape or determine the messages that he wished to convey? Did such symbols stand for all or just some Americans?
2. Rockwell asserts that he put Roosevelt's ideals "in terms everybody can understand." Would "everybody" have understood them, or understood them in the same way?

Since we *[Rockwell and a fellow illustrator]* . . . were too old to enlist, we had decided that the best way for us to contribute to the war effort was by doing posters for the government. We had already worked up some ideas and were going to set off for Washington any day now. The only thing that was delaying us was me. I hadn't come up with a really good idea yet, one I could get excited about. I had a poster of a machine gunner and a couple of other ideas sketched out, but they didn't satisfy me. I wanted to do something bigger than a war poster, make some statement about why the country was fighting the war.

When Roosevelt and Churchill issued their Atlantic Charter, with its Four Freedoms proclamation, I had tried to read it, thinking that maybe it contained the idea I was looking for. But I hadn't been able to get beyond the first paragraph. The language was so noble, platitudinous really, that it stuck in my throat. No, I said to myself, it doesn't go, how am I to illustrate that? I'm not noble enough. Besides, nobody I know is reading the proclamation either, in spite of the fanfare and hullabaloo about it in the press and on the radio.

So I continued to stew over an idea. I tried this and that. Nothing worked. I juggled the Four Freedoms about in my mind, reading a sentence here, a sentence there, trying to find a picture. But it was so darned high-blown. Somehow I just couldn't get my mind around it. . . .

Then one night as I was tossing in bed, mulling over the proclamation and the war, rejecting one idea after another and getting more and more discouraged as the minutes ticked by, all empty and dark, I suddenly remembered how Jim Edgerton had stood up in town meeting and said something that everybody else disagreed with. But they had let him have his say. No one had shouted him down. My gosh, I thought, that's it. There it is. Freedom of Speech. I'll illustrate the Four Freedoms using my Vermont neighbors as models. I'll express the ideas in simple, everyday scenes. Freedom of Speech—a New England town meeting. Freedom from Want—a Thanksgiving dinner. Take them out of the noble language of the proclamation and put them in terms everybody can understand. . . .

I went back to Arlington, rejuvenated, and set right to work. I spent, finally, six months painting the Four Freedoms and it was a struggle. I had a terrible time. I started the first one I did—"Freedom of Speech"—over four times. I practically finished it twice, finding each time when

I had just a few days' work left that it wasn't right. At first I planned to show an entire town meeting, a large hall full of people with one man standing up in the center of the crowd talking. But when I'd got it almost done I found that there were too many people in the picture. It was too diverse, it went every which way and didn't settle anywhere or say anything. So I had to work it over in my mind and, as it turned out, on canvas, until I'd boiled it down into a strong, precise statement: the central figure of the man speaking in the midst of his neighbors. . . .

With "Freedom from Want" and "Freedom from Fear" I had little trouble. I painted the turkey in "Freedom from Want" on Thanksgiving Day. Mrs. Wheaton, our cook (and the lady holding the turkey in the picture), cooked it, I painted it, and we ate it. That was one of the few times I've ever eaten the model. . . .

I never liked "Freedom from Fear" or, for that matter, "Freedom from Want." Neither of them has any wallop. "Freedom from Want" was not very popular overseas. The Europeans sort of resented it because it wasn't freedom from want, it was overabundance, the table was so loaded down with food. I think the two I had the most trouble with—"Freedom of Speech" and "Freedom of Worship"—have more of an impact, say more, better.

_____

Norman Rockwell, *Norman Rockwell: My Adventures as an Illustrator* (Garden City, N.Y.: Doubleday, 1960), 338–39, 341–43.

❧

Freedom from Fear (1943)
NORMAN ROCKWELL

Don't Let That Shadow Touch Them (1942)
LAWRENCE B. SMITH

Why were there no guns or other symbols of the war in Rockwell's images? Freedom from Fear*'s image of protective parents tucking their children into bed, was the only painting that even referred to the conflict (the newspaper headlines mention it). Such omissions seem curious in comparison with other publicly and privately sponsored posters*

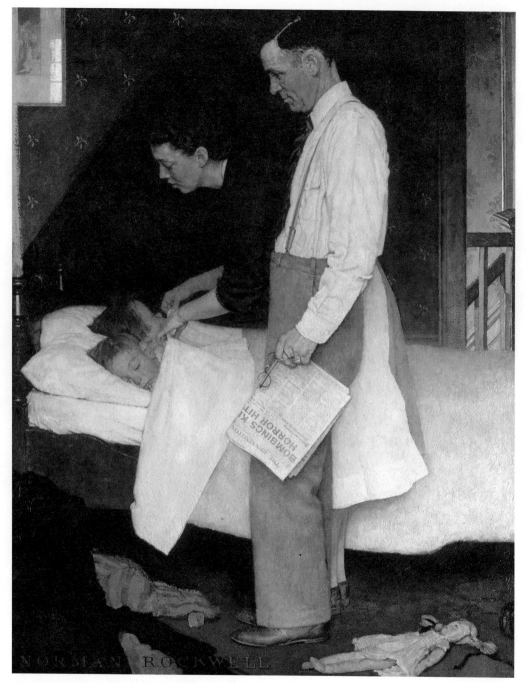

Norman Rockwell, *Freedom from Fear* (1943).

Lawrence B. Smith, "Don't Let That Shadow Touch Them" (1942).

(© Swim Ink 2, LLC/Corbis.)

that encouraged support for the war effort by conjuring up images of the fearful conse-
quences of an American defeat.

PROBLEMS TO CONSIDER

1. Compare Rockwell's poster with this other publicly sponsored image. Did these posters explain why Americans were fighting the war in the same way?
2. What explains the more enduring popularity of Rockwell's poster?

⌁ *Mobilizing American Culture for War* ⌁

World War II was the most destructive war in human history; it also was the most fully industrialized and bureaucratized. Yet the representations of the conflict that have passed down to us—the Marine Corps War Memorial of the American flag raising at Iwo Jima, the American troops landing at Normandy—have given greater attention to the "fighting man" and his enemies than to other equally impor-tant, although less conventionally heroic, dimensions and reasons for the United States' ultimate success: namely, the industrial production and distribution and the organizational management of the war. Some 16.4 million people served in the mil-itary over the course of the conflict and were dispersed around the world. Most of them were young white men, many of them teenagers. The ranks also included 1 million African Americans, 350,000 Mexican Americans, and 350,000 women. It is estimated that only about one-third of those in the armed forces ever saw combat. The great majority of enlisted men and women served in support capacities, behind the lines or even on bases in the United States. Millions more from farming regions or rural towns migrated to new industrial jobs and opportunities in cities such as Los Angeles and Detroit, as wartime federal spending—well beyond anything offered by New Deal programs—ended the Depression and stimulated what would become nearly three decades of economic expansion. The widespread social changes generated by the nearly universal mobilization of the nation for war shook the racial, gender, and sexual status quo. The materials in this section examine these disruptions and their historical impact from two angles: how Americans imagined their unified purposes in fighting the war, and how they imagined the enemy they were fighting against.

⌁ FIGHTING MEN AND WOMEN

For depictions of fighting men, no artist could match the following that Bill Mauldin's cartoons enjoyed among GIs (short for "government issue," a slang term for enlisted men). Mauldin worked for *Stars and Stripes*, the official armed forces newspaper. His cartoons depicted the everyday misery and grim humor of the "dog-face" infantrymen Joe and Willie. Their grimy fatigues and stubble-covered faces showed that they did the war's dirty work, while their commanding officers kept their uniforms and hands clean behind the lines. "I don't make the infantryman look noble," Mauldin explained, "because he couldn't look noble even if he tried."

But Joe and Willie were noble. When Mauldin put their unshaven, weary faces in the same cartoon with the smooth cheeks and over-refined manners of the officer corps, they reaffirmed a gender convention: when men went into battle, they carried the deeply embedded assumption that combat was the supreme test both of one's "manhood" and of one's citizenship. But World War II, as this section demonstrates, also challenged this assumption in unexpected ways. The universal ideals of freedom stated in Roosevelt's speech combined with the severe labor shortage in the military and private sector to democratize the opportunity to prove oneself in war. As a result, many people whose participation in civic life historically had been severely limited, including large numbers of women, seized the chance to expand the meaning and boundaries of their own citizenship.

Masculinity and the Role of the Combat Soldier (1949)
SAMUEL A. STOUFFER ET AL.

Compared to the beating that the breadwinner ideal took over the course of the Depression, waging war promised to rebuild the personal and political authority of men. War cast them as warriors, statesmen, and builders of a better world. American men of all races accepted this truism, although white men believed they were the nation's true fighting race. That presumption explains why African American leaders fought so hard to have men of their race moved from custodial or support roles to the battlefront, where they could prove themselves as men. The following psychiatric study, completed after the war, examines the "codes" that governed the expectations of American soldiers.

PROBLEMS TO CONSIDER

1. What were the markers of a "real soldier"? According to this study, what were the essential features of a "man" or a "guy"?
2. How did soldiers reconcile their valuation of "freedom" with codes of masculinity?

The codes according to which a combat unit judged the behavior of its members, and in terms of which conformity was enforced, differed in their generality. Perhaps the most general was one drawn largely from civilian culture but given its special interpretation in the combat situation: Be a man. Conceptions of masculinity vary among different American groups, but there is a core which is common to most: courage, endurance and toughness, lack of squeamishness when confronted with shocking or distasteful stimuli, avoidance of display of weakness in general, reticence about emotional or idealistic matters, and sexual competency. . . .

Combat posed a challenge for a man to prove himself to himself and others. Combat was a dare. One never knew for sure that he could take it until he had demonstrated that he could. Most soldiers facing the prospect of combat service had to deal with a heavy charge of anticipatory anxiety. The more they heard about how tough the fighting was, the greater the anxiety and the insecurity that came from doubt as to whether they could handle the anxiety. Thus, combat might actually come almost as a relief—it joined the issue and broke the strain of doubt and waiting.

A code as universal as "being a man" is very likely to have been deeply internalized. So the fear of failure in the role, as by showing cowardice in battle, could bring not only fear of social censure on this point as such, but also more central and strongly established fears related to sex-typing. To fail to measure up as a soldier in courage and endurance was to risk the charge of not being a man. ("Whatsa matter, bud — got lace on your drawers?" "Christ, he's acting like an old maid.") If one were not socially defined as a man, there was a strong likelihood of being branded a "woman," a dangerous threat to the contemporary male personality. The generally permissive attitude toward expression of fear . . . mitigated the fear of failure in manliness, but by no means obviated it. A man could show and admit fear without necessarily being branded a "weak sister," but only so long as it was clear that he had done his utmost. . . .

The most direct application of the masculinity code was to the social role of the combat soldier. In fact, the code of the combat soldier can be summarized by saying that behavior in combat was recognized as a test of being a man. When this code was internalized, or enforced by playing on an internalized code of manliness, a man once in combat had to fight in order to keep his own self-respect: "Hell, I'm a soldier." . . .

The attributes [that infantrymen] characteristically ascribed to a good officer differed from those ascribed to a good private. . . . Leadership ability and practices were most often mentioned in the case of officers, while courage and aggressiveness . . . ("guts"), which are central to the masculine ideal, . . . were a prime ingredient of the combat man's notion of the good soldier. . . .

A more concrete impression of some of the elements of masculinity involved in being a combat soldier may be seen in the following fragment of an interview with a wounded Infantry veteran of the North African campaign:

> One time me and another guy were in a hole. The guy says "Let's get out of here." I talked to him (tried to calm him down) but he never was a soldier — did typewriting, ran errands for officers. He was a suck-ass for a colonel,

not a real soldier. A real soldier is a guy — he'll drink and swear — but he relies on himself; a guy that can take care of himself.

Here the combat soldier, the real soldier, is defined partly by contrast with someone who does not qualify as a man.

The man who lived up to the code of the combat soldier had proved his manhood; he could take pride in being a combat man and draw support in his role from this pride. Of this sort was the grim pride in being an "old beat-up Joe," who had suffered and endured and took a perverse satisfaction that things were working out for the worst, just as he had expected they would. A second aspect of this pride of the combat man appears in his typical resentment of the rear echelon. . . . [This] resentment, springing in part from envy of the favored circumstances at the rear, served one function of devaluing what was inaccessible and placing a higher moral value on what had to be put up with. The fact that rear-echelon soldiers accepted the lower status made the right to feel this invidious pride a real support to the combat man.

The pride in being a combat man may be illustrated . . . by a sergeant in a veteran Infantry battalion. He had been wounded and later returned to his outfit through the chain of replacement depots. His account of this revealed that he was indifferent to the physical conditions encountered, but like many combat men of similar experience he was very bitter about the treatment of combat veterans by the permanent personnel of the replacement depots. He complained that the cadre were indifferent to the welfare of replacements, "showed no respect for what the combat men had been through," tried to "shove people around," and so on through a long list. When asked for an example, he told of a corporal who was in charge of a group of veteran combat replacements:

> He kept ordering us around and putting combat men on kitchen details. Finally I got fed up. I told him: "Look here, damn you — you

stay out of here. There are *men* in here, and I don't want them contaminated."

This was recounted with intensely explosive bitterness and contempt.... The code of being a man is here explicit. The rear-echelon soldier is resented and despised because of his misuse of Army authority and his failure to share a community of experience and sentiment. And the

final crushing comment which the combat soldier makes is to imply that the corporal is not a man—because he is not one of the fraternity of front-line fighters....

———

Samuel A. Stouffer et al., "Masculinity and the Role of the Combat Soldier," in *The American Soldier: Combat and Its Aftermath* (Princeton, N.J.: Princeton University Press, 1949), 131–35.

My Personal Hero (1944)

ERNIE PYLE

Ernie Pyle was the most widely read, trusted, and beloved news correspondent covering the war in Europe. Born in Indiana, he had established his reputation as an uncanny chronicler of the "American character" during the 1930s as he wandered across the nation by automobile, writing stories about extraordinary ordinary people, iconic folk with whom he and his readers could identify. As his biographer has observed, people read Pyle not for wisdom or controversial opinion, but "for sustenance in difficult times." During the war, the trust he generated in his readers linked the battlefronts at home and abroad. Personal and concrete, his stories from the European front humanized the violence and sacrifice of the war to domestic readers and bridged the great distance between the two continents. American soldiers welcomed his accounts no less enthusiastically. On the one hand, they treated him as one of their own rather than as an alien presence. To penetrate the soldier's life, Pyle never had to flash his credentials or use his celebrity to cozy up to the brass; he simply greeted GIs, "Hi, I'm Ernie Pyle," and he was in. You "felt at ease immediately with him," a war veteran observed. On the other hand, soldiers regarded Pyle as a specially prized eyewitness who seemed to uniquely appreciate what he called the "semi-barbarian" lives they led. The following accounts of the GI "Buck" Eversole are two of Pyle's best-known and most beloved dispatches from the European front.

PROBLEMS TO CONSIDER

1. What in Pyle's style of writing might have accounted for the popularity of these stories?
2. What made Eversole "heroic"? How did his "heroism" demonstrate "why we fight"?

February 21, 1944
IN ITALY—The company commander said to me, "Every man in this company deserves the Silver Star."

We walked around in the olive grove where the men of the company were sitting on the edges of their foxholes, talking or cleaning their gear.

"Let's go over here," he said. "I want to introduce you to my personal hero."

I figured that the Lieutenant's own "personal hero," out of a whole company of men who deserved the Silver Star, must be a real soldier indeed.

Then the company commander introduced me to Sergt. Frank Eversole, who shook hands sort of timidly and said, "Pleased to meet you," and then didn't say any more.

I could tell by his eyes and by his slow and courteous speech when he did talk that he was a Westerner. Conversation with him was sort of hard, but I didn't mind his reticence for I know how Westerners like to size people up first.

The Sergeant wore a brown stocking cap on the back of his head. His eyes were the piercing kind. I noticed his hands—they were outdoor hands, strong and rough.

Later in the afternoon I came past his foxhole again, and we sat and talked a little while alone. We didn't talk about the war, but mainly about our West, and just sat and made figures on the ground with sticks as we talked.

We got started that way, and in the days that followed I came to know him well. He is to me, and to all those with whom he serves, one of the great men of the war.

Frank Eversole's nickname is "Buck." The other boys in the company sometimes call him "Buck Overshoes," simply because Eversole sounds a bit like "overshoes."

Buck was a cowboy before the war. He was born in the little town of Missouri Valley, Ia., and his mother still lives there. But Buck went West on his own before he was 16, and ever since has worked as a ranch hand. He is 28, and unmarried.

He worked a long time around Twin Falls, Idaho, and then later down in Nevada. Like so many cowboys, he made the rodeos in season. He was never a star or anything. Usually he just rode the broncs out of the chute for pay—$7.50 a ride. . . .

Like any cowboy, he loves animals. Here in Italy one afternoon Buck and some other boys were pinned down inside a one-room stone shed by terrific German shellfire. As they sat there, a frightened mule came charging through the door. There simply wasn't room inside for men and mule both, so Buck got up and shooed him

out the door. Thirty feet from the door a direct hit killed the mule. Buck has always felt guilty about it. . . .

Buck Eversole has the Purple Heart and two Silver Stars for bravery. He is cold and deliberate in battle. His commanders depend more on him than any other man. He has been wounded once, and had countless narrow escapes. He has killed many Germans.

He is the kind of man you instinctively feel safer with than with other people. He is not helpless like most of us. He is practical. He can improvise, patch things, fix things.

His grammar is the unschooled grammar of the plains and the soil. He uses profanity, but never violently. Even in the familiarity of his own group his voice is always low. He is such a confirmed soldier by now that he always says "sir" to any stranger. It is impossible to conceive of his doing anything dishonest.

After the war Buck will go back West to the land he loves. He wants to get a little place and feed a few head of cattle, and be independent.

"I don't want to be just a ranch hand no more," he says. "It's all right and I like it all right, but it's a rough life and it don't get you nowhere. When you get a little older you kinda like a place of your own."

Buck Eversole has no hatred for Germans. He kills because he's trying to keep alive himself. The years roll over him and the war becomes his only world, and battle his only profession. He armors himself with a philosophy of acceptance of what may happen.

"I'm mighty sick of it all," he says very quietly, "but there ain't no use to complain. I just figure it this way, that I've been given a job to do and I've got to do it. And if I don't live through it, there's nothing I can do about it."

February 22, 1944

IN ITALY—Buck Eversole is a platoon sergeant in an infantry company. That means he has charge of about 40 front-line fighting men.

He has been at the front for more than a year. War is old to him and he has become almost the master of it. He is a senior partner now in the institution of death.

His platoon has turned over many times as battle whittles down the old ones and the replacement system brings up the new ones. Only a handful now are veterans.

"It gets so it kinda gets you, seein' these new kids come up," Buck told me one night in his slow, barely audible Western voice, so full of honesty and sincerity.

"Some of them have just got fuzz on their faces, and don't know what it's all about, and they're scared to death. No matter what, some of them are bound to get killed."

We talked about some of the other old-time non-coms who could take battle themselves, but had gradually grown morose under the responsibility of leading green boys to their slaughter. Buck spoke of one sergeant especially, a brave and hardened man, who went to his captain and asked him to be reduced to a private in the lines.

"I know it ain't my fault that they get killed," Buck finally said. "And I do the best I can for them, but I've got so I feel like it's me killin' 'em instead of a German. I've got so I feel like a murderer. I hate to look at them when the new ones come in."

Buck himself has been fortunate. Once he was shot through the arm. His own skill and wisdom have saved him many times, but luck has saved him countless other times. . . .

One day Buck went stalking a German officer in close combat, and wound up with the German on one side of a farmhouse and Buck on the other. They kept throwing grenades over the house at each other without success. Finally Buck stepped around one corner of the house, and came face to face with the German, who'd had the same idea.

Buck was ready and pulled the trigger first. His slug hit the German just above the heart. The German had a wonderful pair of binoculars slung over his shoulders, and the bullet smashed them to bits. Buck had wanted some German binoculars for a long time.

The ties that grow up between men who live savagely and die relentlessly together are ties of great strength. There is a sense of fidelity to each other among little corps of men who have endured so long and whose hope in the end can be but so small.

One afternoon while I was with the company Sergt. Buck Eversole's turn came to go back to rest camp for five days. The company was due to attack that night.

Buck went to his company commander and said, "Lieutenant, I don't think I better go. I'll stay if you need me."

The lieutenant said, "Of course I need you, Buck, I always need you. But it's your turn and I want you to go. In fact, you're ordered to go."

The truck taking the few boys away to rest camp left just at dusk. It was drizzling and the valleys were swathed in a dismal mist. Artillery of both sides flashed and rumbled around the horizon. The encroaching darkness was heavy and foreboding.

Buck came to the little group of old-timers in the company with whom I was standing, to say goodbye. You'd have thought he was leaving forever. He shook hands all around, and his smile seemed sick and vulnerable. He was a man stalling off his departure.

He said, "Well, good luck to you all." And then he said, "I'll be back in just five days." He said goodbye all around and slowly started away. But he stopped and said goodbye all around again, and he said, "Well, good luck to you all."

I walked with him toward the truck in the dusk. He kept his eyes on the ground, and I think he would have cried if he knew how, and he said to me very quietly:

"This is the first battle I've ever missed that this battalion has been in. Even when I was in the hospital with my arm they were in bivouac. This will be the first one I've ever missed. I sure do hope they have good luck."

And then he said:

"I feel like a deserter."

He climbed in, and the truck dissolved into the blackness. I went back and lay down on the ground among my other friends, waiting for the night orders to march. I lay there in the darkness thinking—terribly touched by the great simple devotion of this soldier who was a cowboy—and thinking of the millions far away at home who must remain forever unaware of the powerful fraternalism in the ghastly brotherhood of war.

———————

Ernie Pyle, "My Personal Hero" (February 21 and 22, 1944), courtesy, Manuscripts Department, The Lilly Library, Indiana University, Bloomington, Ind.

⁊

Narrative of Fanny Christina Hill (1987)

Narrative of Beatrice Morales Clifton (1987)

The labor crisis created by the military mobilization for World War II altered the course of many women's lives. Defense industries were massive operations employing, in some cases, tens of thousands of workers and often were desperate to hire people. The opportunity for high wages in good jobs motivated unprecedented numbers of married women to move into the work force and become "Rosie the Riveters." Employers' needs also weakened the gender and racial boundaries that historically had divided men's work from women's work, employment for whites from jobs for nonwhites. The effects of these developments are evident in the oral histories of two young, poor, married women of color who in late 1941 were living in the Los Angeles area, a region that benefited more than any other from wartime military spending and employment. Fanny Christina Hill, originally from Texas, moved there in 1940 at the age of twenty. She found employment as a live-in domestic but always was on the lookout for better work and better pay. Her husband said he married her because she could take care of herself. In 1943, while her husband was serving in the military, she found what she was looking for at North American Aviation, a company that hired more African Americans than most businesses because of pressure from its unionized work force and civil rights groups. Beatrice Morales Clinton was born in Mexico and was living with her husband (a janitor) and four children when the war started. Although poor, she was not looking for work outside the home, and her husband was dead set against the idea. Nonetheless, when she was given the opportunity to work at Lockheed, a major defense contractor, she took it.

PROBLEMS TO CONSIDER

1. Why did these women work outside the home? What obstacles stood in their way? How did the war heighten or weaken those obstacles?
2. What effects did wartime employment have on these women and on their sense of themselves as "wives" or "women"?

NARRATIVE OF FANNY CHRISTINA HILL

I don't remember what day of the week it was, but I guess I must have started out pretty early that morning. When I went there, the man didn't hire me. They had a school down here on Figueroa and he told me to go to the school. I went down and it was almost four o'clock and they told me they'd hire me. You had to fill out a form. They didn't bother too much about your experience because they knew you didn't have any experience in aircraft. Then they give you some kind of little test where you put the pegs in the right hole.

There were other people in there, kinda mixed. I assume it was more women than men. Most of the men was gone, and they weren't hiring too many men unless they had a good excuse. Most of the women was in my bracket, five or six years younger or older. I was twenty-four. . . . I went to work the next day, sixty cents an hour. . . .

[Hill trained for four weeks in a company school before assuming her job.]

I was a good student, if I do say so myself. But I have found out through life, sometimes even if you're good, you just don't get the breaks if the color's not right. I could see where they made a difference in placing you in certain jobs. They had fifteen or twenty departments, but all the Negroes went to Department 17 because there was nothing but shooting and bucking rivets. You stood on one side of the panel and your partner stood on this side, and he would shoot the rivets with a gun and you'd buck them with the bar. That was about the size of it. I just didn't like it. I didn't think I could stay there with all this shooting and a'bucking and a'jumping and a'bumping. I stayed in it about two or three weeks and then I just decided I did *not* like that. I went and told my foreman and he didn't do anything about it, so I decided to leave.

While I was standing outside on the railroad track, I ran into somebody else out there fussing also. I went over to the union and they told me what to do. I went back inside and they sent me to another department where you did bench work and I liked that much better. . . .

I must have stayed there nearly a year, and then they put me over in another department, "Plastics." . . . I worked over there until the end of the war. Well, not quite the end, because I got pregnant, and while I was off having the baby the war was over. . . .

I worked [at the aviation plant] up until the end of March and then I took off [to have my baby]. Beverly was born the twenty-first of June. I'd planned to come back somewhere in the last of August. I went to verify the fact that I did come back, so that did go on my record that I didn't just quit. But they laid off a lot of people, most of them, because the war was over.

It didn't bother me much—not thinking about it jobwise. I was just glad that the war was over. I didn't feel bad because my husband had a job and he also was eligible to go to school with his GI bill. So I really didn't have too many plans—which I wish I had had. I would have tore out page one and fixed it differently; put my version of page one in there.

I went and got me a job doing day work. That means you go to a person's house and clean up for one day out of the week and then you go to the next one and clean up. I did that a couple of times and I discovered I didn't like that so hot. Then I got me a job downtown working in a little factory where you do weaving—burned clothes and stuff like that. I learned to do that real good. It didn't pay too much but it paid enough to get me going, seventy-five cents or about like that.

When North American called me back, was I a happy soul! I dropped that job and went back. That was a dollar an hour. So, from sixty cents an hour, when I first hired in there, up to one dollar. That wasn't traveling fast, but it was better than anything else because you had hours to work by and you had benefits and you come home at night with your family. So it was a good deal.

It made me live better. I really did. We always say that Lincoln took the bale off of the Negroes. I think there is a statue up there in Washington D.C., where he's lifting something off the Negro. Well, my sister always said—that's why you can't interview her because she's so radical—"Hitler was the one that got us out of the white folks' kitchen."

NARRATIVE OF BEATRICE
MORALES CLIFTON

I'd never thought about working. . . .

[The defense plants] had these offices everywhere in Pasadena, of aircraft. I went in there to try and get [my sixteen-year-old niece] something, but they said, "We've got aircraft work right now for everybody, except she's too young." [My brother] says, "Why don't you get it?" I said, "Me?" He said, "Yeah, why don't you get the job?" I said, "Well, I don't know." But the more I kept thinking about it, the more I said, "That's a good idea." So I took the forms and when I got home and told my husband, oh! he hit the roof. He was one of those men that didn't believe in the wife ever working; they want to be the supporter. I said, "Well, I've made up my mind. I'm going to go to work regardless of whether you like it or not." I was determined.

My family and everybody was surprised—his family. I said, "Well, yeah, I'm going to work." "And how does Julio feel?" "He doesn't want me to, but I'm going anyway." When he saw that, he just kept quiet; he didn't say no more. My mother didn't say nothing because I always told her, "Mother, you live your life and I live mine." We had that understanding. When I decided to go to work, I told her, "I'm going to go to work and maybe you can take care of the children." She said, "Yeah." . . .

I filled out the papers and everything and I got the job [at a Lockheed plant]. . . .

They put me way up in the back, putting little plate nuts and drilling holes. They put me with some guy—he was kind of a stinker, real mean. A lot of them guys at the time resented women coming into jobs, and they let you know about it. He says, "Well, have you ever done any work like this?" I said, "No." I was feeling just horrible. Horrible. Because I never worked with men, to be with men alone other than my husband. So then he says "You know what you've

got in your hand? That's a rivet gun." I said, "Oh." What could I answer? I was terrified. So then time went on and I made a mistake. I messed up something, made a ding. He got so irritable with me, he says, "You're not worth the money Lockheed pays you."

He couldn't have hurt me more if he would have slapped me. When he said that, I dropped the gun and I went running downstairs to the rest[r]oom, with tears coming down. This girl from Texas saw me and she followed me. She was real good. She was one of these "toughies"; dressed up and walked like she was kind of tough. She asked me what was wrong. I told her what I had done and I was crying. She says, "Don't worry." She started cussing him. We came back up and she told them all off.

I was very scared because, like I say, I had never been away like that and I had never been among a lot of men. Actually, I had never been out on my own. Whenever I had gone anyplace, it was with my husband. It was all building up inside of me, so when that guy told me that I wasn't worth the money Lockheed paid me, it just came out in tears. . . .

As time went on, I started getting a little bit better. I just made up my mind that I was going to do it. I learned my job so well that then they put me to the next operation. At the very first, I just began putting little plate nuts and stuff like that. Then afterwards I learned how to drill the skins and burr them. Later, as I got going, I learned to rivet and buck. I got to the point where I was very good. . . .

I was just a mother of four kids, that's all. But I felt proud of myself and felt good being that I had never done anything like that. I felt good that I could do something, and being that it was war, I felt that I was doing my part.

I went from 65 cents to $1.05. That was top pay. It felt good and, besides, it was my own money. I could do whatever I wanted with it because my husband, whatever he was giving to the house, he kept on paying it. I used to buy clothes for the kids; buy little things that they needed. I had a bank account and I had a little saving at home where I could get ahold of the money right away if I needed it. Julio never asked about it. He knew how much I made; I showed him. If there was something that had to be paid and I had the money and he didn't, well, I used some of my money. . . .

Fanny Christina Hill and Beatrice Morales Clifton, interviews, in Sherna Berger Gluck, *Rosie the Riveter Revisited: Women, the War, and Social Change* (Boston: Twayne, 1987), 37–38, 41–42, 208–11.

☙

Psychiatry in a Troubled World: Yesterday's War and Today's Challenge (1948)
WILLIAM C. MENNINGER

Another test to the gender-specific categories of the masculine "real soldier" was the enlisted woman. In World War I, women were confined to nursing positions. In World War II, they served in record numbers in all branches of the service and in many capacities short of actual combat. Many of these jobs were conventionally gendered as "women's work," but even these represented an encroachment on what had historically been a male monopoly. In fact, more than 1,000 women flew planes on noncombat missions. These new roles for women in the military provoked anxieties both at home and among the male soldiery. It was feared that such women were guided by suspicious motivations—that they were naive girls who would fall easy prey to predatory men, or were "loose" women out for a fast time, or were secretly lesbians. In other words, there had to be something wrong with a woman who would choose military service. The psychiatrist William C. Menninger served as a consultant to the army and helped develop procedures for screening out the wrong kind of women and men from military service.

PROBLEMS TO CONSIDER

1. What does this document reveal about how fighting men responded to the presence of women in the army?
2. Why would men have such a difficult time with a definition of womanhood that included military service?

Even in our own democracy the approved feminine role is a passive and dependent one. . . . Before 1942 [women] were not supposed to fit into a fighting army except as nurses or Red Cross workers. The average man thought of women in an army as mythical Amazons, or the guerrilla fighters of revolutions, or camp followers with very specific business purposes. It took World War II with its great need for man power to open the doors of military service, as well as of industry, science, and business, to women in any number. Those doors may be hard to close!

The increasing opportunity for American women to modify their traditional position complicates their acceptance of the feminine role. It allows women to choose their pattern of behavior. This is more difficult than it is for men to accept the unchanged concept of the masculine role. Furthermore, our educational philosophy differs from our current standards. The modern girl child in America is not taught to be the passive, dependent individual our culture has conceived of as the normal of adult femininity. So that when grown she is faced with some surprising facts: the "important" work of the world is supposed to be done by men; her early educational, social, and economic preparation for independence conflicts with the limitations of the accepted feminine role; the approved field of her interest seems unbalanced with too much routine for some years and too much leisure in later years. Furthermore, from childhood on, the girl, whether or not she wishes to do so, is expected to assume the role of a "weaker" sex, because of man's greater physical strength. It is reasonable to assume that a girl educated in the American way has to be "broken in" to being feminine. For she was born into what appears as a "man's world," in which she is supposed to "love, honor, and obey" and to make a home for some man. It is not surprising, therefore, that in our culture women should acquire and retain strong masculine strivings.

Psychological significance of WAC [Women's Army Corps] *for women.* In evaluating the psychological significance of the military service for women, one must keep in mind that all WAC members were volunteers. . . . The appeal of an Army experience in time of war had a special attraction for some women, so that appeal was in itself part of the selective process. One must also recognize that conscious reasons for enlisting, while highly commendable (though possibly in some instances reprehensible), are not the total explanation of motivation.

Emancipation from psychological and environmental shackles certainly was a reason for enlistment in some instances. Here was an ideal opportunity to respond to a patriotic call and at the same time to escape the dependence on a home situation or subjection to its responsibilities. No doubt, it was sometimes an escape from what may be regarded as feminine duties. Many women joined against strong protest of their families—probably the most common problem which they had to solve (or ignore). Patriotism was an airtight rationalization for some women who left excellent jobs or apparently comfortable homes. The unconscious motive could have been a resentment toward their civilian (or feminine?) role or situation.

Identification with a specific male person in the Army, or an unconscious masculine identification, must have been the deciding psychological factor in many cases. War and an army always have been the epitome of a strictly masculine activity. This is as well known and accepted by women as by men. Almost every woman at some time in her life, and perhaps for a long period, has wished she were a boy or a man. Perhaps she was envious of the privileges and the opportunities of men, or irked by having to play the traditional role of a woman. Many women have very definite and strong masculine strivings. Often the motivation for joining an essentially male organization was probably stimulated by an unconscious competition with a consciously loved person—the husband, the brother, or the boy friend. Such competition is often evident in sibling rivalry.

Closely allied to the mechanism of identification is the related motive of protest. This is a denial of the feminine role as if the unconscious were saying, "You see, I can even be a soldier, truly serve in a man's job." Undoubtedly, this sometimes took the form of aggressive behavior as if the unconscious were saying, "See here, husband, brother, father, I'll show you I'm as good as you are. I'll join the Army, too." One might well include in this constellation an aggressiveness against the mother who had different hopes and aspirations for her daughter.

Still another motive may have been the need to find a sense of security. This was sometimes fostered further by a sense of boredom or lonesomeness in the woman's civilian role. Joining the WAC was a way of helping the war effort in a commendable fashion which was reasonably safe. It would also give her something to do and provide her, as it does all soldiers, with the security and satisfaction of passively receiving food, a bed, a job, and clothing.

Some women joined the WAC merely as another escape from numerous previous unsuccessful attempts to adjust themselves in civilian life. These were maladjusted individuals who had never been able to fit into their environment and used the Army as an opportunity to make another trial. These were the problem personalities of the WAC.

Probably an unrecognized motive in a certain number of women was the desire to enlist in order to be with other women. Perhaps a very small number were overtly homosexual, though this problem was never a serious one in the WAC. It was anticipated that it would be more prevalent than it actually was. The reaction to homosexuality was interesting. Many women were ignorant of it prior to their coming into the WAC. Some were overconscious of it as a possibility. There was a strong tendency toward "witch-hunting" on the part of some prudish or sadistic officers, who suspected normal friendships of being tinged with homosexuality. On the other hand, it was a surprise to many persons, in and out of the WAC, to learn that some of the most efficient and admirable women had homosexual tendencies.

Finally, a motive in some cases was the search for an opportunity to express femininity. One must suspect, on the basis of psychological knowledge, however, that this was less frequently operative. Some women could have assumed, justifiably, that here was a chance to do an important job within a woman's capacity which would spare a man for a strictly masculine job. They must have hoped that, like Army nurses, they might play something of the mother or the sister role. Normal feminine urges to do secretarial and clerical work, housekeeping and cooking, could find expression in enlistment, regardless of what other desires might have been present. Another aspect of this same motive was seen in those who sought masculine company and felt that the Army was obviously the place to find it. . . .

Psychological significance of the WAC for men. The initial attitude of many of the male personnel in the Army toward the WAC was that the Army was very considerate in providing a female contingent! This psychological response was based in part on the narcissism of the male who too often assumes that women exist to serve him; in part on the automatic exaggeration of the sexual interest in women in an all-male society, and in part on the need for an antidote to the unconscious, vague fears of impotency that exist in a strictly one-sex group. . . .

In spite of the general opinion that the WAC did a very capable job, its existence was accepted by the men with ambivalence. . . .

Men were willing only that women of whom they were not fond should come into the Army. In some way this attitude was less threatening to their supremacy or possibly to their concept of femininity. Undoubtedly it was an expression of their own unconscious simultaneous desires to possess and protect women. In essence it was an expression of their own struggle with the double standard for men and women.

Many men will of necessity be forced by the success of the experiment to make a readjustment in their concepts of the feminine role. . . . [Some psychiatrists] believed that this experience will ultimately beget a new, freer, collaborative and democratic relationship between men and women. This sounds a little optimistic, but among those couples where wives were in the WAC, there is likely to be a new alignment. This will apply equally to families in which wives gained a wider horizon by experience in industry.

William C. Menninger, *Psychiatry in a Troubled World: Yesterday's War and Today's Challenge* (New York: Macmillan, 1948), 104–8.

℘

Advertisement for Women's Army Auxiliary Corps (1943)

The following "letter" was actually part of an advertisement encouraging women to enlist in the Women's Army Auxiliary Corps (WAAC; later changed to Women's Army Corps, or WAC). The message appeared as a handwritten letter.

PROBLEMS TO CONSIDER

1. Why was this letter from "Dad" instead of "Mom"? How did he justify his daughter's role in the fight?
2. How did the ad address the concerns, described in Menninger's report, that women will not remain womanly if they join the WAAC?

My Dear Daughter:

You ask how I feel about your joining the WAAC.

The idea gives me a queer mixture of feelings. You'll have to unscramble them. After all, you—and you alone—must make the decision. I would not have it otherwise.

Your right to decide for yourself is one of the things we're fighting for. When your brother Bill went into the Army I was mighty proud. The men of our family have always put on uniforms when their country called. Frankly, in your case other feelings are involved.

You were our first-born. It's no secret—I wanted you to be a boy. I'll never forget that morning when your mother looked up and said, with a twinkle in her eye, "I'm sorry, Jim,—*he's* a girl." I knew she really wasn't sorry—and I've never been.

You know I like *womanly* women—your mother's kind. And watching you grow up in that pattern has been a delight to me. I am firm in the belief that whatever your decision is, it won't make you any *less* of a woman—just a wiser, steadier, stronger one. You see, your Old Man has a sneaking suspicion you have already decided.

I envy you and Bill. Your lives lie ahead, in a future which you can comprehend better than I, simply because you are closer to it.

The truth is, you *ARE* the future. Long after I am gone, this will still be *your* country. That's the big reason the decision must be yours. Your father and mother must be willing to make *any* sacrifice necessary—even to giving up their son and daughter for a time. We want you and Bill and your friends to have a decent world to live in tomorrow.

So, answering your question, Sis, just this advice—

Never be afraid of doing the thing that in your own heart you know is right. Just be certain you can always look your own conscience and your own country in the face.

Your loving,
Dad

Advertisement for Women's Army Auxiliary Corps, *Saturday Evening Post*, April 3, 1943, 33–34.

✦

✦ KNOWING THE ENEMY, ABROAD AND AT HOME

The potential for political action and social change was generated when an ethnically divided pluralistic nation such as the United States engaged in an international war to spread the Four Freedoms to people of color around the world. The difficulties and opportunities within these contradictions were especially apparent to Asians and Asian Americans. Chinese, Filipinos, Koreans, Japanese, Asian Indians—at different times from the early nineteenth century to the mid-1920s, these peoples had willingly relocated to the United States, where never-ending shortages of low-wage labor created abundant work opportunities that were unavailable in their home countries. Once in the United States, Asians faced continuous cultural and legal discrimination as Americans of European descent sought to establish the racial homogeneity of citizenship and to reserve work opportunities for white men. Since 1790, the federal Naturalization Act had limited the right to become a naturalized citizen to "white" immigrants only. The Chinese Exclusion Act, passed in 1882 (and extended for good in 1902), virtually closed the gate to Chinese immigrants, whom nativists regarded as racially so alien that they were unassimilable to the American way. In 1869, the journalist Henry George called them "utter heathens, treacherous, sensual, cowardly and cruel." Those Asians not excluded by additional legislation were incorporated into the restrictions of the Immigration Act of 1924, which was designed to restore the Nordic character of foreign immigration (see chapters 1 and 4).

The Pacific war placed this history of discrimination in a different and difficult context, overnight turning longtime racial enemies into close cultural friends and political allies. In addition, Hitler's rise to power in Germany had been a subject of intense journalistic scrutiny for a decade; the growing power of Japan in the Pacific and its brutal invasion of Manchuria in 1931, however, had attracted comparatively little attention. In the months after the raid on Pearl Harbor, explaining the Japanese and the savagery of what Roosevelt called the "unprovoked and dastardly attack" on the United States became a major journalistic and scholarly project of experts in foreign affairs, psychology, and anthropology. "The Honorable Enemy," *Fortune* magazine observed in early 1942, "has shown himself to be much more complicated than our casual impressions had painted him." Like the *Fortune* writer, few American observers questioned the governing wisdom that the Japanese were fundamentally and strangely different than themselves and Europeans. The mystery resided in defining how and explaining what made them that way: Was it their culture? Was it their race? If it was race, what made the Japanese different than their racial kin in other Asian nations? The strange circumstances of the world war forced the nation to make sense of its new enemies and friends and to explore the connections among race, national identity, and human behavior.

How to Tell Your Friends from the Japs (1941)

"Japan is not a nation of individuals, but a hive of bees working, buzzing, and fighting in a defense of the hive," observed Hugh Byas, a New York Times *reporter. This common wartime assessment of Japanese culture reworked the stereotype of faceless, numberless Asian societies in which the teeming masses looked and acted alike. Such judgments usually affirmed Westerners' assumptions of their cultural superiority, but they presented troubling problems when Americans allied themselves with the most populous and stereo-*

typed of Asian nations, China, the home of the "treacherous" and "alien" heathens. The attack on Pearl Harbor, a congressman observed in 1943, revealed the "saintly qualities of the Chinese people." Yet how were Americans supposed to distinguish the good Chinese from the bad Japanese when, according to the racial stereotype, all Asians looked so much alike? Two weeks after Pearl Harbor, Time *magazine published a diagram and a "few rules of thumb" to help ease the confusion of its readers. The feature used two pairs of photographic portraits, each contrasting a Chinese man's face and facial expression with that of a Japanese man, to visually explain the difference between America's friends and enemies. The following were the "rules of thumb" that accompanied the photographs.*

PROBLEMS TO CONSIDER

1. How did the article reinvent the Chinese as a racial and cultural stereotype?
2. How did the Chinese and the Japanese compare to the idealized types of Americans portrayed by Ernie Pyle?

Of these four faces of young men and middle-aged men the two on the left are Chinese, the two on the right Japanese. There is no infallible way of telling them apart, because the same racial strains are mixed in both. Even an anthropologist, with calipers and plenty of time to measure heads, noses, shoulders, hips, is sometimes stumped. A few rules of thumb—not always reliable:

• Some Chinese are tall (average: 5 ft. 5 in.). Virtually all Japanese are short (average: 5 ft. 2½ in.).
• Japanese are likely to be stockier and broader-hipped than short Chinese.
• Japanese—except for wrestlers—are seldom fat; they often dry up and grow lean as they age. The Chinese often put on weight, particularly if they are prosperous (in China, with its frequent famines, being fat is esteemed as a sign of being a solid citizen).
• Chinese, not as hairy as Japanese, seldom grow an impressive mustache.
• Most Chinese avoid horn-rimmed spectacles.

• Although both have the typical epicanthic fold of the upper eyelid (which makes them look almond-eyed), Japanese eyes are usually set closer together.
• Those who know them best often rely on facial expression to tell them apart: the Chinese expression is likely to be more placid, kindly, open; the Japanese more positive, dogmatic, arrogant.

In Washington, last week, Correspondent Joseph Chiang made things much easier by pinning on his lapel a large badge reading "Chinese Reporter—NOT Japanese—Please."

• Some aristocratic Japanese have thin, aquiline noses, narrow faces and, except for their eyes, look like Caucasians.
• Japanese are hesitant, nervous in conversation, laugh loudly at the wrong time.
• Japanese walk stiffly erect, hard-heeled. Chinese, more relaxed, have an easy gait, sometimes shuffle.

"How to Tell Your Friends from the Japs," *Time*, December 22, 1941, 33.

ᴘ

As We See It (1942)

"Soul-Stirring Hate" Needed to Wipe Out Japs (1944)

At the outbreak of war, more than 110,000 people of Japanese descent lived on the West Coast of the United States, most of them in California. Fewer than four in ten had been born in Japan (Issei); most were Nisei, or American-born citizens. Citing the nation's need for "every possible protection against espionage and . . . sabotage," President Roosevelt in February 1942 effectively declared all of them potential enemies of the nation and ordered all native-born and foreign-born Japanese Americans as well as resident aliens to report for "relocation" to internment camps in other regions of the country. The sweep was swiftly executed. "By noon Thursday," a California newspaper reported with precision in April 1942, "no person of Japanese ancestry remained in Santa Cruz county for the first time in more than a half-century." The internees were not released until 1945. The following selections from small-town newspapers in Santa Cruz County (located seventy miles south of San Francisco), California, address the "Japanese problem." The letter-writer Gardner was chairman of a local "defense council."

PROBLEMS TO CONSIDER

1. How did these two selections establish the danger posed by Japanese Americans? What made them different from German Americans or Italian Americans? Were the differences racial or cultural in nature?
2. What do you think of the argument that wartime crises justify the suspension of civil liberties? How did that argument affect the question of "why we fight"?

AS WE SEE IT

This is no time for expansive discourses on protection of civil liberties for Japanese residents of the Pacific coast, whether they be American citizens or aliens.

Efficient prosecution of this war demands that we recognize certain facts which make every Japanese in our midst a potential threat to our security, regardless of how admirable he might have been in time of peace. It is a mistake to think that we can clear up the dangers by process of elimination; that is, by depending entirely upon the FBI to ferret out all the treacherous acts and incriminating documents among the 100,000 Japanese living in areas where they could be of greatest service to an invading horde.

An attempted invasion of the Pacific coast is a possibility. Imbued with the doctrine of "The Rising Sun," Japanese on the Pacific coast must be regarded as a potential army already planted behind the American lines.

This is war, and philosophical treatises must give way to practical measures. A few sincere essayists will argue that a deep-rooted conviction for civil liberties cannot be reconciled with "discrimination" and "suspicion" even in time of war. They will maintain devoutly, ever so honest in their opinions, that we must exhaust the processes of law in determining who are our enemies within the borders of the United States.

Our beloved civil liberties will be a thing of the glorious past if the Axis powers win this war. We must employ whatever measures are expedient to defeat the Axis. And it should be clearly evident by now that we must take cognizance of the necessity of eliminating "fifth columnists" *[undercover enemies who subvert the nation's defenses from within].*

The Japanese by their diabolical efficiency and fanatical patriotism have made it easy for us to exercise "discrimination" in dealing with aliens or hyphenated Americans originating from the countries with which we are now at war. They must be considered poles apart from the Italians and Germans, nearly all of whom have been assimilated by American society. The problem of tracking down the enemies of Italian and German origin is not nearly so acute.

We must recognize geographical factors, traditions, and language difficulties in dealing with Japanese communities on the coast. . . .

Even many Japanese who were born in this country have been taught, either at home or at extracurricular Japanese schools, the traditions of Japan, the divine supremacy of the emperor, and the "ultimate destiny of the Rising Sun." . . .

Because of language difficulties, and our regard for civil liberties, we as a nation have been unable to know the extent of indoctrination fostered through Japanese schools and Buddhist Temples in this country.

There are some Japanese who have native loyalty for the United States. If we were at war with any other country than Japan or her allies, it is our judgment that most of the Japanese on the coast would support America.

It is hardly possible under the circumstances to distinguish between a loyal Japanese and a disloyal one. . . .

"As We See It," *Santa Cruz Sentinel-News*, February 19, 1942, 1.

"SOUL-STIRRING HATE" NEEDED TO WIPE OUT JAPS

To the Editor:

For the last two years, some of us, privately and publicly, have asserted that the Japanese, as a race, are absolutely bad, that they are inherently, biologically and traditionally vicious, inherently inhuman, totally unfit for association with any human being, and that every necessary procedure should be adopted for the purpose of expelling from our midst and forever excluding from residence in the United States every creature of such ancestry.

We have maintained that experience with and observation of the members of that race over a half century, their unchangeable nature, as displayed in numerous isolated instances of cruel and inhuman treatment of the Chinese and of members of the white race, their fanatical devotion to their god-emperor, and the known circumstances of their home training and the influence of their instruction in the language schools, are conclusive proof that it is utter folly to assume, as to any particular member of that race, that he, as between the United States and Japan, is loyal to the former.

We have maintained that not the accident of birth, but the inherent nature of the being, his ancient racial traditions, the loyalties of his parents, their training in his home and teaching in the language schools attended by him, determine the loyalty of an individual. A cobra is a cobra whether hatched out on the western or the eastern shores of the Pacific.

We have maintained that in view of these facts, verbal or written protestations of loyalty to this country, as against Japan, made by any Jap, wherever born, are entitled to no credence. . . .

The Japs, as a race, while they are mammals, walk erectly, have a system of oral and written communication, and possess a certain degree of intelligence, by no manner of means may be classified as human beings. Nor does it seem that in placing them we should disgrace any known species of wild beast. For them we must seek an isolated category. . . .

There are two things with which, in respect to the foe which most concerns us, we must equip ourselves if this war is to be won:

a. An intense, tremendous and soul-stirring hate that will impel us, military and civilian alike, to exert ourselves to the ultimate limit of our powers to the accomplishment of one purpose, the complete defeat of the army and navy of Japan, the devastation of its cities, the destruction of its industries and, as nearly as may be possible, the utter extinction of the race.

b. A realization that war is not a Sunday school picnic, nor a friendly but spirited competition between the athletic teams of two nations,

but is the very grim and bloody business of killing or being killed and that a necessary incident to its successful prosecution is a will to kill.

J. E. GARDNER

"'Soul-Stirring Hate' Needed to Wipe Out Japs—Gardner," *Watsonville Register-Pajaronian,* February 1, 1944, 1–2.

ॐ

Nisei Plea for Understanding (1945)

Over the course of the war, 33,000 Nisei served in the U.S. armed forces. Most were from Hawaii, where Japanese Americans, though the largest racial minority, had not had their civil liberties restricted. But many who served were from the West Coast and were drafted while confined to internment camps. The 442nd Regimental Combat Team, which was composed entirely of Nisei, was perhaps the most decorated and honored unit in the war. In the following letter to the editor, Aiko Masada, a Nisei internee, raises this record in confronting an earlier letter-writer. A Mr. Cornell, who described himself as a "red-blooded" American, had insisted that "these unpredictable and unassimilating people" should "take an early boat to Japan."

PROBLEMS TO CONSIDER

1. What arguments did Masada use to refute racial arguments about Japanese disloyalty?
2. Compare how he used the record of Nisei soldiers with other descriptions of Japanese soldiers and American soldiers.

To the editor:
... Perhaps we could have just as easily relocated elsewhere but, my dear Mr. Cornell, because CALIFORNIA was our native land, we have returned.

In the spring of 1942, though charged with no crime, we were forcefully torn from our beloved home and lifelong, dear friends. With a lump in my throat, goodbyes were bade to fellow-freshman classmates, wondering if we'd ever meet again. How clearly that day comes back to me now, the whole world seemed to crumble about us. Some of the evacuees were put behind barbed-wires in dusty Arizona, others in isolated camps in various parts of this country ... our family was fortunate enough to be sent halfway across the continent to a camp in muddy Arkansas.

However, the greatest victim of this unrighteous uprooting of 70,000 American citizens certainly was not the Japanese-Americans themselves ... rather, it was our basic concept of liberty, our standard of justice, and the appeal which we, as free people, should be making to the many oppressed people in the far corners of the world.

We love and intend to serve this great country with its high ideals. Hasn't America climbed to its present height of greatness because of the contributions of all racial groups? Is not our great American hero, Gen. Eisenhower, of German ancestry? It was certainly not for their own health that those Japanese-American boys fought so valiantly, giving of their blood, sweat, and tears, in some of the bitterest battles on the war fronts ... no, they wanted to prove to doubting fellow-citizens of their undivided loyalty and devotion to this great country and the principles for which it stands. . . .

For those of you who still suspect our loyalty, we want you to know that we harbor no hatred toward you. Instead, we'll be praying for that glorious day when everyone all over this world, regardless of race, color, religion, background, or station in life, would all join hands together and live as God intended for us to live . . . as brothers.

Aiko Masada

"Nisei Plea for Understanding," letter to the editor, *Watsonville Register-Pajaronian*, September 26, 1945, 3.

ॐ

ॐ Zoot Suits: Racial Politics and the War at Home ॐ

In 1943, a young African American reported to his draft board in Harlem dressed in a "wild zoot suit": a long-tailed coat with dramatically flared shoulders, baggy pants tapering severely at the ankles, "yellow knob-toe shoes" to match, and hair "frizzled . . . up into a reddish bush of conk." "Crazy-o, daddy-o," he greeted the soldier at the reception desk. Malcolm Little—years later he would become Malcolm X—knew how to perform his "blackness" to offend his white examiners. He was not about to fight a war for freedoms that were denied him in everyday life. Playing on the racism of his examiners, Little got what he wanted—"4F" status, exemption from military service.

The rebellions of zoot-suiters show that cultural style mattered *politically* to those who sought to change as well as to those who sought to conserve the racial status quo. In early 1942, the federal War Productions Board issued standards for men's suits and overcoats—shrinking the cut of jackets, for instance—that aimed to reduce civilian demand for woolen fabrics. One effect of the directive was to outlaw the manufacturing of zoot suits, which seemed an impractical waste of fabric. In the mainstream imagination, the zoot was the ethnic uniform of "hipsters"—young Latino and African American men who delighted in defying convention, relished the new sound of young bebop artists such as Dizzie Gillespie, danced the lindy hop, and spoke the slang of the "hep cat."

Before 1942, many people, usually regardless of class or ethnicity, viewed the wearing of the zoot as a refusal to submit to hard work and breadwinner responsibilities. From the wearers' perspective, however, the zoot was the very emblem of their manhood, the essential element of which was their refusal to bow to (in their minds) the "white man's" canons of respectability. The war standards expanded the rebellious potential of this attire by fusing the gender and class politics of the zoot suit with the politics of citizenship. Without cuffs, lapels, or pleats, the simplicity of military-approved clothing—tight, straight lines; no-nonsense fabric—came to define the only acceptable style for many men. To wear the zoot was no longer just unmanly, but unpatriotic, especially as an underground industry continued to supply the clothing and young nonwhite men continued to wear it. Some such men scoffed at the notion of a campaign against racial tyranny abroad and at home. They sought, like Malcolm Little, to evade dying in a "white man's war." The documents in this section explore the different reactions that zoot suits provoked when African Americans and Latinos manipulated gender, race, and class to challenge the obstacles that institutional and cultural authorities (and middle-class whites in the United States) sought to impose on their behavior and identities in the decade before the postwar civil rights movement.

Why Our Slogan Is "Double V" (1942)

Pursuit of Democracy; Sees Opportunities Broadening for Race Women in Crisis (1942)

MARJORIE MCKENZIE

Not long after the attack on Pearl Harbor, the Pittsburgh Courier, *an African American newspaper, urged its readers to join in a "Double V" campaign for victory over America's fascist enemies abroad and its racist enemies at home. Support for the movement grew quickly, attracting the allegiance of many white and black civil rights leaders. Defenders of racial hierarchies denounced the campaign as "extremist," and other mainstream figures condemned the action as an opportunist and unpatriotic distraction during time of war. Challenges also came from other black leaders, whose criticisms reflected the historic class and cultural divisions in African American agitation for racial reform. A. Philip Randolph, a leader in the black trade union movement, demanded bolder direct confrontation, such as the "Negro March on Washington," which the union organized in early 1941. The demonstration never occurred, but the threat pushed President Roosevelt to install legal guarantees against job discrimination in the expanding defense industries. The following selections from the* Courier —*first, the newspaper's editorial position on the campaign, and second, a female columnist's opinion on the double campaign for black women —provide opportunities for examining the black press's reasons for fighting in light of other assertions of "why we fight."*

PROBLEMS TO CONSIDER

1. Were the aims of African American men and women the same?
2. Compare these explanations of "why we fight" with other documents in this chapter. Did they suggest a unity in war aspirations of all Americans, or a basic division?

WHY OUR SLOGAN IS "DOUBLE V"

We have heard the timid and uninformed ask why, in a National Emergency, do Negro leaders and race periodicals stir up the race question? Why not declare an armistice in the fight for our rights—for the duration?

These questions are premised on the assumption that the fight for race rights during a war is unpatriotic and harmful. This we know is false. We, whose slogan is the "Double V,"

claim for ourselves the highest patriotism, for we would have our country live up to the noble sentiment and principles professed in the Bill of Rights and the Constitution. We would have the flag of Democracy cleansed, and [rid of] discrimination and race prejudice, so that it may wave as a true symbol of Liberty, Justice and Equality, to which the downtrodden of all lands and races could look with confidence and hope. We would take from Japan and Germany their most effective propaganda weapon among the colored races of Asia and Africa if we could, in truth, claim equality for all races under our flag.

Even if we wanted to, we could not hide our country's shame, for it is too universally known; and to be silent concerning these crimes against us would serve no good purpose, and would only deprive us of the opportunity of presenting our cause at a time when we are certain to receive the most sympathetic response. . . .

Our position is that the ranks should be closed. That all races and peoples shielded by our flag should present a solid front for victory. We say to every Negro man, woman and child: do everything within your power to gain victory. Give your property; offer your lives. Our patriotism is not conditional, for this is "Our Country." But we would be less than men if, while we are giving up our property and sacrificing our lives, we do not agitate, contend, and demand those rights guaranteed to all free men. This would be neither patriotism nor common sense.

"Why Our Slogan Is 'Double V,'" *Pittsburgh Courier*, August 8, 1942, 8.

PURSUIT OF DEMOCRACY

In the wake of war's social and economic readjustments, rides a tide of opportunity for the most exploited of all minorities, the Negro woman, the double victim of race and sex. As the war councils make it clear that the country must plan for a long . . . [and] difficult engagement, it becomes equally obvious that American women generally are going to have to assume tasks . . .

Apparently American white women, who are the most emancipated, luxury-surrounded women of the world, have deep reservoirs of courage and willingness to serve which have not been plumbed since the frontiers of the West closed and the suffrage amendment was passed.

As white women are integrated into new fields of training and employment and as Negro men enter the armed forces, Negro women are going to find jobs that will lift them out of their present necessity of accepting their plight as overworked, underpaid domestics, laundry workers and farm laborers. . . .

The great social gains in these developments are not entirely apparent until one remembers that the Negro family in the United States is still, very largely, a matriarchy. This is a polite sociological term meaning that our family is still in the process of growth and that the Negro man in our lower income groups has not assumed his proper responsibilities as chief provider and head of the household. Consequently, the exploited Negro woman worker, has tried to support her children on inadequate wages, with intermittent help either from her husband or a relief agency. This has meant, among other social evils, poor housing, poor health, lack of supervision and juvenile delinquency. Training and new jobs and adequate wages for our women will mean undreamed of progress in our family life.

Marjorie McKenzie, "Pursuit of Democracy; Sees Opportunities Broadening for Race Women in Crisis," *Pittsburgh Courier*, January 17, 1942, 7.

ᴈ

Zoot Suits and Service Stripes: Race Tension Behind the Riots (1943)

Scholars believe that large numbers of minority men actively resisted the draft, even if, in the end, they did not succeed in avoiding it. For instance, they estimate that 35 percent of the war's delinquent registrants were African American. Regardless of zoot-suiters' actual feelings or their qualifications for military service, wearing the "drape shape" came to symbolize in the eyes of reporters, police, and white servicemen an unmanly and un-American selfishness at a time of national self-sacrifice, the most potent ritual of which was submission to the Selective Service. The social tensions provoked by these resentments turned violent in Los Angeles in June 1943, when servicemen from area bases, aided by local police, turned on Latino and black youths in the city's ghettos. The "zoot suit riots" lasted for several days; similar conflicts occurred in other American cities that had been transformed socially by the war. This Newsweek *account provides an overview of the Los Angeles riot.*

PROBLEMS TO CONSIDER

1. How did this account explain the social and political meaning of the zoot suit and the "war" it provoked?
2. What, according to the article, explained why young Latino men wore the zoot suit? Compare the article's tone with the critical reactions against the "Double V" campaign.

"Kill the pachuco bastard!" That was the battle cry. The zoot war began on the West Coast—in Los Angeles—with servicemen doing battle against young civilians of Mexican descent, called pachucos for the Pachuca district in Mexico where natives affect gaudy clothes. It flared up also in Toronto, in Detroit and Philadelphia, and its reverberations reached the State Department in Washington. Though its deeper causes were mixed—including some race prejudice and much resentment of hooliganism—the servicemen's hated target everywhere was the zoot suit.

Between 1914 and 1929 Mexicans by the thousands crossed the border into Southern California to work on section gangs, desert mines, and farms. The depression settled many of them in Los Angeles, where they encountered much of the social ostracism accorded Negroes—in schools, movie houses, playgrounds, community swimming pools. Their American-born children grew up in a jangled environment; at home they were Americans, speaking a language different from their parents; outside they were Mexicans.

Outside, too, they banded into gangs, at first just for sociability, later for plainly vicious purposes. The advent of the zoot suit gave them a distinctive badge of defiance. In bizarre details of drape, pleat, and cuff they outdazzled their Harlem counterparts. They went the limit in porkpie hats, ballooning trousers, and spectacularly long coats. They called themselves the Mateo Bombers, the Main Street Zooters. . . . And for months they engaged in cruel, bludgeoning internecine warfare or came to grips with the law on charges varying from violation of the juvenile curfew to murder, rape, and robbery. . . .

Finally, the gangs had their "cholitas" or "slick chicks," female partners who affected black blouses and slacks or short black skirts and mesh stockings. Sometimes the girls fought side by side with the zooters; sometimes they merely carried their weapons. . . .

A sailor with a pocketful of money has always been fair game for loose women, and the girls of the Los Angeles Mexican quarter were no exception. Soon stories of assaults by zoot suiters on servicemen were getting back to the barracks. Three weeks ago pachucos badly mauled two sailors who tried to steal their girls at a Venice dance hall. The yard was itching for a fight.

On the night of June 4 bands of sailor vigilantes invaded the squalid Mexican quarter on the east side, harrying all zoot suiters they met, thrashing those who refused to discard their fancy clothes, ripping to shreds baggy pants and long coats. By the next night the "sharpies" . . . waded in with tire irons, chains, knives, broken bottles, clubs, steel bars, wrenches, and rope lengths weighted with wire and lead.

And by last Monday night the soldiers and sailors were pouring into Los Angeles by the hundreds seeking a showdown. Downtown a pachuco of 17 tried to sneak through the crowd of civilians following a band of soldiers. Men pushed him back; fists smashed into his frightened brown face. The boy went down; hands ripped off his coat and pants and tossed him into a garbage truck while the crowd roared approval. Dozens of pachucos were stripped and left naked on street corners. The police either could or would do little except make belated arrests. . . .

As a leader of the pachucos, police named Miguel Minijares Guerrero, 26, unmarried, and Texas-born, now serving a 50-day sentence in the county jail. Guerrero has a long record of arrests, chiefly for assault. Like most of the other zooters, Guerrero's draft classification is 4-F— morally unfit because of his police record. . . .

For the zoot war there were almost as many explanations as for any other war. One was the undisputed fact of rising racial tension in America, like that which previously had produced brawls among white and Negro servicemen.

Youth Correction authorities said the basic trouble among zoot suiters was maladjustment, increased by easy relief and brought to a head by the war. Dr. Joseph Catton, San Francisco psychiatrist, thought the zooters suffered from an inferiority complex. Others blamed lack of parental control and lack of supervised night recreation. (Los Angeles playgrounds have been closed by the dimout.) But all sides agreed on one thing: The sight of a young man in a zoot suit in wartime was probably enough to infuriate many servicemen.

"Zoot Suits and Service Stripes: Race Tension Behind the Riots," *Newsweek,* June 21, 1943, 35–36, 38.

৵

César Chavez Recalls "Pachuco Days" (1975)
JACQUES LEVY

Man in Zoot-Suit (c. 1943)
EDDIE WINFRED "DOC" HELM

What kind of a man wore a zoot suit? What kind of man did not? In soldiers' eyes, an army private wrote to Time *magazine in July 1943, "the sight of young loafers of any race, color, creed, religion or color of hair loafing around in ridiculous clothes . . . is enough to make them see red." Zoot suits, he implied, announced a rejection of a national and personal duty that servicemen honored. The way to "avoid trouble," then, was for the "zoot-suit fraternity" to stand up like men, take off their suits, and put on "a uniform or a pair of overalls." From the perspective of the young men who wore them, however, zoot suits were themselves a kind of uniform. In the mid-1960s, César Chavez was a leader in the work stoppages, hunger strikes, and boycotts that led to the unionization of Mexican American farm laborers in the vast commercial agriculture regions of California. In this passage from his autobiography, he describes his rebellious youth in the prewar years as a Latino zoot-suiter, or* pachuco. *Although many pachucos resisted the draft, Chavez enlisted in the navy. The next source is a photograph of a man wearing a zoot suit, taken at a Springfield, Illinois, nightclub around 1943. The photographer, Eddie Winfred "Doc" Helm, had moved there in 1934 to work as a janitor at the state capitol, a good position for an African American man in the Depression. An amateur photographer, he saved up enough money to purchase professional equipment and opened his own studio in*

1943. His photographs compose a rich record of that city's African American community in the war years: church events, weddings, black soldiers at home on leave, and the well-dressed patrons of black nightclubs.

PROBLEMS TO CONSIDER

1. Compare the perspectives of Chavez, the army private quoted above, and Helm's photograph. Did they agree on the meaning of the zoot suit?
2. What was rebellious about the pose and the clothes of the zoot-suiter? What were zoot-suiters rebelling against?

CÉSAR CHAVEZ RECALLS

When I became a teen-ager I began to rebel about certain things. For example, I rebelled against the home remedies and herbs my mother used. I thought no one knew anything but doctors. And I rebelled against Mexican music. This was the age of the big bands, and I really went for Duke Ellington and Billy Eckstine. We would travel from Delano to Fresno to hear the bands, and in San Jose they had them every week.

I also rebelled against some of the religious customs, like the promesa or manda, where you ask the favor of a saint and promise to visit the chapel of the saint's church. It wasn't that I was strong in the church's more formal teachings by then, but just that I didn't approve of it. . . .

And then I rebelled at the conventional way of dressing. I once said I was a pachuco, and I had a very difficult time explaining it. The pachucos wore their hair long, in a ducktail cut; they wore pegged pants and long coats, long key chains, and a pegged, broad flat hat. Today what people remember are the pachuco riots in the forties in San Jose, Oakland, and Delano. But those riots were not the same as when the barrios and ghettos exploded in the sixties. The rioters were not Mexican. They were soldiers, marines, and sailors who raided the barrios attacking the pachucos.

I saw clippings of the Los Angeles papers with pictures of pachuco kids with pants torn to the thighs by police. If they had long hair, police clipped them, and if their coats were long, police cut them short. The pachucos would wear shoes with very thick soles, and police would take the soles off. Today police still act pretty much the same way toward nonconformists. They were pachucos then. Now they're hippies. . . .

We needed a lot of guts to wear those pants, and we had to be rebellious to do it, because the police and a few of the older people would harass us. But then it was the style, and I wasn't going to be a square. All the guys I knew liked that style, and I would have felt pretty stupid walking around dressed differently. At Delano dances, for example, all the squares sat across the room from us, and we had a lot more fun than they did.

My mother wasn't violently opposed to our wearing those clothes, though she and my dad didn't like it much, but little old ladies would be afraid of us. And in Delano there was a whole group in the Mexican-American community who opposed pachuco clothes. . . .

The hard thing, though, was the police. We were so gun shy. For sure the cops would stop you anyplace, any time, and we were prepared for that. But when they stopped us at the theater in Merced, it was humiliating. We were thinking of going to the show, but we weren't sure. We were just looking around to see what was playing. A cop, who was just passing by, saw us and got on his radio. Soon two or three police cars arrived, and the officers lined us up against the wall. It was a bad scene. They made us take our shoes off, they just almost undressed us there. Then they gave us about ten minutes to get out of town.

We were a minority group of a minority group. So, in a way, we were challenging cops by being with two or three friends and dressing sharp. But in those days I was prepared for any sacrifice to be able to dress the way I wanted to dress. I thought it looked sharp and neat, and it was the style.

Jacques Levy, *César Chavez: Autobiography of La Causa* (New York: W. W. Norton, 1975), 81–83.

Eddie Winfred "Doc" Helm, "Man in Zoot-Suit" (c. 1943).

(Winfred "Doc" Helm Photo © 1994.)

At Home with the Cold War: 1947–1960

IN A 1947 ARTICLE in *American* magazine, the director of the Federal Bureau of Investigation, J. Edgar Hoover, posed a frightening question to America's parents: "How Safe Is Your Daughter?" Hoover described an epidemic of violent sex crimes advancing across the United States and imperiling the nation's most innocent and vulnerable citizens. America's "women and children will never be secure," the article warned, "so long as degenerates run wild." Hoover's alert was part of a rash of published reports about sensational murders of children and women in the late 1940s and early 1950s. These reports used the examples of a few indisputably heinous crimes against children to generate a nationwide panic that no shadow was safe in a nation crawling with "deviates."

Hoover's warning and the worries that it expressed and reinforced seem at odds with the images of the 1950s that are most familiar today. They depict the postwar years as a time of comparative innocence and confidence, when America was defined by revitalized nuclear family values, rising prosperity, political complacency and conformity, and domestic tranquility. Central to many of these images is the celebration of a particular model of family life—breadwinner father, homemaker mother, happy child-centered suburban home—in 1950s advertising, women's magazines, and intellectual treatises that defined the naturalness of this order. Magazine ads showing a model housewife in pearls and stylish hairdo rhapsodizing over the year's new colors in kitchen appliances affirm the era's self-satisfaction, founded on a flourishing consumer economy. Rather than being dismissed, this evidence should be combined with the picture that Hoover and others painted. Together, they signal that even before Cold War insecurities and fears of nuclear war began to define the postwar era, Americans were both supremely confident and deeply uneasy about the future of the nation and world that the war had left behind. Such concerns were apparent in the many 1950s movies (*Rebel Without a Cause, I Was a Teenage*

Werewolf) that simultaneously publicized and explained the juvenile crime wave, which many parents and politicians believed was engulfing the nation. These kids, a policeman explains in *Blackboard Jungle* (1955), "were six years old in the last war. Father in the Army. Mother in a defense plant. No home life. No church life."

A close look at the postwar years yields a complicated picture of the broad national and international changes and conflicts: the Cold War abroad and McCarthyism and other manifestations of domestic anticommunism; suburban expansion and affluence, the urbanization of poverty, and the increasing numbers of women in the work force; anxieties about an apparent epidemic of juvenile delinquency on the one hand and child victims of criminal violence on the other; corporate gigantism and the managerial, bureaucratic workplace; the political reorganization of postcolonial Africa and Asia abroad and the beginnings of the civil rights movement at home. This chapter examines how postwar Americans responded, usually confidently, to these developments in the areas of race relations, Cold War politics, and family life.

ᠵ᠊ *Race and Rebellion in the 1950s* ᠵ᠊

In the years between 1947 and 1960, big changes came to the way Americans liked their baseball and their music played, and these changes coincided with and advanced the broader social and cultural shifts in race relations of the postwar civil rights movement. In 1947, Jackie Robinson started at first base for the Brooklyn (New York) Dodgers baseball team and broke the color line imposed by the whites-only policy of Major League Baseball. The Dodgers hired Robinson to be a "whirling demon" on the ball field, and he delivered. His aggressive base-running and base-stealing and agitation of pitchers and fielders alike forced changes in the power-hitting, slowly methodical play that had dominated the all-white big leagues since the days of Babe Ruth in the 1920s. Four years later, in 1951, the white disc jockey Alan Freed began playing rhythm and blues records by black artists on Cleveland radio station WJW. Calling himself the "King of the Moondoggers," Freed addressed listeners in a rapid-fire streetwise voice that his listeners thought sounded more black than white. The songs he played on his *Rock 'n' Roll Party* radio show, broadcast in metropolitan areas east to New York City, introduced white teenagers to rhythm and blues. A new national youth audience wild for the urban African American sound of what Freed called "rock-and-roll" already had amassed by the time Elvis Presley's first record — "That's All Right" on one side, "Blue Moon of Kentucky" on the other — was released in 1954.

It is hard to measure the impact that these cultural developments had on race relations in the United States. In 1956, a headline in *The Cash Box*, a music industry publication, declared "Rock and Roll May Be the Great Unifying Force!" Jackie

Robinson was likewise hailed as the great ambassador for improved race relations. Such pronouncements exaggerated the effects caused by the movement of black music and baseball to the center of American life. White performers continued to dominate baseball and popular music, and the most difficult years of the civil rights fight still lay ahead in the 1960s and early 1970s. Nonetheless, these developments indicate the transformations shaping American life in the 1950s and the role taken by African Americans in pushing for social change. This section, which focuses on Jackie Robinson and the early years of rock-and-roll, explores how popular culture both reordered and reinforced the dominant racial expectations in American society.

ᴖ JACKIE ROBINSON STORIES

Jackie Robinson's ending of the racial segregation of professional baseball is one of the century's most celebrated stories of American sports heroism, the efficacy of individual initiative, and the fight against racial injustice in the United States. Only two generations removed from slavery, Robinson was born in 1919 to a sharecropping family on a Georgia plantation. Months later, his father ran off, never to return. Facing eviction, Mallie Robinson moved her family to Pasadena, California (near Los Angeles), where she worked as a domestic so that her five children could be assured an education. Robinson excelled at every sport he played in high school and college, from football to Ping-Pong. Branch Rickey, general manager of the Brooklyn Dodgers baseball club, hired him away from the Negro League. After a prodigious minor league season, Robinson joined the Dodgers as the century's first African American major leaguer and in his first year helped lead the team to the World Series, which they lost to the New York Yankees.

Robinson's biography of resistance to the racial status quo of segregation did not begin with baseball. While serving in the army during World War II, he had successfully challenged the obstacles to officer training for African Americans; he also had withstood an attempted court-martial, which had been provoked by his refusal to move to the back of a military bus. Rickey knew that Robinson did not go along to get along, but the Dodgers general manager regarded his defiant personality as a strength rather than a liability. Still, from the moment Rickey sent a scout to watch Robinson, a paramount concern was how his style of rebellion against racial segregation—how he presented himself and how he was presented to white America—would affect his teammates, opponents, and baseball fans. None of Robinson's endeavors or achievements occurred as part of an organized protest or a group that we identify with the civil rights movement, but his successes demonstrate how African Americans maneuvered within and against the dominant racial expectations in American society to push for racial equality.

Speech to the "One Hundred Percent Wrong Club" (1956)
BRANCH RICKEY

In addition to being a cagey businessman, Branch Rickey, the thoughtful, college-educated general manager and part owner of the Dodgers, possessed a deeply idealistic belief in racial equality and faith in an American democracy of merit and opportunity. He and Robinson developed an intimate personal relationship; in his 1974 autobiography, Robinson described Rickey as a surrogate father. In this excerpt from a speech delivered in 1956 to an African American audience in Atlanta, Georgia, Rickey explains the "problems" that he had to overcome in hiring Robinson.

PROBLEMS TO CONSIDER

1. What kind of a "man" was Rickey searching for? How did Rickey wish for Robinson to act out his racial identity?
2. Did Rickey's effort to address the "dangers" that the "black race" posed to his experiment stifle or leave room for rebellion in Robinson's quest?

Within the first month in Brooklyn, I approached what I considered the number one problem in the hiring of a negro in professional baseball in this country. . . . Namely,— ownership. Ownership must be in line with you. . . . And when ownership was passed, then five other things presented themselves. . . . The second thing was to find the right man as a player. . . . Then I had to get the right man off the field. I couldn't come with a man to break down a tradition that had in it centered and concentrated all the prejudices of a great many people north and south unless he was good. He must justify himself upon the positive principle of merit. He must be a great player. . . . I must be sure that the man was good on the field, but more dangerous to me, at that time, and even now, is the wrong man off the field. It didn't matter to me so much in choosing a man off the field that he was temper[a]mental,—righteously subject to resentments. I wanted a man of exceptional intelligence, a man who was able to grasp and control the responsibilities of himself to his race and could carry that load. That was the greatest danger point of it all. . . .

[The final problem] was the negro race itself, —over-adulation, mass attendance, dinners, of one kind or another of such public nature that it would have a tendency to create a solidification of the antagonisms and misunderstandings,— over-doing it. And I want to tell you that the committee of 32,—it was called, in Greater New York—eminent negro citizens, [a prominent New York judge], and my secretary and myself,—those 32 men organized all eight cities in the National League and did a beautiful job of it. And for two years not one of those things was attempted or done and I never had any embarrassments in Brooklyn. . . . But the greatest danger, the greatest hazard, I felt was the negro race itself. Not people of this crowd any more than you would find antagonisms organized in a white crowd of this caliber either. Those of less understanding,—those of a lower grade of education frankly. And that job was done beautifully under the leadership of a fine judge in New York who became a Chairman of an Executive Committee . . . [and] the publisher of the Pittsburgh Courier, a very helpful gentleman he was to me. . . .

Branch Rickey, speech to the "One Hundred Percent Wrong Club" banquet, Atlanta, Georgia, January 20, 1956, Branch Rickey Papers, Manuscripts Division, Library of Congress, Washington, D.C.

⁊

Let's Take It in Stride (1947)

WILLIAM G. NUNN

The Pittsburgh Courier *worked closely with the Dodgers general manager not only in breaking the color line but also in urging African Americans to control their pride and enthusiasm when Robinson broke the color line. This editorial, by the newspaper's managing editor, was published the week before Robinson's regular season debut.*

PROBLEMS TO CONSIDER

1. Why did the *Courier* editor give such importance to sports in the struggle against racial discrimination?
2. What did the editor mean by taking Robinson's breakthrough "in stride"? Was he urging his readers to accept the terms for integration of the dominant race or to resist them?

The "Iron Curtain" which has prevented Negroes from participation in major league baseball has finally been lifted!

Jackie Robinson, 27-year-old athlete . . .* with the mental and physical equipment necessary to make the grade . . . has been accepted as a member of the Brooklyn Dodgers baseball club. . . .

Branch Rickey, God-fearing, courageous, powerful, influential head of the far-flung Brooklyn baseball empire, has done his part . . . like a real American. What he did, under terrific pressure and strain, merits the prayerful thanks of millions of Americans, white as well as black.

Jackie Robinson, UCLA graduate and former Army lieutenant, has done his part . . . thus far. He measured up to all that was asked of him . . . he proved on the ball field that he had the ability, the resourcefulness, the personality, the courage, to "come through" when the chips were down. Jackie's conduct . . . on and off the field . . . gave Mr. Rickey the axe he needed to batter down the "iron curtain."

The Pittsburgh Courier, who first mentioned Jackie as a major league prospect and who followed his every move from the moment he first entered the ranks of organized baseball . . . has done its part, thus far.

The Courier interviewed ball players and managers to try and convince ONE owner that the spirit of Democracy in Sports would be questioned until Negroes were given the OPPORTUNITY to make the grade. The Courier fought its battle along the lines of decency and fair play, two inherent American characteristics.

AND NOW . . . the real challenge faces Negro America!

The challenge of taking this tremendous victory in stride!

The challenge to keep our big mouths closed and give Jackie the chance to PROVE he's major league calibre!

The challenge to conduct ourselves at these ball games in the recognized American way!

The challenge to NOT recognize the appearance of Jackie Robinson as the signal for a Roman holiday, with the Bacchanalian orgy complex!

The challenge to leave whiskey bottles at home or on the shelves of the liquor stores . . . and to leave our loud talking, obscene language and indecent dress on the outside of the ball parks.

The challenge to learn something about the game . . . in order that we will know what's going on out on the ball field, and won't humiliate Jackie by our lack of knowledge!

---

*The ellipses in this selection appeared in the original and do not indicate omitted text.

The challenge to stop our booing over some untoward incident which might happen on the ball field. Remember that Jackie might be "roughed up" some, because that's the way they play in the majors . . . for keeps!

The challenge to refrain from holding "Jackie Robinson Days" until he's made the grade!

All of these things might distract his attention from what he has ahead of him . . . and it's a full-time job, too!

Rather than "Jackie Robinson Days" . . . we believe it to be appropriate for civic groups, leaders, Negro newspapers and individuals to conduct "Good Conduct" days wherever the [Brooklyn] "Bums" appear.

Remember . . . today Negro America, whose symbol is Jackie Robinson . . . is on trial! Mr. Rickey opened the door and Jackie's foot is in!

Whether he meets this latest challenge will depend largely on how you act . . . whether you take it "in stride" . . . or whether you make fools of yourselves.

William G. Nunn, "Let's Take It in Stride," *Pittsburgh Courier*, April 19, 1947, 18.

〜

Screenplay, The Jackie Robinson Story (1950)

ARTHUR MANN and LAWRENCE TAYLOR

The movie, The Jackie Robinson Story, *featuring the baseball star playing himself, was filmed after Robinson's all-star 1949 season and released in 1950. This scene, in which Branch Rickey (played by Minor Watson) tests the fitness of the ballplayer's character, was pivotal in the movie, although Robinson hardly mentioned it in his 1948 autobiography.*

PROBLEMS TO CONSIDER

1. Why did the movie emphasize the encounter in this scene?
2. How did the exchange between Rickey and the ballplayer explain the nature of Robinson's resistance to racial discrimination and his heroism?

RICKEY: *(pointing his cigar)* We're tackling something big here, Jackie. If we fail, no one will try it again for twenty years. But if we succeed . . . *(whirls on Jackie)* But we're dealing with rights here. We're dealing with the right of any American to play baseball—the American game. . . . What do you think, Jackie?

JACKIE: I can try.

RICKEY: You think you've got the guts to play the game? No matter what happens? They'll shout insults at you . . . they'll come in to you spikes first . . . they'll throw at your head.

JACKIE: They've been throwing at my head for a long time, Mr. Rickey.

RICKEY: Suppose I'm a player . . . in the heat of an important game. Suppose I collide with you at 2nd base. When I get up I say, "You dirty, black so-and-so." What'd you do?

JACKIE: *(stops and thinks for a moment, then)* Mr. Rickey, do you want a ball player who is afraid to fight back?

RICKEY: I want a ball player with guts enough *not* to fight back. You've got to do this job with base hits and stolen bases and fielding ground balls, Jackie. Nothing else. *(whirls on him)* Now, I'm playing against you in the

World Series and I'm hot-headed. I want to win that game, so I go into you spikes first and you jab the ball in my ribs. The umpire says "Out." I flare—all I see is your face—that black face right on top of me. So I haul off and I punch you right in the cheek. What do you do?

Jackie stops, grinds his right fist into the palm of his left hand, as the CAMERA MOVES IN, then

JACKIE *(slowly)*: Mr. Rickey, I've got two cheeks.

RICKEY *(suddenly grinning)*: Good. . . .

_____

Arthur Mann and Lawrence Taylor, screenplay, *The Jackie Robinson Story* (1950), 33–34, in Arthur Mann Collection, Manuscripts Division, Library of Congress, Washington, D.C.

♁

"Jackie Wouldn't Have Gotten to First Base . . . " (1950)
ARTHUR D. MORSE

Jackie Robinson, along with his many biographers, credited his mother, Mallie Robinson, with extraordinary and positive contributions to his achievements. This account was published in 1950 in Better Homes and Gardens, *a magazine with a predominantly suburban, white female readership, and defines the particulars of her maternal devotion.*

PROBLEMS TO CONSIDER

1. How did the author define Mallie Robinson's mothering of her son? What made her a good mother?
2. How did the author use ideals of domesticity, suburban living, and the social history of the migration of African Americans out of the rural South to northern and western cities to construct this story of Robinson's life?

The three older Robinson boys shared the big bed up-stairs but Jackie, aged 3, still slept with his mother, and that worried her so much that she offered him 25 cents a week to join his brothers. To Mallie Robinson, mother, father, and breadwinner for four sons and a daughter, 25 cents was a lot of money. Her husband had deserted her back in Cairo, Georgia, and now she was working as a domestic to pay for the house on Pepper Street in Pasadena, California.

But Jackie was a little too young to appreciate the buying power of a quarter. It was comfortable to snuggle against his mother, certainly more cozy than having his blankets yanked off by Edgar, Frank, and Mack.

After Mallie had tried every trick, only to find Jackie still curled in her bed, she called upon her greatest weapon—prayer. "Lord," she said, "You never failed me yet. It's time for Jackie to stop being a baby."

Late that night Jackie awakened in terror. "Mama," he cried, "I dreamed a man came through the window to steal me."

"Lord, you're answering my prayer," Mallie whispered. She turned to Jackie. "Look here," she said softly. "The best thing for you is to go upstairs. Nobody could climb up there; and if they did, your brother Edgar is such a light sleeper he'd wake up—"

"—And Edgar's strong," Jackie said excitedly. "He could knock out anyone."

So the three older brothers moved over in their bed for the boy who was to grow up to become the National League's leading batter, win its Most Valuable Player award, and terrorize pitchers with his daring base running.

Mallie Robinson's prayers have guided her family through serious problems as well as minor stratagems like moving Jackie upstairs. In a life of intense self-sacrifice, this gentle, gray-haired woman of 60 has relied on inexhaustible resources of faith, courage, and good humor. Today her son's big-money salary as a Dodger means economic security for her; but her spiritual values, like the modest house on Pepper Street, are unchanged. Mallie's own father was a slave, but it was she who taught Jackie self-control, tenacity, and dignity. The lessons began in 1922 when the family moved to its new home.

When they first arrived in Pasadena, 6 Robinsons and 9 relatives had lived in a two-bedroom flat. There had been no hot water and no sink, and the dishes were washed in a bathtub. Three days after the 15 were settled, Mallie had a job and had organized the household on a cooperative basis so that the rooms were tidy, supper was on time, and someone was always on hand to supervise the children. In a situation which had such roots of juvenile delinquency as overcrowding, inadequate sanitary facilities, and a working mother with no husband, the family flourished. Mallie, who spent the day cleaning other homes, returned to help with dinner and do her own heavy washing. Through it all, she kept her sense of humor, squelched fights among the 15, and found time to mother her own brood. Still, it was with relief and new hope that she moved her youngsters to 121 Pepper Street.

The house had plumbing and a marvelous banister for sliding. But it presented Mallie with a problem serious enough to outweigh these advantages.

The Robinsons were the only colored family on the block, and the neighbors were glowering. Mallie had assumed that the real estate dealer would put them in a neighborhood where they were wanted. Mallie was a peaceful person, but she was also courageous. She decided not to move, but to win the good will of her neighbors. In the beginning, she would keep the children in the house to avoid incidents. This was difficult because she worked all day, and, after all, the young Robinsons had a normal amount of spirit. Mallie told them not to make too much noise and to stay out of fights, tough restrictions on any healthy youngster. But the neighbors hatched their plans anyway. They would raise enough money to buy Mallie out. One day the old widow who lived next door spilled the beans. She had been as aloof as the others, but she called Mallie over to the fence and blurted out her sentiments.

"You must think I'm mean," she said. "If it wasn't for the others, I'd be happy to have you as a neighbor. No one ever kept that house so well, and I've watched the way your children take care of themselves. Why I wouldn't care if you lived in my home."

Mallie smiled, and the widow scampered back to her house so no one would notice the meeting.

The neighbors had difficulty collecting enough money to buy out the Robinsons, and they asked the widow, who had some extra cash, to put up the difference. After all, she lived next door and would gain most by forcing out the Robinsons. But at the crucial neighborhood meeting, the old lady stood up and announced that the Robinsons were the nicest neighbors she had ever had. The plan collapsed, and the Robinson children were allowed outdoors like everyone else. . . .

For all her religious faith, Mallie was no zealot. When she finally persuaded Jack to become active in the Methodist church, the minister hastily scheduled a baptism. But Mallie knew her son was not ready. "Jack's got to be sincere," she told the minister. "He's got to understand what this means and believe in it." So she postponed the baptism, and the next Sunday he was batting a ball in Brookside Park.

The incident was characteristic of Mallie's approach to motherhood. She exposed Jack to the influences she respected. She threw out lead lines and provided as much opportunity as she could, but she aimed for sincerity, not blind obedience. There was no maternal grip on Jackie. He chose his own roads and his own destination. . . .

Her husband Jerrie had been a fine sand-lot baseball player in Georgia, but he had lacked education and was content to work on another man's land at $12 a month. Mallie had implored him to work with her to buy their own farm, but when her efforts brought in extra money, he squandered it on himself. Soon after that he left. Mallie had traveled thousands of miles with her five children so they could go to good schools with an opportunity to succeed by their own merit. . . .

Arthur D. Morse, "Jackie Wouldn't Have Gotten to First Base . . . ," *Better Homes and Gardens*, May 1950, 226, 278–81.

↭

↭ INFLAMING YOUTH WITH TOM-TOMS: THE EARLY YEARS OF ROCK-AND-ROLL

In the postwar 1940s, cultural analysts and parents in general were puzzled by the delirium that the silken voice of Frank Sinatra induced in the nation's "bobbysoxer" population of white teenage girls. By the mid-1950s, the spectacle of frenzied girls and, increasingly, boys was growing ever larger and more disturbing, but Sinatra no longer inspired the excitement; he had become their "parents' music." The new stars were singers of rock-and-roll, which Sinatra called "the most brutal, ugly, desperate, vicious form of expression it has been my misfortune to hear," the "martial music of every side-burned delinquent on the face of the earth." In the mind of Sinatra and other middle-aged American parents, rock-and-roll was the symbol, instrument, and cause of the nation's growing population of seemingly uncontrollable teenagers. "Rock and roll inflames and excites youth like jungle tom-toms," a Catholic priest in Boston warned city authorities in 1956. At a time when social change struck people as evidence of domestic subversion and disorder, communism and rock-and-roll seemed intimately connected.

The sudden rise of "Negro music" in the early civil rights era encouraged people to draw the connection. Since the mid-1950s, rock-and-roll has been the music of white American youth, but its origins are in the vast social and economic dislocations and transformations that working-class Americans experienced with the national mobilization for World War II. During the war years, millions of rural working Americans moved to the growing manufacturing centers invigorated by the war industries—not just Los Angeles, Chicago, and Detroit but also smaller cities such as Toledo, Ohio, and Memphis, Tennessee. Wartime labor shortages made such cities powerful magnets, especially for African Americans from the rural South. In cities such as Chicago or Atlanta, they could multiply their incomes working year-round in laundries, factories, or hotels. The numbers leaving the rural South in the 1940s and 1950s dwarfed earlier phases of black migration and prepared the foundation for rock-and-roll's popularity.

The musical groundwork was rhythm and blues, or R&B, performed by black artists such as Etta James, Fats Domino, "Big" Joe Turner, Hank Ballard and the Midnighters, and Chuck Berry. Unlike the 1920s blueswomen and -men, many of the new artists grew up and lived in cities. Although most still came from working-class backgrounds, they appealed to the experiences, expectations, and tastes of urban working-class communities. Older blues artists such as John Lee Hooker were important influences on them, but they also were shaped by the musical styles that mixed together in the neighborhoods of war-era immigrants: the gospel singing of urban black churches, the country and western ballads of rural white southerners, and the mainstream popular radio music of Tin Pan Alley. Out of these various elements, the new artists developed a diverse but more urban sound — R&B, a tuneful, danceable, and frankly pleasure-oriented music banged out on a new technology, the electric guitar. When Etta James sang "Roll with Me, Henry," everyone knew what kind of tumble she meant. Although such lyrics and sounds stirred reaction when played on black-oriented radio stations, a furor erupted when R&B, led by white disc jockeys such as Alan Freed in Cleveland, became the rage of another population produced by the war: suburban, white, middle-class teenagers.

Why They Rock 'n' Roll—And Should They? (1958)
GERTRUDE SAMUELS

The "Moondog Matinee" concerts that disc jockey Alan Freed staged in Cleveland caught people's attention by attracting packed, mixed-race audiences to hear black artists such as the Dominoes. A former gospel quartet whose hit "Sixty Minute Man" was a musical tribute to male sexual performance, the Dominoes were emblematic of what the entertainment industry daily Variety *called "the specialized jargon of the restricted Negro community." The audience was still limited, though, until WINS in New York City hired the "Moondog" in 1954. The new sounds of R&B hit the popular music business like an earthquake. Before Freed, a fan recalled in 1972, "Radio was school. You heard the things you were supposed to think and never the things you thought." But Freed was "a teen-ager's mind funneled into 50,000 watts." Freed is credited with linking the sound of R&B with the term "rock-and-roll," a familiar expression for sexual intercourse long used in black blues music.*

Rather than defining a specific genre of music, rock-and-roll captured the social and cultural experience of the music's young fans. "Rock and roll was elemental, savage, dripping with sex," the media analyst Jeff Greenfield recalled of his youthful interest. It "was just as our parents feared." Rock-and-roll's popularity rapidly grew beyond its roots in the African American working class. Although black R&B artists sold many thousands of records, the new generation of white artists — Buddy Holly, Bill Haley and His Comets, Jerry Lee Lewis, and the two most popular, Elvis Presley and Pat Boone — sold in the millions. The influential New York Times *was an attentive observer of the social impact and meaning of rock-and-roll's expansion beyond the "Negro market." The journalist Gertrude Samuels provided this levelheaded account of teenagers' reaction to the white rocker Jerry Lee Lewis for the* Times. *Samuels sought to explain the music, the sources of its psychological appeal, and its potential dangers. Although she doubted that teenaged rock 'n' rollers behaved any more hysterically than their fox-trotting grandparents had in their own time, Samuels's account describes the powerful nonverbal ways in which the new music shaped and excited postwar American life.*

PROBLEMS TO CONSIDER

1. According to this article, what was revolutionary about rock-and-roll? Does the article exaggerate rock-and-roll's impact, or was it as rebellious as the reporter suggests?
2. How important was rock-and-roll to being a teenager in the 1950s? In what ways did teenagers regard the music as a part of their generational identity?

Come on over, baby,
Whole lotta shakin' goin' on . . .

"Rocking" the song as though in a life and death struggle with an invisible antagonist was a tall, thin, flaccid youth who pulled his stringy, blond hair over his eyes and down to his chin. He shook his torso about as the beat of the band seemingly goaded him on. Screams from thousands of young throats billowed toward him. In the pandemonium, youngsters flailed the air with their arms, jumped from their seats, beckoned madly, lovingly, to the tortured figure onstage.

The song could scarcely be heard over the footlights. No matter. The kids knew the words. They shrilled them with the singer—and kept up their approving, uninhibited screams. The singer finished off at the piano. The applause and yells all but raised the roof. Then a Negro quartet raced onstage, adjusted the microphones, and a new tune brought on a new cascade of screams and energetic handwaves.

This was the teen-age bedlam at the Paramount Theatre in New York where in recent days Alan Freed emceed a rock 'n' roll show. Now the spectacle is moving on to the national scene. . . .

What is this thing called rock 'n' roll? What is it that makes teen-agers—mostly children between the ages of 12 and 16—throw off their inhibitions as though at a revivalist meeting? What—who—is responsible for these sorties? And is this generation of teen-agers going to hell? . . .

An important source . . . is the music itself. Technically, rock 'n' roll derives from the blues.

But rock 'n' roll is an extension of what was known as Rhythm and Blues, a music of the Thirties and Forties that aimed primarily at the Negro market; that music emphasized the second and fourth beats of each measure. Rock 'n' roll exploits this same heavy beat—by making it heavier, lustier and transforming it into what has become known as The Big Beat. It is a tense, monotonous beat that often gives rock 'n' roll music a jungle-like persistence. . . .

Another rich field for research[ing its appeal] is found among the children themselves. They come from all economic classes and neighborhoods, sometimes lone-wolfing it, but mostly with their pals, dates, clubs and gangs. Outside the theatre they seem to become one class—rocking the neighborhood with wild and emotional behavior. . . .

Like young teen-agers generally, they tend to keep the sexes segregated: girls are mostly with girls; boys with boys. Their clothes and manners bespeak a kind of conformism: so many of the girls wear a sort of uniform—tight, revealing sweaters with colorful kerchiefs, skin-tight toreador pants, white woolen socks and loafers; so many of the boys conform to a pattern—leather or sports jackets, blue jeans, loafers and cigarettes.

Physically, it would seem as though the children feared to look different from one another, or lacked confidence in individuality. . . .

How do the teen-agers feel about rock 'n' roll?

A black-haired, starry-eyed beauty of 15, emerging from the theatre looks as though she had returned from outer space.

"It's just instinct, that's all," murmured Roseann Chasen of Norfolk, Va. . . . "I come to hear it because I can sing and scream here. Because it's not like at home where your parents are watching TV and you can't. Here you can scream all you like. And the stars wave to you, and don't act like they don't care whether you're there or not."...

What does it all prove? ...

A. D. Buchmueller, a psychiatric social worker, ... said:

"Kids, just like adults, get caught up in a mass kind of hysteria, which is contagious. Some get hurt by it, physically and emotionally.

"But it is not helpful, and may even be harmful, for adults to take a strong and condemning attitude and action toward adolescents in their rock 'n' roll behavior. This behavior is part of their individual as well as collective or group rebellion against the strictness of adult society.

"This doesn't mean that I approve of rock 'n' roll. I don't. I think there are many other kinds of music, more beautiful and culturally more valuable, that they might be hearing. And also the suggestiveness of a sexual nature in crude and open exhibitionism, used by some singers, is to be deplored."

Gertrude Samuels, "Why They Rock 'n' Roll—And Should They?" *New York Times*, magazine section, January 12, 1958.
ᴔ

Musical Treatment (1956)

THE SOUTHERNER

Opposition to rock-and-roll came from many quarters. Some cities, such as Boston, tried—usually unsuccessfully—to ban performances. The major entertainment industry publications, Billboard *and* Variety, *weighed in against R&B lyrics, which, if they could understand them, seemed plain dirty. Fearing federal intervention, the papers called for the record business to regulate itself. "Before it's too late for the welfare of the industry—forgetting for the moment the welfare of young Americans,"* Variety *urged, the industry's executives must lead "a strong self-examination of the record business." In the southern United States, the rise of R&B coincided with the general fear of Communist subversion, the* Brown *decision in 1954, the Montgomery bus boycott in 1955–1956, and the massive national and international reaction to the murder in 1955 of Emmett Till, a fourteen-year-old African American boy lynched in Mississippi. The White Citizens Council in Birmingham, Alabama—like councils in other southern states, it came into being to resist the desegregation ruling—was especially concerned about the influence of "Negro music" on the American way of life. Its membership organized efforts to eliminate such music from jukeboxes and the radio. The Birmingham Citizens Council's magazine,* The Southerner, *was edited and in large part written by "Ace" Carter, later a speechwriter for the segregationist Alabama governor George Wallace. Today, Carter is better known under the pen name of Forrest Carter, author of the popular children's book* The Education of Little Tree *(1976).*

PROBLEMS TO CONSIDER

1. How did the author connect musical disorder and social and sexual disorder? How did he link the music to international politics and the Cold War?
2. Compare the demand for resistance to popular music with the strategies for combating domestic subversion presented in some of this chapter's other examples of 1950s popular culture.

Citizens Councils observers attended a "Rock and Roll" Concert held on a Sunday afternoon. . . . The "Concert" was attended by a packed throng of over five thousand teen-agers . . . white teen-agers. The center of their attraction was a negro band and negro singers.

The wildly cheering throng of white children, with girls in the distinct majority, applauded, screamed, swooned and beat time to the heavy throb set by the negroes.

The sensuous negro music, timed to the jungle beat, was accompanied by words shocking in their filthiness. The uninitiated listener feels a physical and soul-quaking blow as the utter beast is brought to the surface; as the vulgarity of the meaning slaps home to the heart.

The words of the negro "singers" are unprintable. The motions of the male negro "musicians" unspeakable. The entire moral structure of man, of Christianity, of spirituality in Holy marriage . . . of all that the white man has built through his devotion to God; all this, was crumbled and snatched away, as the white girls and boys were tuned to the level of the animal. . . .

The program's end was the scene of a frantic, screaming dash by the white girls into the dressing room of the male negro "star," demanding his autograph and picture. . . .

To any white man or woman who retains an ounce of the responsibility of the white race, the scene would be revolting to his decency and disgusting to his sight and hearing. . . .

What has happened to the responsibility supposedly present in our so-called "leaders"?

To drive the white to the level of the negro in order to bring about the integration of the races, is the prime goal of the communist. And in the driving, to destroy the moral fabric, to obliterate Christianity, home and marriage, responsibility, and in truth the soul of man. That is the terrifying battle that rages today, as the war for minds and bodies is waged by the communist. . . .

And as the degradation of communism leads the white toward the status of the negro, he loses his responsibility and his standards that have allowed him in the past to remain a free man, a creator of free governments to be a servant, not a master of man.

Turn on your radio and listen to the rock and roll death song of America and the white race. It is there; put there by those who care little for our race, but rather who hate the white man for standing alone between the communist and world domination.

———————

"Musical Treatment," *The Southerner*, March 1956, 5.

ᔓ

"Shake, Rattle and Roll" (1954)
"BIG" JOE TURNER

"Shake, Rattle and Roll" (1954)
BILL HALEY AND HIS COMETS

The strategy of "self-examination" that Variety *urged on the recording industry actually was well under way by 1955, as major record labels, such as Decca, took established R&B numbers and altered them to fit mainstream broadcasting. Recorded by a white artist and its title changed to "Dance with Me, Henry," Etta James's provocative "Roll with Me, Henry" went to number one on the charts for six weeks. Critics of music censor-*

ship have described this process as sanitizing or diluting the songs for popular white consumption and exploiting the authentic artistry of African American performers. A commonly cited example of this filtering was "Shake, Rattle and Roll," composed by the prolific African American songwriter and arranger Jesse Stone (pen name Charles Calhoun) and recorded by the blues artist "Big" Joe Turner in 1954. Compare Turner's version with that of the all-white rock-and-rollers Bill Haley and His Comets, which went to the top of the charts in 1954.

PROBLEMS TO CONSIDER

1. Did Haley's version "sanitize" this song? What strategies were used both to preserve and to alter the style of Turner's wording?
2. Did Haley's version change the sexual relations between men and women in Turner's version?

"SHAKE, RATTLE AND ROLL" (TURNER)

Get outta that bed, wash your face and hands
Get outta that bed, wash your face and hands
Well, you get in that kitchen, make some noise
    with the pots 'n pans

Way you wear those dresses, the sun comes
    shinin' through
Way you wear those dresses, the sun comes
    shinin' through
I can't believe my eyes, all that mess belongs
    to you

I believe to the soul you're the devil and now
    I know
I believe to the soul you're the devil and now
    I know
Well, the more I work, the faster my money
    goes

Chorus:
I said shake, rattle and roll, Shake, rattle and roll
Shake, rattle and roll, Shake, rattle and roll
Well, you won't do right to save your doggone
    soul . . .
Yeah, blow Joe!

I'm like a one-eyed cat peepin' in a seafood
    store
I'm like a one-eyed cat peepin' in a seafood
    store

Well I can look at you, tell you ain't no child no
    more
(Chorus)

I get over the hill and way down underneath
I get over the hill and way down underneath
You make me roll my eyes, even make me grit
    my teeth
(Chorus)

———

"Big" Joe Turner, "Shake, Rattle and Roll" (1954), transcribed from *The Very Best of Big Joe Turner*, copyright © 1998 Rhino/Atlantic Recording Corp., R2 72968.

"SHAKE, RATTLE AND ROLL" (HALEY)

Get out in that kitchen and rattle those pots
    and pans
Get out in that kitchen and rattle those pots
    and pans
I want my breakfast 'cause I'm a hungry man

Chorus:
I said, Shake, rattle and roll
I said, Shake, rattle and roll
I said, Shake, rattle and roll
I said, Shake, rattle and roll
You never do nothin' to save your doggone
    soul

You're wearin' those dresses, your hair done up
   so nice
You're wearin' those dresses, your hair done up
   so nice
You look so warm, but your heart is cold as ice
(Chorus)

I'm like a one-eyed cat peepin' in a seafood
   store
I'm like a one-eyed cat peepin' in a seafood
   store

I can look at you and tell you don't love me no
   more

I believe you're doin' me wrong and now I know
I believe you're doin' me wrong and now I know
The more I work, the faster my money goes

————

Bill Haley and His Comets, "Shake, Rattle and Roll" (1954), transcribed from *20th Century Masters: The Best of Bill Haley & His Comets* (Millennium Collection), copyright © 1999 MCA, MCAD 11957.

❧

❧ American Strengths and Weaknesses: Domestic Subversion and the Cold War ❧

The opening scenes from the 1952 movie *My Son John* take place on a pleasant residential street in postwar America. Two strapping lads are tossing the football in the front yard on a Sunday morning, wasting some time while Mom readies herself for church. But things are not quite right. The boys' playfulness softens the fact that they have been drafted and are headed that afternoon to Korea. There is an edge to the ribbing they give their awkward father when they pass him the ball and he can't hold on to it. Mom, it appears, always makes them late for church, and today she takes a little too long primping and then runs onto the porch wearing only her slip to tell them she's coming. But someone who is supposed to be there, isn't—John, their oldest son, the head of his class, college graduate, and, now, holder of some fancy title down in Washington. They have not seen him in almost a year. He shows up a week later, but the air of disquiet hanging over this all-American setting prepares us for the gradual but inevitable revelation that there is plenty to worry about in this Cold War nuclear family: their son John is a Communist. Why John or any other American would be a Communist was the question of the era.

What made Americans feel so vulnerable to Communist subversion, especially at a time when the domestic Communist Party had dwindled to almost nothing? Senator Joseph R. McCarthy, Republican of Wisconsin, deserves much of the credit. His name dominates the postwar Red Scare, but that label can be misleading. McCarthy stood out because of the power he amassed for himself and his party from exploiting the attention generated by his reckless and sensational charges of Communist subversives in government. No matter how baseless his accusations, no one—Democrat or Republican—dared to challenge him for fear of appearing soft on communism. But McCarthy's charges had such force because many Americans in the 1950s were prone to believe them. The nation's citizens were in general agreement that American Communist agents had weakened the country's security. Events abroad—revolution in China and Soviet achievements in nuclear weaponry—encouraged this view. How could the Communists have won these major victories in an era of unrivaled American power unless traitors within the nation's own ranks had helped them? Such concerns encouraged unprecedented suspicion of dissidents and nonconformists of any stripe. The documents in this section, most of which are drawn from materials of unusual popularity in the Cold War era, suggest how and why Americans of the 1950s saw themselves, rather than the Soviets, as the source of the problem.

The Doolittle Report (1954)

Under the Eisenhower administration (1953–1961), the Central Intelligence Agency (CIA) emerged as one of the federal government's most powerful foreign policy institutions. In immediate U.S.-Soviet relations, Eisenhower sought to negotiate "peaceful coexistence." But on the periphery of the great nations, especially in the developing post-colonial regions of Africa, Asia, and Central and South America, the American government pursued a more aggressive Cold War strategy in this newly declared battleground against international communism. Problems came with this strategy. In the new age of atomic weaponry and statesmanship, many foreign policy experts regarded conventional battlefield forces and tactics as unwieldy and ineffective tools. What was needed, they believed, was a weapon that operated efficiently and quietly to achieve desired ends. Established in 1947 to gather information ("intelligence") about foreign governments, the CIA after 1953 became the key instrument of countersubversion: secret or covert actions abroad, such as toppling "unfriendly" governments; bankrolling opposition political parties; and clandestinely funding pro-American groups. Broad congressional and public support and admiration for the CIA solidified in 1953 and 1954, when the agency's operatives overturned popularly elected and allegedly pro-Communist governments in Guatemala and Iran and replaced them with leaders aligned with American political and business interests. In 1954, to avert congressional scrutiny of the CIA's "Clandestine Service" operations, Eisenhower requested an investigation by a study group whose members he selected. The Doolittle Committee, named for the famous World War II pilot and Air Force commander who chaired it, prepared a classified endorsement of the agency for the president.

PROBLEMS TO CONSIDER

1. More than reporting on the CIA's covert actions, the Doolittle Report defined the nature of the Soviet threat to the United States. According to the report, where did American weaknesses lie?
2. How did the report use the Soviet Union to reflect on the nature of the United States? Did the major obstacles to effective anticommunism reside abroad or at home?

I. INTRODUCTION

The acquisition and proper evaluation of adequate and reliable intelligence on the capabilities and intentions of Soviet Russia is today's most important military and political requirement. Several agencies of Government and many thousands of capable and dedicated people are engaged in the accomplishment of this task. Because the United States is relatively new at the game, and because we are opposed by a police state enemy whose social discipline and whose security measures have been built up and maintained at a high level for many years, the usable information we are obtaining is still far short of our needs.

As long as it remains national policy, another important requirement is an aggressive covert psychological, political and paramilitary organization more effective, more unique and, if necessary, more ruthless than that employed by the enemy. No one should be permitted to stand in the way of the prompt, efficient and secure accomplishment of this mission.

In the carrying out of this policy and in order to reach minimal standards for national safety under present world conditions, two things must be done. First, the agencies charged by law with the collection, evaluation, and distribution of intelligence must be strengthened and coordinated to the greatest practical degree. This is a primary concern of the National Security Council and must be accomplished at the national policy level. Those elements of the problem that fall within the scope of our directive are dealt with in the report which follows. The second consideration is less tangible but equally important. It is now clear that we are facing an implacable enemy whose avowed objective is world domination by whatever means and at whatever cost. There are no rules in such a game. Hitherto acceptable norms of human conduct do not apply. If the United States is to survive, long-standing American concepts of "fair play" must be reconsidered. We must develop effective espionage and counterespionage services and must learn to subvert, sabotage and destroy our enemies by more clever, more sophisticated and more effective methods than those used against us. It may become necessary that the American people be made acquainted with, understand and support this fundamentally repugnant philosophy.

Because of the tight security controls that have been established by the U.S.S.R. and its satellites, the problem of infiltration by human agents is extremely difficult. Most borders are made physically secure by elaborate systems of fencing, lights, mines, etc., backed by constant surveillance. Once across borders—by parachute, or by other means—escape from detection is extremely difficult because of constant checks on personnel activities and personal documentation. The information we have obtained by this method of acquisition has been negligible and the cost in effort, dollars and human lives prohibitive.

This leads to the conviction that much more effort should be expended in exploring every possible scientific and technical avenue of approach to the intelligence problem. The study group has been extensively briefed by C.I.A. personnel and by the Armed Services in the methods and equipment that are presently in use and under development in this area. We have also had the benefit of advice from certain civilian consultants who are working on such special projects. We are impressed by what has been done, but feel that there is an immense potential yet to be explored. We believe that every known technique should be intensively applied and new ones should be developed to increase our intelligence acquisition by [DELETED].

II. CONCLUSIONS AND RECOMMENDATIONS

With respect to the Central Intelligence Agency in general we conclude: (a) that its placement in the overall organization of the Government is proper; (b) that the laws under which it operates are adequate; (c) that the established provisions for its financial support are sufficiently flexible to meet its current operational needs; (d) that in spite of the limitations imposed by its relatively short life and rapid expansion it is doing a creditable job; (e) that it is gradually improving its

capabilities; and (f) that it is exercising care to insure the loyalty of its personnel. . . .

"Report of the Special Study Group [Doolittle Committee] on the Covert Activities of the Central Intelligence Agency, Sept. 30, 1954," in *The Central Intelligence Agency: History and Documents*, edited by William M. Leary (Tuscaloosa: University of Alabama Press, 1984), 143–44.

☙

We Need Revival! (1949)

BILLY GRAHAM

In 1959, the U.S. census reported, 69 percent of Americans claimed membership in a church, synagogue, or mosque, an astounding rise since 1940, when 49 percent of all Americans described themselves as religious in this way. From many directions, the 1950s were a time of unusually high religious affiliation and activism, a break rather than a continuity with the immediate past. Besides the Reverend Martin Luther King Jr., the most important figure to emerge within American Protestantism during the decade was the Reverend Billy Graham. The North Carolina–born minister was thirty-one years old in 1949 and already a rising youthful force in evangelical Protestantism when he began a revival campaign in America's postwar capital of secular pleasures, Los Angeles, the city, he said, "known around the world because of its sin, crime and immorality." Like earlier generations of American evangelists, Graham appreciated the value of publicity and the power of the communications media that he both denounced and tried to convert to godly purposes. The Los Angeles revival under Graham's "Canvas Cathedral" succeeded initially, converting several minor entertainment figures. The big crowds were not generated until sermons, such as the one reprinted here, were delivered in the aftermath of the Soviet Union's secret testing of an atomic bomb, which President Truman disclosed to the public on September 23, 1949. Graham's denunciations of communism attracted the attention of the fiercely anti-Communist publisher William Randolph Hearst, who made the evangelist front-page news in his Los Angeles newspaper and eventually across the nation. Graham also became one of the most influential figures explaining the nature of the Communist threat to the United States and the world. By the end of the 1950s, public opinion polls consistently identified him as one of the most admired and trusted Americans.

PROBLEMS TO CONSIDER

1. According to Graham, what made Los Angeles (and the United States) "wicked"? What signs of immorality did Graham connect to Communist subversion?
2. What do you think came across more clearly to listeners in his sermon: anxiety or confidence, impending doom or the promise of deliverance?

I want to speak on the subject, "The Choice that is Before Los Angeles During these Next Three Weeks." Remember the verse we just read, "Except the Lord of hosts had left unto us a very small remnant, we should have been as Sodom, and we should have been like unto Gomorrah."

I have been in Europe six times since the war and have seen devastated cities of Germany and the wreckage of war. I believe the only reason that America escaped the ravages and destruction of war was because God's people prayed. Many of these people believe that God can still use America to evangelize the world. I think that we are living at a time in world history when God is giving us a desperate choice, a choice of either revival or judgment. There is no other alternative! And I particularly believe this applies to the city of Los Angeles—this city of wickedness and sin, this city that is known around the world because of its sin, crime and immorality. God Almighty is going to bring judgment upon this city unless people repent and believe—unless God sends an old-fashioned, heaven-sent, Holy Ghost revival.

How desperately we need revival! Think, for a moment, of some of the dreadful things happening throughout the western world. On Friday morning the entire world was shocked. (Sept. 23, 1949.) Across Europe at this very hour there is stark, naked fear among the people, for we all realize that war is much closer than we ever dreamed. The people of Europe stand on the threshold of the unknown. Our President . . . announced to the startled world that Russia has now exploded an atomic bomb. An arms race, unprecedented in the history of the world, is driving us madly toward destruction! And I sincerely believe that it is the providence of God that He has chosen this hour for a campaign—giving this city one more chance to repent of sin and turn to a believing knowledge of the Lord Jesus Christ.

Recalling again our subject, Los Angeles' choice, see the need for a decision in the philo-

sophical realm. The era of Materialism, Paganism and Humanism has been emphasized in the educational circles of this country. Man has steered our course. We have been humanizing God. Throughout our land we have denied the supernatural, outlawed the supernatural, and said that miracles are not now possible. We are taken up with *things* rather than with the *Spirit of God*.

Then look at our moral standard. There was a time a few years ago, which most of you with gray hair can remember, when this country claimed the Ten Commandments as the basis for our moral code. That is no longer true. . . . The home, the basic unit of our society is breaking and crumbling, and the American way of life is being destroyed at the very heart and core of society.

At the same time we see an unchecked crime wave in this country. . . . We need revival! Eight hundred per cent increase in crime in the last ten years in Los Angeles.

Look at the problem of sex. Everywhere, but especially emphasized and underscored here, we see sex placed before American young people. If we want to sell even a motor car tire, we have to use sex to do it. As a result, our high school and college young people are going to the dogs morally—encouraged by the press and radio across this Nation. We need a revival! . . .

Let us look for a moment at the political realm. Let's see what is happening—not only in the city of Los Angeles, but in the western world. The world is divided into two sides. On the one side we see Communism; on the other side we see so-called Western culture. Western culture and its fruit had its foundation in the Bible, the Word of God, and in the revivals of the Seventeenth and Eighteenth Centuries. Communism, on the other hand, has decided against God, against Christ, against the Bible, and against all religion. Communism is not only an economic interpretation of life—Communism is a religion that is inspired, directed and motivated by the Devil himself who has declared war against Almighty God. Do you know that the Fifth Columnists, called Communists, are more rampant in Los Angeles than any other city in America? We need a revival.

Now for the first time in the history of the world we have the weapon with which to destroy ourselves—the atomic bomb. I am persuaded that time is desperately short! . . .

I do want to say that underlying every word I have to say is the basic law of God—"The wages of sin is death." If Sodom and Gomorrah could not get away with sin; if Pompeii and Rome could not escape, neither can Los Angeles! Judgment is coming, as sure as I am standing here! . . .

This may be God's last great call! . . .

I warn you to repent of sin and turn to Jesus Christ as a city before it is too late. Do you know what God is going to do? One of these days—it may not be this year, it may be a hundred years from now, I do not know the time, but I do know this—unless we have a revival, one of these little tremors that you call an earthquake

may shake every building in Los Angeles. . . Do you know the area that is marked out for the enemy's first atomic bomb? New York! Secondly, Chicago; and thirdly, the city of Los Angeles! We don't know how soon, but we do know this, that right now the grace of God can still save a poor lost sinner. We know that the gates of heaven are still open to those who will repent and believe that Jesus is God's Son and our Saviour.

Somebody asked me the other day whether I think we can have a revival. What a foolish question! . . .

In this moment I can see the judgment hand of God over Los Angeles. I can see judgment about to fall. If we repent, if we believe, if we turn to Christ in faith and hope, the judgment of God can be stopped. From the depths of my heart, I believe that this message is God's word today.

Billy Graham, "We Need Revival!" in *Revival in Our Times: The Story of the Billy Graham Evangelistic Campaigns* (Wheaton, Ill.: Van Kampen Press, 1954), 52–57.

ᴖ

One Lonely Night (1951)

MICKEY SPILLANE

Between 1947 and 1952, when domestic unease over the Cold War was intense, Mickey Spillane published six novels. Combined, they sold more than 17 million copies in pulp paperback. No fictional character of the era could match the popularity of Mike Hammer, Spillane's gun-happy private investigator. By established literary as well as middle-class standards, Spillane's novels were in very bad taste. The problem was not only the sadistic violence but also Hammer's sexual adventures with women, most of whom seemed always to be either disrobing for the irresistible detective or touching up after a romp with him. In terms of style, Spillane drew on earlier, more literary masters of 1930s detective fiction, such as Dashiell Hammett. In The Maltese Falcon *and other novels, Hammett's Sam Spade hounds thugs and gangsters who seem to be ugly reflections of himself. At the same time, some of the worst of Hammett's villains contain the populist appeal of the nonconforming outlaw male resisting the oppressive force of social institutions.*

Mickey Spillane's bad guys and gals, although still doubles of his protagonist, did not invite the reader's empathy. They usually deserved worse than the load of lead Hammer pumped into them. Such fates were especially merited once Spillane replaced the gangsters in his fiction with what he called the "real sons of bitches who should have died long ago"— Communist subversives. In One Lonely Night *(1951), Mike Hammer emerged as America's best-selling cold warrior. In the following scene, Hammer discovers that Communist subversives have kidnapped Velda, who is his very attractive fiancée, his secretary, and a virgin. He tracks them to their lair in the ruins of an abandoned paint factory, where he finds Velda in the clutches of Communist subversives.*

PROBLEMS TO CONSIDER

1. What did this scene say about the kinds of women and men who became Communists? According to Spillane, was communism a political ideology or a psychological disorder?
2. Compare the countersubversive methods prescribed by the Doolittle Report with the anti-Communist techniques of Mike Hammer.

The sons-of-bitches had picked the best spot on earth, not a sound would penetrate these walls! In that maze of partitions and cubicles even the brightest beam of light that could escape would be dulled and unseen. I wanted to pull the trigger of the gun and blast the whole dump to bits and wade into the wreckage with my bare hands. I wanted to scream just like the guys outside wanted to scream and I couldn't.

Another minute to make myself cool off. Another minute to let instinct and training take over.

Another minute for my eyes to see and they picked out a path that led through the rubbish, a path I should have seen sooner because it had been deliberately made and often used. Old paint cans had been pushed aside and spilled their thick, gooey mess on the floor. The larger drums had been slop pails for left-over stuff and marked the turns in the trail.

My eyes saw it, my feet followed it. They took me around the bend and through a hall then up the stairs.

And the path that was cleared through the dirt on the floor led to the middle, then the top story. It led to rooms that reeked of turpentine so strong it almost took my breath away. It led to a corridor and another man who stepped out of the shadows to die. It led to a door that swung open easily and into a room that faced on other rooms where I was able to stand in my invisible cloak of blackness with barely the strength to hold the gun.

I stood there and looked at what I was, hearing myself say, "Good God, no, please . . . no!" I had to stand there for a moment of time that turned into eternity while I was helpless to intervene and see things my mind wanted to shut out . . . hear things my ears didn't want to hear.

For an eternal moment I had to look at them all, every one. General Osilov in a business suit leaning on his cane almost casually, an unholy leer lighting his face. My boy of the subway slobbering all over his chin, puking a little without noticing it, his hands pressed against his belly while his face was a study in obscene fascination.

And the guy in the pork-pie hat!

Velda.

She was stark naked.

She hung from the rafters overhead by a rope that chewed into her wrists, while her body twisted slowly in the single light of the electric lantern! The guy in the pork-pie hat waited until she turned to face him then brought the knotted rope around with all the strength of his arm and I heard it bite into her flesh with a sickening sound that brought her head up long enough for me to see that even the pain was dulling under the evil of this thing.

He said, "Where is it? You'll die if you don't tell me!"

She never opened her mouth. Her eyes came open, but she never opened her mouth!

Then there was only beauty to the nakedness of her body. A beauty of the flesh that was more than the sensuous curve of her hips, more than the sharp curve of breasts drawn high under the weight of her body, more than those long, full legs, more than the ebony of her hair. There was the beauty of the flesh that was the beauty of the soul and the guy in the pork-pie hat grimaced with hate and raised the rope to smash it down while the rest slobbered with the lust and pleasure of this example of what was yet to come, even drooled with the passion that was death made slow in the fulfillment of the philosophy that lived under a red flag!

And in that moment of eternity I heard the problem asked and knew the answer! I knew why I was allowed to live while others died! I knew why my rottenness was tolerated and kept alive and why the guy with the reaper couldn't catch me and I smashed through the door of the room with the tommy gun in my hands spitting out the answer at the same time my voice screamed it to the heavens!

I lived only to kill the scum and the lice that wanted to kill themselves. I lived to kill so that others could live. I lived to kill because my soul was a hardened thing that reveled in the thought of taking the blood of the bastards who made murder their business. I lived because I could laugh it off and others couldn't. I was the evil that opposed other evil, leaving the good and the meek in the middle to live and inherit the earth!

They heard my scream and the awful roar of the gun and the slugs tearing into bone and guts and it was the last they heard. They went down as they tried to run and felt their insides tear out and spray against the walls.

I saw the general's head splinter into shiny wet fragments and splatter over the floor. The guy from the subway tried to stop the bullets with his hands and dissolved into a night-mare of blue holes.

There was only the guy in the pork-pie hat who made a crazy try for a gun in his pocket. I aimed the tommy gun for the first time and took his arm off at the shoulder. It dropped on the floor next to him and I let him have a good look

at it. He couldn't believe it happened. I proved it by shooting him in the belly. They were all so damned clever!

They were all so damned dead!

I laughed and laughed while I put the second clip in the gun. I knew the music in my head was going wild this time, but I was laughing too hard to enjoy it. I went around the room and kicked them over on their backs and if they had faces left I made sure they didn't. I saved the last burst for the bastard who was MVD *[Soviet secret police]* in a pork-pie hat and who looked like a kid. A college boy. He was still alive when he stared into the flame that spit out of the muzzle only an inch away from his nose.

I cut her down carefully, dressed her, cradled her in my arms like a baby and knew that I was crying. Me. I could still do that. I felt her fingers come up and touch one of the wet spots on my cheek, heard her say the three words that blessed everything I did, then I went back to the path that led out into the night that was still cold and rainy, but still free to be enjoyed. There was a soft spot on the ground where I laid her with my coat under her head while I went back to do what I had to do. I went back to the room where death had visited and walked under the rafters until I reached the pork-pie hat that lay next to the remains of the thing that wore it. I lifted his wallet out of his back pocket and flipped his coat open so I could rip the inside lining pocket out along with some shreds of the coat fabric. That was all. Except for one thing. When I went down the stairs once more I found a drum of paint whose spilled contents made a sticky flow into some empty cans. When I built up a mound of old papers around the stuff I touched a match to it, stood there until I was satisfied with its flame, then went back to Velda. Her eyes were closed and her breathing heavy. She came up in my arms and I fixed my coat around her.

I carried her that way to my car and drove her home, and stayed while a doctor hovered above her. I prayed. It was answered when the doctor came out of the room and smiled. I said another prayer of thankfulness and did the thing that had to be done to make her comfortable. When the nurse came to sit by her side I picked up my hat and went downstairs.

The rain came down steadily. It was clear and pure. It swept by the curb carrying the filth into the sewer.

We know now, don't we, Judge? We know the answer.

There were only a few hours left of the night. I drove to the office and opened the lamp. I took out the two envelopes in there and spread them out on my desk. The beginning and the end. The complexities and the simplicities. It was all so clever and so rotten.

And to think that they might have gotten away with it!

It was over and done with now. Miles away an abandoned paint factory would be a purgatory of flame and explosions that would leave only the faintest trace of what had been there. It was a hell that wiped away all sins leaving only the good and the pure. The faintest trace that it left would be looked into and expounded upon. There would be nothing left but wonder and the two big words, WHY and HOW. There were no cars at the scene. They wouldn't have been foolish enough to get there that way. The flames would char and blacken. They would leave remains that would take months to straighten out, and in that straightening they would come across melted leaden slugs and a twisted gun that was the property of the investigating bureau in Washington. There would be cover-up and more wonder and more speculation, then, eventually, someone would stumble on part of the truth. Yet even then, it was a truth only half-known and too big to be told.

Only I knew the whole thing and it was too big for me. I was going to tell it to the only person who would understand what it meant.

I picked up the phone.

Mickey Spillane, *One Lonely Night* (New York: Signet, New American Library, 1951), 147–50.

ॐ

How Red Girl Spies Make Suckers of G.I.'s (1954)
DAVID LOEHWING

There was one weapon that was almost as lethal as the bomb and that no healthy American male could defend himself against: the Soviet bombshell or "love spy." Even Mike Hammer, in One Lonely Night, *is unable to contain himself when confronted by a sexually willing Communist woman. A tangle with Hammer typically showed the women just how wrong they were about the American Way. Spillane's fiction exemplified how defenders of America in popular culture and official government positions often represented the threat of communism as the dangers of female sexuality. Defending against such enemies, however, put American men in a difficult position. They had to be careful lest, in resisting the enemy, they be seen as uninterested in women altogether. The following "true" story about the deadly women of communism was published in the* National Police Gazette, *an inexpensive pulp magazine that marketed itself to working-class men with stories about rough sports (boxing and horse racing) and sensational crimes.*

PROBLEMS TO CONSIDER

1. What made American men vulnerable to Communist love spies?
2. Why were the corrupting forces represented by women?

All along the Iron Curtain, from Rostock to the Black Sea, the forces of the free world are locked in a secret underground war of espionage and counter-espionage with the Communists. It's a dirty, no-holds-barred type of gutter fighting, at which the Reds excel because they have no qualms about methods. They resort to kidnapping, torture and cold-blooded murder without the slightest twinge of conscience. . . .

One of the principal Soviet weapons in this war, used mainly against Americans, is sex — glamorous girl "boudoir agents" sent to charm and then betray our soldiers on occupation duty. U.S. intelligence agents say that hundreds of these cold-war Mata Haris *[a term for sexually irresistible female spies]*, trained in the arts of seduction, are slipping through the Iron Curtain. They haunt the bars and night clubs of every town in Germany and Austria where American G.I.s are stationed.

It doesn't occur to G.I.s, taught respect for women at home, that girls could be up to such cold-blooded tricks. "American men are such easy marks for a pretty face, you can depend on it that the Reds will be using more and more girl spies," warned one of them who turned on her Communist masters and gave herself up to the U.S. Counter-Intelligence Corps. She goes by the name of Maria Kazimova, though that's not her real name, and it was from her that the C.I.C. learned much of what it knows about the school in Halle, East Germany, where the top-grade love spies are trained by the MVD — Russia's secret police. . . .

The C.I.C. knew long before Maria Kazimova came along that they had to contend with girl spies from the East. . . .

[YOUNG WOMEN]

The technique used by the fräuleins is simple. As Maria Kazimova points out, a great many Yanks are suckers for a pretty girl, no matter what her nationality or loyalties. It isn't difficult for an attractive, shapely fräulein to find a G.I. to step out with in Berlin. He's lonely and human, and she soon becomes his mistress. That's the first step. Soon he's trading on the black market to provide her with little luxuries, and going A.W.O.L. to enjoy the fruits of illicit love.

Punished by his superior officers, the soldier becomes sullen and resentful, and talks of going "over the hill." The fräulein gets him drunk and then confides that she knows of a place where they can go — a land of milk and honey, where there are no MP's, no officers, no work details or K.P. Just plenty of schnapps. . . .

Maria, a tall, slender, raven-haired beauty with blue-green eyes and very white, almost translucent skin, received her love-spy training at the school in Halle. . . .

At first it wasn't so bad, although she had to study hard to keep up with her lessons in German, French and English. . . . At the same time she had to learn all the lore of espionage work — the use of codes, the sending of messages, how to operate a clandestine radio transmitter, the use of sabotage devices, how to establish and control a Communist underground cell. She spent long hours on the firing range, learning to become a first-rate marksman, since she might be called upon to carry out assassinations from time to time. . . .

She learned how to become irresistible to an unwary male, how to make love to him in order to gain his confidence, and finally, how to extract from him vital military information. At that point her superiors decided she was ready to begin her work. . . .

She slipped through the Iron Curtain and made her way to Frankfurt. Avoiding her MVD contact, who was later arrested, she went directly to the C.I.C. headquarters. . . .

"I was supposed to become your mistress and twist you around my finger," she told the officer in charge, Major Kelly.

Taking in her attractive figure and face at a glance, the Major sighed:

"I guess maybe it's just as well you didn't try."

David Loehwing, "How Red Girl Spies Make Suckers of G.I.'s," *National Police Gazette*, November 1954, 5–7, 32.

❧

❧ Kitchen Debates: Ideal Womanhoods and the New Frontiers of Domesticity ❧

The most popular television comedy of the 1950s was *I Love Lucy*, starring Lucille Ball and her real-life husband Desi Arnaz as Lucy and Ricky Ricardo. The stunning redhead Lucy played housewife to handsome Cuban bandleader Ricky, but the comedy often arose from Lucy's futile attempts to thwart her husband's patriarchal expectations that she satisfy herself with keeping his home. In episode after episode, Lucy managed to scheme her way into Ricky's nightclub act or some other showbiz venture. Tone deaf and more ambitious than talented, she met one humiliating failure after another, each time happily or tearfully concluding that home was, indeed, the better place for her. At least, until the next episode.

The popularity of *I Love Lucy* provides evidence for and against the passivity and conformity of women who lived in the 1950s and experienced firsthand the ideals of domesticity. As on television, actual women and the "ideal woman" rarely coincided in an era when the house-bound housewife was becoming a social anomaly. From 1945 to 1960, the number of women working outside the home actually increased by 2 million. Working women (including Lucille Ball) composed one-third of the nation's labor force, and 40 percent of them had children (again, including Ball). For such women, the high-paying "men's" jobs of the war rarely were an option. The confinement they experienced was determined less by the expectations of domesticity than by the small paychecks and rigid work regimens of gender-segregated employment as secretaries, domestics, and food-service workers. That is not to say that working-class women took what they could get. Their labor activism actually grew in the 1950s. Their confinement in certain job categories—the telephone operators who assisted callers were all women—gave them the numerical strength to organize unions and to combat wage discrimination when men were paid more than women for the same work. Still, even among job-holding women, few were interested in overturning the stereotype that defined womanhood first in terms of marriage, homemaking, and childbearing. Most worked because they needed the income, not because they wanted to challenge the constraints of maternalism or to realize a larger or more exciting life outside the home. In this sense, they were like earlier generations of women, from the young women in 1830s New England who worked in the Lowell mills to the Depression-era women whose low-wage labor made them more employable than their husbands or fathers. To consider how broadly the 1950s ideals of middle-class, heterosexual domesticity applied outside (or even inside) the growing middle-class population of white suburbanites, this section focuses on women who worked both with and against the dominant values and priorities of the era. Their lives suggest the lengths to which those ideals could be stretched to challenge existing social arrangements and relations and to advance new ones.

Encounter (1959)

In July 1959, Vice President Richard Nixon traveled to Moscow ostensibly to open the American National Exhibition, but more importantly to improve diplomatic relations with Soviet premier Nikita Khrushchev in hopes of later setting up a high-level meeting with President Dwight Eisenhower. Their informal meeting in the "model home" on display at the showcase of American goods turned into the famous "kitchen debate," in which the two combative leaders sparred over the issue of whose country had the better standard of living. The kitchen setting inevitably turned the debate toward women, work, and technology, as well as American ideals of domesticity versus Soviet policies that all citizens, regardless of sex or children in their care, should work outside the home.

PROBLEMS TO CONSIDER

1. On what points did Nixon and Khrushchev agree and disagree? Did they view women or women's work in the same way?
2. How did Nixon connect the purchase or ownership of consumer goods and American citizenship and womanhood?

KHRUSHCHEV *(taking Nixon's arm)*: "In another seven years, we shall be on the same level as America. . . . In passing you by, we shall wave. We can stop and say: If you want capitalism you can live that way . . . we feel sorry for you."

NIXON: "You may be ahead of us . . . in the thrust of your rockets . . . We may be ahead . . . in color television."

KHRUSHCHEV *(breaking in)*: "No, we are up with you on this too. . . . We have bested you in one technique and also in the other."

NIXON: "You see, you never concede anything."

KHRUSHCHEV: "I do not give up."

NIXON: *(pointing to a panel-controlled washing machine)*: "In America, these are designed to make things easier for our women."

KHRUSHCHEV: "A capitalist attitude."

NIXON: "I think this attitude toward women is universal."

KHRUSHCHEV *(jeering at the products on display)*: "Don't you have a machine that puts food into the mouth and pushes it down? . . . These are merely gadgets. . . . Newly built Russian houses have all this equipment right now. In America, if you don't have a dollar you have the right to [sleep] on the pavement."

NIXON: "If you were in the Senate, we would call you a filibusterer—you do all the talking and don't let others talk."

KHRUSHCHEV: "On political problems, we will never agree with you. For instance, Mikoyan likes very peppery soup. I do not. But this does not mean that we do not get along."

Then, noting that Nixon was looking approvingly at some girls modeling bathing suits, he added with a wink. "You are for the girls, too."

NIXON: *(showing the Russian a model American house)*: "We hope to show our diversity and our right to choose. We do not wish to have decisions made at the top by government officials. . . . Would it not be better to compete in the merits of washing machines than in the strength of our rockets . . . ?"

That night, as the two men stood at the microphones for the formal opening of the exhibition, their argument was renewed when Khrushchev proposed a toast, in U.S. wine, "to elimination of all bases in foreign lands." Nixon countered with a toast to peace.

KHRUSHCHEV: "We stand for peace [but] if you are not willing to eliminate bases then I won't drink this toast."

NIXON: "He doesn't like American wine."

KHRUSHCHEV: "I like American wine, not its policy. . . . I defend . . . peace. How can peace be assured when we are surrounded by military bases?"

NIXON: "We'll talk about that later. Let's drink to talking . . . not fighting."

Khrushchev approved of that but suddenly pointed to a waitress and suggested: "Let's drink to the ladies."

Nixon agreed: "We can all drink to the ladies."

———

"Encounter," *Newsweek,* August 3, 1959, 16–17.

᧥

Help Yourself to Happiness (1954)
RONALD SCHILLER

Dream Doll: The Ruth Handler Story (1994)
RUTH HANDLER WITH JACQUELINE SHANNON

A short poem published in Better Homes and Gardens *in 1950 explained that women and men have different needs: men have to make a public show of what they do, but women are content to find their rewards at home, where they "warm their hearts at fires / That burn unnoticed, quietly." The pioneering feminist Betty Friedan later called this woman the "happy housewife heroine." Rebellion against such models of womanhood formed the basis of the 1960s women's movement, which ventured that neither happiness nor heroism was possible for women in such a life. Yet the meanings of domesticity and how the boundaries of the homemaking ideal were experienced were not the same for all women. For instance, in 1947 an article in* Ebony, *a new magazine aimed at the growing African American middle class, bid farewell to "Mammy" (the African American domestic) and hello to "Mom." Wartime affluence, the publication asserted, had liberated black women, but liberty for them meant the freedom to be housewives instead of servants and to tend to their own kitchens and children, rather than those of their white employers. For affluent white housewives, however, life sometimes seemed less free when the high cost of postwar labor made hiring full-time domestics (or "mammies") an expensive luxury. For poor women whose husbands' incomes were boosted by wartime and postwar employment, life, while not easy, was becoming better. In the kitchen debates of women's everyday lives, the happy housewife ideal had different meanings, depending on a woman's race or class or employment status.*

Women also could find ways to resist or even to exploit the limitations of the domestic order. For instance, two of the more important figures in postwar American business and consumer culture were women: Brownie Wise, who gave Americans the "Tupperware party," and Ruth Handler, who gave the world the Barbie doll. Beyond their business *achievements, both women consciously identified themselves as mothers, even as they pushed the boundaries of domesticity. Their stories complicate how we might regard the political potential of domesticity and femininity. For instance, it is hard to think of a consumer commodity that seems more symbolic of 1950s suburban domesticity than Tupperware, the handy plastic tumblers, pitchers, and containers that, when sealed with a "burp," protect leftovers from the depredations of refrigeration. Tupperware was named for its inventor, Earl Tupper, a practical Massachusetts chemical engineer who met with little success in marketing his polyethylene product to retail stores. Then, in 1951, he hired an unknown but energetic Detroit woman, Brownie Wise, to revolutionize how Tupperware was sold. Within six years, Tupperware sales were approaching $100 million annually. Wise, whose career is profiled in this article from* Woman's Home Companion, *deservedly gets much of the credit for the company's successes. In early 1959, the Mattel Toy Company introduced a nine-inch-tall, full-figured adult doll named Barbie, which was so unusual that major retailers disregarded it. Ruth Handler, who ran Mattel with her husband, Elliot, had come up with the idea for Barbie and steered it into production at a time when dolls were, by definition, "baby dolls." Handler had an alternative vision of girl's play, which she describes here in an excerpt from her autobiography.*

PROBLEMS TO CONSIDER

1. The following selections describe Wise's and Handler's business techniques. How did they use "domesticity" and "femininity" to define and move into a public business world?
2. Did selling Tupperware or playing with Barbie challenge or reinforce prescribed outlooks for women, especially toward men?

HELP YOURSELF TO HAPPINESS

She walked slowly, fearfully down the hospital steps. Her small son was seriously ill; treatments would cost $5000. She was husbandless, with only her salary as a secretary to live on. Her house was already mortgaged. Where would the money come from?

Brownie Wise remembered hearing about a part-time job, selling on the "party plan." You asked a friend to invite people to her house. Then you demonstrated your wares. You could do this in the evenings.

The night of her first party Brownie was so embarrassed about selling in a friend's home that she was sick. Flustered, she tripped over her sample case and left with a bleeding nose. At home she burst into tears and vowed she would never make another call. But the next night she picked up her 50-pound case and started out again.

Today, only nine years later, Brownie Wise, at the age of 40, heads one of America's largest home-demonstration sales companies—Tupperware Home Parties Inc. She and her son—now a healthy 15-year-old fully recovered from his childhood illness—live on a palatial Florida lakeside ranch, complete with indoor swimming pool, riding horses, Brahman cattle and cabin cruiser. Her income can be guessed by the fact that she recently turned down a salary offer of $125,000 a year from a rival concern.

To people who always imagine top-flight women executives to be strong-faced, coldly efficient, mannishly tailored creatures, the first sight of Brownie Wise is a pleasant shock. She has a slim, youthful figure, wears her prematurely gray hair in a poodle cut. She has a bubbling sense of humor, giggles when amused. Her executives—nearly all of them men younger than herself—call her by her first name, kid her unmercifully. She has a passion for pink roses, usually has bunches of them strewn around her office, even drives a rose-pink convertible with green leather upholstery. . . .

Brownie comes to work in feminine dresses and frilly hats looking like a young matron on her way to a bridge party. Businessmen calling on her for the first time sometimes mistake her for a secretary, ask petulantly: "Why can't we talk to Mrs. Wise herself?" . . .

In spite of her feminine air she has one of the shrewdest business brains in America. "She thinks like a man—and I mean the smartest man I've ever met," says Jack Marshall, the company's general sales manager. . . .

People are always curious as to what drives Brownie to work so hard. "Is it money?" she is asked.

"Partly," she answers. "I like money. Lots of it. And I have a tremendous respect for people who know how to make it. But money alone isn't enough. As a child I was taught that nobody is entitled to his room on earth; he has to pay for it. The real importance of the money and my job is that it lets me pay my way by helping others." . . .

The product Brownie and her dealers sell is "Tupperware." . . . These products are sold only at parties, not in stores.

Since the dealer can arrange her working hours to suit herself, the job is often a godsend to women with young children who need money but cannot be away from home for long periods of time. Other successful dealers are teachers who cannot support families on their low salaries, air-line hostesses with time on their hands between flights, older women who do not want to be a burden on their married children, ministers'

wives who must supplement their husbands' scant incomes in a dignified way. . . .

The people [Brownie] hires are often not born salesmen. Most of them are timid and totally untrained in the arts of selling. Brownie's job is to give them practical advice and—above all—confidence in themselves and respect for the work they do. She is a masterful inspirational speaker—largely because she completely believes in everything she tells her audience. . . . When she talks, she seems almost carried away with fervor, her eyes become brighter and more intense, her voice rings with conviction. . . . Her inspired audience goes out ready to tackle anything.

———

Ronald Schiller, "Help Yourself to Happiness," *Woman's Home Companion*, August 1954, 34, 95–96.

DREAM DOLL:
THE RUTH HANDLER STORY

It was the summer between my husband Elliot's fortieth birthday and my own, and we were smack in the middle of a six-week tour of Europe. The trip combined both business and pleasure, but was heavy on the pleasure side, since we'd brought along our children, Barbara, then 15, and Ken, 12. . . .

The four of us set off on a leisurely shopping expedition down one of the spotless mountain town's [Lucerne] main streets and soon found ourselves in front of a toy store. Ken disappeared inside, and Elliot bounded in behind him. Elliot had more passion for children's toys, to say the least, than your average American adult male. He and I had been building our company, Mattel, for twelve years, and in that time—thanks to his extraordinary talent for toy design and my own marketing and business acumen—we had created and sold some of the hottest toys in America. Mattel had already become the world's third-largest toy company and, because we had a penchant for coming out with something new and different year after year, the *Saturday Evening*

Post magazine had crowned us "the whiz kids of the toy industry."

Instead of following Elliot and Ken, Barbara and I lingered outside that shop for the longest time. We were absolutely transfixed by the window display, which featured six 11-inch-tall adult-style female dolls. . . . Barbara, whom we also called "Barbie" and "Babs," was enchanted. Though she had long since stopped playing with dolls, she still liked to collect and display them in her bedroom.

I was gripped by that window display for another reason. The "Lilli" doll [in the window] was the embodiment of an idea I'd pitched to Elliot and our other Mattel toy designers some five years earlier. Not her face, mind you. Lilli was based on a character in a cartoon strip . . . [her face] was too hard-looking and cartoonish. . . .

But Lilli's body was another story. Here were the breasts, the small waist, the long, tapered legs I had enthusiastically described for the designers all those years ago.

The idea had been the result of the many times I had observed my daughter Barbara playing with paperdolls with her friends. While the toy counters in the early 1950s were heavy with paperdolls of every size, shape, and form, Barbara and her friends always insisted on buying only *adult* female paperdolls. They simply were not interested in baby paperdolls or even those representing ten-year-olds, their own age. Pretending to be doing something else, I'd listen, fascinated, to the girls as they played with these paperdolls hour after hour. And I discovered something very important: They were using these dolls to project their dreams of their own futures as adult women. So one day it hit me: Wouldn't it be great if we could take that play pattern and three-dimensionalize it so that little girls could do their dreaming and role-playing with real dolls and real clothes instead of the flimsy paper or cardboard ones? It dawned on me that this was a basic, much needed play pattern that had never before been offered by the

doll industry to little girls. Oh, sure, there were so-called fashion dolls, those who came with more than one outfit. But these dolls had flat chests, big bellies, and squatty legs—they were built like overweight six- or eight-year-olds. The idea of putting a prom dress on such a doll, had such a dress even been available, was ludicrous. The clothes that *were* available were drab, clumsy, and poorly made.

At Mattel . . . I had approached Elliot and the other designers with my idea. . . . At first, they all looked at me blankly. . . .

But the frowns and head shaking began in earnest as I described in loving detail the fingernail and toenail polish I envisioned on our adult doll, the narrow waist and ankles, the eyelashes and eyeliner.

"Ruth, it won't work," I was told flatly. "We could never make a doll with that much detail in the U.S. and still be able to price it so that people could afford it." . . .

That was the *official* reason my idea was rejected. But I really think that the squeamishness of those designers—every last one of them male—stemmed mostly from the fact that the doll would have *breasts*. . . .

[It took several years for Handler to convince the skeptics at Mattel to back her idea for the Barbie doll, and then another three years to begin actually manufacturing it.]

By early 1959, . . . Barbie was born and ready for Toy Show, the giant annual New York City industry showcase. . . . As Toy Show approached, we were thrilled with Barbie. The marketing people, the sales people, Elliot and I were all fired up about our creation. She came dressed in a black-and-white-striped bathing suit, shoes, and sunglasses and had a modest suggested retail price of $3. It was the razor and the razor blade theory. Sell the razor at a reasonable price and people will buy the razor blades—or clothes, in our case—to go with it. The clothes were packaged separately and priced at $1 to $3. . . .

When the 1959 Toy Show opened on a balmy March morning, the buyers enthusiastically crowded into our display rooms and I could hear the buzz that had become traditional at this event. What had Ruth and Elliot Handler come up with this year? But whenever the buyers picked up and inspected the Barbie doll, that buzz subsided, replaced by a heavy air of disappointment. . . . It's not that we had *no* takers for Barbie. About 25 percent of our usual buyers ordered good-sized quantities of the doll. . . . But fully 50 percent wanted nothing to do with her.

"Ruth, little girls want baby dolls," one said dismissively, setting Barbie aside. "They want to pretend to be mommies."

I heard that one a lot. "No they don't," I said to the buyer, who—like most other industry toy buyers in those days—was male. "Little girls want to pretend to be *bigger* girls."

But just like Mattel's toy designers nearly a decade earlier, the buyers' biggest objection to Barbie by far was her most prominent feature: "Ruth, mothers will never buy their daughters a doll that has . . ."—cough, cough. . . .

I was stunned. And crushed. And horrified. . . . What on earth were we going to do with all that unsold inventory? . . .

I went up to my hotel room and burst into tears of grief. My "baby" had been rejected.

Ruth Handler, with Jacqueline Shannon, *Dream Doll: The Ruth Handler Story* (Stamford, Conn.: Longmeadow, 1994), 1–4, 7, 10–12.

ᴖ

CHAPTER 8

The Politics of Hope and Rage:
The United States in the 1960s

IN 1970, former president Lyndon B. Johnson explained the impossible dilemma he had faced in the mid-1960s as he tried to balance the needs of his Great Society programs to end poverty in the United States and the demands of the mounting military crisis in South Vietnam. He knew he would be "crucified" no matter what he did. "If I left the woman I really loved—the Great Society—in order to get involved with that bitch of a war on the other side of the world, then I would lose everything at home." But if he "lost" Vietnam to the Communists, his political enemies would pounce on him,

> telling everyone that . . . I had let a democracy fall into the hands of the Communists. That I was a coward. An unmanly man. A man without a spine. Oh, I could see it coming all right. Every night when I fell asleep I would see myself tied to the ground in the middle of a long, open space. In the distance, I could hear the voices of thousands of people. They were all shouting at me and running toward me: "Coward! Traitor! Weakling!"*

What was Johnson to do: attend to the domestic needs of the nation, or march into the heroic arena of foreign policy and conflict; care for the needs of "the browns and the blacks and the lame and the poor," or stand tall against the looming Communist menace? For Johnson, the basic question was this: what was a *man* to do? His answer came in July 1965, when he committed 100,000 American ground forces, for the first time, to direct combat action in Vietnam.

In addition to showcasing the earthy Texas vocabulary for which Johnson was notorious, the contrasting descriptions of the Cold War, the War on Poverty, and his own policy decisions highlighted the importance of gender,

---

* Lyndon B. Johnson, quoted in Doris Kearns Goodwin, *Lyndon Johnson and the American Dream* (New York: Harper & Row, 1976), 253.

class, and race to the political and cultural debates that confronted Americans in the 1960s. By the end of the decade, such expectations, whether voiced by the president or Black Power militants, had mobilized massive political and cultural reactions and realignments that continue to shape political conflicts in the United States today. These new directions, however, did not point to a clear path of action through the increasingly visible maze of problems that confronted the country in the 1960s: the extraordinary consumer bounty and the deep strains of poverty in America's cities and towns; the faith in the superiority of American democratic institutions and the violent suppression of minorities; the economy's growing reliance on working women and the continued celebration of the breadwinning man; the imposing might of America's industries and technologies and the deepening worries about the power of the military-industrial complex. The problem that would override them all by the middle of the decade was the war in Indochina, where American policymakers from both parties agreed that the United States could not, under any circumstances, allow any more foreign territory to go Communist.

By the end of the decade, many Americans from across the political and social spectrum shared Johnson's feeling of impotence and confusion and the suspicion that the nation's problems were too complicated and vast for political action to solve. Others—working-class women and men, people of color, gays and lesbians, as well as disaffected people who resisted the countercultural directions of antiwar protesters, feminists, and militant civil rights activists— felt motivated and empowered to assert themselves from the margins of American society. The documents in this chapter track the confidence, confusion, and rage of the 1960s, starting with the civil rights activism that initially inspired and eventually polarized the political hopes of the decade. We may imagine the sixties as a time of growing militancy in response to the evolution of the American war in Vietnam, but the texts and images here remind us how activists from across a broad political spectrum shaped the agendas of the 1960s and the decades that followed.

ᴥ Why We Can't Wait: From Civil Rights to Black Power ᴥ

In early 1957, civil rights leader Martin Luther King Jr. traveled to the new African nation of Ghana to celebrate its independence from Great Britain. For King, civil rights reform in the United States was only one dimension of a global movement of peoples of color against their histories of subordination to whites. In Ghana, he saw that new age dawning. Back at his Montgomery, Alabama, church, King told his congregation that the "throbbing desire" for freedom inside every man could no longer be denied. "To rob a man of his freedom," he said, "is to take from him the essential basis of his manhood."

Better than anyone else, King was able to describe the immoral disjunction between the rhetoric of freedom, equality, and boundless opportunity that was trumpeted so loudly in Cold War America, and the reality of injustice and limitation that African Americans continued to experience as their destiny. By the early 1960s, his example had combined with those of other African Americans, including college students leading lunch-counter sit-ins and voter registration drives in the Deep South, to inspire growing numbers of women and men to end this contradiction. Civil rights activists showed they would accept nothing less than the elimination of Jim Crowism and discrimination in all aspects of southern life. They demanded not only the basic American rights of voting and equal education but also the freedom to drink from the same water fountain or to use the same restroom or to compete for the same jobs as whites. One measure of their success was public opinion. Whereas early agitators were commonly denounced as irresponsible troublemakers or Communist subversives, by the summer of 1964—when Congress passed the landmark Civil Rights Act—a majority of all Americans could imagine nothing more reasonable or more fundamentally American than the campaign for legal and political equality for African Americans.

However, the movement's demands for equality and "power to the people" regardless of race rarely addressed questions about the *gender* of a truly free person. Raising this point draws attention to the many women—black and white, old and young, famous and little known—who made a difference in the fight for racial justice. The omission also signals how race *and* gender shaped the goals and tactics of the civil rights campaign. Were activists, in defying the social conditions of their day, seeking to challenge or to reinforce conventional gender and sexual hierarchies that gave priority to the experience and freedom of men? Were women supposed to be their helpmates or their equals? Such questions, which always were present, came to the forefront of activism in 1965 and afterward as the movement increasingly divided along reformist and liberationist paths.

The Sword That Heals (1964)

MARTIN LUTHER KING JR.

King and the Southern Christian Leadership Council (SCLC) that he led came to symbolize the "New Negro" who took the movement to reform American institutions out of the courts and into the streets. Instead of only filing lawsuits, the new civil rights activists employed a form of civil disobedience called nonviolent direct action—marches, sit-ins, boycotts, pray-ins. Demonstrators deliberately provoked reactions by peacefully refusing to abide by unjust laws and then willingly suffering violent abuse and incarceration. Refusing to retaliate or to resist arrest showed the justness of their cause and their respect for the rule of law. Inspired by the example of Mahatma Gandhi's protests against

British colonial rule in India, African American activists had used nonviolent tactics in the early 1940s. The Montgomery bus boycott in 1955, instigated when Rosa Parks refused to give up her bus seat to a white rider, and its success in ending segregated seating on that city's buses popularized the tactic. Demonstrators, however, had to endure cruel violence in order to win even small victories against racial segregation. In the spring of 1963, when the SCLC targeted the system of segregation in Birmingham, Alabama, King knew that the movement's culture of nonviolence itself would be on trial. The ferocity of local white resistance, which television cameras broadcast around the world, provoked new sympathy for the civil rights movement and resulted in one of its most important victories. At the core of King's account of the Birmingham demonstrations, Why We Can't Wait, *was a defense of nonviolent direct action.*

PROBLEMS TO CONSIDER

1. What assumptions did King have to refute in order to convince his readers of the effectiveness and appropriateness of nonviolent demonstrations?
2. Examine the vocabulary that King used to describe nonviolence. Why did he call the nonviolent movement a "war"?

Fortunately, history does not pose problems without eventually producing solutions. The disenchanted, the disadvantaged and the disinherited seem, at times of deep crisis, to summon up some sort of genius that enables them to perceive and capture the appropriate weapons to carve out their destiny. Such was the peaceable weapon of nonviolent direct action, which materialized almost overnight to inspire the Negro, and was seized in his outstretched hands with a powerful grip.

Nonviolent action, the Negro saw, was the way to supplement—not replace—the process of change through legal recourse. It was the way to divest himself of passivity without arraying himself in vindictive force. Acting in concert with fellow Negroes to assert himself as a citizen, he would embark on a militant program to demand the rights which were his: in the streets, on the buses, in the stores, the parks and other public facilities. . . .

Like his predecessors, the Negro was willing to risk martyrdom in order to move and stir the social conscience of his community and the nation. Instead of submitting to surreptitious cruelty in thousands of dark jail cells and on countless shadowed street corners, he would force his oppressor to commit his brutality openly—in the light of day—with the rest of the world looking on.

Acceptance of nonviolent direct action was a proof of a certain sophistication on the part of the Negro masses; for it showed that they dared to break with the old, ingrained concepts of our society. The eye-for-an-eye philosophy, the impulse to defend oneself when attacked, has always been held as the highest measure of American manhood. We are a nation that worships the frontier tradition, and our heroes are those who champion justice through violent retaliation against injustice. It is not simple to adopt the credo that moral force has as much strength and virtue as the capacity to return a physical blow; or that to refrain from hitting back requires more will and bravery than the automatic reflexes of defense.

Yet there is something in the American ethos that responds to the strength of moral force. I am reminded of the popular and widely respected novel and film *To Kill a Mockingbird.*

Atticus Finch, a white southern lawyer, confronts a group of his neighbors who have become a lynch-crazed mob, seeking the life of his Negro client. Finch, armed with nothing more lethal than a lawbook, disperses the mob with the force of his moral courage, aided by his small daughter, who, innocently calling the would-be lynchers by name, reminds them that they are individual men, not a pack of beasts.

To the Negro in 1963, as to Atticus Finch, it had become obvious that nonviolence could symbolize the gold badge of heroism rather than the white feather of cowardice. In addition to being consistent with his religious precepts, it served his need to act on his own for his own liberation. It enabled him to transmute hatred into constructive energy, to seek not only to free himself but to free his oppressor from his sins. This transformation, in turn, had the marvelous effect of changing the face of the enemy. The enemy the Negro faced became not the individual who had oppressed him but the evil system which permitted that individual to do so.

The argument that nonviolence is a coward's refuge lost its force as its heroic and often perilous acts uttered their wordless but convincing rebuttal in Montgomery, in the sit-ins, on the freedom rides, and finally in Birmingham. . . .

As the broadcasting profession will confirm, no shows are so successful as those which allow for audience participation. In order to be somebody, people must feel themselves part of something. In the nonviolent army, there is room for everyone who wants to join up. There is no color distinction. There is no examination, no pledge, except that, as a soldier in the armies of violence is expected to inspect his carbine and keep it clean, nonviolent soldiers are called upon to examine and burnish their greatest weapons—their heart, their conscience, their courage and their sense of justice. . . .

The striking thing about the nonviolent crusade of 1963 was that so few felt the sting of bullets or the clubbing of billies and nightsticks. Looking back, it becomes obvious that the oppressors were restrained not only because the world was looking but also because, standing before them, were hundreds, sometimes thousands, of Negroes who for the first time dared to look back at a white man, eye to eye. . . .

Nonviolence had tremendous psychological importance to the Negro. He had to win and to vindicate his dignity in order to merit and enjoy his self-esteem. He had to let white men know that the picture of him as a clown—irresponsible, resigned and believing in his own inferiority—was a stereotype with no validity. . . . The Negro was able to face his adversary, to concede to him a physical advantage and to defeat him because the superior force of the oppressor had become powerless.

Martin Luther King Jr., *Why We Can't Wait* (New York: Harper & Row, 1964), 26–31.

⁊

"We're Not Afraid . . . We're Gonna Die for Our People" (1968)
STOKELY CARMICHAEL

Three weeks before he was murdered in Memphis, Tennessee, in April 1968, Martin Luther King visited that city to lend his support to the striking African American sanitation workers. King's interest in a labor action, rather than a voting or an equal employment rights demonstration, was significant. The nonviolent tactics of sit-ins, boycotts, and quietly suffering brutal retaliation had won a broad national sympathy for racial integration and brought landmark civil rights legislation in 1964 and 1965. But in the succeeding years, King and other activists redirected their activism toward social injustices that locked poor and minority Americans out of mainstream middle-class life. Poor housing and health care, substandard wages and schools, and other inequities, which once seemed peculiar to the backward, rural South, now appeared rooted in the very foundation of American life.

At the same time that King's trenchant criticisms of the Vietnam War and social injustices called for actions that went beyond adjusting legal rights, growing numbers of black activists grew disillusioned with the early movement's integrationist vision and nonviolent approach. Proudly standing up for oneself and one's blackness seemed to offer a greater sense of personal power than nonviolently suffering brutal abuse in order to show the world the savagery of American racists. If black activists were going to make real changes in American life, they would have to organize in more powerful ways. In the days after King's assassination, riots broke out in cities throughout the United States, including—perhaps most dramatically—Washington, D.C. To explain the outrage of America's black citizens, newspaper and television news frequently turned to Stokely Carmichael, one of the leaders of the Student Nonviolent Coordinating Committee (SNCC), a youth organization. Journalists treated Carmichael as the representative of the new militancy of "black power" in the civil rights movement.

PROBLEMS TO CONSIDER

1. In what ways did Carmichael repudiate the defense of nonviolence offered by Martin Luther King? Was there any significance in his consistent reference to "white America" as "she"?
2. How did the reporter seek to define King's message and murder through the questions he asked? How did Carmichael respond?

Carmichael: . . . I think white America made its biggest mistake when she killed Dr. King last night because when she killed Dr. King last night, she killed all reasonable hope. When she killed Dr. King last night, she killed the one man of our race that this country's older generations, the militants and the revolutionaries and the masses of black people would still listen to. Even though sometimes he did not agree with them, they would still listen to him. . . .

When they got rid of Brother Martin Luther King they had absolutely no reason to do so. He was the one man in our race who was trying to teach our people to have love, compassion, and mercy for what white people had done. When white America killed Dr. King last night, she declared war on us. There will be no crying and there will be no funeral.

The rebellions that have been occurring around these cities and this country is just light stuff to what is about to happen.

We have to retaliate for the deaths of our leaders. The execution for those deaths will not be in the court rooms. They're going to be in the streets of the United States of America.

The kind of man that killed Dr. King last night made it a whole lot easier for a whole lot of black people today. There no longer needs to be intellectual discussion. Black people know that they have to get guns. White America will live to cry since she killed Dr. King last night. It would have been better if she killed [SNCC's chairman] Rap Brown and/or Stokely Carmichael. But when she killed Dr. King, she lost it. . . .

Q: What do you say to black people who have to die to do what you say?

Mr. Carmichael: That they take as many white people with them as they can. We die every day. We die in Vietnam for the honkies. Why don't we come home and die in the streets for our people? We die every day. We die cutting and fighting each other inside our own communities. We cut and fight and kill each other off. Let's kill off the real enemies.

Black people are not afraid to die. We die all the time. We die in your jails. We die in your ghettos. We die in your rat-infested homes. We die a thousand deaths every day. We're not afraid to die, because now we're gonna die for our people. . . .

Q: Mr. Carmichael, are you declaring war on white America?

Mr. Carmichael: White America has declared war on black people. She did so when she stole the first black man from Africa. The black man has been . . . has been patient, has been resisting—and today the final showdown is coming.

That is clear. That is crystal clear. And black people are going to have to find ways to survive. The only way to survive is to get some guns. Because that's the only way white America keeps us in check, because she's got the guns.

Q: What do you see this ultimately leading to? A blood bath in which nobody wins?

Mr. Carmichael: First, my name is Mr. Carmichael, and secondly, black people will survive the bath. Last question.

Q: What accomplishments or objectives do you visualize from the encounter? What do you think you will accomplish?

Mr. Carmichael: The black man can't do nothing in this country. Then we're going to stand up on our feet and die like men. If that's our only act of manhood, then Godd----t we're going to die. We're tired of living on our stomachs.

"We're Not Afraid . . . We're Gonna Die for Our People," *Washington Post*, April 6, 1968, 16.

✦

SNCC Position Paper (1964)

[CASEY HAYDEN AND MARY KING]

In 1964, two young white women, Casey Hayden and Mary King, enlisted in "Freedom Summer," the voter registration drive in Mississippi led by SNCC. SNCC started as a biracial coalition of young college students. The group organized lunch-counter sit-ins and freedom rides to contest segregation in public facilities and led the dangerous voter registration campaigns in the Deep South. Even as white Mississippians threatened and assaulted SNCC workers in order to enforce racial divisions and hierarchies, Mary King herself gradually came to the conclusion that an unquestioned double standard was at work within the movement for racial equality. No matter how competent or qualified, movement women were expected to defer to the leadership of men, who reserved for themselves the big decisions. Still several years before the feminist movement, King and Hayden used the following position paper, which they presented at a SNCC staff retreat in 1964, to expose the pervasive sexual discrimination they faced within the organization. When Stokely Carmichael was asked, in reaction to the paper, what position women should occupy in the organization, he joked, "prone." He later regretted the remark, which revealed the sexual and gender politics at work in SNCC.

PROBLEMS TO CONSIDER

1. Why were labor and leadership divided by gender in an organization that promoted civil rights? Were Hayden and King upholding the ideals of the movement, or were they injecting a peripheral concern?
2. In examining how this protest arose, what role did the women's race play? Did their race make the protest more divisive than constructive?

1. Staff was involved in crucial constitutional revisions at the Atlanta staff meeting in October. A large committee was appointed to present revisions to the staff. The committee was all men.

2. Two organizers were working together to form a farmers league. Without asking any questions, the male organizer immediately assigned the clerical work to the female organizer although both had had equal experience in organizing campaigns.

3. Although there are women in the Mississippi project who have been working as long as some of the men, the leadership group in COFO [*a coalition of civil rights organizations*] is all men.

4. A woman in a field office wondered why she was held responsible for day-to-day decisions, only to find out later that she had been appointed project director but not told.

5. A fall 1964 personnel and resources report on Mississippi projects lists the number of people in each project. The section on Laurel, [Mississippi], however, lists not the number of persons but "three girls."

6. One of SNCC's main administrative officers apologizes for appointment of a woman as interim project director in a key Mississippi project area.

7. A veteran of two years' work for SNCC in two states spends her day typing and doing clerical work for other people in her project.

8. Any woman in SNCC, no matter what her position or experience, has been asked to take minutes in a meeting when she and other women are outnumbered by men.

9. The names of several new attorneys entering a state project this past summer were posted in a central movement office. The first initial and last name of each lawyer was listed. Next to one name was written: (girl).

10. Capable, responsible, and experienced women who are in leadership positions can expect to have to defer to a man on their project for final decision making.

11. A session at the recent October staff meeting in Atlanta was the first large meeting in the past couple of years where a woman was asked to chair.

Undoubtedly this list will seem strange to some, petty to others, laughable to most. The list could continue as far as there are women in the movement. Except that most women don't talk about these kinds of incidents, because the whole subject is not discussable—strange to some, petty to others, laughable to most.

The average white person finds it difficult to understand why the Negro resents being called "boy," or being thought of as "musical" and "athletic," because the average white person doesn't realize that *he assumes he is superior*. And naturally he doesn't understand the problem of paternalism. So too the average SNCC worker finds it difficult to discuss the woman problem because of the assumption of male superiority. Assumptions of male superiority are as widespread and deep-rooted and every much as crippling to the woman as the assumptions of white supremacy are to the Negro. Consider why it is in SNCC that women who are competent, qualified, and experienced are automatically assigned to the "female" kinds of jobs such as: typing, desk work, telephone work, filing, library work, cooking, and the assistant kind of administrative work but rarely the "executive" kind.

The woman in SNCC is often in the same position as that token Negro hired in a corporation. The management thinks that it has done its bit. Yet, every day the Negro bears an atmosphere, attitudes, and actions which are tinged with condescension and paternalism, the most telling of which are seen when he is not promoted as the equally or less skilled whites are.

This paper is anonymous. Think about the kinds of things the author, if made known, would have to suffer because of raising this kind of discussion. Nothing so final as being fired or outright exclusion, but the kinds of things which are killing to the insides—insinuations, ridicule, overexaggerated compensations.

This paper is presented anyway because it needs to be made known that many women in the movement are not "happy and contented" with their status. It needs to be made known

that much talent and experience are being wasted by this movement, when women are not given jobs commensurate with their abilities. It needs to be known that just as Negroes were the crucial factor in the economy of the cotton South, so too in SNCC, women are the crucial factor that keeps the movement running on a day-to-day basis. Yet they are not given equal say-so when it comes to day-to-day decision making. . . .

Maybe the only thing that can come out of this paper is discussion. . . . And maybe some women will begin to recognize day-to-day discriminations. And maybe sometime in the future the whole of the women in this movement will become so alert as to force the rest of the movement to stop the discrimination and start the slow process of changing values and ideas so that all of us gradually come to understand that this is no more a man's world than it is a white world.

[Casey Hayden and Mary King], "SNCC Position Paper," in Mary King, *Freedom Song: A Personal Story of the 1960s Civil Rights Movement* (New York: Morrow, 1987), 567–69.

～

The Special Plight and the Role of Black Women (1971)
FANNIE LOU HAMER

One part of the civil rights leadership was drawn largely from the southern African American middle class of professionals, small-business owners, educators, and college students. Many of the agitators, though, were like Fannie Lou Hamer—very poor working people, often women with families, who scraped by on the margins of American society. Hamer herself had been picking cotton since she was six years old. During the voter registration drive of 1962, she and her husband were sharecroppers on a plantation near Indianola, Mississippi. Her activism began that summer when she successfully opposed local white authorities who tried to intimidate her into silence. Hamer later achieved national attention for her leadership of the Mississippi Freedom Democratic Party, which challenged the Democratic Party to recognize them, instead of the all-white delegation from Mississippi, as the only democratically elected and legitimate representatives of their state at the party's national convention in 1964. In this selection, from 1971, Hamer reflects on nearly a decade of activism and on what "liberation" meant specifically to black women.

PROBLEMS TO CONSIDER

1. How did Hamer's poverty affect her actions? Did her economic vulnerability restrict or enhance her political actions?
2. Hamer was a wife and mother at the time she joined the civil rights movement. How did these roles affect her actions, the resistance she faced, and the assistance she received?

The special plight and the role of black women is not something that just happened three years ago. We've had a special plight for 350 years. . . .

It's been a special plight for the black woman. I remember my uncles and some of my aunts—and that's why it really tickled me when you talked about integration. Because I'm very black, but I remember some of my uncles and some of my aunts was as white as anybody in here, and blue-eyed, and some kind of green-eyed—and my grandfather didn't do it, you know. So what the folks is fighting at this point is what they started. . . . And right now, sometimes, you know I work for the liberation of all people, because when I liberate myself, I'm liberating other people. But you know, sometimes I really feel more sorrier for the white woman than I feel for ourselves because she been caught up in this thing, caught up feeling very special. . . . You thought that you was *more* because you was a woman, and especially a white woman, you had this kind of angel feeling that you were untouchable. You know that? There's nothing under the sun that made you believe that you was just like me, that under this white pigment of skin is red blood, just like under this black skin of mine. So we was used as black women over and over and over. . . . So all of these things was happening because you *had* more. You had been put on a pedestal, and then not only put on a pedestal, but you had been put in something like a ivory castle. So what happened to you, we have busted the castle open and whacking like hell for the pedestal. And when you hit the ground, you're

gone have to fight like hell, like we've been fighting all this time.

In the past, I don't care how poor this white woman was, in the South she still felt like she was more than us. In the North, I don't care how poor or how rich this white woman has been, she still felt like she was more than us. But coming to the realization of the thing, her freedom is shackled in chains to mine, and she realizes for the first time that she is not free until I am free. The point about it, the male influence in this country—you know the white male, he didn't go and brainwash the black man and the black woman, he brainwashed his wife too. . . . He made her think that she was a angel. . . .

We have a problem, folks, and we want to try to deal with the problem in the only way that we can deal with the problem as far as black women. And you know, I'm not hung up on this about liberating myself from the black man, I'm not going to try that thing. I got a black husband, six feet three, two hundred and forty pounds, with a 14 shoe, that I don't *want* to be liberated from. But we are here to work side by side with this black man in trying to bring liberation to all people. . . .

We have a job as black women, to support whatever is right, and to bring in justice where we've had so much injustice. . . .

A few years ago throughout the country the middle-class black woman—I used to say not really black women, but the middle-class colored women, c-u-l-l-u-d, didn't even respect the kind of work that I was doing. But you see now, baby, whether you have a Ph.D., D.D., or no D, we're in this bag together. And whether you're from Morehouse *[a historically black college]* or Nohouse, we're still in this bag together. Not to fight to try to liberate ourselves from the black men—this is another trick to get us fighting among ourselves—but to work together with the black man, then we will have a better chance to just act as human beings, and to be treated as human beings in our sick society.

Fannie Lou Hamer, "The Special Plight and the Role of Black Women" (1971), in *Black Women in White America: A Documentary History*, edited by Gerda Lerner (New York: Vintage, 1992), 609–13.

❧ *Quagmires: The Vietnam War and American Culture* ❧

In July 1959, a *Time* magazine story from South Vietnam described how "six Communist terrorists" had sneaked up on a group of American servicemen watching a movie and gunned down Master Sergeant Chester Ovnand and Major Dale Buis in a "murderous hail of bullets." Ovnand and Buis were advisers to the South Vietnamese military and were symbols, according to *Time*, of why the "new nation" was "still independent and free and getting stronger all the time." They were also the first Americans to die in Vietnam. When *Life* magazine observed the anniversary of this event a decade later, much had changed. The story, called "One Week's Dead," included two paragraphs of text followed by another eleven pages with the names and photographs of the 242 Americans killed from May 28 through June 3—in statistical terms, an average number for seven days in 1969. What these Americans symbolized no longer seemed clear. The only certainty the magazine could read in the "gallery of young American eyes" was the "anguish" their deaths had brought to "hundreds of homes all over the country."

These two reports, published at opposite ends of a decade of war in Vietnam and of protest against racial injustice at home, plot the erosion of Americans' faith in the Cold War dualisms of good and evil that justified the war. In the 1950s, Vietnam had been a test case for the Truman Doctrine's strategy of containing communism. As Senator John F. Kennedy ominously described the little-known nation in 1956, South Vietnam was the one "finger in the dike" preventing "the red tide of Communism" from swamping the region and, from there, the world. America had the best weaponry for the fight: its pragmatic know-how, superior technology, and invincible manpower. What he believed the nation lacked was the vital will to take action. No matter how vigorously the political leadership of the 1960s—Kennedy, Johnson, and Nixon—engaged the "enemy," however, setbacks in Southeast Asia and deepening social and cultural divisions at home steadily weakened confidence in the nation's military and moral vitality. As the carnage mounted (by 1969, 36,000 Americans and many hundreds of thousands of Vietnamese had died) and the end seemed nowhere in sight, first a new generation of college students and eventually a broad spectrum of people came to question the war and the nature of the society that had undertaken it. As previous chapters have shown, wars and national crises have tended both to broaden cultural unity and to expose, or even heighten, existing social divisions. Within the context of a historic movement for racial justice, the failures of a war undertaken in part as a bold exercise of decisive national vigor encouraged Americans in some cases to reassess, and in others to reassert, the certainties that had traditionally organized life in the United States.

Debates about the Vietnam War—over the strategies by which the American military deployed its forces, the morality of the Cold War campaign, the character of the soldiers who fought or chose not to fight there—often took the form posed by President Johnson: what would or should a *man* do? Using just such terms, the selections in this section assess, directly or indirectly, Cold War strategies, political ideals, and policy aims in the 1960s.

The Presidency in 1960 (1960)
SENATOR JOHN F. KENNEDY

John F. Kennedy campaigned for the presidency in 1960 calling for a generational rebellion against the tired ways of the old men of the 1950s. The national election in November, however, showed the country evenly split in choosing between promises of continuity from the Republican Richard M. Nixon and the demand for change from Kennedy. The Massachusetts senator had many liabilities as a candidate. He would be the nation's first Catholic president, and he possessed little national recognition compared to Vice President Nixon, who served in the administration of the still-popular Eisenhower. Those weaknesses diminished after the first televised presidential debate. With an audience of 70 million watching, Kennedy appeared youthful and dynamic compared to Nixon, who looked tired and weak. Kennedy's following rose enough to squeak by Nixon in the popular vote. But Kennedy's rebellion was not a matter of looks alone. He said he would invigorate U.S. foreign policy and government. He defined the kind of president he would and would not be in this speech before the National Press Club during his campaign in early 1960.

PROBLEMS TO CONSIDER

1. What did it mean to Kennedy to make the president "the vital center of action"?
2. What importance did gender have in the way Kennedy distinguished his view of the presidency from that of Eisenhower?

The modern presidential campaign covers every issue in and out of the platform from cranberries to creation. But the public is rarely alerted to a candidate's views about the central issue on which all the rest turn. That central issue . . . is not the farm problem or defense or India. It is the Presidency itself.

Of course a candidate's views on specific policies are important, but Theodore Roosevelt and William Howard Taft shared policy views with entirely different results in the White House. Of course it is important to elect a good man with good intentions, but Woodrow Wilson and Warren G. Harding were both good men of good intentions; so were Lincoln and Buchanan; but there is a Lincoln Room in the White House and no Buchanan Room.

The history of this Nation—its brightest and its bleakest pages—has been written largely in terms of the different views our Presidents have had of the Presidency itself. This history ought to tell us that the American people in 1960 have an imperative right to know what any man bidding for the Presidency thinks about the place he is bidding for, whether he is aware of and willing to use the powerful resources of that Office; whether his model will be Taft or Roosevelt, Wilson or Harding. . . .

During the past 8 years, we have seen one concept of the Presidency at work. Our needs and hopes have been eloquently stated—but the initiative and follow-through have too often been left to others. . . .

The American people in 1952 and 1956 may have preferred this detached, limited concept of the Presidency after 20 years of fast-moving, creative Presidential rule. Perhaps historians will regard this as necessarily one of those frequent periods of consolidation, a time to draw breath, to recoup our national energy. . . .

But the question is what do the times—and the people—demand for the next 4 years in the White House?

They demand a vigorous proponent of the national interest—not a passive broker for conflicting private interests. They demand a man capable of acting as the commander in chief of the Great Alliance, not merely a bookkeeper who feels that his work is done when the numbers on the balance sheet come out even. They demand that he be the head of a responsible party, not rise so far above politics as to be invisible—a man who will formulate and fight for legislative policies, not be a casual bystander to the legislative process.

Today a restricted concept of the Presidency is not enough. For beneath today's surface gloss of peace and prosperity are increasingly dangerous, unsolved, long postponed problems—problems that will inevitably explode to the surface during the next 4 years of the next administration—the growing missile gap, the rise of Communist China, the despair of the underdeveloped nations, the explosive situations in Berlin and in the Formosa Straits, the deterioration of NATO, the lack of an arms control agreement, and all the domestic problems of our farms, cities, and schools. . . .

In the decade that lies ahead—in the challenging revolutionary sixties—the American Presidency will demand more than ringing manifestoes issued from the rear of the battle. It will demand that the President place himself in the very thick of the fight, that he care passionately about the fate of the people he leads, that he be willing to serve them, at the risk of incurring their momentary displeasure.

Whatever the political affiliation of our next President, whatever his views may be on all the issues and problems that rush in upon us, he must above all be the Chief Executive in every sense of the word. He must be prepared to exercise the fullest powers of his Office—all that are specified and some that are not. He must master complex problems as well as receive one-page memorandums. He must originate action as well as study groups. He must reopen the channels of communication between the world of thought and the seat of power. . . .

"The President is at liberty, both in law and conscience, to be as big a man as he can." So wrote Prof. Woodrow Wilson. But President Woodrow Wilson discovered that to be a big man in the White House inevitably brings cries of dictatorship.

So did Lincoln and Jackson and the two Roosevelts. And so may the next occupant of that office, if he is the man the times demand. But how much better it would be, in the turbulent sixties, to have a Roosevelt or a Wilson than to have another James Buchanan, cringing in the White House, afraid to move.

Nor can we afford a Chief Executive who is praised primarily for what he did not do, the disasters he prevented, the bills he vetoed—a President wishing his subordinates would produce more missiles or build more schools. We will need instead what the Constitution envisioned: a Chief Executive who is the vital center of action in our whole scheme of Government.

_____

Senator John F. Kennedy, "The Presidency in 1960," January 18, 1960, reprinted in *Congressional Record* 106, pt. 1:710–11.

☙

The Making of a Quagmire (1965)

DAVID HALBERSTAM

War, like Cold War politics, Kennedy believed, required a new kind of warrior. Early in his presidency, Kennedy authorized the formation of the "Green Berets," a Special Forces unit within the army who were to be the lead figures in countering insurgent Communist guerrilla movements in the postcolonial battlefields of Africa and Asia. The Green Berets were a kind of armed version of the Peace Corps—the best, brightest, and most idealistic young men, committed to defeating communism by winning the hearts and minds of the people whose freedom they were defending. This strategy was called counterinsurgency. These experts in unconventional warfare trained indigenous forces (such as the South Vietnamese army, or ARVN) to defend their nations themselves. American advisers would not be seen as a foreign occupying force because they would nurture a fight against communism that grew out of native soil instead of being imposed from outside.

In 1965, the Johnson administration rapidly replaced counterinsurgent methods in Vietnam with conventional tactics of military force. The "Rolling Thunder" bombing campaign in North Vietnam was launched, and some 165,000 American troops were in Vietnam by the end of the year. That same year, two important and widely read accounts of the war and of the American men who fought it were published. Robin Moore's dramatization of unconventional warfare, The Green Berets, *sold 3.1 million paperbacks in 1966 alone. Moore's book was inspiringly patriotic, but the author was not uncompromisingly hawkish on the war itself. As a civilian journalist, he had voluntarily undergone Special Forces training and then, carrying a rifle, followed units into combat in Vietnam. Moore believed that the real enemies in the war against international communism were not the Vietcong, but Washington politicians, career military officers, and corrupt Asians who prevented the nation's best fighting men from doing what it took to win the war. In 1966, he and Barry Sadler (himself a Green Beret) produced one of the year's biggest hit songs. "The Ballad of the Green Berets" did not mention Vietnam, but its lyrics left no doubt that the Special Forces soldiers who had been deployed there were courageous and honorable men. The other book, David Halberstam's* The Making of a Quagmire, *was likewise a study of the American warrior. Like Moore, Halberstam was a Harvard graduate, a journalist (he covered the war from 1961 to 1962 for the* New York Times*), and an eyewitness to what he, too, regarded as a confusing, heartbreaking* *war in Vietnam. "No Westerner can return from Vietnam a proud or satisfied man," he concluded. "If he has any conscience at all he goes home with a profound sense of inadequacy, along with whatever scars and sympathies and experience he has acquired." In this selection, Halberstam presents a portrait of army officer John Paul Vann, whom he and others regarded as among the most admirable and qualified military advisers assigned to Vietnam in the years before the buildup.*

PROBLEMS TO CONSIDER

1. What aspects of Vann's character won the reporter's admiration? Compare Halberstam's portrait of Vann with the men described by Kennedy.
2. How did Halberstam use Vann's character to comment on the way the United States conducted the war in Vietnam?

For Lieutenant Colonel John Vann, the battle of Ap Bac and the subsequent Vietnamese and American reaction to it were a bitter disappointment. Many Americans considered him one of the two or three best advisers in the country. . . .

Vann was a man of curious contrasts. Thirty-seven years old, one of the younger lieutenant colonels in the Army, he was clearly on his way to becoming a full colonel, with a very good chance of eventual promotion to general. (His recognizable superiority is the reason that some of the high people in the Pentagon wish that Vann had never happened, for his case documented and symbolized so many embarrassments that might otherwise have been swept under the rug.) He was clearly about to take off in his career—one of those men who reaches his mid-thirties and suddenly begins to pull away from his contemporaries.

Yet most Army officers of this type tend to be sophisticated and polished, usually with a West Point background, often from second- or third-generation Army families—in contrast to some of their colleagues who excel as combat officers, but who find other aspects of the Army a bit baffling. Vann, however, could hardly have been more different from the traditional gentleman-soldier. There was little polish to him: he was a poor boy from Virginia, who always reminded me of a good old Appalachian South redneck—and it was literally true that on operations his neck and arms always turned an angry red.

Vann had risen by sheer drive, vitality and curiosity. After one year of college he had enlisted at the age of eighteen, and became a B-29 navigator at the end of World War II. In 1950 and 1951 he commanded the first air-borne Ranger company to be sent to Korea, specializing in actions behind enemy lines and against North Korean guerrillas who were trying to harass UN forces behind our lines. . . .

Vann had volunteered for duty in Vietnam. Once there, he had shaken a desk job; then, knowing that he was to [command] . . . the Seventh Division, he had gone on as many helicopter missions in the Delta as possible while preparing to take over; by the time he left Vietnam he had participated in more than two hundred helicopter assault landings. As a result, he knew as much or more about his area of Vietnam than any other adviser—or indeed than any Vietnamese officer—that I ever met. . . .

Vann also tried to set an example by his personal courage, and his [routine practice of] walking in the field [with ordinary soldiers] on major operations had a considerable effect on the Vietnamese troops, who had never seen any of their own officers above the rank of captain in the field. But the walks had another purpose: they were a futile attempt to shame Vietnamese officers into walking in the paddies too. What Vann, and many others like him who tried similar tactics, failed to realize was the power of the mandarin legacy: the whole point of being a major or colonel was that you *didn't* have to go into the field, and therefore the distinction and class separation of such officers from their juniors was much sharper than in a Western army, and the prerogatives of a high rank were more fondly cherished.

What the Americans were attempting to do, by setting examples like this, epitomized our entire problem in Vietnam. They were trying to persuade an inflexible military ally, who had very little social or political sense about its own people, to do what the Americans knew must be done, but this would force the Vietnamese officers to give up the very things that really mattered to them and that motivated them in the first place. How could anyone make the Vietnamese officers see, almost overnight, that the purpose of promotion was not primarily to separate them from the misery whence they came, but to get them to inspire or lead others? . . .

If Vann had any shortcoming, it was one typical of the best of the American advisers in Vietnam: the belief that the adviser's enthusiasm, dedication and effort could, through diplomatic guidance of his Vietnamese counterpart, successfully buck the system. This naïveté was the result of favorable encounters with other systems, and an overly optimistic view that in time of war common sense will prevail and allies will be inclined to agree on basic goals. This hope was doomed in Vietnam; the system was stronger than the men bucking it. . . .

We reporters admired Vann greatly . . . because he cared so desperately about Vietnam, because he knew so much about his area, and because whenever we were with him we had a sense that a very real war was being fought—and not fought on a peacetime footing with peacetime hours and peacetime arrogance toward an Asian enemy. The remarkable thing about Vann, and a few others of his caliber who were fully aware of the shortcomings of the war, was that they still believed that under certain circumstances the war could be pursued successfully. This was the best kind of optimism; it was not the automatic we-are-winning push-button chant of Saigon, but a careful analysis of all the problems on both sides, and a hope that there were still time and human resources enough to change the tide. . . .

The first time I ever met Vann he shook hands, told me that I was lucky because there would be an operation the next day that I could go out on, and then said, "Well, Halberstam, the first thing you'll learn is that these people may be the world's greatest lovers, but they're not the world's greatest fighters." He paused, and then added, "But they're good people, and they can win a war if someone shows them how." . . .

There was nothing ideological in Vann's make-up; he was simply a man of consuming curiosity and drive. . . . It was hard for him to compromise; he once told me that the trouble with compromise was that often it meant taking a position between something that was right and something that was wrong, with the result that you ended up with something that was neither right nor wrong. In war, Vann said, that's not good enough. It was this sense of commitment, and this unwillingness to compromise and blend in with the system—the American system, which was fast becoming a parallel of the Vietnamese—that finally brought Vann to a showdown with his superiors.

David Halberstam, *The Making of a Quagmire* (New York: Random House, 1965), 163–68.

⌇

⌁ *Gender and Protest:*
Campus Rebels and Radical Feminists ⌁

In 1961, *Time* magazine reported a new phenomenon on American university campuses: white students, inspired by the lunch-counter demonstrations of their courageous counterparts at Southern black institutions, were exhibiting a new spirit of social and political commitment. The new "involvementalism," as the magazine called it, rejected the superficial material comfort and "ironbound conformity" of their parents' generation for lives of intense, vigorous engagement with issues that mattered. Some students said they were taking up the challenge of President John F. Kennedy's inaugural address: "Ask not what your country can do for you—ask what you can do for your country." Reports of the generational revolt of 1960s college students come as no news today. The decade of the sixties is well known as the era of the youth movement, of angry protest and activism that rejected old ways of thinking and acting for lives of passionate engagement. The rebellion that *Time* described in 1961, however, involved "a sharp turn" not to the left, but "to the political right." Conservatism was sweeping college campuses. "My parents thought Franklin D. Roosevelt was one of the greatest heroes who ever lived," twenty-two-year-old Robert Schuchman explained. "I'm rebelling from that concept."

The media attention devoted to radical countercultural youth in the middle of the 1960s and to the escalating antiwar movement has tended to obscure other popular and more conservative rebellions by college youth of the era. Nonetheless, movements on the left and right had important traits in common. First, both modeled their actions and their attitudes on the defiant protests of civil rights activists. Second, both regarded themselves as a revolt of the young against the tired orthodoxies of the less involved and less vigorous older generation, often that of their parents. Third, both voiced their impatience with the 1950s and their hopes for reinvigorating the nation, which they often expressed as their determination to achieve and demonstrate an authentic masculinity. However, the solutions they offered for the perceived problems of the day usually differed, often radically. This section on the rebellions of the 1960s examines two areas to shed light on the cultural attitudes that united and divided the decade of protest: the countercultural student revolts of the 1960s and the radical feminist rebellion at the end of the decade.

⌁ CAMPUS RADICALS

Unlike earlier periods of intense social protest in the United States, the era of student activism and rebellion at American universities began in the midst of unprecedented prosperity, especially for the leaders of these movements—young, college-educated men and women. Millions of Mexican Americans, African Americans, and rural Americans of all races remained the exception to this development; they constituted large pockets of poverty across the country. But for the middle class and upwardly mobile, the 1950s had turned out a blessing. By the end of that decade, the intensity of the Red Scare was in decline and America's consumer economy was booming. The nation's gross national product alone had grown by more than a third in that period and disposable family incomes with it. The new prosperity of the post–World War II era was especially evident on America's public university campuses, which grew dramatically over the decade. The growth reflected, more than anything else, the impact of the GI Bill of Rights — federal legislation from 1944 that awarded veterans an array of valuable benefits, including modest stipends to help with the cost of higher education. But postwar federal investment in scientific and medical research and the more general economic expansion further fueled the demand for college-educated workers (usually men), which led even more Americans (including those from less advantaged parts of the population) to seek post-secondary degrees. In 1950 about 14 percent of the population age eighteen to twenty-four were pursuing college or graduate degrees; in 1970, more than 32 percent, or 7.9 million, were doing so. What some scholars call the democratization of higher education was evident in the universities themselves, growing numbers of which were massive, city-like agglomerations of laboratories, classroom buildings, and dormitories, with faculty numbering in the thousands and student populations of 20,000 or more. The University of California system under the leadership of its president, the economist Clark Kerr, was at the forefront of these developments. Kerr optimistically imagined his modern "multi-versity" as the foundation of the "knowledge industry" that served America's national greatness. But by the early 1960s, a growing minority of students was questioning the educational world that Kerr and others had created, which to them seemed impersonal, bureaucratic, and corrupted by their close partnership with the military and industrial giants of corporate America. As the Berkeley activist Mario Savio saw them, universities seemed geared to manufacture "well-behaved children" who accepted the world as it was as the price of getting a good job. The rejection of the "multi-versity" and the American "utopia of sterilized, automated contentment" found many ready listeners among students. Prosperity, for them, was itself a cause for discontent as they demanded, not more and better access to consumer bounty, but preparation for lives of vital, authentic engagement with the great problems afflicting the world. These demands often were expressed in terms of a liberated and revitalized masculinity. The documents in this section on Sixties activism examine how such concerns figured in the scope of efforts to reform, reinforce, or reject altogether the politics and culture of the 1960s.

Images of Student Protest (1964 and 1968)

Two well-known images of young people "acting up" suggest the changes and the continuities in student activism over the course of the 1960s. The photo of the "Free Speech Movement" at the University of California, Berkeley, in the fall of 1964 shows students (including Mario Savio, in front, hands behind his back) and some faculty demonstrating against university restrictions on political expression. The Berkeley marchers — politely dressed in jackets and ties or skirts, self-consciously restrained, reasonable, respectable — modeled their protests on the nonviolent but forceful civil rights protests of young African Americans. The second photograph from 1968 shows antiwar activists confronting a hostile Chicago police force during the Democratic National Convention. The obscene gesture of a shirtless man, aiming his finger at the Chicago police, indicates how the divisive political and social conflicts of the 1960s altered the aims, style, and vocabulary of political speech and behavior in the United States. Yet, as different as the incidents shown in these two images appear, both protests provoked bewilderment and eventual outrage from the demonstrators' elders. In the context of their time, each was regarded and denounced as the dangerously irresponsible and radical actions of reckless young people, who themselves defended their actions as constructive, moral, and necessary. For protesters as well as their critics, evaluating student demonstrators often involved reading and assessing how the young people used gender — how they placed themselves in relation to figures of authority and how the sexes were positioned in relation to each other. What, for instance, did the gesture of the bare-chested demonstrator of 1968 signal? Was he an insolent boy "fixated at the age of the temper tantrum" and desperate to prove his manhood, as Bruno Bettelheim, the eminent Freudian psychologist, described student radicals to a congressional committee in 1969? Or did he symbolize what many radicals of the time demanded: a powerful assertion of individual defiance of both political authority and the oppressive rules of middle-class respectability? Considering such questions enables us to examine whether activists, in defying the political and social conditions of the day, also sought to challenge or to reinforce common expectations about how men and women should behave.

PROBLEMS TO CONSIDER

1. Compare these two images of student protesters in the 1960s. In what ways did student demonstrations change or remain the same in the four years between 1964 and 1968?
2. In examining these images, consider how the photographs used symbols of gender, race, and class to explain the nature of student unrest. What, for instance, was the effect of centering the lens on the bare-chested demonstrator?

Student demonstrators lead the free speech movement march at the University of California, Berkeley, 1964.

(Courtesy of The Bancroft Library, University of California, Berkeley.)

Demonstrators protest the Vietnam War during the Democratic National Convention in Chicago, 1968.

(As published in *Chicago Daily News*, Copyright 1968 by Chicago Daily News, 350 North Orleans Street, Chicago, IL 60654.)

෴

The Sharon Statement (1960)
YOUNG AMERICANS FOR FREEDOM

The Port Huron Statement (1962)
STUDENTS FOR A DEMOCRATIC SOCIETY

The two important early manifestos of the 1960s youth movement were, on the political right, "The Sharon Statement" and, on the political left, "The Port Huron Statement." In the fall of 1960, young conservatives gathered in Sharon, Connecticut, at the estate of the wealthy National Review *editor William F. Buckley. They drafted their creed and designated themselves Young Americans for Freedom (YAF), an organization still in operation today. YAF conservatives were committed activists; they initially supported the free speech movement at Berkeley. They tied their political hopes to the eloquent and energetic Republican senator from Arizona, Barry Goldwater, whose presidential campaign lost in a landslide in 1964 to President Kennedy's successor, Lyndon Johnson. At the Republican convention that year, Goldwater was introduced by YAF member Ronald Reagan, whose cause YAF would embrace for the next sixteen years. "The Port Huron Statement" was the "agenda for a generation" that the radical Students for a Democratic Society (SDS) issued at their general meeting in 1962. Founded at the University of Michigan two years earlier, SDS became the leading student activist organization from the mid-1960s until the early 1970s. Its membership of college and graduate students identified themselves as the "New Left," distinct from the "Old Left" because they rejected the hierarchical bureaucracies of previous generations of Communist, socialist, and labor organizers. SDS focused initially on two areas of concern: countering the repressive apparatus of the Cold War state, and grass-roots mobilization of the inner-city poor to fight against their oppression and misery. Released early in the decade, before the Vietnam War pushed all other political concerns to the margins, "The Port Huron Statement" offered a cultural and political critique of 1960s America that served to define the organization's political mission and the generational identity of its membership. By 1964, SDS had 1,200 members on twenty-seven college campuses. The escalation of the Vietnam War sent membership skyrocketing to as many as 100,000 in 1968. At that point, SDS was the leading antiwar organization, but its unity diminished rapidly as internal disagreements about strategy and infiltration by the FBI reduced it to bitterly divided factions by 1971.*

PROBLEMS TO CONSIDER

1. In what ways were campus activists of either political stripe leading a generational revolt? Which characteristics or attitudes of their parents were they rejecting? What qualities of American society of the 1950s were they rejecting?
2. Compare YAF's call for freedom with that of "The Port Huron Statement." In what ways were their rebellions alike, and in what ways were they different? Was "The Sharon Statement" any more or less an "agenda for a generation"?

THE SHARON STATEMENT

IN THIS TIME of moral and political crisis, it is the responsibility of the youth of America to affirm certain eternal truths.

We, as young conservatives, believe:

That foremost among the transcendent values is the individual's use of his God-given free will, whence derives his right to be free from the restrictions of arbitrary force;

That liberty is indivisible, and that political freedom cannot long exist without economic freedom;

That the purpose of government is to protect these freedoms through the preservation of internal order, the provision of national defense, and the administration of justice;

That when government ventures beyond these rightful functions, it accumulates power, which tends to diminish order and liberty;

That the Constitution of the United States is the best arrangement yet devised for empowering government to fulfill its proper role, while restraining it from the concentration and abuse of power;

That the genius of the Constitution—the division of powers—is summed up in the clause that reserves primacy to the several states, or to the people in those spheres not specifically delegated to the Federal government;

That the market economy, allocating resources by the free play of supply and demand, is the single economic system compatible with the requirements of personal freedom and constitutional government, and that it is at the same time the most productive supplier of human needs;

That when government interferes with the work of the market economy, it tends to reduce the moral and physical strength of the nation; that when it takes from one man to bestow on another, it diminishes the incentive of the first, the integrity of the second, and the moral autonomy of both;

That we will be free only so long as the national sovereignty of the United States is secure; that history shows periods of freedom are rare, and can exist only when free citizens concertedly defend their rights against all enemies. . . .

That the forces of international Communism are, at present, the greatest single threat to these liberties;

That the United States should stress victory over, rather than coexistence with, this menace; and

That American foreign policy must be judged by this criterion: does it serve the just interests of the United States?

———

Young Americans for Freedom, "The Sharon Statement" (1960), *National Review*, September 24, 1960, 173.

THE PORT HURON STATEMENT

We are people of this generation, bred in at least modest comfort, housed now in universities, looking uncomfortably to the world we inherit.

When we were kids the United States was the wealthiest and strongest country in the world; the only one with the atom bomb, the least scarred by modern war, an initiator of the United Nations that we thought would distribute Western influence throughout the world. Freedom and equality for each individual, government of, by, and for the people—these American values we found good, principles by which we could live as men. Many of us began maturing in complacency.

As we grew, however, our comfort was penetrated by events too troubling to dismiss. First, the permeating and victimizing fact of human degradation, symbolized by the Southern struggle against racial bigotry, compelled most of us from silence to activism. Second, the enclosing fact of the Cold War, symbolized by the presence of the Bomb, brought awareness that we ourselves, and our friends, and millions of abstract "others" we knew more directly because of our common peril, might die at any time. We might deliberately ignore, or avoid, or fail to feel all other human problems, but not these two, for these were too immediate and crushing in their impact, too challenging in the demand that we as individuals take the responsibility for encounter and resolution.

While these and other problems either directly oppressed us or rankled our consciences and became our subjective concerns, we began to see complicated and disturbing paradoxes in our surrounding America. The declaration "all men are created equal . . . " rang hollow before the facts of Negro life in the South and the big cities of the North. The proclaimed peaceful intentions of the United States contradicted its economic and military investments in the Cold War status quo.

We witnessed, and continue to witness, other paradoxes. With nuclear energy whole cities can easily be powered, yet the dominant nation-states seem more likely to unleash destruction greater than that incurred in all wars of human history. Although our own technology is destroying old and creating new forms of social organization, men still tolerate meaningless work and idleness. While two-thirds of mankind suffers under nourishment, our own upper classes revel amidst superfluous abundance. Although world population is expected to double in forty years, the nations still tolerate anarchy as a major principle of international conduct and uncontrolled exploitation governs the sapping of the earth's physical resources. Although mankind desperately needs revolutionary leadership, America rests in national stalemate, its goals ambiguous and tradition-bound instead of informed and clear, its democratic system apathetic and manipulated rather than "of, by, and for the people."

Not only did tarnish appear on our image of American virtue, not only did disillusion occur when the hypocrisy of American ideals was discovered, but we began to sense that what we had originally seen as the American Golden Age was actually the decline of an era. The worldwide outbreak of revolution against colonialism and imperialism, the entrenchment of totalitarian states, the menace of war, overpopulation,

international disorder, supertechnology—these trends were testing the tenacity of our own commitment to democracy and freedom and our abilities to visualize their application to a world in upheaval.

Our work is guided by the sense that we may be the last generation in the experiment with living. . . .

Unlike youth in other countries we are used to moral leadership being exercised and moral dimensions being clarified by our elders. But today, for us, not even the liberal and socialist preachments of the past seem adequate to the forms of the present. . . . All around us there is astute grasp of method, technique—the committee, the ad hoc group, the lobbyist, the hard and soft sell, the make, the projected image—but, if pressed critically, such expertise is incompetent to explain its implicit ideals. . . .

We regard *men* as infinitely precious and possessed of unfulfilled capacities for reason, freedom, and love. In affirming these principles we are aware of countering perhaps the dominant conceptions of man in the twentieth century: that he is a thing to be manipulated, and that he is inherently incapable of directing his own affairs. We oppose the depersonalization that reduces human beings to the status of things. . . .

Men have unrealized potential for self-cultivation, self-direction, self-understanding, and creativity. It is this potential that we regard as crucial and to which we appeal, not to the human potentiality for violence, unreason, and submission to authority. The goal of man and society should be human independence: a concern not with image or popularity but with finding a meaning in life that is personally authentic; a quality of mind not compulsively driven by a sense of powerlessness, nor one which unthinkingly adopts status values, nor one which represses all threats to its habits, but one which has full, spontaneous access to present and past experiences; one which easily unites the fragmented parts of personal history; one which openly faces problems which are troubling and unresolved; one with an intuitive awareness of possibilities, an active sense of curiosity, an ability and willingness to learn.

This kind of independence does not mean egotistic individualism—the object is not to have one's way so much as it is to have a way that is one's own. Nor do we deify man—we merely have faith in his potential.

Students for a Democratic Society, *The Port Huron Statement* (1962; reprint, Chicago: Charles H. Kerr, 1990), 7–8, 10–12.

↷

Chicago Retrospective (1968)

STEWART ALBERT

The counterculture, as one of its partisans defined it, "was an attempt to rebel against the values our parents had pushed on us. We were trying to get back to touching and relating and living." Such young people, who shared many of the discontents that motivated YAF, SDS, and other political movements, became visible nationwide in the mid-1960s, drawing their inspiration from earlier generations of cultural rebels, poets, and writers. But the counterculturalists who converged in "Psychedelphia" (San Francisco's Haight-Ashbury district) and nearby Golden Gate Park had a large, if diffuse, agenda for cultural—as opposed to strictly political—revolution. That agenda was summarized in the list of essential tools for achieving intense, authentic, and, many of them hoped, mind-altering experiences: sex, drugs, and rock-and-roll. Whereas YAF and SDS insisted on organized planning and mobilization to effect measurable political and institutional change, countercultural groups tried to change the world by first altering consciousness. Rather than following the leader, they spontaneously did their "own thing" or moved entirely off the grid of conventional time and space with the assistance of hallucinogenic drugs.

The Yippies—the hippie followers of the Youth International Party, led by pranksters Jerry Rubin and Abbie Hoffman—claimed to be the political arm of the counterculture. During the 1968 Democratic National Convention in Chicago, they descended on the city to demonstrate their opposition to the war (for president, they nominated Pigasus, a pig). As debate about the Vietnam War divided the party delegates, the 20,000-strong police force that Chicago mayor Richard Daley assembled to preserve order turned on thousands of antiwar demonstrators with clubs and tear gas, with the Yippies serving as prime targets. The images of the nation at war with itself left the audience watching the riots live on television outraged—whether they sympathized with the demonstrators or with the police. A Yippie provided the following account of the riots for an underground newspaper, the Berkeley (California) Barb.

PROBLEMS TO CONSIDER

1. According to this account, what were the aims of the demonstrators, such as the Yippies? How did the Yippies distinguish themselves from the "moderate forces"?
2. Why was the demonstration an event to be proud of, according to the writer?

In Chicago, teargas was a very democratic experience. On the last two nights, it impartially choked throats of Yippies, Women for Peace, TV cameramen, and even some delegates to the Democratic Convention.

The moderate forces tried to lead orderly marches on the sidewalk policed by monitors who must have taken a semester of piggery at some academy. [Civil rights activist] Dick Gregory made an appearance, as did Eugene McCarthy *[an antiwar candidate who ran for the Democratic presidential nomination in 1968]*, but it served for nothing.

Richard Daley saw every demonstrator in Chicago as Ho Chi Minh *[North Vietnam's president]* with a reefer in his mouth, out to rape his daughter.

The marches were broken up by teargas, riflebutts (the National Guard occasionally joining the pigs *[a derogatory term for police]*), and nightsticks. We all went back into the streets, breaking store windows, throwing rocks at cops and tossing garbage.

The action centered around the heavily guarded Hilton Hotel, in which the delegates hoped to avoid any contact with Chicago.

It did not work. The teargas seeped through the air conditioning and even [Vice President] Hubert Humphrey got sick and had to take a bath. *[Humphrey was the Democratic Party's nominee for president in 1968.]*

The teargas scenes were grotesque—people running, vomiting, burning, choking and praying for some decency that it all stop.

Chicago was a revolutionary wet-dream come true. One night a thousand longhairs joined at the picket-line of striking black bus drivers. On the following night, striking cab-drivers left a picket-line to join the march on the Amphitheatre. . . .

What happened that week was the prototypical formation of the alliance necessary to bring the man down and keep him down. It all happened without a single leaflet being given to anyone and without a single white missionary getting a factory job.

This wasn't the way I was told it would happen. The catechism of orthodox American Leninism is to shave off your beard, get a haircut and stop smoking pot. A revolutionary act is to give leaflets to dockworkers. . . .

It is by our example of rebellion that we will steer the workers into realizing their own dreams. We won't do it by collapsing before the mediocratic cleanshaven alcoholic comformities and telling the prolies to read this after they have read that. . . .

At first, our own reaction [to the Chicago police] was one of terror and frenzied running. Then a more confident move-just-as-far-back-as-you-have-to walk, and finally the discovery that tear gas cannisters could be hurled back and a cop-car taken out of action if enough people surrounded it. A lot of manhood emerged in Chicago, and for that we must be ironically grateful to the Democratic party.

Our revolution is going to be a chaotic, funky mud type of thing. . . . It is being made in the streets right now. On its appearance, you laugh with joy at its absolute originality.

Stewart Albert, "Chicago Retrospective," *Berkeley Barb,* September 6–12, 1968, 9. Obtained from Underground Press Collections, 1963–1985, microfilm.

❧

"GIRLS SAY YES to Boys Who Say NO" (c. 1968)

By the late 1960s, much of the antiwar movement had organized itself around the one issue that affected all young men: the draft. Combat—facing death in defense of the nation—has conventionally been regarded as the ultimate proving ground of manhood. Then how were Americans to view the young men who refused to fight in Vietnam? Were they heroically defying the "system," or were they disguising their cowardice as prin-

ciple? Even the most committed draft resisters agonized over these questions. Focusing on the draft also potentially marginalized activist women because, presumably, they could know war only through men. Furthermore, women who voiced a feminist consciousness in anger at being overlooked for leadership positions or at having to watch the kids so that the men could do the movement's work were accused of putting their petty concerns above the real *political issues. From this perspective, what did* war *have to do with women, aside from their supporting roles as mothers, lovers, wives, or mourners? This poster from 1968, featuring folksinger and antiwar activist Joan Baez (left) and her sisters, addressed these questions.*

PROBLEMS TO CONSIDER

1. How did this image convey women's support for opposition to the draft?
2. How did sleeping with a draft resister express women's relation to war and to antiwar protest? Did the poster represent women in a conventional or an unconventional relationship to men?

(National Museum of American History, Smithsonian Institution, Division of Politics and Reform, photomechanical lithograph ca. 1968 by an unidentified postermaker, gift of William Mears, photographed by Larry Gates.)

ॐ THE CHALLENGES OF FEMINISM

Young women, too, were vital members of the era's rebellion. White women especially benefited from the expanding number of educational and job opportunities in the post–World War II economy. Many such women embraced the demands of the New Left for social reforms and new, more "real" ways of living. Although they felt empowered by their activism, they also were awakened to the double standard that Casey Hayden and Mary King encountered in SNCC. They sensed that the attack on the injustice and inequality of the "system" excluded a questioning of women's designated place as followers and supporters, but never leaders, of men. By the end of the decade, many of the same issues that motivated the civil rights and antiwar movements combined with the discrimination that women experienced as activists to generate an organized women's movement. The sixties generation of feminists split into two major groups, according to their related but different understandings of the problems confronting American women. So-called liberal feminists, such as those who founded the National Organization for Women (NOW) in 1966, followed the strategies that civil rights organizations had pioneered. With strong ties to organized labor, NOW was sensitive to the needs of working women and rejected the cultural primacy of the breadwinning man/housekeeping woman division of labor and responsibility. They also sought legal reforms and protections by suing public and private employers for sex discrimination and lobbying governments for legal protections for working women. Self-consciously "radical" feminists, on the other hand, believed that women needed more than legal protection; they needed liberation from a social order founded on male dominance. Rather than working within the system, "women's liberation" attacked *structural* conditions that were built into the very foundation of American life, starting with the norm of the patriarchal family. They followed the direction of the Black Power and antiwar radicals of the time and often called for separatist women-only organizations.

Despite their great differences, the liberal and liberationist branches of sixties feminism shared certain tendencies. First, both built on the idea of *sisterhood*, the bonds that joined all women in a common experience of sex oppression and the shared cause of gaining equality with men. Second, both strands of feminism questioned gender determinism, namely the assumption that a woman must sacrifice every interest to her supposedly natural calling: motherhood. Feminists of the 1960s raised a number of questions: Was selflessness rooted in women's "natures"— a mainstay position of earlier generations of American women who sought to mold the world outside the home? Or were women conditioned by their subordination in a patriarchal society to be nurturing and maternal figures? Did all women experience oppression or discrimination in the same way, regardless of race, class, or sexuality? Rather than settling these issues, the many directions that feminism took after 1965 exercised enormous influence on the debates over gender, class, race, sexuality, and ethnicity that have preoccupied Americans for the last four decades.

No More Miss America! (1968)

NEW YORK RADICAL WOMEN

"Women's liberation" arrived most famously in 1968 when radical feminists staged a loud and theatrical protest against the Miss America beauty pageant in Atlantic City, New Jersey. No bras were burned, as mythical accounts of the protest have contended ever since, but the protesters made a name for themselves and their cause by destroying other symbols of women's objectification — hair-curling irons, girdles, makeup. This "consciousness-raising" demonstration made the point that the "personal is political." The ways in which American cultural industries, such as those sponsoring the beauty pageant, instructed women to wear or color their hair, deodorize and shave their bodies, and reveal their legs or breasts, supposedly belonged to the realm of women's private choices, which were not relevant subjects for public concern. Radical feminists contended, however, that such practices and products were overtly political in nature and contributed to the general oppression of women. The following pamphlet, which was circulated prior to the demonstration, stated the positions and aims of the protest.

PROBLEMS TO CONSIDER

1. What made the Miss America demonstration a radical, rather than a liberal, protest? How did the protesters connect the exploitation of women to larger social and political issues?
2. Consider this protest in light of the other movements discussed in this chapter — those involving civil rights, the counterculture, and college conservatives and radicals. What similarities and differences can you identify?

We Protest:

1. *The degrading Mindless-Boob-Girlie Symbol.* The Pageant contestants epitomize the roles we are all forced to play as women. The parade down the runway blares the metaphor of the 4-H Club county fair, where the nervous animals are judged for teeth, fleece, etc., and where the best "specimen" gets the blue ribbon. So are women in our society forced daily to compete for male approval, enslaved by ludicrous "beauty" standards we ourselves are conditioned to take seriously.

2. *Racism with Roses.* Since its inception in 1921, the Pageant has not had one Black finalist, and this has not been for a lack of test-case contestants. There has never been a Puerto Rican, Alaskan, Hawaiian, or Mexican-American winner. Nor has there ever been a *true* Miss America — an American Indian.

3. *Miss America as Military Death Mascot.* The highlight of her reign each year is a cheerleader-tour of American troops abroad — last year she went to Vietnam to pep-talk our husbands, fathers, sons and boyfriends into dying and killing with a better spirit. She personifies the "unstained patriotic American womanhood our boys are fighting for." The Living Bra and the Dead Soldier. We refuse to be used as Mascots for Murder.

4. *The Consumer Con-Game.* The Pageant is sponsored by Pepsi-Cola, Toni [*hair-styling product*], and Oldsmobile — Miss America is a walking commercial. Wind her up and she plugs your

product on promotion tours and TV—all in an "honest, objective" endorsement. What a shill.

5. *Competition Rigged and Unrigged.* We deplore the encouragement of an American myth that oppresses men as well as women: the win-or-you're-worthless compe[ti]tive disease. The "beauty contest" creates only one winner to be "used" and forty-nine losers who are "useless."

6. *The Woman as Pop Culture Obsolescent Theme.* Spindle, mutilate, and then discard tomorrow. What is so ignored as last year's Miss America? This only reflects the gospel of our society, according to Saint Male: women must be young, juicy, malleable—hence age discrimination and the cult of youth. And we women are brain-washed into believing this ourselves!

7. *The Unbeatable Madonna-Whore Combination.* Miss America and Playboy's centerfold are sisters over the skin. To win approval, we must be both sexy and wholesome, delicate but able to cope, demure yet titillatingly bitchy. Deviation of any sort brings, we are told, disaster: "You won't get a man!!"

8. *The Irrelevant Crown on the Throne of Mediocrity.* Miss America represents what women are supposed to be: unoffensive, bland, apolitical. If you are tall, short, over or under what weight The Man prescribes you should be, forget it. Personality, articulateness, intelligence, commitment—unwise. Conformity is the key to the crown—and, by extension, to success in our society.

9. *Miss America as Dream Equivalent To—?* In this reputedly democratic society, where every little boy supposedly can grow up to be President, what can every little girl hope to grow to be? Miss America. That's where it's at. Real power to control our own lives is restricted to men, while women get patronizing pseudo-power, an ermine cloak and a bunch of flowers; men are judged by their actions, women by their appearance.

10. *Miss America as Big Sister Watching You.* The Pageant exercises Thought Control, attempts to sear the Image onto our minds, to further make women oppressed and men oppressors; to enslave us all the more in high-heeled, low-status roles; to inculcate false values in young girls; to use women as beasts of buying; to seduce us to prostitute ourselves before our own oppression.

NO MORE MISS AMERICA!

New York Radical Women, "No More Miss America!" from the personal archives of Carol Hanisch, reprinted with her permission.

✂

A Critique of the Miss America Protest (1968)
CAROL HANISCH

Deferring to men in the movement left feminists with a keen awareness of and sensitivity to authoritarianism in any form. In the following selection, Carol Hanisch, a feminist with experience in the civil rights struggle, subjected the Miss America protest to the same searching examination that women's liberation aimed at contemporary mainstream and radical politics—and found much to criticize. Her objections reveal many of the core features of radical feminism, especially the importance of "consciousness-raising" demonstrations. These actions were designed in part to expose how male domination operated invisibly in women's everyday lives. But the events also were deployed to embolden women to speak out about forbidden subjects such as sexuality and abortion. So successful was consciousness-raising as an organizing and protest tactic that its use was adopted by later social and political reform movements, including both those conservative and radical in nature.

PROBLEMS TO CONSIDER

1. What did Hanisch find objectionable about the protest of the Miss America pageant itself? What model of political action did she propose instead?
2. How did Hanisch connect the politics of the protest with the larger political goals of feminists such as herself?

The protest of the Miss America Pageant in Atlantic City in September told the nation that a new feminist movement is afoot in the land. Due to the tremendous coverage in the mass media, millions of Americans now know there is a Women's Liberation Movement. . . .

When I proposed the idea to our group, we decided to go around the room with each woman telling how she felt about the pageant. We discovered that many of us who had always put down the contest still watched it. Others, like myself, had consciously identified with it, and had cried with the winner.

From our communal thinking came the concrete plans for the action. We all agreed that our main point in the demonstration would be that all women were hurt by beauty competition— Miss America as well as ourselves. We opposed the pageant in our own self-interest, e.g. the self-interest of all women.

Yet one of the biggest mistakes of the whole pageant was our anti-womanism. A spirit of every woman "do[ing] her own thing" began to emerge. Sometimes it was because there was an open conflict about an issue. Other times, women didn't say anything at all about disagreeing with a group decision; they just went ahead and did what they wanted to do, even though it was something the group had definitely decided against. Because of this egotistic individualism, a definite strain of anti-womanism was presented to the public to the detriment of the action.

Posters which read "Up Against the Wall, Miss America," "Miss America Sells It," and "Miss America Is a Big Falsie" hardly raised any woman's consciousness and really harmed the cause of sisterhood. Miss America and all beautiful women came off as our enemy instead of as our sisters who suffer with us. A group decision

had been made rejecting these anti-woman signs. A few women made them anyway. . . .

A more complex situation developed around the decision of a few women to use an "underground" disruptive tactic. The action was approved by the group only after its adherents said they would do it anyway as an individual action. As it turned out, we came to the realization that there is no such thing as "individual action" in a movement. We were linked to and were committed to support our sisters whether they called their action "individual" or not. . . . We need to reach as many women as possible as quickly as possible with a clear message that has the power of our person behind it. At this point women have to see other women standing up and saying these things. That's why draping a women's liberation banner over the balcony that night and yelling our message was much clearer. We should have known, however, that the television network, because it was not competing with other networks for coverage, would not put the action on camera. It did get on the radio and in newspapers, however.

The problem of how to enforce group decisions is one we haven't solved. It came up in a lot of ways throughout the whole action. The group rule of not talking to male reporters was another example.

One of the reasons we came off anti-woman, besides the posters, was our lack of clarity. We didn't say clearly enough that we women are all FORCED to play the Miss American role—not by beautiful women but by men who we have to act that way for and by a system that has so well institutionalized male supremacy for its own ends.

This was none too clear in our guerrilla theater either. Women chained to a replica, red, white and blue–bathing-suited Miss America could have been misinterpreted as against beautiful women. Also, crowning a live sheep Miss America sort of said that beautiful women *are* sheep. However, the action did say to some women that women are *viewed* as auction-block, docile animals. The grandmother of one of the participants really began to understand the action when she was told about the sheep, and she ended up joining the protest.

There is as great a need for clarity in our language as there is in our actions. The leaflet that was distributed as a press release and as a flyer at the action was too long, too wordy, too complex, too hippy-yippee-campy. Instead of an "in" phrase like "Racism with Roses" (I still don't know exactly what that means), we could have just called the pageant RACIST and everybody would have understood our opposition on that point. If we are going to reach masses of women, we must give up all the "in-talk" of the New Left/Hippie movements—at least when we're talking in public. (Yes, even the word F--K!) We can use simple language (*real* language) that everyone from Queens to Iowa will understand and not misunderstand.

We should try to avoid the temptation to say everything there is to say about what is wrong with the world and thereby say nothing that a new person can really dig into [to] understand. Women's liberation itself is revolutionary dynamite. When other issues are interjected, we should clearly relate them to our oppression *as women*.

We tried to carry the democratic means we used in planning the action into the actual *doing* of it. We didn't want leaders or spokesmen. It makes the movement not only *seem* stronger and larger if everyone is a leader, but it actually *is* stronger if not dependent on a few. It also guards against the time when such leaders could be isolated and picked off one way or another. And of course many voices are more powerful than one. . . .

The Miss America protest was a zap action, as opposed to person to person group action. Zap actions are using our presence as a group and/or the media to make women's oppression into social issues. In such actions we speak to men as a group as well as to women. It is a rare opportunity to talk to men in a situation where they can't talk back. (Men must begin to learn to listen.) Our power of solidarity, not our individual intellectual exchanges will change men.

We tried to speak to individual women in the crowd and now some of us feel that it may not have been a good tactic. It put women on the spot in front of their men. We were putting them in a position which we choose to avoid ourselves when we don't allow men in our discussion groups.

It is interesting that many of the non-movement women we talked to about the protest had the same reaction as many radical women. "But I'm not oppressed," was a shared response. "I don't care about Miss America," was another. If more than half the television viewers in the country watch the pageant, somebody cares! And many of us admitted watching it too, even while putting it down.

It's interesting, too, that while much of the Left was putting us down for attacking something so "silly and unimportant" or "reformist," the Right saw us as a threat and yelled such things as "Go back to Russia" and "Mothers of Mao" at the picket line. Ironically enough, what the Left/Underground press seemed to like best about our action was what was really our worst mistake—our anti-woman signs. . . .

Unfortunately the best slogan for the action came up about a month after when Ros Baxandall came out . . . with "Every day in a woman's life is a walking Miss America Contest." We shouldn't wait for the best slogan; we should go ahead to the best of our understanding. We hope all our sisters can learn something as we did from our first foray.

Carol Hanisch, "What Can Be Learned: A Critique of the Miss America Pageant," November 27, 1968, from the Marxism and Aesthetics Collection of Lee Baxandall; Tamiment 151; Box 3, Folder 26, Tamiment Library and Wagner Labor Archives, Bobst Library, New York University, New York, N.Y.

⤳

Colonized Women: The Chicana (1970)
ELIZABETH SUTHERLAND MARTÍNEZ

The Older Woman: A Stockpile of Losses (1972)
TI-GRACE ATKINSON

Even as the radical feminist critique of the Miss America pageant, as well as the feminist objections to the protest's implied antiwomanism, was gaining unprecedented attention, other feminist voices—those of lesbian women, African American and other women of color, and older women—were calling into question the whole notion of sisterhood. They were pointing out the unexamined gender, ethnic, age, and class biases implicit even in radical feminism. The following two selections called attention to the feminism of such marginalized groups. The first, by Elizabeth Sutherland Martínez, addressed the circumstances of Chicanas (Mexican American women). The second document, Ti-Grace Atkinson's keynote address at the 1972 OWL (Older Women's Liberation) Conference, spoke up for older women.

PROBLEMS TO CONSIDER

1. What did Martínez mean by "colonized women"? Compare her assertions about the condition of Chicanas with the protests against the Miss America pageant.
2. Was "sisterhood" a workable ideal for feminists, or were the experiences of women too diverse for them to unite across the divisions the writers identify?

COLONIZED WOMEN: THE CHICANA

For the woman of a colonized group, even the most political, her oppression as a woman is usually overshadowed by the common oppression of both male and female. Black and brown people in this country are fighting for sheer survival against the physical genocide or wars (including a high draft rate), police brutality, hunger, deprivation—and against the cultural genocide of white Anglo institutions and values. The overused word "minority" becomes significant here; any colonized woman will feel an impulse toward unity with her brothers rather than challenge against them, but when the colonized group is the minority, as in the United States, this becomes even truer. . . .

The sensitive woman from a colonized people also recognizes that many times it has been easier for her economically than for the men of her group. Often she can get a job where a man cannot. She can see the damage done to the men as a result, and feels reluctant to risk threatening their self-respect even further. This may be a short-range viewpoint involving false definitions of manhood, but it is created by immediate realities whose force cannot merely be wished away. It is also a fact that in many Chicano families, the woman makes many of the important decisions—not just consumer decisions—though the importance of her role will be recognized only privately. This may seem hypocritical or like a double-standard, but the knowledge of having real influence affects how the Chicana feels.

There is something else, and larger. It has been eloquently described by Maria Varela, now working in the Chicano movement of the Southwest:

When your race is fighting for survival—to eat, to be clothed, to be housed, to be left in peace—as a woman, you know who you are. You are the principle of life, of survival and endurance. No matter how your husband is—strong but needing you to keep on, or weak and needing you for strength, or brutal and using you to keep his manhood intact—no matter what *he* is, your children survive and survive only through your will, your day-to-day battle against inimical forces. You know who you are. This is even more true when, as a woman, you are involved in battling the forces of oppression against your race. For the Chicano woman battling for her people, the family—the big family—is a fortress against the genocidal forces in the outside world. It is the source of strength for a people whose identity is constantly being whittled away. The mother is the center of that fortress.

For the young, alienated Anglos, on the other hand, the family as it has functioned in the past often reflects a bundle of false values in a lying society of which she is part. Her position is almost the opposite of the Chicana's. And the family is but one example of how the culture or life-style of a colonized people becomes a weapon of self-defense in a hostile world—hostile to any signs of unity among them, hostile to their very existence. It is a weapon against the oppressor's tactic of "divide and conquer," with which he has sustained his rule these many centuries.

That life-style may have other roots as well, but to challenge it today means to risk being seen as the oppressor. "We don't want to become like the dominating Anglo women," you can hear Chicanas say. The comment shows a great lack of understanding of the Anglo woman's struggle, but it also reveals how deeply cultural integrity is interwoven with survival for a colonized people. The middle-class Anglo woman must therefore beware of telling her black or brown sisters to throw off their chains—without at least first understanding the origins and reasons for those "chains." And also without first asking themselves: are there perhaps some aspects of these other life-styles from which we, with our advanced ideas, might still learn? . . .

———

Elizabeth Sutherland Martínez, "Colonized Women: The Chicana," reprinted with permission of the author.

THE OLDER WOMAN: A STOCKPILE OF LOSSES

The issue of the older woman is the strategic Achilles' heel of Women's Liberation. The definition of her problem was evaded from the beginning—its existence even denied at first. The definition of "older woman" *is* "woman." This definition exposes the softness of the feminist analysis.

"Woman"—bluntly put—means "garbage"—waste. Woman is "potential." The older woman is "past potential." A contradiction in terms? Not if you understand the meaning of "potential."

"Potential" means "not actualized"—"nonexistent." The non-older woman has hope. She may still be used. The older woman is use-less, past the possibility of use. She is no longer in danger of—has lost the "opportunity" of—being politically raped by one man. The older woman is *guaranteed* ravishment by the whole f--king system.

The older woman no longer has potential. She's *had* it. Or rather she can no longer *have* it. The older woman has had it: she's been ejected from the system. She is a stockpile of losses—a walking history of lost potentials. She should, of course, have the good taste to lie down and die like a lady. Be that as it may, for better or for worse, the "older woman" hangs in. And I say—"as long as we're gonna hang in—we might as well hang *out*, too."

In 1966, the older woman *was* the Women's Movement, only the older woman wasn't *in* the Women's Movement. I was *one* of the, if not *the*, youngest active members in NOW (the OW of

"Never"). But most of the women prefaced nearly all their major statements with: "It's too late for me; I'm fighting for my daughters." Charitable kamikazes have always seemed a dubious lot to me. These proved no exception.

The older woman in the Women's Movement didn't "care" enough for the future of their daughters to fight for it in the only way the future can ever be fought for: on the battleground of your own present. If the older woman isn't worth the fight, then neither are women as a class worth the fight. My thesis, here, is that the older woman is the conceptual nub of the class of woman.

The convenors of the present conference have had the tenacity and, yes, courage to hack out the area of "older women" as a special section within the Women's Movement. My question is: Do you have the guts to take it over? It is only when the older woman becomes the Women's Movement that we will have a movement. It's only when you're all the way in the s--t that the shoveling is worth it in the long run.

Do older women care enough about all women to hammer home within the movement that the truth about the older woman is the truth about *all* women?

Ti-Grace Atkinson, "The Older Woman: A Stockpile of Losses," *Prime Time*, October 1972, 1, 3, reprinted with permission of the author.

⁊

CHAPTER 9

All in the Family:
American Culture, 1969–1992

IN THE HALF-HOUR debut episode of *All in the Family* that CBS television broadcast in 1971, the character Archie Bunker managed to insult, slander, and demean virtually every social and cultural grouping that had organized politically by the end of the 1960s. A regular blue-collar working stiff, Archie hated everything about the America of his day: the "break-down in law and order," the "sob sisters" with their "bleeding heart" concern for "spics" and "spades," the "girls with skirts up to here" and "men with hair down to there." The show's theme song, "Those Were the Days," described a faded past when guys like Archie had it made. Back then, we "didn't need no welfare states" because "everybody pulled his weight." The country would be better off, if only we had "a man like Herbert Hoover again." The Hoover line always got a reaction from the show's laugh track. Archie was a political and cultural dinosaur. Actual Americans loved to laugh at him, whether he was raging at his "dingbat" wife, Edith, or explaining the ethnic profiles of "yids" and "coloreds." By the end of the first season, his verbal brawls with "Meathead" (his liberal, unemployed, college-student son-in-law Mike) were attracting 50 million viewers weekly, the largest audiences of the time.*

The popularity of *All in the Family* marked a new era in network entertainment. After the political and cultural turmoil of the previous decade, television, it seemed, was free to confront the great social conflicts of the day. Norman Lear, the show's writer and producer, tried to do just that. Lear did not bother to conceal his liberal political sympathies for the social reform movements of the 1960s. In fact, he believed that comedy could discredit bigotry and igno-

---

* "Meet the Bunkers," written and produced by Norman Lear, directed by John Rich, copyright © 1970 Tandem Productions, Inc., from *All in the Family* videotape 02129, copyright © 1998 Columbia TriStar Home Video.

rance and reform America more effectively than could reasoned debate. Every time Archie opened his foul mouth, he was supposed to point viewers in the direction of a new and better future. People laughed, but the show's impact on American society is hard to measure. What audiences heard when Archie ventured an opinion may not have been what Lear wanted them to hear. Even contemporary observers wondered if laughing at Archie discredited his politics or affirmed his view of himself as the true victim of the era's misguided reformers.

The ability of Lear's comedy to make Americans of varying political outlooks join in laughter demonstrates how popular culture can give voice to, interpret, and explain the common concerns of its day—even if it does so in ways that its producers had not intended. Few people endorsed Archie's ugliest bigotries, yet his tirades on behalf of the little guy against big government and the social disorder of his day voiced a growing sentiment that after a decade of protest and government activism, the nation had strayed from its destiny and was far worse off than it had been in the 1950s. As earlier chapters have shown in the case of other cultural artifacts, the show's nostalgia for a bygone age of harmony in America was just that—nostalgia. But *All in the Family* did get history right in one respect. Although Archie was supposed to be a political and cultural dinosaur who had lived past his time, he actually forecast a political shift to the right, a backlash against the very reform agenda that *All in the Family* was supposed to promote. The show mapped out, with uncanny accuracy, the conflicts that split Americans into organized political and cultural blocs in the 1970s and afterward. Far from going away, these divisions—ethnic, racial, gender, class, and sexual—have shaped the nation's history in the decades since the Vietnam War. This chapter focuses on three regions of cultural terrain around which Americans have organized with and against one another in their determination to set the nation on its proper course: the "sexual revolution," environmentalism, and the AIDS epidemic.

ᢒ *Sexual Revolutions: The Matter of Women's Sexuality* ᢒ

Few things infuriated Archie Bunker more than having to witness the eager sexual attraction between his miniskirted daughter and longhaired son-in-law. Gloria and Mike spoke for the "sexual revolution," and they were apt to exercise its new freedoms at any moment on the living room sofa. In his day, Archie protested, "there was nothin', I mean absolutely nothin', not until the wedding night." "Yeah," agreed his wife, "and even then . . ." The audience's laughter affirmed the unpleasant contrast between the Bunkers' sadly dried-up romance and the frisky young couple. Gloria and Mike literally embraced the new attitude that the enjoyment of sexual pleasure before and during marriage and at any hour of the day was natural, healthy, and appropriate. Sexuality, in the new view, was a vital source of personal liberty, meaning, and identity, equally for women and for men. Sex also was nothing to be ashamed of, although, this being television, the couple had to be married if they were going to be amorous on the sofa.

The new erotic environment, or "sexual revolution," began in the late 1950s with the discrediting of the sexual double standard, which traditionally defined women as less sexual than men. Although the sexual revolution was commonly associated with the "free love" counterculture of the 1960s, by the early 1970s, when the first baby boom generation was reaching young adulthood, the broad middle of American culture had embraced the new outlook on sex. Assisted by new contraceptive technologies such as the birth control pill (introduced in 1960), heterosexual women and men were able to view sex as natural, penalty-free, personally liberating, and fun. The consumer marketplace reinforced these messages. *The Joy of Sex* (1972)— a "Gourmet Guide to Love Making"—was a best-selling fixture of middle-class bedrooms across the country. In a 1971 ad campaign, the "stewardesses" of National Airlines implicitly promised an erotic adventure when they invited male passengers to "Fly me to Miami." At the same time, the gay and lesbian movements were challenging the heterosexual norm with new urban public spaces—neighborhoods, bars, beaches—where homosexual women and men sought their sexual preferences. Sexuality appeared more visible and unrestrained in American public life, more central to how people affirmed their identities, and no longer a taboo subject, even among populations that did not think of themselves as countercultural. In *The Total Woman* (1973), Marabel Morgan, an evangelical Christian, advised fellow housewives to greet their husbands at the end of the day in an adventurously sexy outfit. "He'll feel more alive just coming home to you, when your whole countenance and attitude say, 'Touch me, I'm yours!'"

These examples indicate that Americans' valuation of sexuality and their tolerance for expanded and even unconventional sexual frontiers had changed dramatically by the mid-1970s, yet efforts to alter expectations about what constituted natural and normal sexuality and gender identities often met with forceful resistance—especially when innovation challenged the expected relations between women and men. Did new attitudes about sexuality affect or "liberate" women and men equally and in the same way? In what ways was the sexual revolution revolutionary? The documents in this section explore these issues, in part, by exploring the conflicts over gender that were sparked by an industrially manufactured and market-oriented sexual technology: the birth control pill.

An End to Woman's "Bad Days"? (1962)

J. D. RATCLIFF

The Pill: How It Is Affecting U.S. Morals, Family Life (1966)

In 1960, the federal Food and Drug Administration approved the first contraceptive hormonal pill, Enovid, manufactured by G. D. Searle & Company. Containing much higher levels of estrogen than the versions used today, "the pill" promised 99 percent effectiveness in preventing conception. By the end of the decade, millions of American women — most of them middle-class, including one-quarter of all married women — were taking it, usually to protect against unwanted pregnancy. The pill was the most important technology affecting the sexual revolution. Many women (and men) believed its ease of use liberated sexual passion: once a day a woman swallowed a little pill. The pill supposedly allowed for the spontaneity and pleasure that were compromised by both fear of pregnancy and doubts about the reliability of other birth control methods. Finally, and perhaps most significant, the pill divorced sexual relations from reproduction. This development troubled many people who believed women's sexuality should be governed by their biological role as childbearers. Women who took the pill could enjoy sex the way men did and could plan, with or without their partners, if, when, or how often they became pregnant. "Modern woman," a female journalist proclaimed in 1969, "is at last free, as a man is free, to dispose of her own body, to earn her living, to pursue the improvement of her mind, to try a successful career." Such reflections, more than describing some women's experiences, underscore the political ramifications of the new technology. For most women (and men), the pill became part of the complicated history of the politics of women's bodies — how they were perceived, who controlled them, and for what purposes they could be used.

The following documents implicitly address these questions. The first piece, from the mass-circulation Reader's Digest, *celebrates the wonders of the new technology, including its supposed ability to free women from their biological limitations. The second, from the weekly* U.S. News & World Report, *is more cautionary, allowing a panel of mostly male experts on moral authority to identify and assess how the pill contributed to new sexual outlooks and affected traditional controls on sexual behavior.*

PROBLEMS TO CONSIDER

1. How did these articles explain the purposes and functions of women's bodies and sexuality?
2. In measuring the desirable or undesirable effects of using the pill, what are the values or assumptions that connected women's sexuality and social order?

AN END TO WOMAN'S "BAD DAYS"

"It appears quite likely that this may be the last generation of women to menstruate. A means is now at hand to control this event—to hasten it, postpone it, or eliminate it entirely."

The author of this intentionally dramatic statement is Dr. Ralph I. Dorfman of the respected Worcester Foundation for Experimental Biology, who chose these words to emphasize the astonishing strides now being made in hormonal control of the menses.

Already a sizable number of women with special problems are welcoming a newly developed means to postpone monthly periods and the tension that accompanies them: opera singers about to undertake difficult roles, business women on the eve of important conferences, athletes about to enter competition, young women about to be married. Many women undergoing medical treatment for a uterine disorder have gone two years without periods and, on present evidence, could do so indefinitely without harm.

All these possibilities are opened by the new hormonal birth-control pills. One of the outstanding research accomplishments of our day, the new pills—on the average, 20 times as effective as "safe period" control, 10 times as effective as the most commonly used contraceptive devices—promise protection against unwanted pregnancies to a degree never before possible. Yet, control of birth is only one of the applications of these remarkable medicines. Indeed, their usefulness appears to broaden constantly. They are proving invaluable aids in controlling threatened miscarriage, permitting women to have babies that might otherwise be lost. They are useful in treating some types of sterility, in bringing order to irregular periods, controlling excessive loss of blood, reducing severe pain that frequently accompanies menstruation, and lessening the tension that goes with the menstrual period.

Menstruation has been called "nature's physiological flaw." Once a month the womb is prepared for pregnancy, when an egg cell erupts from an ovary. Tissue proliferates, new blood supply lines are laid to nourish a new life. When pregnancy fails to develop, this tissue is discarded. "The womb weeps for its loss," one poetically-minded researcher observes.

Not until the 1930's did researchers begin to discover the complex chemistry involved in the cessation of menstruation with pregnancy. With fertilization of the ovum a whirlwind of hormonal activity begins. The ovaries increase production of the female sex hormones, estrogen and progesterone: levels rise to dozens of times normal. The increased progesterone quiets the rhythmic contractions of the uterus so the new life will not be dislodged and discharged. It also exerts a smothering effect on the ovaries. No further eggs will be produced during the span of pregnancy. In sum, normal events of the female cycle, including menstruation, come to a halt.

The birth-control pills, containing synthetic versions of the two female sex hormones, achieve much of the same results—producing in effect a pseudo-pregnancy. Ovarian activity is suppressed. No egg cells are produced and without the egg cells there can be no pregnancy. To use the pill as a contraceptive without suppressing menstruation, women swallow one a day for 20 days, beginning on the fifth day of the menstrual cycle. Suppression of menstruation is achieved by taking the pills continuously, usually in larger doses.

Early work at the Ortho Research Foundation, G. D. Searle and other pharmaceutical houses indicated that contraceptive pills would suppress menstruation in monkeys. Dr. Robert W. Kistner of Harvard Medical School and other physicians thought this effect might be useful in treating women for endometriosis, a condition in which flecks of the endometrium, the lining of the womb, become detached, implant and begin growing in the vagina. Or, bits of this tissue may slip through the Fallopian tubes into the pelvic cavity, or reach other parts of the body, and there grow like a hardy weed—at times choking off or obstructing vital organs. And each month this tissue, wherever it may be, responds to hormone stimulus and menstruates—*i.e.*, bleeds.

Physicians long ago noted that when menstruation was suppressed, random endometrial tissue tended to wither, die and be absorbed by the body. In general there were two ways of achieving suppression: by performing a hysterectomy and removing ovaries, uterus, tubes; or by one or more pregnancies. Difficulty with the latter course often arose from the fact that many women with endometriosis were made sterile by the disease.

Why not, Dr. Kistner reasoned, use large doses of birth-control pills on a daily, round-the-calendar basis to induce a false pregnancy and suppress menstruation? It worked, without causing the serious side effects he had observed with other hormones tried for this purpose. A number of Kistner patients have been free of the menses for two or more years. In better than four of five women treated, endometriosis has been satisfactorily controlled. Such work by Kistner and others provides evidence that menstruation can be completely suppressed for long periods, with no harmful permanent effects as yet detected—to resume again in normal fashion when the pills are stopped.

Women in whom only postponement of menses is wanted—swimming stars, actresses on opening nights, women about to take rugged motor trips—are given the pills to take on a daily basis. Menstruation can then be retarded as long as wanted, but will occur three to five days after pill taking ceases. In cases where it is desirable to hasten the event, small doses are taken during the first five days of the normal cycle. Again, the menses follow a few days after the pills are omitted. In all cases, of course, the physician must adjust dosages to fit individual needs.

Is such control over a natural body function ethically sound, morally valid? Is it wise to tinker with nature in such fashion? Physicians are quietly debating these questions. Some doctors even contend that menstruation itself is an *abnormal* event, that nature apparently intended women to follow one pregnancy with another, continuously.

While menstruation is reasonably trouble-free for a majority of women, for others it is a period of genuine trial. Both French and U.S. studies of women convicted of crimes of violence showed that about 80 percent of such crimes were committed during the stressful time preceding menstruation or the first few days of the period. A British study showed that accident rates take a dramatic upswing during this period of irritability, depression and lethargy.

For the millions of women who have severe nervous reactions or real physical agony, the avoidance of menstruation could be a blessing—to themselves, to their long-suffering families, and also to their employers.

What are the possible dangers of interfering with the normal cycle? After seven years' experience with these pills, dangers appear to be minimal. At first there were fears that continued use might produce a permanent sterility. All evidence indicates that the reverse is true, that there is a "rebound": apparently fertility heightens once a woman ceases taking the pills. In one study, 60 percent of women who desired pregnancy achieved it within one month of omitting the pills. This "rebound phenomenon" is today being utilized to treat *infertility*.

The question of cancer arises. Again, all studies to date indicate that the incidence of cancer is no greater among pill-users than among non-users. Might the pills do permanent harm to glands? Might they damage microscopic egg cells in the ovary, destined to mature at some later date? Studies by Dr. John Rock, clinical professor of gynecology at Harvard, have produced no evidence of this.

Last December the question arose whether a birth-control pill might be associated with blockages in blood vessels by clots (embolism); at that time the American Medical Association undertook a careful scientific review of oral contraceptives and found absolutely no evidence to connect the pills with the blood-clotting condition.

In sum, evidence so far indicates safety. Many conservative physicians feel, nonetheless, that more years of experience must accumulate before a final answer can be given.

The pills, admittedly, do have drawbacks. Approximately one woman in five will get reactions much like those of pregnancy. Breasts swell and become tender, morning sickness and weight gains are noted—all symptoms that vanish after two or three months, just as they vanish after two or three months of pregnancy.

Almost surely, better pills with fewer side effects are on the way. In research laboratories scientists are busy building new synthetic hormones. They have made thousands, and among this vast number it seems probable that some will be virtually troublefree.

The debatable question of whether it would ever be desirable to suppress menstruation totally will, in all likelihood, be resolved on an individual basis. For millions of women it would be bliss to avoid monthly disability; for millions of others it might be unwise. But the really important point is this: for the first time in history there is an element of choice. A physiological function that has been a source of misery for countless women over countless thousands of years can now be controlled at will.

J. D. Ratcliff, "An End to Woman's 'Bad Days'?" *Reader's Digest*, December 1962, 73–76.

THE PILL: HOW IT IS AFFECTING
U.S. MORALS, FAMILY LIFE

What is "the pill" doing to the moral patterns of the nation?

Growing popularity of oral contraception is raising profound questions among sociologists, educators, churchmen and others.

Is the pill regarded as a license for promiscuity? Can its availability to all women of childbearing age lead to sexual anarchy? Are old fears of the social stigma of illegitimacy about to become a thing of the past?

Here is a report, based on extensive inquiry, on birth-control pills of the present and future, and what leading authorities say about the pills' possible impact on American culture.

An era of vast change in sexual morality now is developing in America.

Fear is being expressed that the nation may be heading into a time of "sexual anarchy."

Just six years ago the birth-control pill came onto the market. Today—

• College girls everywhere are talking about the pill, and many are using it. The pill is turning up in high schools, too.
• City after city is pushing distribution of the pill to welfare recipients, including unmarried women.
• Tens of thousands of Roman Catholic couples are turning to the pill as a means of practicing birth control.

These and other trends are expected to accelerate in times just ahead as laboratories perfect the long-term "contraceptive shot" and the retroactive pill which wards off pregnancy even if taken after sexual intercourse.

Result: Widespread concern is developing about the impact of the pill on morality.

Being asked are these questions: With birth control now so easy and effective, is the last vestige of sexual restraint to go out the window?

Will mating become casual and random—as among the animals?

Recently, John Alexander, general director of the Inter-Varsity Christian Fellowship, which has its headquarters in Chicago, said:

"I think it is certain that the pill will tear down the barriers for more than a few young people hitherto restrained by fear of pregnancy—and this will be even more true when the 'retroactive' pill comes on the market." . . .

Disquiet is voiced even by an official of Planned Parenthood-World Population, which actively promotes birth control. Dr. Donald B. Strauss said:

"The two great supports of sexual morality in the past—fear of disease and fear of pregnancy—have now, happily, been largely removed. . . .

"This, I submit, leaves our generation of parents with a problem that largely remains unsolved."

Early promiscuity. The dimensions of that problem are being outlined daily by signs of growing sexual promiscuity among America's young. . . .

Almost countless incidents have been reported, across the U.S., of teen-age girls in high school carrying birth control pills.

In some cases, these have been supplied by their parents. . . .

"A whole new world." As many clergymen and educators see it, the pill is becoming a major element in the crumbling of past standards of sexual morality—especially among the young. A woman teacher at a small college in upstate New York said:

"When you talk to the girls today, you're talking in a whole new world. They know how to get the pill. They think a girl is a fool not to use it if—and it's a big 'if'—she is seriously in love. Promiscuity is still frowned upon, but it's not equated with morals. It's a matter of personal pride." . . .

In the medical profession . . . some uneasiness is beginning to be felt on the problem. It is being pointed out by some physicians that a doctor could be sued by a girl's parents—or charged with contributing to the delinquency of a minor—if he prescribes the pill without her parents' consent.

As a result, some physicians are prescribing the pills for unmarried girls only on a restricted basis. For example, a Washington, D.C., gynecologist said:

"If a young woman over 18 years old came in and told me that she wanted a prescription because she was getting married, I would be inclined to give it to her. But, of course, I would have no way of knowing for sure that she really was getting married." . . .

Recently the Right Rev. Richard S. Emrich, Episcopal Bishop of Michigan, said:

"The existence of the pill opens up dangerous possibilities. . . . It provides an invitation to pre-marital sex. There must be limitations and restrictions on the use of sex if we are to remain a civilized people."

"The Pill: How It Is Affecting U.S. Morals, Family Life," *U.S. News & World Report,* July 11, 1966, 62–65.

ᘒ

"The Pill" (1975)

LORETTA LYNN

Why did American women use the pill? In 1975, Loretta Lynn, the "coal miner's daughter" who became one of the era's best-loved country music singers, explained why in her hit song "The Pill." Country music is supposed to be the most apple-pie conservative genre in American popular music; in fact, some radio stations refused to play "The Pill." But Lynn often challenged conventional expectations of women and men by singing about sensitive subjects drawn from women's experiences as abused or unwanted wives. She also did not shy away from singing about sexuality, as her tribute to the contraceptive here demonstrates.

PROBLEMS TO CONSIDER

1. How did using the pill change women's lives, according to this song? Did the song confirm or refute the effects of the pill as outlined in the *U.S. News & World Report* article?
2. According to the song, how did the pill affect the gender relations between women and men? In what ways did Lynn find the pill liberating?

You wined me and dined me, when I was your girl
Promised if I'd be your wife, you'd show me the world
But all I've seen of this ol' world is a bed and a doctor bill
I'm tearin' down your brooder house, 'cause now I've got the pill

All these years I've stayed at home, while you had all your fun
And every year that's gone by, another baby's come
There's gonna be some changes made right here on nursery hill
You've set this chicken your last time 'cause now I've got the pill

This old maternity dress I've got is goin' in the garbage
The clothes I'm wearin' from now on, won't take up so much yardage
Miniskirts, hot pants and a few little fancy frills
Yeah, I'm makin' up for all those years, since I've got the pill

I'm tired of all your crowin', how you and your hens play
While holdin' a couple in my arms, another's on the way
This chicken's done tore up her nest, and I'm ready to make a deal
And you can't afford to turn it down, 'cause you know I've got the pill

This incubator is overused, because you've kept it filled
The feelin' good comes easy now, since I've got the pill
It's gettin' dark, it's roostin' time, tonight's too good to be real
Ah but daddy don't you worry none, 'cause mama's got the pill
Ah daddy don't you worry none, 'cause mama's got the pill

Loretta Lynn, "The Pill," transcribed from Loretta Lynn, *Blue Eyed Kentucky Girl*, copyright © 1985, MCA Records Inc., MCAD-20261.

ᴐᴐ

Our Bodies, Ourselves (1973)
BOSTON WOMEN'S HEALTH BOOK COLLECTIVE

In 1969, Barbara Seaman published The Doctor's Case Against the Pill, *an exposé of the serious health risks to women who took hormonal contraceptives. Seaman, a magazine writer, demanded that drug makers and physicians inform women of the risks associated with the pill and allow them to decide for themselves whether to use it. In doing so, she directed attention to the unequal distribution of power implicit in the relation-*

ships between drug maker and drug taker, physician and patient, male doctor and female client. The pharmaceutical industry, physicians, population-control and family-planning agencies, and book reviewers ridiculed Seaman's case against the pill as sentimental and "scatterbrained." In early 1970, however, the U.S. Senate investigated her charges. The hearings eventually prompted historic regulations favoring consumers: drug makers were required to include warning labels on their products, and physicians had to obtain "informed consent" before administering treatment to their patients.

The Senate hearings also inadvertently encouraged the women's health movement of the 1970s when senators subpoenaed an all-male roster of witnesses and refused to call Seaman to testify. With network television cameras rolling, feminist protesters in the audience disrupted the hearings, demanding testimony from women taking the pill. One senator advised the "girls" to control their behavior. The protests brought national attention not only to the risks of taking hormonal contraceptives but also to the feminists' more radical critique of the male-dominated medical establishment and how it treated women's health needs. In the aftermath, one poll found that pill usage dropped by 18 percent. At the same time, the women's health movement flourished, developing a far-reaching critique of the health care industry's control of information about women's bodies. In 1971, a group of feminist women, who had been meeting in Boston for several years to discuss women's health issues, published Our Bodies, Ourselves, *a landmark health manual about, by, and for women. The book has been updated several times and still is in print; according to its publisher, total sales have exceeded 4 million copies. The following selections are from the preface to the first mass-audience edition, which appeared in 1973.*

PROBLEMS TO CONSIDER

1. What made the women's efforts to acquire knowledge about their bodies a political struggle? How did their achievement affect their consciousness of themselves?
2. Compare the discussions of women's bodies and health care in *Our Bodies, Ourselves* to those in the *Reader's Digest* article. What assumptions about women and their bodies did *Our Bodies, Ourselves* challenge?

The history of this book, *Our Bodies, Ourselves*, is lengthy and satisfying.

It began at a small discussion group on "women and their bodies" which was part of a women's conference held in Boston in the spring of 1969. These were the early days of the women's movement, one of the first gatherings of women meeting specifically to talk with other women. For many of us it was the very first time we got together with other women to talk and think about our lives and what we could do

about them. Before the conference was over some of us decided to keep on meeting as a group to continue the discussion, and so we did.

In the beginning we called the group "the doctor's group." We had all experienced similar feelings of frustration and anger toward specific doctors and the medical maze in general, and initially we wanted to do something about those doctors who were condescending, paternalistic, judgmental and non-informative. As we talked and shared our experiences with one another, we realized just how much we had to learn about our bodies. So we decided on a summer project—to research those topics which we felt were particularly pertinent to learning about our bodies, to discuss in the group what we had learned, then to write papers individually or in small groups of two or three, and finally to present the results in the fall as a course for women on women and their bodies.

As we developed the course we realized more and more that we really were capable of collecting, understanding, and evaluating medical information. Together we evaluated our reading of books and journals, our talks with doctors and friends who were medical students. We found we could discuss, question, and argue with each other in a new spirit of cooperation rather than competition. We were equally struck by how important it was for us to be able to open up with one another and share our feelings about our bodies. The process of talking was as crucial as the facts themselves. Over time the facts and feelings melted together in ways that touched us very deeply. . . .

From the very beginning of working together, first on the course that led to the book and then on the book itself, we have felt exhilarated and energized by our new knowledge. Finding out about our bodies and our bodies' needs, starting to take control over that area of our life, has released for us an energy that has overflowed into our work, our friendships, our relationships with men and women, and for some of us our marriages and our parenthood. In trying to figure out why this has had such a life-changing effect on us, we have come up with several important ways in which this kind of body education has been liberating for us and may be a starting point for the liberation of many other women.

First, we learned what we learned equally from professional sources—textbooks, medical journals, doctors, nurses—and from our own experiences. The facts were important, and we did careful research to get the information we had

not had in the past. As we brought the facts to one another we learned a good deal, but in sharing our personal experiences relating to those facts we learned still more. Once we had learned what the "experts" had to tell us, we found that we still had a lot to teach and to learn from one another. For instance, many of us had "learned" about the menstrual cycle in science or biology classes—we had perhaps even memorized the names of the menstrual hormones and what they did. But most of us did not remember much of what we had learned. This time when we read in a text that the onset of menstruation is a normal and universal occurrence in young girls from ages ten to eighteen, we started to talk about our first menstrual periods. We found that, for many of us, beginning to menstruate had not felt normal at all, but scary, embarrassing, mysterious. We realized that what we had been told about menstruation and what we had not been told, even the tone of voice it had been told in—all had had an effect on our feelings about being female. . . .

A second important result of this kind of learning is that we are better prepared to evaluate the institutions that are supposed to meet our health needs—the hospitals, clinics, doctors, medical schools, nursing schools, public health departments, Medicaid bureaucracies, and so on. For some of us it was the first time we had looked critically, and with strength, at the existing institutions serving us. The experience of learning just how little control we had over our lives and bodies, the coming together out of isolation to learn from each other in order to define what we needed, and the experience of supporting one another in demanding the changes that grew out of our developing critique—all were crucial and formative political experiences for us. We have felt our potential power as a force for political and social change.

The learning we have done while working on *Our Bodies, Ourselves* has been such a good basis for growth in other areas of life for still another reason. For women throughout the centuries, ignorance about our bodies has had one major consequence—pregnancy. Until very recently pregnancies were all but inevitable, biology was our destiny—that is, because our bodies are designed to get pregnant and give birth and lactate, that is what all or most of us did. . . . When we first started talking to each other about this we found that that old expectation had nudged most of us into a fairly rigid role of wife-and-motherhood from the moment we were born female. . . . It was not until we researched carefully and learned more about our reproductive systems, about birth-control methods and abortion, about laws governing birth control and abortion, not until we put all this information together with what it meant to us to be female, did we begin to feel that we could truly set out to control whether and when we would have babies. . . .

There is a fourth reason. . . . For us, body education is core education. Our bodies are the physical bases from which we move out into the world; ignorance, uncertainty—even, at worst, shame—about our physical selves create in us an alienation from ourselves that keeps us from being the whole people that we could be. . . . Learning to understand, accept, and be responsible for our physical selves, we are freed of some of these preoccupations and can start to use our untapped energies. Our image of ourselves is on a firmer base, we can be better friends and better lovers, better *people*, more self-confident, more autonomous, stronger, and more whole.

Boston Women's Health Book Collective, *Our Bodies, Ourselves: A Book by and for Women* (New York: Simon and Schuster, 1973), 1–3.

ᔛ

ᔛ *Keep America Beautiful:* *Fashioning the New Environmental Consciousness* ᔛ

Until the mid-1950s, environmental concerns were mostly confined to debates about the fate of wilderness areas of the public domain, especially in the mountain, old-growth forest, and desert regions of western federal lands. Experts in government bureaucracies, private "naturalist" groups, and business interests wrangled over how to balance the desire to preserve parklands and wilderness areas in an unspoiled state with the determination of farmers, ranchers, loggers, extractive industries, and tourists to use the federal domain for their own purposes. The paradoxical determination to preserve and to manage nature still shapes debates about the fate of the natural environment, although the scope of concern expanded dramatically in the 1960s and 1970s. By that time, people had begun to worry about the less direct but vastly more destructive effects of unchecked population growth and industrial expansion in the United States since 1941. Initially, the new movements were sparked by federal dam projects in the West, which flooded wilderness desert areas with artificial lakes to provide water to sprawling new populations in California and the Southwest.

By the 1960s, the problems were no longer confined to the vanishing wilderness; they encompassed American life in its totality. Residents of urban areas were choking on the air they breathed; dead fish floated in nearby rivers and estuaries; sewage contamination closed beaches to swimmers; middle-class kitchens were stocked with harmful pesticides. Industries were largely unregulated in deciding where and how they dumped their waste materials. In 1969, when Cleveland's Cuyahoga River briefly "burst into flames," the flaming waterway symbolized the polluted nation. "Some river!" *Time* magazine gasped. "Chocolate-brown, . . . it oozes rather than flows." Individual people were no better than industrial dumpers, as they littered parks, beaches, and streets with the refuse of a throwaway consumer economy. The new environmentalism (itself a new word in the American reform vocabulary) identified progress itself—its hallmark industries and consumer conveniences— as the principal danger to the quality of life that Americans regarded as their birthright. No person or place was safe from the effects of pollution.

The mounting ecological disasters engendered a new environmental conscious-ness. This broadly shared sensibility was critical of American culture for its waste-fulness and detachment from nature, yet optimistic that the destruction could be reversed. Environmentalism changed the terms in which ordinary Americans, poli-cymakers in Washington and state capitals, and business interests debated the best way to protect and use the American Eden. Did Americans have to sacrifice the benefits and pleasures of life in an advanced industrial and technological society, or could the air, water, and food necessary for life be made safe by regulating industries and developing new and cleaner technologies? Could the environment be saved by changing people's behaviors or lifestyles, or was the American way of life itself the root of the problem? The documents in this section explore how Americans under-stood and sought to address the environmental crisis of the 1970s.

Silent Spring (1962)

RACHEL CARSON

The 1962 publication of Rachel Carson's Silent Spring *was a landmark in recent American history. Her book generated a popular reexamination of the culture of abundance, the costs of suburban affluence, and the price of technological progress. Carson brought the environmental crisis—the "toxicity of modern life," as one historian has described it— directly into the fabric and consciousness of everyday life in the United States. Carson was a trained scientist with a master's degree in zoology who worked for the federal Department of the Interior. In the 1940s and 1950s, she grew increasingly alarmed by the environmental impact of the widespread use of synthetic pesticides and herbicides. Many of these substances—including DDT, an insecticide used to kill typhus-causing lice—had been employed during World War II. Afterward, chemical manufacturers and the U.S. Department of Agriculture (USDA) marketed such products to farmers, to public wilderness and land-management agencies, and to suburban homeowners who were replacing rural fields and forest with lawns of manicured grass. The determination to wipe out weeds and bugs, said Carson, fomented a "war on nature" that reflected the dangerously misguided belief that human beings could control or harness nature. She contended that the use of such poisons caused unexpected consequences as they traveled through the food chain, harming everything they touched, including songbirds. Where had they gone? she asked, explaining the title of her book.*

The book's influence was based on more than just the persuasive information she compiled against the chemical industry and its support network in the USDA and academic science. Carson translated technical information into stories that used familiar cultural images and conventions to unsettle confidence in the inviolable safety of domestic life. She exploited anxieties about the atomic bomb and the invisible dangers of radiation poisoning. The following selections include her introduction and a later section on the toxicity of ordinary household chemicals.

PROBLEMS TO CONSIDER

1. What effects did Carson try to achieve with her introduction, entitled "A Fable for Tomorrow"? How did her "fable" make the image of a "silent spring" so disturbing? Did such imagery draw, consciously or unconsciously, on anxieties stemming from the Cold War?
2. Did the section on poisons undermine assumptions about middle-class domesticity? Was Carson's critique narrowly directed at the use of pesticides, or was she also critical of modern lifestyles in the United States?

A FABLE FOR TOMORROW

There was once a town in the heart of America where all life seemed to live in harmony with its surroundings. The town lay in the midst of a checkerboard of prosperous farms, with fields of grain and hillsides of orchards where, in spring, white clouds of bloom drifted above the green fields. In autumn, oak and maple and birch set up a blaze of color that flamed and flickered across a backdrop of pines. Then foxes barked in the hills and deer silently crossed the fields, half hidden in the mists of the fall mornings.

Along the roads, laurel, viburnum and alder, great ferns and wildflowers delighted the traveler's eye through much of the year. Even in winter the roadsides were places of beauty, where countless birds came to feed on the berries and on the seed heads of the dried weeds rising above the snow. The countryside was, in fact, famous for the abundance and variety of its bird life, and when the flood of migrants was pouring through in spring and fall people traveled from great distances to observe them. . . . So it had been from the days many years ago when the first settlers raised their houses, sank their wells, and built their barns.

Then a strange blight crept over the area and everything began to change. Some evil spell had settled on the community: mysterious maladies swept the flocks of chickens; the cattle and sheep sickened and died. Everywhere was a shadow of death. The farmers spoke of much illness among their families. In the town the doctors had become more and more puzzled by new kinds of sickness appearing among their patients. There had been several sudden and unexplained deaths, not only among adults but even among children, who would be stricken suddenly while at play and die within a few hours.

There was a strange stillness. The birds, for example—where had they gone? Many people spoke of them, puzzled and disturbed. The feeding stations in the backyards were deserted. The few birds seen anywhere were moribund; they trembled violently and could not fly. It was a spring without voices. On the mornings that had once throbbed with the dawn chorus of robins, catbirds, doves, jays, wrens, and scores of other bird voices there was now no sound; only silence lay over the fields and woods and marsh. . . .

In the gutters under the eaves and between the shingles of the roofs, a white granular powder still showed a few patches; some weeks before it had fallen like snow upon the roofs and the lawns, the fields and streams.

No witchcraft, no enemy action had silenced the rebirth of new life in this stricken world. The people had done it themselves.

This town does not actually exist, but it might easily have a thousand counterparts in America or elsewhere in the world. I know of no community that has experienced all the misfortunes I describe. Yet every one of these disasters has actually happened somewhere, and many real communities have already suffered a substantial number of them. A grim specter has crept upon us almost unnoticed, and this imagined tragedy may easily become a stark reality we all shall know.

What has already silenced the voices of spring in countless towns in America? . . .

BEYOND THE DREAMS OF THE BORGIAS

The contamination of our world is not alone a matter of mass spraying. Indeed, for most of us this is of less importance than the innumerable small-scale exposures to which we are subjected day by day, year after year. Like the constant dripping of water that in turn wears away the hardest stone, this birth-to-death contact with dangerous chemicals may in the end prove disastrous. Each of these recurrent exposures, no matter how slight, contributes to the progressive buildup of chemicals in our bodies and so to cumulative poisoning. Probably no person is immune to contact with this spreading contamination unless he lives in the most isolated situation imaginable. Lulled by the soft sell and the hidden persuader, the average citizen is seldom aware of the deadly materials with which he is surrounding himself; indeed, he may not realize he is using them at all.

So thoroughly has the age of poisons become established that anyone may walk into a store and, without questions being asked, buy substances of far greater death-dealing power than the medicinal drug for which he may be required to sign a "poison book" in the pharmacy next door. A few minutes' research in any supermarket is enough to alarm the most stouthearted customer—provided, that is, he has even a rudimentary knowledge of the chemicals presented for his choice.

If a huge skull and crossbones were suspended above the insecticide department the customer might at least enter it with the respect normally accorded death-dealing materials. But instead the display is homey and cheerful, and, with the pickles and olives across the aisle and the bath and laundry soaps adjoining, the rows upon rows of insecticides are displayed. Within easy reach of a child's exploring hand are chemicals in *glass* containers. If dropped to the floor by a child or careless adult everyone nearby could be splashed with the same chemical that has sent spraymen using it into convulsions. These hazards of course follow the purchaser right into his home. A can of a mothproofing material containing DDD, for example, carries in very fine print the warning that its contents are under pressure and that it may burst if exposed to heat or open flame. A common insecticide for household use, including assorted uses in the kitchen, is chlordane. Yet the Food and Drug Administration's chief pharmacologist has declared the hazard of living in a house sprayed with chlordane to be "very great." Other household preparations contain the even more toxic dieldrin.

Use of poisons in the kitchen is made both attractive and easy. Kitchen shelf paper, white or tinted to match one's color scheme, may be impregnated with insecticide, not merely on one but on both sides. Manufacturers offer us do-it-yourself booklets on how to kill bugs. With push-button ease, one may send a fog of dieldrin into the most inaccessible nooks and crannies of cabinets, corners, and baseboards.

If we are troubled by mosquitoes, chiggers, or other insect pests on our persons we have a choice of innumerable lotions, creams, and sprays for application to clothing or skin. Although we are warned that some of these will dissolve varnish, paint, and synthetic fabrics, we are presumably to infer that the human skin is impervious to chemicals. . . .

We can polish our floors with a wax guaranteed to kill any insect that walks over it. We can hang strips impregnated with the chemical lindane in our closets and garment bags or place them in our bureau drawers for a half year's freedom from worry over moth damage. The advertisements contain no suggestion that lindane is dangerous. . . .

Gardening is now firmly linked with the super poisons. Every hardware store, garden-supply shop, and supermarket has rows of insecticides for every conceivable horticultural situation. Those who fail to make wide use of this array of lethal sprays and dusts are by implication remiss, for almost every newspaper's garden page and the majority of the gardening magazines take their use for granted. . . .

Little is done, however, to warn the gardener or homeowner that he is handling extremely dangerous materials. On the contrary, a constant stream of new gadgets make it easier to use poisons on lawn and garden—and increase the gardener's contact with them. . . .

The mores of suburbia now dictate that crabgrass must go at whatever cost. Sacks containing chemicals designed to rid the lawn of such despised vegetation have become almost a status symbol. These weed-killing chemicals are sold under brand names that never suggest their identity or nature. To learn that they contain chlordane or dieldrin one must read exceedingly fine print placed on the least conspicuous part of the sack. The descriptive literature that may be picked up in any hardware- or garden-supply store seldom if ever reveals the true hazard involved in handling or applying the material. Instead, the typical illustration portrays a happy family scene, father and son smilingly preparing to apply the chemical to the lawn, small children tumbling over the grass with a dog.

Rachel Carson, *Silent Spring* (Boston: Houghton Mifflin, 1962), 1–3, 173–78.

᷒

Advertisement for Earth Day (1970)

The first Earth Day observance was held in April 1970 and was organized by environmental activists with the support of Senator Gaylord Nelson of Wisconsin. From the start, the designers of the event disavowed militancy, aiming instead to spread environmental awareness and concern among the broad middle of the American population. They succeeded. Earth Day attracted some 20 million participants across the nation. The popular response added fuel to the fire under Congress, which passed the Clean Air Act several months later and approved legislation establishing Environmental Protection Agency later that year. The following ad, paid for by Environmental Teach-In, Inc., announced the plans for a "national day of environmental education," or Earth Day, in early 1970.

PROBLEMS TO CONSIDER

1. How did Earth Day's organizers characterize the environmental crisis? According to them, who was to blame for the crisis?
2. How effective was the message in appealing to what one organizer called its targeted national constituency—the middle class?

April 22. Earth Day.

A disease has infected our country. It has brought smog to Yosemite, dumped garbage in the Hudson, sprayed DDT in our food, and left our cities in decay. Its carrier is man.

The weak are already dying. Trees by the Pacific. Fish in our streams and lakes. Birds and crops and sheep. And people.

On April 22 we start to reclaim the environment we have wrecked.

April 22 is the Environmental Teach-In, a day of environmental action.

Hundreds of communities and campuses across the country are already committed.

It is a phenomenon that grows as you read this.

Earth Day is a commitment to make life better, not just bigger and faster; To provide real rather than rhetorical solutions.

It is a day to re-examine the ethic of individual progress at mankind's expense.

It is a day to challenge the corporate and governmental leaders who promise change, but who short change the necessary programs.

It is a day for looking beyond tomorrow. April 22 seeks a future worth living.

April 22 seeks a future. . . .

No list of famous names accompanies this ad to support our plea, though many offered without our asking.

Big names don't save the environment. People do.

Help make April 22 burgeon.

For you. For us. For our children.

Advertisement for Earth Day, *New York Times*, January 18, 1970, 13.

⤳

Advertisement for Keep America Beautiful Foundation (c. 1971)

In the early 1960s, Keep America Beautiful (KAB), an organization founded "to develop and promote a national cleanliness ethic," and the Ad Council, an association of advertising industry professionals who donated their services in designing public-service ads, teamed up to develop a campaign against littering. Early television commercials featured "Susan Spotless," a little girl in a white dress who scolds her father when he thoughtlessly tosses trash on the ground: "Daddy, you forgot; every litter bit hurts!" Although that commercial is long forgotten, the one the Ad Council developed for KAB in 1970–1971, featuring the "crying Indian," is legendary in the ad industry and has been celebrated as one of the most effective TV commercials ever created. The Indian was played by Iron Eyes Cody, an actor who claimed to be Cherokee (actually, he was Italian American) and became a cultural icon as a result of the KAB campaign. In the television spot, Cody, clad in the buckskin of a Hollywood "noble savage," paddles a canoe down an American waterway, moving from a scene of natural beauty to the horrors of modern civilization. The movement through time and space is marked first by litter floating past and then by a shore lined with heavy industries belching smoke. As Cody steps onto a filthy beach, the voice-over announces, "Some people have a deep abiding respect for the natural beauty that was once this country." The Indian walks up to a highway choked with traffic, and as a bag of trash hurled from a car window bursts at his feet, the voice-over continues: "And some people don't." The Indian turns his gaze from the highway to look America in the eye. The camera zooms in on his face to show a tear welling up and dropping under his right eye: "People start pollution. People can stop it." The commercial became so well known that KAB print ads, such as the one shown here, had only to include the image of Cody's tearful eye; no explanation was necessary.

PROBLEMS TO CONSIDER

1. Why was a Native American man a potent symbol to awaken Americans to the problems of pollution? What beliefs about Native Americans did viewers have to share in order for the commercial's message to come across?
2. Compare the ad's message with that of Earth Day. Why did the ad resonate so effectively with Americans?

Pollution: It's a crying shame

But it won't be, if we start doing something about the problems. Things as easy as using a hand mower if your lawn is small. Or not overtaxing sewage systems by running water needlessly. Or actively supporting programs to clean up our rivers, lakes and streams. Let's restore the natural beauty that was once this country.

**People start pollution.
People can stop it.**

Keep America Beautiful

advertising contributed
for the public good

(1971 *Crying Indian* advertisement courtesy of Keep America Beautiful, Inc. www.kab.com.)

"*Forward!*" *in* Ecodefense: A Field Guide to Monkeywrenching (1985)

EDWARD ABBEY

Earth Day and the "Crying Indian" campaign helped bring together broad national constituencies founded on a new environmental consciousness and faith that people, working together, could stop the madness. In the eyes of more angry critics, however, such demonstrations failed to address the real menace to the environment, which was modern America itself. This critique was advanced by writer Edward Abbey, who in 1975 published The Monkey Wrench Gang, *one of the decade's iconic texts, a satirical and comic adventure tale and an inspiration to succeeding generations of outraged environmentalists. The background to the novel was Glen Canyon Dam (completed by 1964), a federal project on the Utah-Arizona border that backed up the Colorado River to create a reservoir (Lake Powell) for water-hungry urban populations and industries in the region. The dam flooded Glen Canyon, a region of unmatched (and unprotected) natural beauty. Abbey's novel imagines a vigilante campaign of vengeance against the dam, led by a posse of eco-guerrillas. The book introduced the term "monkeywrenching," or nonviolent ecological sabotage. Abbey, who died in 1989, claimed that he never meant to advocate actual sabotage; he was only writing a story. But in the 1980s and 1990s, environmental militants read him with dead seriousness. When they chained themselves to redwoods, toppled highway billboards, or burned down coastal mansions, they believed they were monkeywrenching. In 1985, Abbey wrote a foreword to a monkeywrenching how-to manual for the "serious saboteur." The editors—Dave Foreman and Bill Haywood—maintained that the book's detailed instructions describing, for instance, how to disable massive earth-moving machinery by pouring sand into its fuel tanks were "for entertainment purposes only."*

PROBLEMS TO CONSIDER

1. What was the significance of Abbey's description of monkeywrenching as a tactic of "self-defense" of the American "wilderness home"? Were monkeywrenchers a righteous militia or a band of terrorists?
2. Compare the tone of Abbey's statement with that of the Earth Day and KAB projects. What distinguished Abbey's critique? Was it more radical?

If a stranger batters your door down with an axe, threatens your family and yourself with deadly weapons, and proceeds to loot your home of whatever he wants, he is committing what is universally recognized—by law and morality—as a crime. In such a situation the householder has both the right and the obligation to defend himself, his family, and his property by whatever means are necessary. This right and this obliga- tion is universally recognized, justified and even praised by all civilized human communities. Self-defense against attack is one of the basic laws not only of human society but of life itself, not only of human life but of all life.

The American wilderness, what little remains, is now undergoing exactly such an assault. Dave Foreman has summarized the character and scale of the assault in the first chapter of this excellent and essential book. With bulldozer, earth mover, chainsaw and dynamite the international timber, mining and beef industries are invading our public lands—property of all Americans—bashing their way into our forests, mountains and rangelands and looting them for everything they can get away with. This for the sake of short-term profits in the corporate sector and multi-million dollar annual salaries for the three-piece-suited gangsters (M.B.A., Harvard, Yale, University of Tokyo, *et alia*) who control and manage these bandit enterprises. Cheered on, naturally, by *Time*, *Newsweek*, and the *Wall Street Journal*, actively encouraged by those jellyfish Government agencies which are supposed to protect the public lands, and as always aided and abetted in every way possible by the quisling politicians of our Western states (such as Babbitt, DeConcini, Goldwater, Hatch, Garn, Symms, Hansen, Wallop, Domenici—to name but a few) who would sell the graves of their own mothers if there's a quick buck in the deal, over or under the table, what do they care.

Representative democracy in the United States has broken down. Our legislators do not represent those who elected them but rather the minority who finance their political campaigns and who control the organs of communication—the Tee Vee, the newspapers, the billboards, the radio—that have made politics a game for the rich only. Representative government in the USA represents money not people and therefore has forfeited our allegiance and moral support. We owe it nothing but the taxation it extorts from us under threats of seizure of property, or prison, or in some cases already, when resisted, a sudden and violent death by gunfire.

Such is the nature and structure of the industrial megamachine (in Lewis Mumford's term) which is now attacking the American wilderness. That wilderness is our ancestral home, the primordial homeland of all living creatures including the human, and the present final dwelling place of such noble beings as the grizzly bear, the mountain lion, the eagle and the condor, the moose and the elk and the pronghorn antelope, the redwood tree, the yellowpine, the bristlecone pine, even the aspen, and yes, why not say it?, the streams, waterfalls, rivers, the very bedrock itself of our hills, canyons, deserts, mountains.

For many of us, perhaps for most of us, the wilderness is as much our home, or a lot more so, than the wretched little stucco boxes, plywood apartments, and wallboard condominiums in which we are mostly confined by the insatiable demands of an overcrowded and ever-expanding industrial culture. And if the wilderness is our true home, and if it is threatened with invasion, pillage and destruction—as it certainly is—then we have the right to defend that home, as we would our private rooms, by whatever means are necessary. (An Englishman's home is his castle; an American's home is his favorite fishing stream, his favorite mountain range, his favorite desert canyon, his favorite swamp or patch of woods or God-created lake.)

The majority of the American people have demonstrated on every possible occasion that they support the ideal of wilderness preservation; even our politicians are forced by popular opinion to *pretend* to support the idea; as they have learned, a vote against wilderness is a vote against their own re-election. We are justified in defending our homes—our private home and public home—not only by common law and common morality but also by common belief. We are the majority; they—the greedy and powerful—are the minority.

How best defend our wilderness home? Well, that is a matter of strategy, tactics and technique, which is what this little book is about. Dave Foreman explains the principles of ecological defense in the complete, compact and conclusive pages of his short introduction. I can think of nothing I could add nor of anything I would subtract; he says exactly what needs to be said, no more and no less.

I am happy to endorse the publication of *Ecodefense*. Never was such a book so needed, by so many, for such good reason, as here and now. Tomorrow might well be too late. This is a book that will fit handily in any saddlebag, in any creel, in any backpack, in any river runner's ammo can—and in any picnicker's picnic basket. No good American should ever go into the woods again without this book and, for example, a hammer and a few pounds of 60-penny nails. Spike a few trees now and then whenever you enter an area condemned to chainsaw massacre by Louisiana Pacific and its affiliated subsidiary the U.S. Forest Service. You won't hurt the trees; they'll be grateful for the protection; and you may save the forest. My Aunt Emma back in West Virginia has been enjoying this pleasant exercise for years. She swears by it. It's good for the trees, it's good for the woods, it's good for the earth, and it's good for the human soul. Spread the word—and **carry on!**

Edward Abbey, "Forward!" in *Ecodefense: A Field Guide to Monkeywrenching*, edited by Dave Foreman and Bill Haywood (1985; repr., Chico, Calif.: Abbzug Press, 1993), 3–4.

᧞

᧞ *The Virus in Our System:* ᧞ *AIDS and the Culture Wars* ᧞

The AIDS outbreak in the United States in the early 1980s was caused by the human immunodeficiency virus (HIV). The virus is spread through the exchange of bodily fluids, such as blood or semen, most commonly during sexual intercourse or when intravenous drug users share needles. Public health officials and politicians either ignored or avoided the subject of AIDS before the mid-1980s, in part because they did not want to identify themselves with the population it struck most visibly: homosexual men. Such neglect meant that even as the terror of infection grew, AIDS was mistakenly regarded as a "gay disease" that was irrelevant to the welfare of the heterosexual majority. This misperception persisted even as infection and death spread widely through the American population and caused a national public health crisis by the end of the decade. At the same time, cases among heterosexual men and women around the world spiked to disastrous levels, especially in developing regions. In the United States, about 550,000 persons had died of AIDS through 2005. Today, there is no cure for AIDS, but in the developed world, mortality has slowed with the use of antiretroviral drug therapy (ART). In the developing world (especially on the African continent), however, drug prices limit the availability of ART, and the rates of HIV infection and AIDS death remain astoundingly high. The Joint United Nations Programme on HIV/AIDS estimates that global deaths from AIDS in 2003 alone reached 2.9 million.

The deadliness of AIDS shattered the widely shared confidence that modern medicine had conquered sexually transmitted diseases, such as syphilis and gonorrhea. "Our species," the late paleontologist Stephen Jay Gould grimly observed in 1987, "has not won its independence from nature, and we cannot do all that we can dream." Its spread in the United States, however, was not a natural phenomenon. Rather, the AIDS epidemic began amid particular historical social, cultural, and technological changes, all of which affected how and among whom it spread and how Americans understood the disease. The outbreak of AIDS among gay men resulted from the changes associated with the weakened traditional constraints on sexual activity. Many young women and men were having casual sexual relations with little concern for pregnancy, disease, or social sanction. For many gay men, this sexual freedom was no less important than their demands for social recognition and legal protection from discrimination.

AIDS challenged these behaviors and views by adding the risk of deadly infection to sexual freedom. It also focused attention on modern sexuality, fueling a divisive public debate that marked out the fault lines of the 1980s "culture wars." The term refers to the battles between newly organized and politically active conservative groups (many of them led by evangelical Christians, a group that played an important part in Ronald Reagan's election in 1980) and their more secular opponents (Norman Lear's People for the American Way, for example). The issues over which they fought—abortion and women's rights, social welfare programs, prayer in public schools, rising crime rates, federal support of the arts, affirmative action— highlighted the fact that many Americans remained deeply troubled by the social and cultural changes of the 1960s and blamed the social crises of the time on what they perceived as the breakdown of authority and the decline of personal responsibility. The investigation of AIDS, therefore, involved not only the study of a mysterious virus but also a debate about the character of sexuality itself. The documents in this section, most of them from the critical years 1987–1991, focus on debates about the meaning of AIDS and the actions taken by the victims themselves, which were influential in shifting public perception and fears.

The Normal Heart (1985)
LARRY KRAMER

Remarks on Amendment No. 956 (1987)
SENATOR JESSE HELMS

Was AIDS a medical condition, that is, an illness that needed treatment? or a biological phenomenon caused by a virus that did not discriminate in choosing its host? or a consequence of personal morality that reflected the good or bad choices individuals made? In other words, what or who was to blame for AIDS: the infected persons or the virus? As scientists such as Stephen Jay Gould saw it, diseases are an ordinary part of nature, and epidemics have periodically marked human history, often disastrously. From this perspective, "AIDS represents the ordinary workings of biology, not an irrational or diabolical plague with a moral meaning." Nonetheless, scientific detachment rarely governed the larger debate about the causes, consequences, and treatment of AIDS in the United States, especially once homosexual men and women organized to secure adequate health services for stricken populations and to force public authorities to confront the epidemic. Their demands generated bitter political conflicts over policies that determined federal drug regulations and development, health insurance and medical treatment for infected persons,

*and programs (such as needle exchange for users of illegal intravenous drugs) for prevent-
ing further spread of the disease.*

*Two perspectives are included here. The first is a scene from Larry Kramer's celebrated
play* The Normal Heart, *which was produced in 1985 at New York City's Public Theater. Kramer, a gay activist who in 1982 helped found the Gay Men's Health Crisis (one
of the earliest organizations of its kind), is a contentious and uncompromising figure. In
person and in his drama, he pushed fellow homosexuals no less than public authorities to
take decisive action against the disease. In this scene, set in the early 1980s when little
was known about the disease, a no-nonsense physician, Emma (who is wheelchair bound
from polio), demands that Ned (a character based on Kramer himself) tell the city's
homosexuals to restrain their sexual freedom. Many people, including conservative leaders such as Senator Jesse Helms (R-N.C.), believed that AIDS was spread, not by unsafe
sex, but by the immorality of homosexuality. In the Senate speech reprinted here, Helms
condemns an erotic comic promoting safe sex that was published by the Gay Men's Health
Crisis, apparently using federal funds. Helms's amendment, which passed 94–2, banned
federal money for AIDS projects that "promote or encourage . . . homosexual activities."*

PROBLEMS TO CONSIDER

1. How did Kramer and Helms understand the relation of the disease-causing
   virus to sexuality in general and to homosexuality in particular? How could sexual freedom and public health be reconciled?
2. Both Kramer and Helms, from differing perspectives, advocated behavioral
   changes as a defense against the AIDS epidemic. What were their major points
   of agreement or disagreement?

THE NORMAL HEART

NED: How many of us do you think already
have the virus in our system?

EMMA: In this city—easily over half of all gay
men.

NED: So we're just walking time bombs—waiting for whatever it is that sets us off.

EMMA: Yes. And before a vaccine can be discovered almost every gay man will have been
exposed. Ned, your organization is worth-
less! I went up and down Christopher Street
last night and all I saw was guys going in the
bars alone and coming out with somebody.
And outside the baths, all I saw was lines of
guys going in. And what is this stupid publication you finally put out? (*She holds up a
pamphlet.*) After all we've talked about? You

leave too much margin for intelligence. Why
aren't you telling them, bluntly, stop! Every
day you don't tell them, more people infect
each other.

NED: Don't lecture me. I'm on your side.
Remember?

EMMA: Don't be on my side! I don't need you
on my side. Make your side shape up. I've
seen 238 cases—me: one doctor. You make
it sound like there's nothing worse going
around than measles.

NED: They wouldn't print what I wrote. Again.

EMMA: What do you mean "they"? Who's they?
I thought you and Bruce were the leaders.

NED: Now we've got a board. You need a board
of directors when you become tax-exempt. It
was a pain in the ass finding anyone to serve

on it at all! I called every prominent gay man I could get to. Forget it! Finally, what we put together turns out to be a bunch as timid as Bruce. And every time Bruce doesn't agree with me, he puts it to a board vote.

EMMA: And you lose.

NED: *(Nods.)* Bruce is in the closet; Mickey works for the Health Department; he starts shaking every time I criticize them—they won't even put out leaflets listing all the symptoms; Richard, Dick, and Lennie owe their jobs somehow to the mayor; Dan is a schoolteacher; we're not allowed to say his last name out loud; the rest are just a bunch of disco dumbies. I warned you this was not a community that has its best interests at heart.

EMMA: But this is death.

NED: And the board doesn't want any sex recommendations at all. No passing along anything that isn't a hundred percent certain.

EMMA: You must tell them that's wrong! Nothing is a hundred percent certain in science, so you won't be saying anything.

NED: I think that's the general idea.

EMMA: Then why did you bother to start an organization at all?

NED: Now they've decided they only want to take care of patients—crisis counseling, support groups, home attendants . . . I know that's important, too. But I thought I was starting with a bunch of Ralph Naders and Green Berets, and the first instant they have to take a stand on a political issue and fight, almost in front of my eyes they turn into a bunch of nurses' aides.

EMMA: You've got to warn the living, protect the healthy, help them keep on living. I'll take care of the dying.

NED: They keep yelling at me that I can't expect an entire world to suddenly stop making love. And now I've got to tell them there's absolutely no such thing as safe sex . . .

EMMA: I don't consider going to the baths and promiscuous sex making love. I consider it the equivalent of eating junk food, and you can lay off it for a while. And, yes, I do expect it, and you get them to come sit in my office any day of the week and they'd expect it, too. Get a VCR, rent a porn film, and use your hands!

NED: Why are you yelling at me for what I'm not doing? What the f--k is your side doing? Where's the g-dd----d AMA in all of this? The government has not started one single test tube of research. Where's the board of directors of your very own hospital? You have so many patients you haven't got rooms for them, and you've got to make Felix well. . . . So what am I yelling at you for?

EMMA: Who's Felix? Who is Felix?

NED: I introduced you to him at that Health Forum you spoke at.

EMMA: You've taken a lover?

NED: We live together. Emma, I've never been so much in love in my life. I've never been in love. Late Friday night he showed me this purple spot on the bottom of his foot. Maybe it isn't it. Maybe it's some sort of something else. It could be, couldn't it? Maybe I'm over-reacting. There's so much death around. Can you see him tomorrow? I know you're booked up for weeks. But could you?

EMMA: Tell him to call me first thing tomorrow. Seven-thirty. I'll fit him in.

NED: Thank you.

EMMA: God d--n you!

NED: I know I should have told you.

EMMA: What's done is done.

NED: What are we supposed to do—be with nobody ever? Well, it's not as easy as you might think. *(She wheels herself directly in front of him.)* Oh, Emma, I'm so sorry.

EMMA: Don't be. Polio is a virus, too. I caught it three months before the Salk vaccine was announced. Nobody gets polio anymore.

NED: Were you in an iron lung?

EMMA: For a while. But I graduated from college and from medical school first in my class. They were terrified of me. The holy terror in the wheelchair. Still are. I scare the s--t out of people.

NED: I think I do, too.

EMMA: Learn how to use it. It can be very useful. Don't need everybody's love and approval. *(He embraces her impulsively; she comforts him.)* You've got to get out there on the line more than ever now.

NED: We finally have a meeting at City Hall tomorrow.

EMMA: Good. You take care of the city—I'll take care of Felix.

NED: I'm afraid to be with him; I'm afraid to be without him; I'm afraid the cure won't come in time; I'm afraid of my anger; I'm a terrible leader and a useless lover. . . . *(He holds on to her again. Then he kisses her, breaks away from her, grabs his coat, and leaves. Emma is alone.)*

Larry Kramer, *The Normal Heart*, act 2, scene 8, in *The Normal Heart; and, The Destiny of Me* (New York: Grove Press, 2000), 69–73.

SENATOR JESSE HELMS'S REMARKS

Mr. President, the amendment . . . will offer some assurance that the hard-earned tax dollars of the American people are not to be used to perpetuate the AIDS problem. Specifically, my amendment states that any funds authorized under this act shall not be used to promote, condone, or encourage sexual activity outside a sexually monogamous marriage, including homosexual activity, or the intravenous use of illegal drugs. . . .

This Senator was naive enough at one time to believe that AIDS education meant simply telling people about the deadly AIDS virus. How wrong I was!

[Recently] I received a copy of some AIDS comic books that are being distributed by the Gay Men's Health Crisis, Inc., of New York City, an organization which has received $674,679 in Federal dollars for so-called AIDS education and information. These comic books told the story, in graphic detail, of the sexual encounter of two homosexual men.

The comic books do not encourage and change any of the perverted sexual behavior. In fact, the comic book promotes sodomy and the homosexual lifestyle as an acceptable alternative in American society. . . .

These comic books . . . were defended . . . [as] a valid method of educating homosexuals. I do not agree. . . . I believe that if the American people saw these books, they would be on the verge of revolt. . . .

So . . . I went down to the White House and I visited with the President. . . .

The President opened the [comic] book, looked at a couple of pages, closed it up, and shook his head, and hit his desk with his fist. . . .

In 1966 . . . the Gay Men's Health Crisis . . . grant proposal . . . laid out in great detail how the money would be spent. Let me read the grantees' statement of the problem:

As gay men have reaffirmed their gay identity through sexual expression, recommendations to change sexual behavior may be seen as oppressive. For many, safe sex has been equated with boring, unsatisfying sex. Meaningful alternatives are often not realized. These perceived barriers must be considered and alternatives to high-risk practices promoted in the implementation of AIDS risk-reduction education.

. . . I am not a goody-goody two-shoes. I have lived a long time. I have seen a lot of things. . . . But every Christian, religious, moral ethic within me cries out to do something. . . .

We can talk about condoms and clean needles until we are blue in the face, but until we are ready and willing to discourage and do our dead level best to eliminate the types of activities which have caused the spread of the AIDS epidemic, I do not believe we are ever going to solve it. . . .

Think about it. . . . Every AIDS case can be traced back to a homosexual act. A hemophiliac who contracts AIDS from a blood bank has gotten it from a homosexual with AIDS who contributed blood or a heterosexual infected by an infected bisexual. For the prostitute, she got it from an infected man who had had sexual relations with a bisexual or a homosexual. For the drug addict, somewhere along the line the needle has been used by a homosexual or a bisexual man or a heterosexual woman infected by a bisexual or homosexual. Heterosexuals are infected only from bisexuals or other heterosexuals who have had sexual relations with bisexuals.

So it seems quite elementary that until we make up our minds to start insisting on distributing educational materials which emphasize abstinence outside of a sexually monogamous marriage — including abstinence from homosexual activity and . . . from intravenous use of illegal drugs — and discourage the types of behavior which brought on the AIDS epidemic in the first place, we will simply be adding fuel to a raging fire which is killing a lot of people. And . . . this will take courage. It will force this country to slam the door on the wayward, warped sexual revolution which has ravaged this Nation for the past quarter of a century.

Senator Jesse Helms, remarks on Amendment No. 956, October 14, 1987, in *Congressional Record* 133, pt. 20: 27752–54.

ঽ

Interview with Gregg Bordowitz (2002)

In 1987, Larry Kramer and other AIDS activists were outraged at the refusal of public authorities to respond to the health crisis, the growing public hostility toward AIDS victims, and fellow homosexuals' reluctance to take bold action to force the government's hand or to protect themselves. President Ronald Reagan, for the first six years of the epidemic, never publicly mentioned AIDS. The Supreme Court, in its Bowers v. Hardwick *decision in 1986, had upheld Georgia's antisodomy law, a ruling that many AIDS activists believed only encouraged proposals to quarantine HIV-infected persons. In 1988, a public opinion poll found that 60 percent of Americans had "no" or "not much" sympathy for persons who had contracted HIV from homosexual sex.*

In this atmosphere of hostile neglect and timid silence, activists formed ACT UP (AIDS Coalition to Unleash Power), a militant "direct action" group that used the nonviolent tactics of the civil rights movement to embolden AIDS activism and to garner sympathetic public attention. The organization involved homosexual men as well as women and included many New Yorkers who worked in the arts and theater, public relations, and advertising and thus were skilled at manipulating images and performances to attract mass-media attention. From their first demonstrations on Wall Street in 1987, ACT UP demanded massive public education and action to stop the spread of the disease, bans on discriminating against HIV-positive persons, and a "coordinated, comprehensive, and compassionate national policy on AIDS." On October 11, 1988, ACT UP "took over" the headquarters of the Food and Drug Administration (FDA) near Washington to force the agency to speed the approval of AIDS treatments, which were bogged down in regulatory procedures while thousands were dying. The dramatic demonstration generated international media attention and heightened public pressure on the FDA, which was forced to change its handling of AIDS-related drugs. The action is described here in an oral interview with Gregg Bordowitz, a principal organizer of the demonstration. Bordowitz places his involvement with ACT UP in the context of the evolution of his identity as a gay man and of the epidemic in the 1980s.

PROBLEMS TO CONSIDER

1. How did the evolution of AIDS and of the AIDS political movement affect Bordowitz's sense of himself as a homosexual? How did the experience of getting information about the disease fuel Bordowitz's political consciousness?
2. How did ACT UP's demonstrations change perceptions of homosexual AIDS victims? of homosexuals in general? Compare the FDA demonstration with protest actions (the disruption of Senate birth control hearings; Earth Day; Edward Abbey's defense of "monkeywrenching"). How indebted were these actions to the civil rights demonstrations of the 1960s?

The first time I heard the term "gay cancer" . . . I was in high school. It was in 1982, I guess. I had befriended my high school art teacher, who was a gay man, and who was really good to me, and was very friendly. We used to talk about gay issues without ever saying the word "gay." This was out on Long Island. He used to take me into the city and he introduced me to the Village. We used to walk around. He was kind of introducing me to gay culture. Upon my graduation, he said to me, "Gregg, when you go to New York, there will be people who tell you that you can get cancer from certain kinds of gay sex. That's not true. They just want us not to be able to have sex. So you can't get cancer from anal sex. There's no such thing as gay cancer."

So I came to New York with that information in my head. . . . When was I first aware of AIDS? It was around, I think, 1983/1984. It was like after a year after I came into Manhattan. . . . There was some buzz around the bars, and there were people who knew people who were getting sick. But I don't really remember the first time I heard the word "AIDS." . . . By 1985, I was most certainly aware of AIDS, to the extent that I thought I might have contracted AIDS from having unprotected sex with men. . . .

I went out seeking [information about AIDS]. . . . I was hanging out in the East Village, and I was going to bars, mostly gay bars. I was also living with a girlfriend, living a kind of bisexual downtown hip existence. I didn't know anyone who was identified as gay, although I knew plenty of guys who had sex with other guys and women who had sex with other women. . . .

But I did become aware, either through knowing people who were getting sick, or television reports on the news . . . I became aware that I might have exposed myself to a virus through unprotected sex . . . with men. So I went to the Gay Community Center. How did I know to go to the Gay Community Center? I don't really know, but that was the only place you could go at that time—1986—to get information. And that was a profound experience for me. I went and they directed me upstairs to the Community Health Project. I was given a free examination and much needed education, and this was all done without any judgment, whatsoever. And I felt that I could talk freely there. There was nowhere else . . . I could ask the kinds of questions about the information that I needed.

That was a very profound experience for me and it changed a lot of things. First, it was then and there that I decided I would become a citizen of this gay community, whatever that meant. I felt very indebted to the gay community. I remember looking up at the sign, pondering what the notion of community was, and realizing that a community is a group of people who need each other. The people at the Community Center and the Community Health Project didn't know me, but I could tell that they had dealt with a lot of people like me. So I felt very indebted . . . and decided that I would join this community and make a contribution to this community. That was the pivotal turning point in my life around that time. That is when I started to get more politicized about issues of identity and became much more knowledgeable about AIDS issues. . . . I became very knowledgeable about safer-sex, and started telling people about safer-sex, and passing out information. . . .

So I was developing this consciousness. . . . I met David Meieran, who was a videomaker. . . . We were these young gay artists who were interested in doing serious video work about the growing AIDS crisis. That's when *Hardwick* hit. . . . We started showing up to the protests around *Hardwick* in the Village, with cameras, and we started documenting those. . . .

[I became aware of ACT UP after] David and I saw a poster at the Christopher Street subway stop for a protest at Wall Street. We said, "We're gonna go there with cameras. That's the next step. That's what the *Hardwick* protests are leading us to. This is the most important issue that's confronting the gay community." And *Hardwick* also was framed . . . in terms of AIDS issues. One of the opinions . . . said that in the context of the AIDS epidemic it was legitimate to intervene in the sex lives of gay men because of the dangers of spreading HIV. . . .

So we had been making these links. We were aware of the growing homophobia around us. . . .

The most important [direct action] to me . . . was . . . the non-violent takeover of the Food and Drug Administration. . . .

The idea was to cut through the bureaucratic red tape of the Food and Drug Administration.

But more than that, that people with AIDS should be involved in every level of decision-making concerning research for a treatment and a cure for our disease. . . .

There was a history . . . that predated the action, which had to do with sluggishness on drugs. There was an unwillingness to test HIV drugs. There were like thirty drugs in the pipeline that we thought were promising, that the FDA had back-burnered and not pushed through to the testing process. . . .

There was a contingent of people that thought we should . . . be demonstrating in front of Congress, why bother with this regulatory institution, the FDA, and go to the White House, the president. . . . We had to [show them that] to make the AIDS activist movement significant, and singular, and directly address the issues that were specific to us demanded a new kind of thinking, a savvier notion of what the target should be, a savvier way of dealing with the media. . . .

So I had come up with this slogan, "Seize Control of the FDA." That was frightening to many people, this notion of seizing control. But I was very insistent: "This is what has to be. It has to be that we are just going to take over the agency. The agency is not being run in our interests. People with AIDS are going to take over the agency and run it in our own interests." This is very much the idea, which I think was the lasting historical contribution of ACT UP, that people with AIDS be in control of all decisions concerning our health. It was very significant and it's very consistent within the history of civil rights movements. Primarily, the core principle is self-determination. . . .

What the FDA [action] did was shift the group away from a defensive posture to an offensive posture. The FDA action . . . enabled us to come up with a vision for the way that healthcare should be done in this country, the way that drugs should be researched, and sold, and made available. Most importantly . . . was the idea that people with AIDS should be at the center of the public discussion on AIDS. . . . We had wrested control of the public discussion on AIDS away from the hands of the right wing in this country and towards the direction of, or in the hands of, people with the disease itself. . . .

The FDA [action] was beautiful because the media following the FDA was amazing. . . . We completely won. . . . We shifted the ground and wrested the discussion on AIDS out of the hands of the right wing. All of a sudden, we had people from the group representing people with AIDS in the conversation. . . .

———

Interview with Gregg Bordowitz, December 17, 2002, 1–3, 5–6, 21–24, 27, 31–32, 60; conducted by Sarah Schulman for the ACT UP Oral History Project (www.actuporal history.org), codirected by Schulman and Jim Hubbard.

⌇

Statement to the Presidential Commission on the HIV Epidemic (1988)
RYAN WHITE

A revealing demonstration of how much AIDS terrified Americans occurred in 1984, when the superintendent of the Kokomo, Indiana, school system banned thirteen-year-old Ryan White from school property because he had AIDS. White, who had been infected during treatment for the rare blood disease hemophilia, had to attend school through a telephone hookup. His family's discrimination lawsuit against the schools attracted national attention and broad sympathy for this victim. Celebrities—Elton John, Michael Jackson, and others—lent their support, while White himself became an articulate and courageous voice for the humanity of all AIDS victims, as shown here in his testimony before a federal government commission. In 1989, ABC broadcast The Ryan White Story, *which reshaped public concern for AIDS victims. After White's death in 1990, a commission spokesman explained that "a fine and loving and gentle person" such as Ryan made it "hard for people to justify discrimination against people" with AIDS. The major funding bill for AIDS treatment and care that Congress passed later that year was called the Ryan White Comprehensive AIDS Resource Emergency Act. Two years earlier, federal funding had been denounced by Senator Jesse Helms and others who blamed AIDS on homosexual acts. White's death, as one congressman explained, "brought it home to many, many people" that AIDS is not "an issue just affecting the gay community."*

PROBLEMS TO CONSIDER

1. Compare Ryan White's actions with ACT UP's demonstration at the FDA, both of which were effective in provoking federal responses to AIDS. Were these two responses to the AIDS crisis alike in any way?
2. What factors in White's story made him a unifying "face" of AIDS? Did he represent all AIDS victims?

My name is Ryan White. I am sixteen years old. I have Hemophilia, and I have AIDS.

When I was three days old, the doctors told my parents I was a severe Hemophiliac, meaning my blood does not clot. Lucky for me, there was a product just approved by the Food and Drug Administration. It was called Factorate, which contains the clotting agent found in blood.

While I was growing up I had many bleeds or hemorrhages in my joints which made it very painful. Twice a week I would receive injections or I.V.'s of Factorate which clotted the blood and then broke it down. A bleed occurs from a broken blood vessel or vein. The blood then had nowhere to go so it would swell up in a joint. You could compare it to trying to pour a quart of milk into a pint-sized container of milk.

The first five to six years of my life were spent in and out of the hospital. All in all I led a pretty normal life.

Most recently my battle has been against AIDS and the discrimination surrounding it. On December 17, 1984 I had surgery to remove two inches of my left lung due to pneumonia. After two hours of surgery the doctors told my mother I had AIDS. I contracted AIDS through my Factorate which is made from blood. When I came out of surgery, I was on a respirator and had a tube in my left lung. I spent Christmas and the next 30 days in the hospital. A lot of my time was spent searching, thinking, and planning my life.

I came face to face with death at 13 years old. I was diagnosed with AIDS: a killer. Doctors told me I'm not contagious. Given 6 months to live and being the fighter that I am, I set high goals for myself. It was my decision to live a normal life, go to school, be with my friends, and enjoy day to day activities. It was not going to be easy.

The school I was going to said they had no guidelines for a person with AIDS. The school board, my teachers, and my principal voted to keep me out of the classroom . . . for fear of someone getting AIDS from me; by casual contact. Rumors of sneezing, kissing, tears, sweat, and saliva spreading AIDS, caused people to panic.

We began a series of court battles for 9 months, while I was attending classes by telephone. Eventually, I won the right to attend school, but the prejudice was still there. Listening to medical facts was not enough. People wanted 100% guarantees. There are no 100% guarantees in life, but concessions were made by mom and me to help ease the fear. We decided to meet everyone half way.

(1) separate restrooms
(2) no gym
(3) separate drinking fountain
(4) disposable eating utensils and trays

Even though we knew AIDS was not spread through casual contact. Nevertheless, parents of 20 students started their own school. They were still not convinced.

Because of the lack of education on AIDS, discrimination, fear, panic, and lies surrounded me.

(1) I became the target of Ryan White jokes
(2) Lies about me biting people
(3) Spitting on vegetables and cookies
(4) Urinating on bathroom walls
(5) Some rest[a]urants threw away my dishes
(6) My school locker was vandalized inside and folders were marked FAG and other obscenities

I was labeled a trouble maker, my mom an unfit mother, and I was not welcome anywhere. People would get up and leave, so they would not have to sit anywhere near me. Even at Church; people would not shake my hand.

This brought on the news media, TV crews, interviews, and numerous public appearances. I became known as the AIDS boy. I received thousands of letters of support from all around the world, all because I wanted to go to school. . . . Entertainers, athletes, and stars started giving me support. . . . All of these [celebrities] . . . became my friends, but I had very few friends at school. How could these people in the public eye, not be afraid of me, but my whole town was.

It was difficult, at times, to handle; but I tried to ignore the injustice, because I knew the people were wrong. My family and I held no hatred for those people because we realized they were victims of their own ignorance. We had great faith that with patience, understanding, and education, that my family and I could be helpful in changing their minds and attitudes around.

Financial hardships were rough on us, even though mom had a good job. . . . The more I was sick, the more work she had to miss. Bills became impossible to pay. . . . AIDS can destroy a family if you let it, but . . . mom taught us to keep going. Don't give up, be proud of who you are, and never feel sorry for yourself.

After 2½ years of declining health, two attacks of pneumocystis, shingles, a rare form of whooping cough, and liver problems, I faced fighting chills, fevers, coughing, tiredness, and vomiting. I was very ill and being tutored at home. The desire to move into a bigger house, to avoid living AIDS daily, and a dream to be accepted by a community and school, became

possible and a reality with a movie about my life, *The Ryan White Story.*

My life is better now. At the end of the school year (1986–87), my family and I decided to move to Cicero, Indiana. We did a lot of hoping and praying that the community would welcome us, and they did. For the first time in three years, we feel we have a home, a supportive school, and lots of friends. . . . I'm feeling great.

I am a normal happy teenager again. . . . I'm just one of the kids, and all because the students at Hamilton Heights High School [which serves Cicero, Indiana] listened to the facts, educated their parents and themselves, and believed in me.

I believe in myself as I look forward to graduating from Hamilton Heights High School in 1991.

Hamilton Heights High School is proof that AIDS EDUCATION in schools work[s].

Ryan White speech, March 3, 1988, in National Commission on Acquired Immune Deficiency Syndrome Records, MS C544, reprinted courtesy of the National Library of Medicine, Bethesda, Md.

✌

American Culture at the Turn of the Twenty-First Century

FOR MANY AMERICANS, the late 1990s were glory years. Stock markets, riding the Internet bubble, reached record highs; low interest rates encouraged home construction and consumer purchasing; and unemployment dropped to levels that few experts earlier in the decade had dreamed possible. Moreover, statistics showed, and experience confirmed, that the rate of violent crime, once the plague of America's big cities and a chief symbol of the nation's woes, was falling dramatically, even among juveniles. Despite these hopeful developments, Americans of all political leanings still worried about the future of the nation and its children. Perhaps the most disturbing events began in October 1997, when the media reported school shootings in Mississippi, Oregon, Kentucky, and Arkansas. The deadliest school violence occurred in Littleton, Colorado, in April 1999, when two teenagers, Eric Harris and Dylan Klebold, armed themselves with homemade bombs and semiautomatic guns; traveled to their suburban high school, Columbine High; and began shooting their classmates and teachers. They killed thirteen people, wounded twenty-eight others, and then shot themselves. As television displayed graphic scenes of the violence and of the terrified students to audiences around the world, the killings seemed to be both unimaginable horrors and all-too-predictable signs of the times. In this light, the carnage at Columbine struck contemporaries not as the isolated actions of two deeply troubled individuals, but as symptoms of a deeper crisis of alienation and moral decline in the nation as a whole.

As this volume has shown, optimism contending with anxiety has marked all periods of the history of the United States. In the 1880s, Americans marveled at the rapid expansion of the industrial nation while fearing that the new economic order threatened to destroy the republic. In the years after the atomic bomb was dropped on Hiroshima, when the United States was the leading world power, Americans worried that they were falling behind the Soviet Union because their own citizens were betraying the nation. As the new millennium approached, similar questions and doubts preoccupied Americans: Had the nation's wealth and power weakened the character of its people? Did social and political change bring progress, or did it foster national decline? Was American life marked by too little freedom or too much? These questions were in the minds of contemporaries as they searched for and identified the causes of the Columbine killings, from loosely regulated gun manufacturers and sellers to the decline of religion and the secularization of cultural value systems. But in the weeks after the event, the mainstream of speculation focused on two overlapping concerns. One was the state of America's families. The other involved multinational entertainment industries, which were accused of racking up profits from the sale of ultra-violent video games and movies that fostered a "culture of violence" among children, especially boys. Most notorious were computer games such as Doom and Quake, which the Harrises and Klebolds had let their sons play. These strains merged when President Bill Clinton said that parents, not government regulation, were the first line of defense against future Columbines. Parents "should turn off the television, pay attention to what's on the computer screen," and make "sure your children know you care about what they're doing."

While the horror of Columbine was unique, the alarm it set off intensified the divisions that marked the culture wars in the United States. In the 1990s and afterward, Americans continued to argue over whether it was possible both to strengthen community ties and to encourage diversity. They struggled to reconcile the free range of individual choices with the restrictive bonds of civic and family obligations. In these cases, too, Americans strove to define for themselves and their children the precise meaning of manhood and womanhood in a time when social and cultural developments made the definitions of those concepts appear less secure or stable than they supposedly had been for past generations. This chapter examines how these concerns about individual identity, community, and gender shaped the cultural conversation about two aspects of American life peculiar to the last fifteen years: the efforts to define the shape and purpose of "family" in the new century, and the cyberculture, of which computer games such as Doom were an integral part.

ᕱ Family Values: Marriage, Parenthood, and Children in Recent American History ᕱ

Historians generally agree that the family has been a centrally important institution in the social life of Americans. They also agree, however, that the ways families are organized and the values that people attach to them have been in continuous flux since the earliest European settlements in the Americas. For instance, the "family values" debate was evident in the pre–Civil War period, when slave marriages and families had no legal standing or protection. No matter how vigorously bondsmen and -women defended their unions and kinship ties as real, their owners usually resisted recognizing their legitimacy—a stance that fueled abolitionists' denunciations of slavery. Moreover, at any moment in American history, a variety of family models have coexisted. These models reflected the different values and preferences of ethnic and racial groups, social classes, and rural and urban populations; they also were shaped by the choices that economic circumstances allowed people to make. In short, there has been no "traditional family" or universally recognized set of "family values" in American history.

Many people today are neither comforted nor convinced by this argument. Their resistance is understandable. One constant in American history is the practice of assigning high value to family life and debating the significance and desirability of the changes that have marked the institution's history. That debate reached a new phase of intensity after 1970—the period when civil rights activists, feminists, gays, lesbians, and others were effectively challenging conventional understandings of racial and gender difference. If these developments are added to rising divorce rates, growing numbers of unwed mothers, and the declining fertility of married couples, it is no surprise that substantial numbers of Americans came to believe that the bedrock of the nation's comfort and security—the strength of its supposedly traditional families of husband, wife, and children—was crumbling. Although worries about the family cut across political divisions, the new conservative political organizations that coalesced around these concerns (and helped elect Ronald Reagan president in 1980) have been especially influential ever since in shaping the cultural dispute about the family and the nation.

The documents in this section focus on the phase of the family values debate since the mid-1990s, an era of two major developments. First, the model of two-parent heterosexual households with children no longer corresponded to the family life of the majority of Americans. Second, gay and lesbian Americans sought, often successfully, to participate in family life on an equal basis with heterosexual Americans. Although these developments reflected the long-term dynamism of family life in the United States, the recent family values debate raises an important historical question: did the relative decline of the heterosexual nuclear family and the growing prevalence of alternative family arrangements change, or instead reinforce, conventional ideas about the purposes of the family and the gender definitions that support it? In spite of the bitterness of the debate, have Americans been divided or united in what they think the family ought to be and do?

Marriage Under Fire: Why We Must Win This Battle (2004)
JAMES DOBSON

In 1993, the Hawaii Supreme Court ruled that the state's refusal to grant marriage licenses to same-sex couples violated the state constitution's equal-protection provisions. The decision opened the door for gays and lesbians in Hawaii to marry persons of the same sex. Although Hawaii voters later amended their constitution to ban such unions, the court's decision provoked a nationwide argument about whether all *states would be forced to grant legal recognition to Hawaii's married gay couples. Most constitutional scholars believed that it would not, but the presumed legal limitations on the reach of that decision did not comfort people who believed that marriage was, by definition, the "union between one man and one woman as husband and wife." That phrase is from the Defense of Marriage Act (DOMA), which Congress, responding to the outrage over Hawaii's actions, passed by an overwhelming majority and which President Clinton signed in September 1996. In addition to defining marriage in federal law, the act outlined a state's right to refuse recognition of legal same-sex marriages from another state.*

The DOMA initiative had the broad support of both political parties and a clear majority of Americans, although its most vigorous proponents were evangelical Christian organizations. Among the influential and active supporters was Focus on the Family, which began in 1977 as a radio program hosted by Dr. James Dobson. At the time, Dobson was a professor of pediatric medicine who was alarmed by what he regarded as the rapid disintegration of the family in a time of national moral decay. The organization has since expanded into a publishing and broadcasting giant with more than 2 million supporters. In 2005, Time *magazine named Dobson, then sixty-eight years old, one of the "most influential evangelicals" in the United States. In this selection, Dobson explains why same-sex marriage threatens the survival of the family.*

PROBLEMS TO CONSIDER

1. In Dobson's view, what makes marriage the foundation of social order?
2. According to Dobson, why can marriage occur only between a man and a woman? Which mattered more to him: preserving traditional marriage or reinstituting traditional definitions of manhood and womanhood?

To put it succinctly, the institution of marriage represents the very foundation of human social order. Everything of value sits on that base. Institutions, governments, religious fervor, and the welfare of children are all dependent on its stability. When it is weakened or undermined, the entire superstructure begins to wobble. That is exactly what has happened during the last thirty-five years, as radical feminists, liberal lawmakers, and profiteers in the entertainment industry have taken their toll on the stability of marriage. Many of our pressing social problems can be traced to this origin.

Made for Each Other

One reason the preservation of the family is critical to the health of nations is the enormous influence the sexes have on each other. They are specifically designed to "fit" together, both physically and emotionally, and neither is entirely comfortable without the other. There are exceptions, of course, but this is the norm. George Gilder, the brilliant sociologist and author of the book *Men and Marriage*, states that women hold *the* key to the stability and productivity of men. When a wife believes in her husband and deeply respects him, he gains the confidence necessary to compete successfully and live responsibly. She gives him a reason to harness his masculine energy—to build a home, obtain and keep a job, help her raise their children, remain sober, live within the law, spend money wisely, etc. Without positive feminine influence, his tendency is to release the power of testosterone in a way that is destructive to himself and to society at large.

We see Gilder's insight played out in the inner city. Our welfare system, in the aftermath of the Great Society programs, rendered millions of men superfluous. Indeed, government assistance to women and children was reduced or denied when a father was present in the home. Food stamps put groceries in the pantry. The Department of Housing and Urban Development sent repairmen to fix maintenance problems. When children were in trouble, social workers stepped in to help. Thus men became unnecessary beyond the act of impregnation. Who needed 'em? . . . Men were separated from their historic role as providers and protectors, which stripped them of masculine dignity and robbed them of meaning and purpose. Thus, as Gilder said, their energy became a destructive force instead of powering growth and personal development.

Stated positively, a man is dependent for stability and direction on what he derives from a woman, which is why the bonding that occurs between the sexes is so important to society at large. Successful marriages serve to "civilize" and domesticate masculinity, which is not only in the best interests of women, but is vital for the protection and welfare of the next generation.

Conversely, a woman typically has deep longings that can only be satisfied through a romantic, long-term relationship with a man. Her self-esteem, contentment, and fulfillment are typically derived from intimacy, heart-to-heart, in marriage. Unfortunately, most young husbands find these emotional needs in their wives to be not only confusing, but downright baffling at times. That was certainly true of my early relationship with my wife, Shirley. It took me several years of marriage to "get it," and we experienced some bumps in the road while I was sorting things out. . . .

What I was beginning to understand in those early days were the ways my wife was uniquely crafted, and how I alone could meet her most important emotional needs. Shirley was also learning some new things about me. She observed that I needed her to respect me, to believe in me, and to listen to my hopes and dreams. . . . The way she looked up to me gave me confidence . . . and empowered me to take risks professionally and to reach for the sky. She was meeting a critical need for me. . . .

When the predominate needs of one sex go unmet or ignored by the other, something akin to "soul hunger" occurs. It cannot be explained by cultural influences that are learned in childhood. . . . It is deeply rooted in the human personality. . . .

Hurtling Toward Gomorrah

In short, marriage, when it functions as intended, is good for everyone—for men, for women, for children, for the community, for the nation, and for the world. Marriage is the means by which the human race is propagated, and the means by which spiritual teaching is passed down through the generations. Research consistently shows that heterosexual married adults do better in virtually every measure of emotional and physical health than people who are divorced or never married. They live longer and have happier lives. . . . These and countless other benefits of marriage serve to validate (although no validation is necessary) the wisdom of the Creator, who told us what was best for mankind. . . .

A life in keeping with God's design and instruction brings the greatest possible fulfillment, while any deviation from His design invites disaster. This is why the Bible warns against all harmful forms of sexual behavior, including premarital sex, adultery, prostitution, incest, bestiality, and pedophilia. Homosexuality is only one of the several ways we can wound ourselves and devastate those around us. Ironically, homosexual activists strive with all their energies to achieve "freedom" from the shackles of moral law and traditional institutions. But the Scripture teaches that true freedom and genuine fulfillment can be found only when we live in harmony with our design.

The traditional family and marriage as defined from the dawn of time are among the few institutions that have, in fact, stood the test of time. If we now choose to stand idly by while these institutions are overthrown, the family as it has been known for millennia will be gone. And with its demise will come chaos such as the world has never seen before.

This is why I am profoundly concerned today about the effort to tamper with this time-honored institution. For nearly sixty years, the homosexual activist movement and related entities have been working to implement a master plan that has had as its centerpiece the utter destruction of the family. Now the final battle is at hand: The institution of marriage and the Christian church are all that stand in the way of the movement's achievement of every coveted aspiration. . . .

There is hope. We can still turn the tide. Most Americans want marriage to survive. But we need a widespread awakening that will shake the nation, and we need it soon.

Isn't it worth our utmost efforts to protect the health and vitality of the traditional family? On that one institution rests the welfare of future generations and the viability of this great land. Indeed, Western civilization itself appears to hang in the balance. We must not throw this God-ordained institution on the ash heap of history.

———

James Dobson, *Marriage Under Fire: Why We Must Win This Battle* (Sisters, Ore.: Multnomah Publishers, 2004), 9–12, 15–19, 26–27.

ᴣᴏ

Here Comes the Groom: A (Conservative) Case for Gay Marriage (1989)
ANDREW SULLIVAN

Andrew Sullivan, a former editor of the political magazine The New Republic, *has been both a leading conservative writer since the early 1990s and a pioneer "blogger" using the Internet as a forum for engaged political debate and discussion. As a practicing Roman Catholic and an HIV-positive homosexual, however, he has frequently been at odds with fellow conservatives, Republican Party politicians, and Americans in general on questions about the morality of homosexuality and the social impact of same-sex marriage, which he supports on conservative grounds. The following article, which appeared in 1989 when he was still a Harvard graduate student, was the basis of his book* Virtually Normal: An Argument About Homosexuality *(1995). He framed his argument as an opposition to the "domestic partnership" laws that several cities had passed to extend limited legal benefits and protections, well short of marriage, to same-sex couples.*

PROBLEMS TO CONSIDER

1. What made Sullivan's argument a "conservative" case for same-sex marriage?
2. How could two conservatives such as Andrew Sullivan and James Dobson reach such opposing conclusions about same-sex marriage? Did they agree on any points?

The concept of domestic partnership . . . chips away at the prestige of traditional relationships and undermines the priority we give them. This priority is not necessarily a product of heterosexism. Consider heterosexual couples. Society has good reason to extend legal advantages to heterosexuals who choose the formal sanction of marriage over simply living together. They make a deeper commitment to one another and to society; in exchange, society extends certain benefits to them. Marriage provides an anchor, if an arbitrary and weak one, in the chaos of sex and relationships to which we are all prone. It provides a mechanism for emotional stability, economic security, and the healthy rearing of the next generation. We rig the law in its favor not because we disparage all forms of relationship other than the nuclear family, but because we recognize that not to promote marriage would be to ask too much of human virtue. In the context of the weakened family's effect upon the poor, it might also invite social disintegration. One of the worst products of the New Right's "family values" campaign is that its extremism and hatred of diversity has disguised this more measured and more convincing case for the importance of the marital bond.

The concept of domestic partnership ignores these concerns, indeed directly attacks them. This is a pity, since one of its most important objectives—providing some civil recognition for gay relationships—is a noble cause and one completely compatible with the defense of the family. But the way to go about it is not to undermine straight marriage; it is to legalize old-style marriage for gays.

The gay movement has ducked this issue primarily out of fear of division. Much of the gay leadership clings to notions of gay life as essentially outsider, anti-bourgeois, radical. Marriage, for them, is co-optation into straight society. For the Stonewall generation [*of gay activists from the late 1960s*], it is hard to see how this vision of conflict will ever fundamentally change. But for

many other gays—my guess, a majority—while they don't deny the importance of rebellion 20 years ago and are grateful for what was done, there's now the sense of a new opportunity. A need to rebel has quietly ceded to a desire to belong. To be gay and to be bourgeois no longer seems such an absurd proposition. Certainly since AIDS, to be gay and to be responsible has become a necessity.

Gay marriage squares several circles at the heart of the domestic partnership debate. Unlike domestic partnership, it allows for recognition of gay relationships, while casting no aspersions on traditional marriage. It merely asks that gays be allowed to join in. Unlike domestic partnership, it doesn't open up avenues for heterosexuals to get benefits without the responsibilities of marriage, or a nightmare of definitional litigation. And unlike domestic partnership, it harnesses to an already established social convention the yearnings for stability and acceptance among a fast-maturing gay community.

Gay marriage also places more responsibilities upon gays: it says for the first time that gay relationships are not better or worse than straight relationships, and that the same is expected of them. And it's clear and dignified. There's a legal benefit to a clear, common symbol of commitment. . . .

Legalizing gay marriage would offer homosexuals the same deal society now offers heterosexuals: general social approval and specific legal advantages in exchange for a deeper and harder-to-extract-yourself-from commitment to another human being. Like straight marriage, it would foster social cohesion, emotional security, and economic prudence. Since there's no reason gays should not be allowed to adopt or be foster parents, it could also help nurture children. And its introduction would not be some sort of radical break with social custom. As it has become more acceptable for gay people to acknowledge their loves publicly, more and more have committed themselves to one another for life in full view of their families and their friends. A law institutionalizing gay marriage would merely reinforce a healthy social trend. It would also, in the wake of AIDS, qualify as a genuine public health measure. Those conservatives who deplore promiscuity among some homosexuals should be among the first to support it. . . .

The argument that gay marriage would subtly undermine the unique legitimacy of straight marriage is based upon a fallacy. For heterosexuals, straight marriage would remain the most significant—and only legal—social bond. Gay marriage could only delegitimize straight marriage if it were a real alternative to it, and this is clearly not true. To put it bluntly, there's precious little evidence that straights could be persuaded by any law to have sex with—let alone marry—someone of their own sex. The only possible effect of this sort would be to persuade gay men and women who force themselves into heterosexual marriage (often at appalling cost to themselves and their families) to find a focus for their family instincts in a more personally positive environment. But this is clearly a plus, not a minus: gay marriage could both avoid a lot of tortured families and create the possibility for many happier ones. It is not, in short, a denial of family values. It's an extension of them.

Of course, some would claim that any legal recognition of homosexuality is a de facto attack upon heterosexuality. But even the most hardened conservatives recognize that gays are a permanent minority and aren't likely to go away. Since persecution is not an option in a civilized society, why not coax gays into traditional values rather than rail incoherently against them?

There's a less elaborate argument for gay marriage: it's good for gays. . . . Legal gay marriage could also help bridge the gulf often found between gays and their parents. It could bring the essence of gay life—a gay couple—into the heart of the traditional straight family in a way the family can most understand and the gay offspring can most easily acknowledge. It could do as much to heal the gay-straight rift as any amount of gay rights legislation.

If these arguments sound socially conservative, that's no accident. It's one of the richest ironies of our society's blind spot toward gays that essentially conservative social goals should have the appearance of being so radical. But gay marriage is not a radical step. It avoids the mess of domestic partnership; it is humane; it is conservative in the best sense of the word. It's also practical. Given the fact that we already allow legal gay relationships, what possible social goal is advanced by framing the law to encourage those relationships to be unfaithful, undeveloped, and insecure?

Andrew Sullivan, "Here Comes the Groom: A (Conservative) Case for Gay Marriage," *The New Republic*, August 28, 1989, 20, 22.

❧

Single Mothers by Choice: A Guidebook for Single Women Who Are Considering or Have Chosen Motherhood (1994)
JANE MATTES

The 2000 census reported that 32 percent of all births in the United States were to unmarried women; in 1960, the figure was 5.3 percent. Such statistics confirmed the views of many people who already were alarmed about the apparent decline of the traditional family. Out-of-wedlock births historically have been regarded as a cause for public concern and as an indicator of the moral disorder and social instability that breed poverty and crime. But other people reading the same numbers regarded them as evidence, not necessarily of family and social deterioration, but of the increasing diversity of choices that Americans—and American women in particular—can make in forming their families. By the mid-1990s, the percentage of single women in their thirties in the United States was rising; white educated professional women constituted the fastest-growing category of unmarried motherhood. This new demographic profile was antici-pated in 1981 when Jane Mattes founded Single Mothers by Choice. A support organization for women who, like her, chose to bear or adopt a child even though they were not married, Single Mothers by Choice now has chapters nationwide. In 1994, Mattes published a landmark guidebook on voluntary single motherhood, from which the following selection is taken.

PROBLEMS TO CONSIDER

1. What is the argument for single motherhood advanced here? Did Mattes seek to redefine or reinforce traditional understandings of what family is?
2. Does Mattes's defense of mothers such as herself agree or disagree with the arguments of James Dobson and Andrew Sullivan?

A single mother by choice is a woman who starts out raising her child without a part-ner. She may or may not marry later on, but at the outset she is parenting alone. This definition excludes unmarried couples, heterosexual or ho-mosexual, because although they are not legally married, they will be coparenting, and it also ex-cludes women who became mothers while they were married and then later were widowed or divorced. . . .

Most of us were raised with the dream of falling in love with a wonderful man, getting married, and raising a child in a loving relation-ship. To be happy being an SMC you need to come to terms with giving up your dream of parenting a child from the beginning with a lov-ing partner. Perhaps you will get married in the future, perhaps you won't. You may decide to have a child but may never get married, or you may decide not to have a child and try harder to find a mate, only to end up having neither. There are no guarantees. . . .

Single motherhood by choice is an adventure through relatively uncharted territory. It is not for everyone and there are many things you need to consider when making this choice. But most of all, *make a decision.* The worst thing you can do is not think about the issue at all and not

make a decision. . . . You may then, like Sleep-ing Beauty, wake up one day, only to discover that Prince Charming never came! . . .

There are probably a number of reasons for the increase in older single women having ba-bies, but I believe that the one that underlies them all is the women's movement. By refusing to accept the premise that all women should find their fulfillment solely within the family as wives and mothers, and by identifying and fighting for women's rights, the women's move-ment has made it possible for women today to have choices. We can have satisfying careers out of the home, or we can stay home and raise a family, or both. Whichever path we choose, we have a better sense of self-esteem and feel more empowered than ever before. The days when a woman had to be married to feel that she could have a rewarding and satisfying life are long over, and women who do not marry have many other ways to find fulfillment. . . .

Thanks in great part to the women's move-ment, many of us now feel capable of running countries and businesses, not to mention being heads of households. We are not only finan-cially more able to support a family, but also feel more capable of being a good parent and raising a child, even raising a child alone. We may be interested in marriage to a man whom we feel would be a loving partner, but we do not need, nor are we willing, to marry a man who is not right for us solely in order to have a child, particularly in light of the fact that so many marriages in recent years have been ending in divorce. . . .

It is no longer the case that if a woman doesn't marry she is considered an "old maid" with no other sources of satisfaction in her life. Not that long ago, an unmarried woman was an object of pity, seen as a "nothing" or a "nobody" unless she was legally attached to a man. . . . Today a woman who is not married can have a successful and rewarding career, she can have a social and sexual life, and she can have a family by adopting or conceiving a baby. Marriage is not her only path to happiness. . . .

I think that we need to keep in mind that we are living in changing times, and that the so-called "alternative family" (stepparent family, single-parent family, and gay or lesbian or heterosexual couple living together) is now more common than the traditional family. We all surely would agree that having a child in a family with two loving parents is the ideal situation, but after many years of overidealizing the traditional family, we now also know that it was not perfect. The fact that children can be raised successfully in other kinds of families is becoming more accepted. I believe that our energies would be best invested in trying to learn more about what things work in all families, both traditional and alternative ones, where the children turn out well, rather than continuing to be fearful of change and insisting that alternative families cannot work.

———————

Jane Mattes, *Single Mothers by Choice: A Guidebook for Single Women Who Are Considering or Have Chosen Motherhood* (New York: Times Books, 1994), 4–5, 8, 12–13, 19–20.

༞

The Expectant Father: Facts, Tips and Advice for Dads-to-Be (1995)
ARMIN BROTT

Additional evidence that the cultural boundaries of family, motherhood, and fatherhood were changing in the mid-1990s appeared in the first line of Armin Brott's 1995 guide to fatherhood: "When my wife and I got pregnant with our first child . . ." Brott's career as an adviser to "expectant fathers" began in 1992, when he wrote a Newsweek *column lamenting that children's literature contained so few admirable father figures. His publications since then suggest how the shift in the equation of single motherhood with unwomanly immorality was accompanied by a weakening in the bias that fathers who engaged in active nurturing of their children were unmanly and weak. Brott's work coincided with the contemporary "men's movement," a loose array of organizations founded to counter what some regarded as the excessive influence of feminist critiques of modern men and manhood. Some of these groups encouraged men both to reclaim their presumed natural savagery, which women had softened out of them, and to release their emotional reserves, which they had repressed lest they appear weak. Brott, an ex-Marine, was well positioned to advocate a type of fatherhood that crossed over into the emotional territory traditionally assigned to women.*

PROBLEMS TO CONSIDER

1. Why would "dads-to-be" need an advice book on how to be a father?
2. Was Brott redefining fatherhood, or was he refortifying traditional understandings of the male role in parenting?

Unconditional Love

Sooner or later, almost every writer takes a crack at trying to describe love. And for the most part, they fall short. But there's a line in Maurice Sendak's classic children's book *Where the Wild Things Are* that captures the feeling of loving one's own child exactly: "Please don't go—we'll eat you up—we love you so." As crazy as it may sound, that's precisely what my love for my daughters feels like to me. Whether we're playing, reading a book, telling each other about our days, or I'm just gazing at their smooth, peaceful faces as they sleep, all of a sudden I'll be overcome with the desire to pick them up, mush them into tiny balls, and pop them in my mouth. If you don't already know what I mean, believe me, you will soon. Just you wait. . . .

Feeling, Well, Paternal

Despite all the excitement, you may be filled with a sense of calm and peacefulness. You may feel less like going to work and more like hanging out with the new family. If so, you certainly aren't alone. Canadian researcher Anne Storey found that new fathers' testosterone levels often drop by as much as a third right after the birth of their children. Storey speculates that this kind of testosterone reduction would make a man feel more parental or more like "settling down."

Awe at What the Female Body Can Do

Watching your partner go through labor is truly a humbling experience; chances are, your own physical courage, strength, and resolve have rarely been put to such a test. But there's nothing like seeing a baby come out of a vagina to convince you that women are really different from men.

I know that vaginal birth has been around for millions of years and that that's the way babies are supposed to be born. Yet in a strange way, there's something almost unnatural about the whole process—the baby seems so big and the vagina so small. . . . You'd think that with all the technological advances we've made in other areas, we'd have invented a quicker, easier, less painful way to have children.

Jealousy

"The single emotion that can be the most destructive and disruptive to your experience of fatherhood is jealousy," writes Dr. Martin Greenberg in *The Birth of a Father.*

There's certainly plenty to be jealous about, but the real question is, "Whom are you jealous of?" Your partner for being able to breastfeed and for her close relationship with the baby, or the baby itself for taking up more than his or her "fair share" of your partner's attention, and for having full access to your partner's breasts while you aren't even supposed to touch them? The answer is, "Both."

Now that the baby's born, communication with your partner is even more important than before. . . . So if you're feeling jealous, tell her about it. But if you can't bring yourself to discuss your feelings on this issue with your partner, take them up with a male friend or relative. You'll be surprised at how common these feelings are.

Feeling Pushed Away or Left Out

Another common feeling experienced by new fathers is that of being pushed away or excluded from the parenting experience. . . .

While it's easy to give in to your feelings, throw up your hands, and leave the parenting to your partner, don't do it. Encourage her to talk about what she's feeling and thinking, and ask her specifically to involve you as much as possible.

A good way to cut down on your potential feelings of jealousy or of being pushed away is to start getting to know your baby right away — even before you leave the hospital. Change as many diapers as you can . . . , give the baby a sponge bath, or take him or her out for a walk while your partner gets some rest. . . .

Bonding with the Baby
No one knows exactly where or when it started, but one of the most widespread — and most enduring — myths about child rearing is that women are somehow more nurturing than men and are therefore better suited to parenting.

In one of the earliest studies of father-infant interaction, researcher Ross Parke made a discovery that might shock the traditionalists: the fathers were just as caring about, interested in, and involved with their infants as the mothers were, and they held, touched, kissed, rocked, and cooed at their new babies with at least the same frequency as the mothers did. Several years later, Martin Greenberg coined a term, *engrossment*, to describe "a father's sense of absorption, preoccupation, and interest in his baby."

Parke and a number of other researchers . . . have concluded that what triggers engrossment in men is the same thing that prompts similar nurturing feelings in women: early infant contact. . . .

But What If I Don't Bond Right Away?
Although we've spent a lot of time talking about the joys of loving your child and how important it is to bond with the infant as soon as possible, many new fathers (and mothers, for that matter) don't feel particularly close to the new baby immediately after the birth. . . .

So, if you haven't established an instant attachment with your baby, there's absolutely nothing wrong with you. And, more important, there's no evidence whatsoever that your relationship with or feelings for your child will be any less loving than if you'd fallen head over heels in love in the first second. Just take your time, don't pressure yourself, and don't think for a second that you've failed as a father.

There's a lot of evidence that parent-child bonding comes as a result of physical closeness. So if you'd like to speed up the process, try carrying the baby every chance you get, taking him with you whenever you can, and taking care of as many of his basic needs as possible. . . .

Armin Brott, *The Expectant Father: Facts, Tips, and Advice for Dads-to-Be* (1995; repr., New York: Abbeville Press, 2001), 207–11.

⌇

Heather *and Her Critics* (1997)
LESLÉA NEWMAN

Since its publication in 1990, Heather Has Two Mommies *and* Daddy's Roommate *have been two of the books that conservative parent and religious groups have most frequently tried to ban from school and public libraries.* Heather, *written by Lesléa Newman and illustrated by Diane Souza, is about the preschool daughter of a lesbian couple, who conceived her through artificial insemination. Michael Willhoite's* Daddy's Roommate *is told from the perspective of a young boy who, after his parents divorce because his father is gay, comes to understand his father's sexuality and new relationship. The pub-*

lisher of both books, Alyson Wonderland books, dedicated itself "to providing children of gay and lesbian parents books which reflected the reality of their lives." The stories were written to provide positive support for children of alternative families, but they also proposed to normalize gay and lesbian families in the eyes of the heterosexual majority. The boy in Daddy's Roommate, *for instance, learns that "being gay is just one more kind of love." The publisher initially imagined a narrow readership for the books; however, conservative groups nationwide that protested their affirmation of homosexuality generated a national audience for the books and turned them into library standards. In this selection, the author of* Heather Has Two Mommies, *Lesléa Newman, explains why she wrote the children's book and answers her critics.*

PROBLEMS TO CONSIDER

1. What definition of "family" does Newman advocate in *Heather Has Two Mommies?*
2. What did the book's message suggest to readers about the meaning and importance that Americans assign to "family"? Did Newman radically redefine family, or did she reinforce traditional meanings?

As an out lesbian author of six picture books, five of which depict families with gay or lesbian members, I have been called one of the most dangerous writers living in America today. In fact, in 1994, my book *Heather Has Two Mommies* was the second most challenged book in the nation, following closely on the coattails of Michael Willhoite's *Daddy's Roommate,* another book about a family that includes a gay parent. When I wrote *Heather* in 1988, I had no idea my work would cause such a fuss. Though I have been repeatedly accused of having a political agenda, my goal was simply to tell a story.

The idea for *Heather* came about one day when I was walking down Main Street in Northampton, Massachusetts, a town that bears the slogan "small town charm, big city excitement." Northampton is also known for its liberalism, tolerance of difference, and large lesbian population. On this particular day, I ran into a woman who along with her female partner had recently welcomed a child into their home. "We have no books to read our daughter that show our type of family," the woman said. "Somebody should write one." Is it important for children to

see their own image reflected back to themselves within the culture at large? Speaking from personal experience, my answer is a resounding YES.

As a child, I grew up in a Jewish family, in a Jewish neighborhood. I was surrounded with families that looked like my family, families that dressed in similar clothes, families that ate similar foods, families that spoke in similar phrases. Yet I asked my parents over and over, "Why can't we have a Christmas tree? Why can't I hunt for Easter eggs?" Since I had never read a book or seen a TV show or movie about a young Jewish girl with frizzy brown hair eating matzo ball soup with her Bubbe on a Friday night, I was convinced there was something the matter with my family. My family didn't look like any of the families I saw in my picture books or on my television set. My family was different. My family was wrong.

Of course, as a child, I was not aware of the power of the media. I was not aware of this yearning to see a family like my own reflected in the culture at large. Nor could I articulate this need. As a grown woman who happens to be a Jewish lesbian, I am painfully aware of the lack of positive images, or even any images of myself in the media. I believe that had I had those images and role models at an early age, they would have greatly enhanced my self-esteem.

And so I took on the challenge of writing *Heather Has Two Mommies*, hoping to create a book that would help children with lesbian mothers feel good about themselves and their families.

Heather was written in 1988. The premise of the book is that Heather's favorite number is two. She has two hands, two feet, two pets, and two moms. Her family goes on picnics together and celebrates holidays together. When Heather goes to day care for the first time, she realizes that her family is not the same as everyone else's family. Her teacher has all the children draw pictures of their families, explaining that "the most important thing about a family is that all the people in it love each other." . . .

In December of 1989, the first copies of *Heather Has Two Mommies* rolled off the presses. . . . I have not yet heard of a child having an adverse reaction to the book. Adults, however, are another story. . . .

The first conflict occurred in Portland, Oregon, where Lon Mabon had launched an anti-gay campaign, trying to amend the state constitution to allow discrimination against lesbians and gay men. During meetings of his organization, the Oregon Citizen Alliance (OCA), copies of *Heather* and *Daddy* were passed around as evidence of "the militant homosexual agenda" Mabon felt was sweeping the nation. In 1992, the citizens of Oregon defeated the OCA measure, though anti-gay legislation was voted into effect that same year in Colorado. (In 1996, Colorado's anti-gay amendment was declared unconstitutional by the United States Supreme Court.)

The second arena of controversy surrounding *Heather Has Two Mommies*, *Daddy's Roommate*, and another title of mine, *Gloria Goes to Gay Pride*, took place in school and public libraries around the country when the books began disappearing from library shelves from coast to coast. When Alyson Publications learned of this, the company offered to send free replacement copies to the first five hundred libraries who called. Almost as soon as word went out, five hundred calls came in. Librarians, for the most part, rallied around the books and defended freedom of expression as a vital principle upon which this country is based. . . .

I continue to be amazed by all this fuss. It seems to me that a disproportionate number of parents live in fear of their child reading just one book with a gay character in it, for such exposure will, in these parents' minds, cause their child to grow up to be lesbian or gay. It is usually useless to point out that the vast majority of lesbians and gay men were brought up by heterosexual parents and spent countless hours of their childhood reading books with heterosexual characters. Fear is irrational. It is also about control. I have no problem with parents deciding their child cannot read *Heather Has Two Mommies*. I do have a problem with these same parents deciding that *nobody* can have access to it—or to any other book, for that matter. . . .

Heather Has Two Mommies and *Daddy's Roommate* are not about sex. They're about families. Clearly it's the adults, not the children, who can't take the sex out of homosexuality. . . .

For those who do not want children exposed to this type of family, I ask this: what leads you to believe that every child sitting in your child's classroom or library comes from a home with a mother and father? Why do you think that there are no children in your child's classroom or library with lesbian or gay parents, siblings, aunts, uncles, grandparents, neighbors and friends? What messages are you giving to all children, when you pretend there is only one type of family, and render the rest invisible?

Lesléa Newman, "*Heather* and Her Critics," *The Horn Book Magazine*, March–April 1997, 149–53.

∽

ᕽ *Electronic Frontiers: Radical Individualism,*
Virtual Community, and the Internet ᕽ

Some thirty years ago, the invention and popularization of the personal computer, or PC, launched the era of potent mechanized tools in the hands of people outside mammoth corporations and government agencies—what radicals of the 1960s called the "system." Americans have responded with an uneasy excitement about the liberty and happiness promised by the apostles of advanced communications and technologies. Although they have benefited in many ways from the wide distribution of these machines, some still believe that machinery is essentially hostile to human existence and more likely to enslave than to liberate them. Others worry that such technologies encourage the decline of politics and community in American life as people turn away from civic engagement and inward toward private fulfillment. They note teenagers' absorption in computer games, or marvel at the explosion of pornography on the World Wide Web, or regret that Americans are more likely to watch DVD movies at home or in their automobiles than on theater screens.

Defenders of market and individual freedom and technological innovation counter that machines themselves—whether semiautomatic weapons or crime-oriented video games such as Grand Theft Auto—are neutral. Bad people make them bad. The National Rifle Association, facing renewed efforts to regulate firearm sales, insisted that Eric Harris and Dylan Klebold, not guns, were responsible for the killings at Columbine. Proponents of the digital revolution similarly assert the liberating potential of information technology. In the right hands, the general class of inexpensive technologies such as computers and the Internet can redistribute power to the people and reconnect them in renewed and revitalized communities. "From the Internet to the iPod," declares the Electronic Frontier Foundation (EFF), a civil libertarian organization, "technologies of freedom are transforming our society and empowering us as speakers, citizens, creators, and consumers." EFF, whose slogan is "Defending Freedom in the Digital World," was founded to fight efforts by government and private or corporate interests to control ownership of or access to the resources of the "electronic frontier."

Using words such as "freedom" and "frontier" casts the profound changes generated by the digital revolution in mythic terms that are very familiar to Americans (see chapter 2). The frontier stands for self-reliant individualism, endless freedom and opportunity, and gun-blazing conflict between the forces of civilized good and those of savagery or tyranny. No matter how American or personally empowering the digital revolution promises to be, many people remain uneasy about the concentrated power of the entertainment conglomerates that profit from information technologies and the effects that the tools of the electronic frontier have on the fabric of community life. These concerns frequently are framed in terms similar to the descriptions of the disintegrating family. Does the digital world cause a deterioration of traditional ways of participating as individuals in a collective community, or does it lead to a diversification of how American communities are organized? Do "first-person shooter" computer games that revel in virtual carnage desensitize players to the real consequences of actual violence? The documents in this section examine debates about the virtual communities of the digital world—whether they are real or counterfeit, socially productive or destructive.

Bowling Alone: The Collapse and Revival of American Community (2000)
ROBERT D. PUTNAM

In 2000, Robert D. Putnam, a professor of government at Harvard University, published Bowling Alone, *a dense analysis of what he saw as the pervasive fraying of the fabric of social and civic life in the United States. The book became a bestseller. Putnam's diagnosis of the nation's ills describes the decline of social capital, the bonds of trust and commitment that arise from individuals' involvement in shared community responsibilities and activities. In recent decades, Americans have become more active as individuals than as members of collective groups.* Bowling *is Putnam's central metaphor for the deterioration of community and civic engagement. Americans are bowling in record numbers, he says, but membership in bowling leagues has fallen steeply. Putnam held out the possibility for social renewal but warned that without a concerted effort by Americans, the effects of declining social capital—poverty, ruptured families, crime, violence, and intolerance—were likely to get worse over time. In this section from his book, Putnam seeks to measure the Internet's effects on the nation's reserves of social capital.*

PROBLEMS TO CONSIDER

1. What kind of social identity and commitment does Putnam value? What factors account for their decline, according to Putnam?
2. In what ways does the Internet encourage or discourage the social engagement that Putnam prescribes? Do the interests of market capital (the producers) take precedence over social capital?

As the twenty-first century opens we are only a few years into the era of widespread access to the Internet. . . . The speed of diffusion of this new technology has been substantially greater than that of almost any other consumer technology in history—rivaled only by television. . . .

Like virtually all technical consumer innovations, this one caught on most rapidly and fully among younger generations. One study in 1999 found that although young people were in general much less likely to seek out political information than older cohorts, they were more likely to use the Internet as their preferred means of access. . . .

Within a few years of the Internet's launch, simulacra of most classic forms of social connectedness and civic engagement could be found on-line. Mourners could attend virtual funerals over the Web. . . . Virtual vows arrived. . . . Yahoo mentioned more than five hundred places where one could pray virtually. . . . All these forms of virtual social capital and more could be found in cyberspace.

One central question, of course, is whether "virtual social capital" is itself a contradiction in terms. There is no easy answer. . . . Very few things can yet be said with any confidence about the connection between social capital and Internet technology. One truism, however, is this: The timing of the Internet explosion means that it cannot possibly be causally linked to the crumbling of social connectedness. . . . Voting, giving, trusting, meeting, visiting, and so on had all begun to decline while Bill Gates was still in grade school. . . . Whatever the future implications of the Internet, social intercourse over the last several decades of the twentieth century was not simply displaced from physical space to cyberspace. The Internet may be part of the solution to our civic problem, or it may exacerbate it, but the cyberrevolution was not the cause.

We also know that early users of Internet technology were no less (and no more) civically engaged than anyone else. . . . The absence of any correlation between Internet usage and civic engagement could mean that the Internet attracts reclusive nerds and energizes them, but it could also mean that the Net disproportionately attracts civic dynamos and sedates them. . . . I consider here some of the *potential* advantages and disadvantages of computer-mediated communication for American civic life, recognizing in advance that neither the apocalyptic "gloom and doom" prognosticators nor the utopian "brave new virtual community" advocates are probably on target. How are "virtual" communities likely to be different from the "real" thing?

Community, communion, and communication are intimately as well as etymologically related. Communication is a fundamental prerequisite for social and emotional connections. Telecommunications in general and the Internet in particular substantially enhance our ability to communicate; thus it seems reasonable to assume that their net effect will be to enhance community, perhaps even dramatically. Social capital is about networks, and the Net is the network to end all networks. . . .

Very much like nineteenth-century futurists, . . . enthusiasts for "virtual community" see computer networks as the basis for a kind of utopian communitarianism. Starr Roxanne Hiltz and Murray Turoff, early prophets of computer-mediated communication, predicted that "we

will become the Network Nation, exchanging vast amounts of both information and socioemotional communications with colleagues, friends and 'strangers,' who share similar interests . . . we will become a 'global village.'" . . .

Some of the allegedly greater democracy in cyberspace is based more on hope and hype than on careful research. The political culture of the Internet . . . is astringently libertarian, and in some respects cyberspace represents a Hobbesian state of nature, not a Lockean one. . . .

Nevertheless, the potential benefits of computer-mediated communication for civic engagement and social connectedness are impressive. The Internet offers a low-cost and in many respects egalitarian way of connecting with millions of one's fellow citizens, particularly those with whom one shares interests but not space or time. In fact, liberating our social ties from the constraints of time . . . may turn out to be a more important effect of the Internet than liberation from the constraints of space.

Against this promise . . . must be weighed . . . serious challenges to the hope that computer-mediated communication will breed new and improved communities. . . .

Computer-mediated communication . . . masks the enormous amount of nonverbal communication that takes place during even the most casual face-to-face encounter. . . . Eye contact, gestures, . . . nods, a faint furrowing of the brow . . . —none of this mass of information that we ordinarily process almost without thinking in face-to-face encounters is captured in text. . . .

The poverty of social cues . . . inhibits interpersonal collaboration and trust, especially when the interaction is anonymous and not nested in a wide social context. Experiments that compare face-to-face and computer-mediated communication confirm that the richer the medium of communication, the more sociable, personal, trusting, and friendly the encounter. . . .

Face-to-face networks tend to be dense and bounded, whereas computer-mediated communication networks tend to be sparse and unbounded. Anonymity and fluidity in the virtual world encourage "easy in, easy out," "drive-by" relationships. That very casualness is the appeal of computer-mediated communication for some denizens of cyberspace, but it discourages the creation of social capital. If entry and exit are too easy, commitment, trustworthiness, and reciprocity will not develop. . . .

The final potential obstacle is more conjectural and yet more ominous: Will the Internet in practice turn out to be a niftier telephone or a niftier television? In other words, will the Internet become predominantly a means of active, social communication or a means of passive, private entertainment? Will computer-mediated communication "crowd out" face-to-face ties? It is, in this domain especially, much too early to know. . . . [One] early experimental study found that extensive Internet usage seemed to cause greater social isolation and even depression. Amid these scattered straws in the wind, a final caution: The commercial incentives that currently govern Internet development seem destined to emphasize individualized entertainment and commerce rather than community engagement. If more community-friendly technology is to be developed, the incentive may need to come from outside the marketplace. . . .

The most important question is not what the Internet will do to us, but what we will do with it. How can we use the enormous potential of computer-mediated communication to make our investments in social capital more productive? How can we harness this promising technology for thickening community ties? How can we develop the technology to enhance social presence, social feedback, and social cues? How can we use the prospect of fast, cheap communication to enhance the now fraying fabric of our real communities, instead of being seduced by the mirage of some otherworldly "virtual community"? In short, how can we make the Internet a part of the solution? . . .

Robert D. Putnam, *Bowling Alone: The Collapse and Revival of American Community* (New York: Simon and Schuster, 2000), 169–71, 173–77, 179–80.

๛

Blood Sport (1997)
DAVID KUSHNER

The violent computer games Doom and Quake were the most notorious forms of computer-mediated communication that critics identified with the socially corrosive and alienating effects of life in the Information Age. Doom, which a team of computer-game fiends and gifted software designers calling themselves id Software released in late 1993, changed the course of computer gaming history. Featuring astonishing three-dimensional graphics, Doom created an immersive world of depth, texture, and adventure for players. The immersion also seemed total because instead of watching a figure that they manipulated, players inhabited the virtual world of Doom. They ran from room to room, taking in the action as though they actually were behind the gun they carried and fired. Doom was not the first "first-person shooter" game, but its advanced graphics made that virtual perspective unusually convincing and the standard in computer gaming. As one reviewer explained, "You, the player, enter this adventure game's other reality." That reality was a labyrinthine world of blood-and-guts-spattering violence unmatched by any game before it. Monstrous characters did not simply get shot and disappear but also suffered agonizing, disfiguring deaths—as did the players. Doom pioneered multiplayer gaming, which allowed individuals linked through computer networks to compete against and kill one another. An instant cult sensation, Doom was played by millions around the world.

The popularity of Doom and its successor, Quake, made id's founders, John Carmack and John Romero, superstars of the Information Age, but the games' violent action also generated opposition. Parent groups and members of Congress already had expressed their concerns that Doom and Quake made children violent and antisocial when the Columbine killings occurred in 1999. Within days, news media reported that the killers, Eric Harris and Dylan Klebold, had both been Doom fanatics. Doom and similar games "romanticize and sanitize extreme forms of violence and teach our children that killing is cool," said Senator Joseph Lieberman, responding to the bloodshed at Columbine. For Lieberman and other critics, computer games diminished players' capacity to distinguish real life from virtual life, imaginary carnage from actual death. The following article is a journalist's account of the "Super Bowl" for computer gamers, a Quake tournament that was held in Lawrence, Kansas, in early 1997. It explores the worlds of Doom and Quake from the perspective of the games' fanatics, instead of its critics.

PROBLEMS TO CONSIDER

1. What attracted fans of Doom and Quake to these games?
2. Does this article suggest that playing Quake and Doom fosters what Robert Putnam calls social capital or erodes it?

In a dark room pulsing with blood-red shadows, Dr. Rigormortis sits hunched over a computer, twitching his body as if he were repeatedly and intentionally sticking his toe in a socket.

"Doh!" he yelps as the digitized soldier on his screen hits an unanticipated blizzard of nails. Or, in the parlance of Quake, the computer game he's playing, "Telefraged!"

This is in Lawrence, Kansas, moments before the start of the online gaming underground's unofficial Super Bowl. Like the few dozen others convulsing throughout his University of Kansas student flophouse, Dr. Rigormortis, 21, has been up two nights straight practicing for a match between his team, Impulse 9, and their rivals from Michigan, the Ruthless Bastards. For the past year, their contests have been part of a growing Internet subculture of computer gamers called clans: groups of players who eat, sleep, and dream Quake's violent fantasy. Along with the hundreds of thousands of other Quake addicts . . . , these two clans usually wage their battles on the Net, but on this tornado-gray New Year's weekend, they've assembled here for

a LAN party—an informal gathering where clans patch their computers into a local area network—to settle the score in the flesh. . . .

Since its release online last June, Quake has spawned clans from Portland to Moscow, mostly on college campuses where Internet access is free and unlimited. On one level, the phenomenon might come down to the beautiful nightmare of the game itself: a futuristic military hellscape where players hunt each other down in a wild panic to kill or be killed. But on another, it could be how Quake is the first game specifically designed for team competition over the Internet. And with that, we may be witnessing something far more compelling: the dawn of cybersports.

Network war games are nothing new. In the early 1980s, Net pioneers inspired by the role-playing craze Dungeons & Dragons invented MUDs, "multi-user domains," live chat-based adventures that were about as exciting as typing "Isis hurls meta cleaver at Thor" and imagining the bloodshed. A decade later came Doom, the breakthrough title in the so-called "twitch" genre of quasi-3-D shoot-'em-ups; for the first time, instead of just battling a computerized enemy, up to four players could link PCs and take on a spontaneous human being. At 1.7 million copies worldwide, [it was] the best-selling computer game in history.

After creating the Doom series, "we basically said, 'Hmm, let's see how many people we can get into a network game,'" recalls Barrett Alexander of id Software. What they came up with was Quake, which allows players to connect with up to 15 marauders over the Net in a real-time free-for-all—or even break up into paintball-like teams. "We knew it was going to be big," Alexander says, "but not mind-numbing." . . .

Now there is a growing perception in the $10 billion video- and computer-game industry (even bigger than film) that network gaming could become more than just idle entertainment. "Electronic games are the extreme games of the mind," insists Terry Torok, creator of XS New York, a chain of virtual-reality arcades. . . .

"I hate the smell of blood and guts." _fo0k, the closest thing to a network-gaming superstar, is standing in his parents' garage surrounded by the jaws of death: Rows of black steel animal traps line the walls like some medieval torture chamber. _fo0k's father runs a small trapping business and skins minks here at the house. "Sometimes I find all these carcasses hanging from the ceiling," _fo0k says. "It's pretty weird."

Though _fo0k is sheepish around real weapons, he's an expert at virtual ones. As the 28-year-old cocaptain of the Ruthless Bastards, he's led his clan to the top of the ClanRing (the NFL of Quake), a feat accomplished by only one other team, his main rivals, Impulse 9. Watch _fo0k play Quake . . . and you'll realize just how much talent it takes to be a world-class clanner. Along with preternatural hand-eye coordination, _fo0k possesses what Torok has called "an amazing ability to assimilate electronic information in a nanosecond." . . .

Since Quake came out last year, _fo0k has spent evenings buried in his parents' basement, a windowless room filled with twisted piles of joy-sticks and keyboards, mammoth speakers, and a scattering of videogame cartridges. . . .

Videogames, _fo0k says, have been his favorite pastime ever since Space Invaders "first melted my mind," back in the late '70s. At the time, _fo0k was simply Clint Richards, the new kid on the block who regularly escaped into the fantasy worlds of sci-fi novels and Atari 2600. After seeing *Star Wars* a few dozen times, he decided his life's ambition was to "fly to other planets and battle aliens." Unlike most kids, he never gave up.

Following a failed stab at rock stardom . . . , Richards found the answer to his childhood dreams with Quake. Using the handle _fo0k (a satire of self-conscious hacker typescript) and a high-speed modem hustled from his job as a cable installer, he cofounded the Ruthless Bastards, a team of ex-Doom junkies in Michigan who've since become his closest friends. _fo0k says he probably wouldn't be hanging out with clanners if it wasn't for the game—most are younger than he is, and he says it's a fairly geeky scene, but their friendships run deep.

Maybe that's because these last-in-the-lineup guys are experiencing for the first time in their lives the agony and ecstasy of team sports. And maybe that's also why they spend up to six hours a night together online. "The Internet is my real home," _fo0k explains. "At work, I'm sentient, but I find myself walking around in a daze because I'm so bored with the usual stuff: my job, meeting people who aren't interesting. When I get home and start shooting the s--t with the guys and start playing, that's when I get excited." . . .

It's just seconds before the start of 19/RB's death match, and the clanners are all on edge . . .

Down the hall in the Bastard's room, _fo0k sucks the last breath from his cigarette and reaches for the keyboard. "Okay, brothers," he says, "let's win."

David Kushner, "Blood Sport," *Spin*, June 1997, 104, 106–7.

~

The Unreal Estate Boom (2003)

JULIAN DIBBLE

A different kind of clan experience occurs in the role-playing computer games popularly known as MMORPGs (massively multiplayer online role-playing games). Today they are one of the fastest-growing forms of computer gaming. For a yearly membership fee (usually about $50), players can log on to what Julian Dibble has called the "semifictional digital otherworlds" of games such as EverQuest (and its many sequels), Ultima Online, or World of Warcraft, which has 9 million members and generates more than $1 billion in revenue. Players choose an online identity, or avatar, through which they inhabit this three-dimensional world. They are joined in action and conversation by perhaps millions of avatars around the world. The MUDs (multiuser dimensions) of MMORPGs are called persistent worlds *because they as well as the avatar exist even when a player is not logged in. Dibble has long been a role-playing resident of MUDs, an observer of the moral complications of citizenship in a virtual world, and a curious explorer of the shifting and uncertain boundary between real life and digital life. In this article, he examines the absorption of* Ultima Online *players and how their motivations and behaviors make virtual life seem no less authentic than real life.*

PROBLEMS TO CONSIDER

1. Does life in Britannia confirm the Internet's promise of freedom and happiness?
2. How does Britannia's economy differ from and resemble the real economy? Does Britannia's economy foster or diminish social capital?

Not long ago, a 43-year-old Wonder Bread deliveryman named John Dugger logged on to eBay and, as people sometimes do these days, bought himself a house. Not a shabby one, either. Nine rooms, three stories, rooftop patio, walls of solid stonework—it wasn't quite a castle, but it put to shame the modest redbrick ranch house Dugger came home to every weeknight after a long day stocking the supermarket shelves of Stillwater, Oklahoma. Excellent location, too; nestled at the foot of a quiet coastal hillside, the house was just a hike away from a quaint seaside village and a quick commute from two bustling cosmopolitan cities. It was perfect, in short, except for one detail: The house was imaginary.

Equally unreal were the grounds the house stood on, the ocean it overlooked, the neighboring cities, and just about everything else associated with it—except Dugger himself, the man he bought it from, and the money he shelled out. At $750, Dugger's winning bid on the property set him back more than a week's wages and was, on the face of it, an astonishing amount for what he actually bought: one very small piece of Britannia, the fantasy world in which the networked role-playing game *Ultima Online* unfolds.

Yet there was nothing particularly unusual about the transaction. On any day you choose, dozens of Britannian houses can be found for sale online at comparable prices. And houses are just the start of it. Swords, suits of armor; iron ingots, lumber, piles of hay; tables, chairs, potted plants, magic scrolls; or any other little cartoon item the little cartoon characters of Britannia might desire can be had at auction, priced from $5 for a pair of sandals to $150 for an exceptionally badass battle-ax to $1,200 for a well-located fortress. A simple, back-of-the-envelope calculation puts the estimated sum of these transactions at $3 million per year.

Which in turn is just a fraction of the total wealth created annually by the residents of Britannia. For every item or character sold on eBay and other Web sites, many more are traded within the game itself—some bartered, most bought with Britannian gold pieces (a currency readily convertible into US legal tender at about 40,000 to the dollar, a rate that puts it on par with the Romanian lei). The goods exchanged number in the millions, nearly every one of them brought into existence by the sweat of some player's virtual brow. . . .

Last year—in an academic paper analyzing the circulation of goods in Sony Online's 430,000-player *EverQuest*—an economist calculated a full set of macro- and microeconomic statistics for the game's fantasy world, Norrath. Taking the prices fetched in the $5 million *EverQuest* auctions market as a reflection of in-game property values, professor Edward Castronova of Cal State Fullerton multiplied those dollar amounts by the rate at which players pile up imaginary inventory and came up with an average hourly income of $3.42. He calculated Norrath's GNP at $135 million—or about the same, per capita, as Bulgaria's. . . .

The traffic in virtual goods . . . isn't just another new market. It's a whole new species of economy—perhaps the only really new economy that . . . the Internet has yet given rise to. . . . For years, the world's economy has drifted further and further from the solid ground of the tangible: Industry has given way to postindustry, the selling of products has given way to the selling of brands. . . . This was all supposed to culminate in what's been called the virtual economy. . . . And so it has. But who would have guessed that this culmination would so literally consist of the buying and selling of castles in the air?

These little economies raise big questions, therefore, and by no coincidence, they tend to be the big questions of the economic age. How, for instance, do we assign value to immaterial goods? What defines ownership when property becomes as fluid as thought? What defines productivity when work becomes a game and games become work?

And, of course, the question of questions—the one that in a sense asks them all: How, exactly, did a 7-Kbyte piece of digital make-believe become John Dugger's $750 piece of upmarket real estate?

At a construction site in Indianapolis, Troy Stolle sits with a hard hat in his lap and a Big Mac in his hands. . . . Stolle's job, as a form carpenter, is to build the wooden molds the concrete gets poured into. . . .

Asked how this job compares to the work of building a virtual tower in Britannia two years ago, he answers like it's obvious: "That was a lot more stressful." . . .

Through high school, . . . and well into his first years as a carpenter, Stolle spent vast stretches of his free time immersed in the intricacies of D&D [*Dungeons & Dragons*], Warhammer, BattleTech, and other tabletop role-playing and strategy games.

Then came [Electronic Arts'] *Ultima Online*. The first true massively multiplayer online role-playing game, *UO* went live in September 1997, and by December, Stolle had a character: a blacksmith he called Nils Hansen. The business of bettering Nils' lot in life quickly came to absorb him more intensely than any game ever had. In short order, he added two other characters. . . . And to give this little team a base of operations . . . he paid about 40,000 gold coins for a deed permitting him to build a small house. He found a nice, secluded spot in northern Britannia, placed his cursor there, and double-clicked the building into existence.

The house worked out fine for a while, but in a game about accumulation, no house stays big enough for long. Stolle's trio needed new digs, and soon. By now, though, . . . there was nowhere left to build. . . . At last, EA announced a solution that could work only in a make-believe world—a whole new continent was being added to the map.

Stolle started preparing for the inevitable land rush months before it happened. He scrimped and saved, sold his house for 180,000 gold, and finally had enough to buy a deed for the third-largest class of house in the game, the so-called Large Tower.

On the night the new continent's housing market was set to open, Stolle showed up early at a spot he had scouted out previously, and found 12 players already there. No one knew exactly when the zero hour was, so Stolle and the others just kept clicking on the site, each hoping to be the first to hit it when the time came. . . .

Finally, at about 1 in the morning, the housing option switched on, and as a couple thousand "Build" commands went through at once, the machine that was processing it all swooned under the load. ". . . For like 10 minutes, everything's frozen. You see people kind of disappearing here and there. And then it starts to let up. And a tower appears! . . . I double-clicked on it, and I couldn't tell. And so then I double-clicked again—and there was my key to the tower." . . .

Throughout history, whenever human beings have tried to imagine the best of all possible worlds, they've pictured . . . a place of abundance and ease. Not too long ago, people insisted the Internet was just such an environment, with its effortlessly reproducible wealth of data and light-speed transcendence of geography and time. In the emerging online universe, it was said, scarcity had no place. . . .

Yet scarcity has turned out to be a feature, not a bug. . . . The worlds [that people] actually want to be in . . . are the ones that make the digital goods hard to get to and even harder to copy. The addictive appeal of online role-playing games suggests that people will choose the constraining and challenging world over the one that sets them free. . . .

Which in turn makes the fact that you can log on to eBay this minute and buy 10,000 imaginary iron ingots for $4.50 seem not only a little less improbable but in fact inevitable. Scarcity, after all, breeds markets, and markets will seep like gas through any boundary that gives them the slightest opening—never mind a line as porous as the one between real and make-believe.

Julian Dibble, "The Unreal Estate Boom," *Wired*, January 2003, 108, 110–11, 113.

ᴄ

↙ TEXT CREDITS

Edward Abbey. "Forward!" from *Ecodefense: A Guide to Monkeywrenching*. Reprinted by permission of Don Congdon Associates, Inc. Copyright © 1985 by Edward Abbey.

Ad for Earth Day. U.S. EPA History.

Stewart Albert. "Chicago Retrospective," *Berkeley Barb*, September 6–12, 1968, p. 9. Reprinted with permission of Judy Gumbo Albert. For more information, please visit www.stewalbert.com.

"As We See It," editorial, *Santa Cruz Sentinel-News*, February 19, 1942, p. 1. Reprinted by permission of Santa Cruz Sentinel-News.

Ti-Grace Atkinson. "The Older Woman: A Stockpile of Losses" by Ti-Grace Atkinson. Copyright © 1972 by Ti-Grace Atkinson. Originally published in *Prime Time*, Volume 1, October 1972. Reprinted by permission of Georges Borchardt, Inc., for the author.

Boston Women's Health Collective. From the Preface to *Our Bodies, Ourselves*, Second Edition by Boston Women's Health Book Collective. Copyright © 1971, 1973 by The Boston Women's Health Book Collective, Inc. Abridged by permission of Simon & Schuster Adult Publishing Group.

Armin Brott, *The Expectant Father: Facts, Tips and Advice for Dads-To-Be*, 2001, pp. 207–211. Reprinted by permission of Abbeville Press.

Stokely Carmichael. "We're Not Afraid . . . We're Gonna Die for Our People." Reprinted by permission of the Estate of Stokely Carmichael.

Dale Carnegie. From "The Big Secret of Dealing with People" in *How to Win Friends and Influence People* by Dale Carnegie. Copyright 1936 by Dale Carnegie. Copyright renewed © 1964 by Donna Dale Carnegie and Dorothy Carnegie. Abridged by permission of Simon & Schuster Adult Publishing Group.

Rachel Carson. Excerpt from *Silent Spring* by Rachel Carson. Copyright © 1962 by Rachel L. Carson, renewed 1990 by Roger Christie. Reprinted by permission of Houghton Mifflin Company. All rights reserved.

A. P. Carter. "No Depression (in Heaven)," lyrics by A. P. Carter, transcribed from *The Carter Family: The Later Years of the First Family of American Music, 1935–1941*, Disc C, 1936–1937, JSP Records JSP7708C.

Frank Churchill. "Who's Afraid of the Big Bad Wolf?," by Frank Churchill. © Copyright 1933 (Copyright Renewed). World Wide Rights Assigned to Bourne Co. All Rights Reserved. International Copyright Secured. ASCAP.

Beatrice Morales Clifton. From Sherna Berger Gluck, *Rosie the Riveter Revisited: Women, the War and Social Change*. New York: Meridian, 1987. To listen to the original audio recording of these interviews, go to www.csulb.edu/voaha.

Noel Coward. "I Went to a Marvellous Party." Words and Music by Noel Coward. © 1938 (Renewed) Chappell Music Ltd. All Rights Administered by Chappel & Co. for the United States and Canada. All Rights Reserved. Used by Permission of Alfred Publishing Co., Inc.

Ida Cox, "Wild Women Don't Have the Blues" transcribed from *Ida Cox Complete Recorded Works 1923–1938, Volume 2: c. March 1924 to April 1925*, Document Records DOCD-5323. Written by Ida Cox, 1924.

David Kushner. "Blood Sport," *Spin*, June 1997, pp. 104, 106–107. Reprinted by permission of the author.

Jacques Levy. *Cesar Chavez: Autobiography of La Causa*. Reprinted by permission of the Estate of Jacques Levy.

Alain Locke. "Toward a Critique of Negro Music," *Opportunity* 12, November 1934, pp. 328–331. Reprinted by permission.

David Loehwing. "How Red Girl Spies Make Suckers of G.I.'s," *National Police Gazette* 159, November 1954, pp. 5–7, 32.

Loretta Lynn. "(Since I've Got) The Pill." © Copyright 1973, Renewed 2001. Guaranty Music/BMI/Coal Miners Music, Inc./BMI (admin. by ICG). All rights reserved. Used by permission.

Arthur Mann and Lawrence Taylor. Screenplay, *The Jackie Robinson Story*, 1950, pp. 33–34. Reprinted by permission of the Estate of Marion Mann.

Elizabeth Sutherland Martinez. "Colonized Women: The Chicana." Copyright © 1969. Reprinted by permission of the author.

Jane Mattes. From *Single Mothers by Choice: A Guidebook for Single Women Who Are Considering or Have Chosen Motherhood* by Jane Mattes, copyright © 1994, 1997 by Jane Mattes. Used by permission of Three Rivers Press, a division of Random House, Inc.

Marjorie McKenzie. "Pursuit of Democracy; Sees Opportunities Broadening for Race Women in Crisis," *Pittsburgh Courier*, January 17, 1942, p. 7. Reprinted by permission of GRM Associates, Inc.

William C. Menninger. *Psychiatry in a Troubled World: Yesterday's War and Today's Challenge*, 1948, pp. 104–108. William C. Menninger papers, Menninger Archives, Kansas State Historical Society. Reprinted by permission.

Clarence LeRoy Mitchell. Letter to the editor, *The Afro-American*, February 15, 1930, p. 6. Reprinted by permission of the Afro-American Newspapers.

Robin Morgan. "No More Miss America" from *The Word of a Woman: Feminist Dispatches, Second Edition (1968–1992)* by Robin Morgan. Copyright © Robin Morgan, 1994. By permission of Edite Kroll Literary Agency Inc.

Arthur D. Morse. "Jackie Wouldn't Have Gotten to First Base." Reprinted by permission of International Creative Management, Inc. Copyright © 1950 by Arthur D. Morse.

"Musical Treatment," *The Southerner*, March 1, 1956, p. 5.

Lesléa Newman. "*Heather* and Her Critics." Copyright © 1997 by Lesléa Newman. First appeared in *The Horn Book Magazine*. Reprinted by permission of Curtis Brown, Ltd.

"Nisei Plea for Understanding," *Watsonville Register-Pajaronian*, September 26, 1945, p. 3. Reprinted by permission of Register-Pajaronian.

William G. Nunn. "Let's Take It in Stride," *Pittsburgh Courier*, April 19, 1947, p. 18. Reprinted by permission of GRM Associates, Inc.

"The Pill: How It Is Affecting U.S. Morals, Family Life," *U.S. News & World Report* 61, July 11, 1966, pp. 62–65. Copyright 1966 U.S. News & World Report, L.P. Reprinted with permission.

Cole Porter. "Love for Sale." Words and Music by Cole Porter. © 1930 (Renewed) WB Music Corp. All Rights Reserved. Used by Permission of Alfred Publishing Co., Inc.

Protest Petition Against Amos 'n' Andy, *Pittsburgh Courier*, September 12, 1931, p. 2. Reprinted by permission of GRM Associates, Inc.

Robert D. Putnam. Reprinted with the permission of Simon & Schuster Adult Publishing Group from *Bowling Alone: The Collapse and Revival of American Community* by Robert D. Putnam. Copyright © 2000 by Robert D. Putnam.

Ernie Pyle. "My Personal Hero." Courtesy Lilly Library, Indiana University, Bloomington, IN.

J. D. Ratcliff. "An End to Woman's 'Bad Days'?" *Reader's Digest* 81, December 1962, pp. 73–76.

Grantland Rice. "What Draws the Crowd," *Colliers* 75, June 20, 1925, pp. 10, 44. Reprinted by permission.

Branch Rickey. Speech to the "One Hundred Percent Wrong Club" banquet, Atlanta, Georgia, January 20, 1956. Reprinted by permission.

Norman Rockwell. *Norman Rockwell: My Adventures as an Illustrator*. Printed by permission of the Norman Rockwell Family Agency. Copyright © 1960 the Norman Rockwell Family Entities.

"Ruth Fined $5000; Costly Star Banned for Acts Off Field," *New York Times*, August 30, 1925, p. 1. Copyright © 1925 by The New York Times Co. Reprinted with permission.

Gertrude Samuels. "Why They Rock 'n' Roll—and Should They?," *New York Times Magazine*, January 12, 1958, pp. SM 16–18. Reprinted by permission of the Estate of Gertrude Samuels.

Ronald Schiller. "Help Yourself to Happiness," *Woman's Home Companion* 81, August 1954, pp. 34, 95–96.

Sarah Schulman. Interview conducted with Gregg Bordowitz by Sarah Schulman as part of the ACT UP Oral History Project, December 17, 2002, pp. 1–3, 5–6, 21–24, 27, 31–32, 60. This project was co-directed by Sarah Schulman and Jim Hubbard. Reprinted by permission.

Bessie Smith. *Mistreatin' Daddy*. Words and Music by Porter Grainger and Bob Ricketts. © Copyright 1923 by Bourne Co. Copyright Renewed. All Rights Reserved. International Copyright Secured. ASCAP.

"'Soul Stirring Hate' Needed to Wipe Out Japs—Gardner," *Watsonville Register-Pajaronian*, February 1, 1944, pp. 1–2. Reprinted by permission of Register-Pajaronian.

Mickey Spillane. From *One Lonely Night* by Mickey Spillane, copyright 1951 by E. P. Dutton, renewed © 1979 by Mickey Spillane. Used by permission of Dutton, a division of Penguin Group (USA) Inc.

Samuel A. Stouffer. "Masculinity and the Role of the Combat Soldier." *The American Soldier*. © 1949 Princeton University Press, 1977 renewed PUP. Reprinted by permission of Princeton University Press.

Students for a Democratic Society. "The Port Huron Statement," 1962, 1990, pp. 7–8, 10–12. Reprinted by permission of Charles H. Kerr Publishing Company, Chicago.